Sport, Representation and Evolving Identities in Europe

Cultural Identity Studies

Volume 19

Edited by
Helen Chambers

PETER LANG
Oxford · Bern · Berlin · Bruxelles · Frankfurt am Main · New York · Wien

Philip Dine and Seán Crosson (eds)

Sport, Representation and Evolving Identities in Europe

PETER LANG

Oxford · Bern · Berlin · Bruxelles · Frankfurt am Main · New York · Wien

Bibliographic information published by Die Deutsche Nationalbibliothek.
Die Deutsche Nationalbibliothek lists this publication in the Deutsche National-
bibliografie; detailed bibliographic data is available on the Internet at
http://dnb.d-nb.de.

A catalogue record for this book is available from the British Library.

Library of Congress Cataloguing-in-Publication Data:

Sport, representation and evolving identities in Europe / Philip Dine and Seán Crosson
(eds).
    p. cm.
 Includes bibliographical references and index.
 ISBN 978-3-03911-977-6 (alk. paper)
 1. Sports--Social aspects--Europe. 2. Sports and state--Europe. 3. Europe--Social life and
customs. I. Dine, Philip. II. Crosson, Seán.
 GV706.5.S7363 2010
 306.483094--dc22
                              2010026646

This book is based on original research funded by the
Irish Research Council for the Humanities and Social Sciences (IRCHSS).

This publication was grant-aided by the Publications Fund
of **National University of Ireland, Galway**.

ISSN 1661-3252
ISBN 978-3-03911-977-6

© Peter Lang AG, International Academic Publishers, Bern 2010
Hochfeldstrasse 32, CH-3012 Bern, Switzerland
info@peterlang.com, www.peterlang.com, www.peterlang.net

Contents

viii

Acknowledgements

The case studies collected here put forward original research which was initially outlined at a series of expert seminars held at the National University of Ireland, Galway, in 2008 and 2009. These were made possible by primary funding from the Irish Research Council for the Humanities and Social Sciences (IRCHSS) under its Thematic Project Grants scheme (2006–2009). The editors of the present volume are most grateful for this financial support and are very pleased to acknowledge it here. We would also wish to express our thanks for the additional funding and administrative support received from the following bodies at the National University of Ireland, Galway: the Millennium Fund for Research; the Research Office; the College of Arts, Social Sciences and Celtic Studies; the School of Languages, Literatures and Cultures; and the discipline of French Studies. Particular thanks are extended to the Huston School of Film & Digital Media, its director, Rod Stoneman, and its administrator, Dee Quinn. We are also grateful to Murdo McLeod for kindly allowing us to make use of his excellent photographic image of Roy Keane for conference publicity. Thanks for their specialist guidance and support are extended to Graham Speake, Joe Armstrong and their colleagues at Peter Lang Ltd, with particular gratitude due to Helen Chambers, as General Editor of the Cultural Identity Studies series in which this volume appears. Finally, we wish to record our appreciation of the expertise and cooperation of our contributors, who have, without exception, been a pleasure to work with on the present volume. Our sincere thanks to them, and to all those who have helped us to bring this research project to fruition.

List of Illustrations

Chapter 5

Chapter 6

Chapter 7

Chapter 9

Chapter 15

Every effort has been made to trace copyright holders and to obtain their permission for the use of copyright material. The publisher apologizes for any errors or omissions in the above list and would be grateful for notification of any corrections that should be incorporated in future reprints or editions of this book.

List of Diagrams

PADDY AGNEW

Foreword
Football and Evolving National Identity

> Sport represents the exaltation of the moral and physical force of youth
> and enhances a country's prestige. Sport will become the trademark of
> Fascist Italy.[1]

It comes as no surprise to learn that the above speaker was *Il Duce*, Benito
Mussolini. What is interesting is that he made that statement in January
1923, in a private conversation just three months after the de facto coup of
his infamous 'March on Rome'. *Il Duce* had summoned Giorgio Vaccaro,
an ambitious young Fascist militant and First World War veteran, who
had boldly introduced himself at a Fascist Congress in Rome in November
1921. As he prepared to establish his dictatorship, Mussolini was keen to
draft in trusted lieutenants. Vaccaro had already declared a major interest
in sport, so *Il Duce* had plans for him.

Mussolini's own interest in sport was twofold. Firstly, he was convinced
that his totalitarian regime would have to stake out a moral dominion over
every sphere of the individual citizen's life, including sport and recreation.
Secondly, he was equally convinced that sport, in particular football, could
have a hugely important unifying role in the new Fascist Italy. In those
early meetings with the young Vaccaro, recalled by sports historian Mario
Pennacchia in his book, *Il Generale Vaccaro* (2008), *Il Duce* stressed that
sport could in no way be allowed to remain the preserve of a privileged
minority.

---

1   M. Pennacchia, *Il Generale Vaccaro: L'epopea dello sport italiano da lui guidato a
vincere tutto* (Rome: Lucarini, 2008), p.11.

To put it another way, from very early on Mussolini perceived the potential of sport in helping to enhance and consolidate national identity. In a foreword for a book by the Olympic athlete Ugo Frigiero in 1934, *Il Duce* wrote:

> Sporting achievements enhance the nation's prestige and they also prepare men for combat in the open field and in that way they testify to both the physical well being and moral vigour of the people.[2]

Thus it was that, in 1926, Mussolini opted to reorganize Italian football along lines 'more consonant with the new life of the Nation'. For a start he tried (and failed) to convince Italians that football was not in fact an importation from the dreaded 'Inglesi', but rather the logical development of the old Florentine 'calcio'.

More importantly, though, his 1926 reforms gave him direct control of the governing body of Italian football, the FIGC (*Federazione Italiana Giuoco Calcio*). Thus it was a Fascist-controlled FIGC which, in the 1929 season, instigated the first truly national league championship (until then, there had been Northern and Southern leagues). In a sense, then, it was Mussolini who invented 'Serie A'.

The preparations, too, for that new Serie A indicated clearly just what role Mussolini attributed to sport. Under the original rules, the new Serie A would have had to start off without Triestina (the side from Trieste on the border with Slovenia) and without either Napoli or Lazio. The new Serie A was to combine the first eight in the Northern and Southern leagues – the problem was that Triestina had finished ninth in the north and Lazio and Napoli had tied for eighth in the south.

Vaccaro, knowing all too well what Mussolini required of him, was having none of it. With splendid 'flexibility', he simply changed the rules and decided that the new Serie A would have 18 rather than 16 teams, thus making way for all three sides. Shortly afterwards, Mussolini summoned Vaccaro to government house to congratulate him on his handling of the

---

2   U. Frigerio, *Marciando nel nome dell'Italia* [Walking in the Name of Italy], foreword by *Il Duce* Benito Mussolini (Rome: UTEP, 1934).

problem, and in particular on how he had overcome the resistance of senior Fascist figure and Under-Secretary at the Ministry of the Interior, Leandro Arpinati:

> The single league championship represents the unity of Italy and that would have been a deformed unity without Trieste. I don't understand Arpinati [...] Football is a sport of the 'popolo', we must never forget that. This new national championship will improve our best players and generate great enthusiasm for the national team. And now we have a new horizon to conquer, the World Cup.[3]

Mussolini was not the first, nor the last, political leader to realize that football could provide priceless popular consensus, not to mention positive PR and photo-ops for himself and his regime. It was under Mussolini that football became the national sport. State funding was pumped into the building of a 'stadio communale' in towns such as Milan (the original San Siro), Bologna, Florence, Genoa, Pisa, Palermo, Rome, Trieste and Turin. (Ironically, today's top Italian clubs suffer economically from this Fascist investment because they continue to use increasingly outdated, local authority run stadiums, thus missing out on the valuable revenue that could be generated by having their own modern stadiums).

Mussolini was particularly quick to recognize the value of the then fledgling World Cup. He lobbied hard to have the second World Cup in 1934 staged in Italy, and he then worked even harder to make sure that Italy would have a team capable of winning the tournament. With pragmatic cynicism, legislation banning foreign players was reversed and suddenly the Italian national team was able to field a number of Argentine stars of Italian origin, with three of them, Raimundo Orsi, Luis Monti and Enrique Guaita, playing a key role in Italy's 1934 World Cup triumph. (All three had played for Argentina before switching allegiance to Italy.)

The Italian team which won two World Cups, 1934 and 1938, for Mussolini came with a very clear Fascist tag. In his book, *Football and Fascism: The National Game Under Mussolini* (2004), Simon Martin argues that, when they travelled outside Italy during the 1930s, both Italian clubs and

---

3   Pennacchia, *Il Generale Vaccaro*, p.30.

the national team were closely identified with the Mussolini regime.[4] For example, Italy were bitterly jeered by the crowd at their opening game in Marseille during the 1938 World Cup finals, when, as was their wont, the *Azzurri* greeted the fans with the Fascist salute. Police were called in to restrain anti-fascist protesters (doubtless including many Italian political exiles). Despite such moments, however, football was, by and large, good for Italian Fascism and Italian Fascism was good for football. *Il Duce* clearly used it effectively in the process not just of empire building, but also in the consolidation of a national identity.

Sixty years after *Il Duce*, another powerful Italian with autocratic tendencies, namely media mogul and centre-right Prime Minister Silvio Berlusconi, has also piggy-backed on that same sporting identity. As the owner of Serie A club AC Milan, Berlusconi is a genuine fan. Yet, somewhere along the way and almost by accident, he discovered that being the boss of one of Italy's most successful clubs did him no harm as he attempted to win populist consensus.

Obviously, Berlusconi's media empire, his wealth and, above all, political alliances with such as the late, disgraced, Socialist Prime Minister, Bettino Craxi, were fundamental to preparing the way for his entry into politics in 1994. But, the AC Milan factor weighed in too. As the silverware piled up on the AC Milan sideboard, Berlusconi began to enjoy the populist experience. This is hardly surprising – just try walking out into the San Siro stadium to be greeted by wild applause from 70,000 fans at the mere mention of your name and not be moved by the experience.

It is at least arguable that nothing quite plugged Berlusconi into the psyche of the 'popolo' as effectively as regular spectacular success at the nation's favourite game. Long before he entered the political arena, the 'popolo' was only too familiar with the name Berlusconi – he was a winner not just via the creation of his multi-billion Fininvest empire, but also via a football team that he had rescued from imminent financial collapse and then led on to (very stylish) Italian, European and World club tournament success.

4   S. Martin, *Football and Fascism: The National Game under Mussolini* (London: Macmillan, 2004).

When Berlusconi did decide to enter politics, his carefully prepared entrance was heavily underlined with populist, football language. In an American-style presidential TV address from his study in his Arcore villa, outside Milan, on 26 January 1994, Berlusconi solemnly announced:

> I have chosen to take to the field and involve myself in public life because I don't want to live in an illiberal country governed by immature forces and by men [the ex-Communists] who are still closely linked to a past that proved both a political and economic disaster ...[5]

The key phrase was 'take to the field'. His new party was to be called 'Forza Italia' or 'Up Italy', a cry which until then had applied only to an Italian national team, and his party deputies were to be referred to as *Azzurri*, a term previously used for national team players. As he campaigned in the Rome no. 1 constituency for the 1994 election, he even taunted his opponent, economist Luigi Spaventa, saying to him, 'Before running against me, go win yourself two Champions Cups'.[6]

The Berlusconi story is far from over. Yet what links his story to that of Mussolini is the use of sport, intentional or otherwise, in the formation of an identity. Mussolini desperately needed sport to help create a national identity, whereas Berlusconi has found it useful in the creation of a populist, Peronist identity. Both men are just two examples of the role of sport in evolving European identities. There was a time when sports commentators would piously urge us not to 'mix politics and sport'. The reality, as we all know, is that professional sport is not only intrinsically 'mixed up' with politics, but also with 'evolving' social, cultural and national identities.

In this volume, you will find many different examples of just such identities, ranging from Hungarian to Northern Irish footballers and from Roy Keane to fictional athlete Alf Tupper. All of them are worth consideration and an attentive read.

---

5   P. Agnew, *Forza Italia: A Journey in Search of Italy and its Football* (London: Ebury Press, 2006), p.120.
6   Ibid.

Bibliography

Agnew, P. *Forza Italia: A Journey in Search of Italy and its Football* (London: Ebury Press, 2006).

Frigerio, U. *Marciando nel nome dell'Italia* [Walking in the Name of Italy], foreword by *Il Duce* Benito Mussolini (Rome: UTEP, 1934).

Martin, S. *Football and Fascism: The National Game under Mussolini* (London: Macmillan, 2004).

Pennacchia, M. *Il Generale Vaccaro: L'epopea dello sport italiano da lui guidato a vincere tutto* (Rome: Lucarini, 2008).

PHILIP DINE AND SEÁN CROSSON

Introduction
Exploring European Sporting Identities: History, Theory, Methodology

In his groundbreaking investigation of the emergence of the world sports system, *Global Games* (2001), the Dutch historian and sociologist Maarten Van Bottenburg charted the evolution of modern sport from its origins in locally varied pastimes to the international standardization that renders possible today's mega-competitions, such as the football World Cup and the Olympic Games. The point of departure for this sports-based transformation of the world was Europe, which was primarily responsible for the development, codification and then exportation of these new corporeal practices, simultaneously transforming itself and its inhabitants. As Van Bottenburg notes:

> In European societies everyday life was conducted at the local or regional level well into the nineteenth century. [...]
>
> In the latter half of the nineteenth century geographical and social relations were quickly transformed, partly through the advent of new transportation and communications networks. [...] All this had the effect of bridging cultural differences. Variations between regional costumes became blurred, standard languages came to predominate over dialects, national feast days demoted local festivities to the status of folklore, and nationally standardized sports became more important than local recreational activities. Without these processes of integration and increases in scale it would have been impossible for sportsmen and sportswomen from different regions (let alone countries) to compete with any regularity or for competitions to be organized and coordinated with set rules at the national and eventually international level.[1]

---

1   M. Van Bottenburg, *Global Games* (trans. B. Jackson; Urbana, IL: University of Illinois Press, 2001), pp.3–4.

Thus regarded, the development of modern sport may legitimately be considered as a precursor of the processes of administrative integration and, within important limits, cultural homogenization that characterized the project of European construction in the wake of the Second World War, and which has been significantly extended since the fall of the Berlin Wall in 1989 and the final collapse of the Soviet Union in 1991. Yet, paradoxically, a central theme of the present volume is the remarkable extent to which local, regional and national variations continue to exist, and even to predominate, in European sport, where they show no sign of ceasing to elicit meanings for individuals and communities which our contributors reveal to be both historically determined and contextually specific.

The point of departure for this survey of 'the state of play' in European sport is the sheer scale and ubiquity of this characteristically social (both associative and societal) phenomenon. For sport annually mobilizes millions of people across Europe: as practitioners in a wide variety of competitive, educational, recreational and, increasingly, health-related contexts; and as spectators, whether physically present or, more typically, following events via the mass media. In so doing, sporting practices and representations contribute significantly to the social construction of identities, through the elaboration of discourses and networks of power relations that, together, both shape and serve to legitimize highly distinctive processes of socialization. These mechanisms may be regarded negatively, for instance, by Marxist, Foucauldian and feminist critics respectively, as alienating, disciplinary and/or patriarchal.[2] They may also be interpreted more positively, as permitting self-expression and even self-actualization of various kinds, in a tradition of linking the playing of games to the education of the young that stretches at least as far back as the Roman concept of *mens sana in corpore sano* (a healthy mind in a healthy body). However, perhaps most persuasively, sport may be understood as combining both positive and negative features, depending on the specific situations in which it is practised, watched, listened to, read about or otherwise consumed, and thus on the variety of individual and collective experiences to which

2   P. Markula and R. Pringle, *Foucault, Sport and Exercise: Power, Knowledge and Transforming the Self* (London: Routledge, 2006), pp.98–103.

it may give rise. This is the consciously broad approach that underpins this collaborative investigation of sporting Europe and Europeans.

The inherent tensions and even contradictions of modern sport, and particularly its complex existence as a site of both personal liberation and institutional control, are necessarily an integral part of the case studies that follow. Whether the focus is on such conventionally negative manifestations of sport's social resonance as its use as an instrument of totalitarian rule in Fascist Italy (investigated by Paul Dietschy in Chapter 5), or on such apparently positive incarnations as the return of the Olympic Games to their ancient homeland on the occasion of the Athens 2004 Olympiad (discussed by Eleni Theodoraki in Chapter 3), the frequently paradoxical impacts of modern games come regularly to the fore. Moreover, as Patrick Mignon reminds us, in a putatively postmodern age of globalization and instant digital communication, the new individual and collective identities made – and unmade – by ephemeral sporting events require, if anything, an even greater focus on complexity and ambiguity.[3]

The essays collected here put forward original research into sport in modern and contemporary Europe, with their common aim being to examine its distinctive contribution to the construction of identities. To this end, they focus scholarly attention on sport's social significance, as a set of mass-mediated practices and spectacles giving rise to a complex network of images, symbols and discourses. The individual chapters and the work as a whole seek to explore, and ultimately to explain, the processes of representation and mediation involved in the sporting construction, and subsequent renegotiation, of local, national and, increasingly, global identities. Our study thus offers a survey of key developments in sporting Europe – from the mid-nineteenth century to the present, and from the Atlantic to the Urals – presenting findings by acknowledged international experts and emerging scholars at the level of individuals, communities, regions, nations and Europe as a whole, both in its geographical and political incarnations. The work's focus on representation offers a broadly conceived, and consciously inclusive, approach to issues of 'European-ness' in modern and contemporary sport.

3   P. Mignon, 'Le football investi par les capitaux', *Esprit*, January 1999, pp.121–33; see especially pp.132–3.

The present collaborative study is thus intended to contribute to the ongoing elucidation of the role of sport in the processes of identity construction in contemporary societies. Since the pioneering work of Eric Hobsbawm and Terence Ranger on 'the invention of tradition' (1983), and Benedict Anderson on 'imagined communities' (1983),[4] modern games have regularly been identified as a core component in the construction of Europeans' individual and communal senses of self, particularly at the level of the modern nation-state. Our volume seeks to build on these still solid conceptual foundations, as well as on more recent and more specifically targeted work in this area, such as the important edited volumes by Jeremy MacClancy (*Sport, Identity and Ethnicity*, 1996), and by Adrian Smith and Dilwyn Porter (the latter a contributor to the present volume) (*Sport and National Identity in the Post-War World*, 2004).[5] As a result of these and related interventions in what has become an expanding field of study, few academic commentators would today doubt sport's significance as a mode of individual and communal interaction, and, *a fortiori*, of cultural representation. Indeed, a persuasive case can be made for regarding participation, broadly conceived, in mass sporting activities as among the most important modes of perception, both of ourselves and others, available to contemporary societies. Since their emergence and codification in the mid-nineteenth century, modern sports have exerted a powerful influence on both personal and collective self-images, and have thus impacted extensively on local and national politics, and even on the international order itself. At the core of this evolving system of signification, sport's distinguishing input to the imaginative life and the identity politics of modern European nation-states has been a constant for well over a century.

This book, like the research project on which it is based, is consciously European in orientation and ambition. However, it is no coincidence that the funding which allowed the editors to invite sports specialists from

---

4   E. Hobsbawm and T. Ranger (eds), *The Invention of Tradition* (Cambridge: Cambridge University Press, 1983); B. Anderson, *Imagined Communities: Reflections on the Origin and Spread of Nationalism* (London: Verso, 1983).

5   J. MacClancy (ed.), *Sport, Identity and Ethnicity* (Oxford: Berg, 1996); A. Smith and D. Porter (eds), *Sport and National Identity in the Post-War World* (London: Routledge, 2004).

across the continent to gather and debate their findings should have been Irish, nor that the venue for their deliberations should have been a small city on Europe's Atlantic periphery. For, while Ireland may be located on the geographical – and even, perhaps, the economic and political – margins of Europe, there can be no doubting the centrality of the Irish case in any informed analysis of sports-related identity construction. In fact, the pivotal importance of the Gaelic Athletic Association (GAA) in the development of cultural and political nationalism in Ireland – and in the subsequent establishment and consolidation of a distinctively Irish state – can hardly be overstated. Founded in 1884, the GAA celebrated its 125th anniversary in 2009 and is widely hailed not only as the most important sports association right across the still politically divided island, but also as one of its foremost forces of social cohesion (notwithstanding its inevitably contested position in the 'Six Counties' of British-administered Northern Ireland).[6] As a particularly clear exemplar, the case of the GAA stands as a paradigm of sport's multifaceted social role, and this at both the national and local levels, additionally serving to underline the broader value of the academic study of the history and sociology of modern sport. Again, significant contributions in this field have been made by analysts such as John Sugden and Alan Bairner (the latter a contributor to the present volume) in their pioneering *Sport, Sectarianism and Society in a Divided Ireland* (1986), as well as in subsequent works, including especially their edited volume on *Sport in Divided Societies* (1999).[7]

While the quintessentially home-grown sphere of Gaelic games will not be focused on in this European volume, other Irish sporting traditions do figure here. More specifically, the most global of sports, association football, is discussed in two of its most intriguing incarnations, north and south of the still divided island's political border, by Alan Bairner

6   See, among others, M. Cronin, M. Duncan and P. Rouse, *The GAA: A People's History* (Cork: The Collins Press, 2009); M. Cronin, W. Murphy and P. Rouse (eds), *The Gaelic Athletic Association, 1884–2009* (Dublin: Irish Academic Press, 2009); J. Scally, *The GAA: An Oral History* (Edinburgh: Mainstream, 2009).

7   J. Sugden and A. Bairner, *Sport, Sectarianism and Society in a Divided Ireland* (Leicester: Leicester University Press, 1986); J. Sugden and A. Bairner (eds), *Sport in Divided Societies* (Aachen: Meyer and Meyer, 1999).

(in Chapter 10) and Marcus Free (in Chapter 9) respectively. These Irish analyses are juxtaposed with case studies taken from the United Kingdom and across continental Europe to highlight both perceptual and structural commonalities as well as important situational divergences. The editors' aim has not been, and clearly cannot be, comprehensiveness in such a richly diverse area of study. Rather, they have sought to encourage a methodologically coherent and thematically representative eclecticism, so as to derive the maximum possible benefit from this gathering of specialists from across Europe and from a broad range of disciplinary backgrounds, including sports administration, anthropology, art criticism, geography, history, literature, film and media studies, and sociology, as well as having a variety of practical engagements with the sports under discussion, up to and including personal involvement in elite competition. The fifteen individual contributions collected here together highlight the magnitude, diversity and consequent social complexity of modern European sport. The dual function of contemporary sporting practices, which are typically experienced as participant activities and/or mass-mediated spectacles, is reflected in the attention given by our contributors both to 'playing the game' and to the mechanics of fandom. The closely related issue of the symbiotic relationship between sport and the media – previously explored by scholars including Raymond Boyle and Richard Haynes in their co-authored *Power Play: Sport, the Media and Popular Culture* (2000), Alina Bernstein and Neil Blain in their edited volume on *Sport, Media, Culture: Local and Global Dimensions* (2003) and David Rowe in his edited volume on *Critical Readings: Sport, Culture and the Media* (2004)[8] – is also, inevitably, an important focus of our own volume, in which attention is regularly drawn to their mutually dependent economies and systems of representation.

8   R. Boyle and R. Haynes, *Power Play: Sport, the Media and Popular Culture* (London: Longman, 2000); A. Bernstein and N. Blain (eds), *Sport, Media, Culture: Local and Global Dimensions* (London: Frank Cass, 2003); D. Rowe (ed.), *Critical Readings: Sport, Culture and the Media* (Maidenhead, Open University Press, 2004).

Sport is undoubtedly a privileged site for studying European modes of social organization and their associated mindsets. In the final analysis, as Fred Inglis explained three decades ago in a pioneering study of modern games, 'Sports tell us stories; they make sense of the world'.[9] This is at least as true in the European context as it is in any other. More specifically, sport serves to explain a Europe that is constantly evolving, often in apparently bewildering ways, offering interpretative schemata that are increasingly mobilized as a result of sport's exceptionally visible location at the interface between local, national and global cultures. Inevitably, issues of governance are raised by sports policy and sports administration at both national and international levels. Our study consequently includes an analysis of the role of European sporting bodies such as the Union of European Football Associations (UEFA), concentrating not only on their management of key tournaments (such as the European club and nations cup competitions), but also on their role in the supra-national governance of European sport. Additionally considered is the impact on traditional, nationally based management structures of interventions by other key agencies, such as the European Court of Justice, whose Bosman ruling of 1995 was a landmark in the regulation of the transfer market in professional football players. Patterns of migration affecting both elite performers and broader populations are themselves an important component of evolving European identities, and thus of the constantly evolving sporting context with which the present volume seeks to engage.

Part 1 of the volume consequently focuses on the shift from Europe-led sporting diffusion in the nineteenth century to contemporary sports governance within the European Union, as discussed respectively by Sébastien Darbon and Borja García (Chapters 1 and 2). Their analysis is complemented by that of Eleni Theodoraki (Chapter 3), whose reading of the 2004 Athens Olympics explores the ways in which both the ancient history and entrepreneurial modernity of Greece were mobilized to maximize the positive impacts for national self-images of this most global of

---

9   F. Inglis, *The Name of the Game: Sport and Society* (London: Heinemann, 1977), p.71.

sporting mega-events. Later in the volume, Gyozo Molnar investigates
the concrete impact on individual identities of the increasing mobility of
elite sports players, focusing on the under-researched topic of Central and
Eastern European professionals, represented here by Hungarian footballers (Chapter 11).

The following section of the book concentrates the contributors'
attention on the national level, still arguably the most dynamic sphere of
sporting investments, both moral and material, notwithstanding the much
anticipated withering away of the nation-state in the era of globalization.
All three of the constituent chapters in Part 2 thus underline sport's significance as a remarkably rich field of nation-based representations, exploring its impact on both the 'high' and 'popular' cultures of Europe, from
the fine arts, through print and audio-visual media, to the contemporary
communications and information industries. The national sporting narratives explored here range from Jeffrey Hill's analysis of the class-bound
Englishness of the 'Tough of the Track' comic series (Chapter 4), through
Paul Dietschy's survey of the Italian sporting press under Fascism (Chapter
5), to the mediation of Spanish social values in the sports films discussed
by Álvaro Rodríguez Díaz (Chapter 6).

As Richard King and David Leonard comment, in the introduction
to their edited volume on *Visual Economies of/in Motion: Sport and Film*
(2006), the representational economies of sport serve 'to simultaneously
fashion magical spaces and to unfold metaphors for the social'.[10] In terms
of cinematic representations, the 'sports film' has become one of commercial cinema's most recognizable products. While Hollywood has largely
defined and popularized the form since at least Harold Lloyd's *The Fresh-
man* (Fred C. Newmeyer and Sam Taylor, 1925), through classics such as
Rocky (John G. Avildsen, 1976) and *Raging Bull* (Martin Scorsese, 1980),
and the more recent Oscar winner *Million Dollar Baby* (Clint Eastwood,
2004), there have also been important European contributions to the
genre. Moreover, while sport has played a crucial role in the articulation of

---

10   C. R. King and D. J. Leonard (eds), *Visual Economies of/in Motion: Sport and Film*
     (New York: Peter Lang, 2006), p.3.

local, regional and, particularly, national identities, this role has similarly been identified by scholars with regard to cinema, with Susan Hayward noting that 'film functions as a cultural articulation of a nation'.[11] European sports films have included work from Britain (*The Loneliness of the Long Distance Runner*, Tony Richardson, 1962; *This Sporting Life*, Lindsay Anderson, 1963; *Chariots of Fire*, Hugh Hudson, 1981); Norway (*Flåklypa Grand Prix* [*Pinchcliffe Grand Prix*], Ivo Caprino, 1975); Germany (*Die Angst des Tormanns beim Elfmeter* [*The Goalkeeper's Fear of the Penalty*], Wim Wenders, 1972; *Das Wunder von Bern* [*The Miracle of Bern*], Sönke Wortmann, 2003); France (*Les Triplettes de Belleville* [*Belleville Rendez-Vous*], Sylvain Chomet, 2003); and Ireland (*The Boxer*, Jim Sheridan, 1997), as well as the many Spanish examples Rodríguez Díaz discusses. Indeed, as King and Leonard further contend, 'sport cinema matters because sport matters and because popular culture matters in the creation, construction, dissemination, and articulation of dominant tropes and discourses of race, gender, class, sexuality and nation'.[12]

Located at the interface of the individual and the social, such sporting representations offer valuable insights into the creation and circulation of identities, particularly as regards their articulation with collective memory. Part 3 of the volume foregrounds such magical spaces and such social metaphors, especially as illuminated by the creative application of feminist critical paradigms to the analysis of conventionally gendered masculinity, the constitutive ambivalence of which is again very much in evidence. This is variously revealed by the relevant chapters: in the hyper-masculinity of boxing, as read both textually and visually by David Scott (Chapter 7); in the consciously ironic surfing culture of Mediterranean France, as explored by Cathal Kilcline (Chapter 8); and in the confected Ireland and Irish-ness communicated by the Irish media through its conflicting representations of the former Manchester United football star Roy Keane, as decoded by Marcus Free (Chapter 9).

---

11 Susan Hayward, *French National Cinema* (London: Routledge, 1993), p.x.
12 King and Leonard, *Visual Economies of/in Motion*, p.237.

Contested and reinvented identities remain to the fore in Part 4 of the volume, with the initial focus being on the often traumatic complexities of Northern Ireland's historical, political and cultural status as both a part of the island of Ireland and a 'province' of the United Kingdom. A recognized specialist in the area, Alan Bairner delves into the individual negotiations and representational ambiguities resulting from the selection of Catholic players for Northern Ireland's (Protestant and Unionist dominated) association football team (Chapter 10). The very different engagements with personal and cultural displacements experienced by elite Hungarian footballers playing in the professional leagues of Western Europe are then explored by Gyozo Molnar (Chapter 11). In contrast, in his own study of another contested Celtic identity, that of Cornwall, Dilwyn Porter reveals that objectively insignificant sporting competitions (such as English rugby union's traditional county championship, a competition effectively superseded by professionalism and its media-dependent league and cup tournaments) may actually be reinvested and even reinvented, albeit temporarily, by self-conscious and media-aware supporters, as a means of affirming cultural continuity and, indeed, political will (Chapter 12).

In the final section of the book, which focuses on the new sporting Europe, our contributors examine the changes which have occurred in two of the continent's sports superpowers, under the combined impacts of the political, economic and social restructuring that has taken place in Central and Eastern Europe since the fall of the Berlin Wall and the collapse of the Soviet Union. Two acknowledged experts in the field, and long-time pioneers of European sports history, Arnd Krüger and James Riordan, reflect here on developments since 1989, providing fresh insights into sport and identity in Germany since reunification (Chapter 13), and into sport and politics in Russia and the former Soviet Union (Chapter 14). Finally (in Chapter 15), John Bale, the respected sports geographer and cultural historian, brings the volume back to the issues of diffusion and representation raised by Sébastien Darbon in Chapter 1, drawing attention to Europe and its Others, specifically as regards Europeans writing (about) the African Olympian, of this and earlier generations.

By investigating a selection of particularly significant practices, locations and representations, the work as a whole seeks to assess the contribution of modern sports, both as participatory activities and sporting spectacles, to the ongoing construction of identities. It explores both 'traditional' identities (conceived as unitary and fixed) and the emergence of eclectic and unstable forms of identification. The study consequently draws on familiar sociological paradigms (such as age, class, gender and ethnicity), but also seeks to foreground processes of negotiation and reinvention, and the consequent emergence of various forms of hybridization in the sporting and broader public spheres. This includes particularly the emergence of multicultural and trans-national identities in sport and closely related issues of citizenship, empowerment and social inclusion. While sporting practices, locations and representations are prominent concerns throughout the work, individual chapters focus on the moral and material investment made by European citizens, and very often European states, in targeted events, institutions and figures.

This last point highlights the significance both of intra-European and extra-European sports exchanges and influences, as regards both individual practitioners and communities with a shared sporting identity, as well as competitive models imported from outside Europe and most obviously from the United States of America. Examples of such patterns analysed in this volume include the elite Hungarian footballers studied by Gyozo Molnar (in Chapter 11), the case study of Greek national readings of the supposedly universal symbolism of the Olympics at the 2004 Athens Games presented by Eleni Theodoraki (in Chapter 3) and David Scott's semiotic approach to European intellectual and artistic engagements with American constructions of masculinity in and through boxing (in Chapter 7). The last of these contributions is particularly suggestive of the attention to issues of representation that informs the present volume, as well as being exemplary in its broadly conceived, inherently interdisciplinary and consciously inclusive approach to issues of 'European-ness' in modern and contemporary sport. While the concept of 'Europe' itself may be destined to remain a weak marker of sporting identity in the face of more deeply entrenched, and periodically re-imagined, local, regional and national affiliations, there can be no doubting sport's broader contribution to the construction of evolving European identities. The goal of this collaborative study is precisely the scholarly elucidation of those identities and their sports-related interactions.

Bibliography

Anderson, B. *Imagined Communities: Reflections on the Origin and Spread of Nationalism* (London: Verso, 1983).

Bernstein, A. and N. Blain (eds). *Sport, Media, Culture: Local and Global Dimensions* (London: Frank Cass, 2003).

Boyle, R. and R. Haynes. *Power Play: Sport, the Media and Popular Culture* (London: Longman, 2000).

Cronin, M., M. Duncan and P. Rouse. *The GAA: A People's History* (Cork: The Collins Press, 2009).

Cronin, M., W. Murphy and P. Rouse (eds). *The Gaelic Athletic Association, 1884–2009* (Dublin: Irish Academic Press, 2009).

Hayward, S. *French National Cinema* (London: Routledge, 1993).

Hobsbawm, E. and T. Ranger (eds). *The Invention of Tradition* (Cambridge: Cambridge University Press, 1983).

Inglis, F. *The Name of the Game: Sport and Society* (London: Heinemann, 1977).

King, C. R. and D. J. Leonard (eds). *Visual Economies of/in Motion: Sport and Film* (New York: Peter Lang, 2006).

MacClancy, J. (ed.) *Sport, Identity and Ethnicity* (Oxford: Berg, 1996).

Markula, P. and R. Pringle. *Foucault, Sport and Exercise: Power, Knowledge and Transforming the Self* (London: Routledge, 2006).

Mignon, P. 'Le football investi par les capitaux', *Esprit*, January 1999, pp.121–33.

Scally, J. *The GAA: An Oral History* (Edinburgh: Mainstream, 2009).

Smith, A. and D. Porter (eds). *Sport and National Identity in the Post-War World* (London: Routledge, 2004).

Sugden, J. and A. Bairner. *Sport, Sectarianism and Society in a Divided Ireland* (Leicester: Leicester University Press, 1986).

——(eds). *Sport in Divided Societies* (Aachen: Meyer and Meyer, 1999).

Van Bottenburg, M. *Global Games* (trans. B. Jackson; Urbana, IL: University of Illinois Press, 2001).

PART I

From Diffusion to Governance

SÉBASTIEN DARBON

Chapter 1
An Anthropological Approach to the Diffusion of Sports: From European Models to Global Diversity

Researchers who have chosen sport as a field of investigation are obliged to reflect at some length on what they mean precisely by the term 'sport'. This is especially true when they engage with the process of sporting diffusion. Of course, this word has a generally accepted meaning upon which we may all agree, for instance if we are discussing sport in the pub. The broader this general meaning, the easier it is to arrive at a consensus about it. But if our intention is to conduct a serious analysis, as researchers working on the social and cultural dimensions of sport, we simply must use the term as an efficient tool; this means that the word 'sport' is rather more than a conventional notion – it is an analytical concept. Clearly, this may be the case for many words that are pivotal to any intellectual investigation, but it is even more important when dealing with sport. This is because of the extraordinary importance that sports activities have attained in everyday life in all countries, whether traditional or modern, and where they are now so deeply embedded in language, behaviours and representations. The researcher has consequently to be able to give clear answers to many questions of the following kind: 'When I am jogging every morning before going to work, am I doing sport?'; or 'Is ballet dancing a sport?'; or 'Is bullfighting a sport?' These are simple questions, but the answers are not so simple.

Another kind of trap lies in the historical use of the word sport, which can cover many different things. For instance, in England during the seventeenth and eighteenth centuries, for a member of the aristocracy or gentry, 'to have good sport' was a very common expression, which typically referred to activities like 'hunting, shooting and fishing'. I would like to show why it is important to make a clear distinction between such heterogeneous notions and a concept of sport that is genuinely useful, and thus broadly applicable, especially when we deal with the process of diffusion: *what*, precisely, has that continuing process diffused?

Many researchers have attempted to provide definitions of sport. They are so numerous that it would be tedious to list them. Nevertheless, in my opinion at least, those definitions are both frustrating and of strictly limited applicability, as they do not allow us to delimit with adequate precision a set of ill-assorted activities and thereby to give them a real conceptual unity. The problem may be that such attempts to define sport come from 'above', by which I understand a viewpoint that is overly theoretical. It seems to me that the best way to deal with that problem is to derive the concept of sport from a deep and rigorous historical analysis. The point of departure for such an approach must be the acknowledgement that, in nineteenth-century England, there progressively emerged a highly original system, the 'sports system', which constituted a radical break with the system that had prevailed hitherto – let us call the latter the 'athletic games system'. It was this new sports system that would subsequently be diffused across Europe and then throughout the whole world, and with it the specific sports upon which it was constructed.

Sports and athletic games have in common the fact that they are both physical and competitive activities between human beings, but we can identify a number of characteristics that may serve to distinguish radically between them. Such a perspective has been initiated by eminent historians and sociologists, the first systematic attempt probably being Allen Guttmann's delineation of the seven characteristics of what he called 'modern sports'.[1] Other attempts have been made since, but I think we could all agree on a list which would include the following:

1   A. Guttmann, *From Ritual to Record: The Nature of Modern Sport* (New York: Columbia University Press, 1978).

- The supplanting of the sacred by the secular;
- The profoundly innovative perception of the spatiotemporal framework of the relevant practices, and particularly the extraordinary importance given to the standardization and normalization of spaces devoted to play;
- The constant quest for equality – even if it cannot always be fulfilled;
- The emergence of very complex 'rules of the game', along with the need to write them down (which was crucial to the diffusion process), and particularly the fact that those rules became universal – that is, they were applied in any context where the sport was played;
- The bureaucratization of physical activity, with competitions being standardized in space and time, and administrative organs established to regulate and ensure respect for these and other relevant norms;
- The drive for rationalization and specialization, together with quantification, which reminds us that the sports system was also a product of the industrial revolution and exploded on to the scene in a period when Taylorism was in the ascendant.

All of this is well known and widely accepted.[2] Nevertheless, I propose to ask some rather broad questions about it.

The first question concerns the designation, or the naming, of that qualitatively new situation. Following Guttmann, we call it 'modern sport', as opposed to 'Greek sport', 'Roman sport', or 'medieval sport'. I have even come across the designation 'prehistoric sport', referring presumably to mammoth hunting or some such activity. This is puzzling, because it introduces a kind of evolutionist perspective that contradicts what Guttmann himself, and many others, describe as a radically new conception. Speaking of 'modern sport' is thus a kind of pleonasm, for sport has always been modern, and if we do not take this into account, we help to conceal what

---

2   Nevertheless, the relative importance of the various items is open to debate. For instance, in my opinion, the entirely new conception of space that is one of the main characteristics of sports has not been sufficiently stressed.

was precisely the main strength of all the efforts made to bring a historical perspective to the definition of sport. What happened in the nineteenth century with the emergence of the sports system was not simply the product of an evolution; it was, in fact, more akin to a revolution.

A second set of questions may give rise to some hostility. Arguably, the difference between the emergence of specific sports (tennis, football, golf, and so on) and what we call the 'sports system' has not been sufficiently stressed. Fuller appreciation of this deficit would allow us to understand more clearly a number of historical facts concerning the origins, and especially the diffusion, of sports. Of course, the two are intimately connected. It is precisely because some of the old athletic games were profoundly transformed, in particular by the then prevailing education system in England, that the advent of an entirely new conceptual framework, the sports system, became possible. However, by accentuating the distinction, we make clearer the possibility of temporal differences between the emergence of the sports system (an entity invented in Britain and nowhere else) and the emergence of a few specific sports (which in some cases were invented elsewhere). For instance, a sport like Olympic (or field) handball was born in Germany and has its roots in old German or central European athletic games.[3] Yet, it became a sport only in the 1920s, when all the characteristics of the sports system were already well established. It was the same process with such quintessentially American sports as basketball (Naismith, 1891) and volleyball (Morgan, 1895).

Thus, it would be preferable to make the distinction between, on the one hand, 'early' sports (such as cricket, rowing, golf, football and rugby), all of which were born in Britain – remembering that baseball and American football are respectively American versions of 'rounders' and rugby – and all having contributed by their early development to the creation of the sports system; and on the other hand, more recent sports (like handball, basketball and volleyball), which benefited from the existence of the sports system and immediately adopted its main features.

3   This game is the subject of the discussion that follows and should not to be confused with the varieties of traditional handball played against a wall, such as Fives in Great Britain (in its Eton Fives and Rugby Fives variants), Gaelic handball in Ireland, and pelota in the Basque Country.

Even if we know that forms of handball-like games were played all over the world in antiquity, handball as we (approximately) know it today was introduced in Germany in about 1890 by Konrad Koch, and thus may be considered to be a 'second-generation' sport, in the same way as basketball (1891) or volleyball (1895). In each case, the influence of a single man was important (respectively Koch, Naismith and Morgan), even if the role of the social and cultural environment was also crucial. But the similarities stop there. If volleyball, and especially basketball, were helped by the powerful structures of the YMCA, and were thus diffused very rapidly across the USA and all over the world, handball did not become popular at once. Rather, it was revived after the First World War, thanks to the efforts of Hirschman and Schelenz, who adapted it to the rules of association football;[4] it then became a regular sport within the educational system. The 'eleven-a-side' version of handball played outdoors (on a football field) was initially the most popular, and the 'seven-a-side' version played indoors on a much smaller court (almost exclusively in Scandinavia) became the prevailing game only at the beginning of the 1950s. The first countries to adopt it were those of Western Europe, but in Great Britain the first handball club was formed only in 1957, while the British Handball Association was not founded until 1967. The game's first incarnation as an International Amateur Handball Federation dates from 1928.

This general process of 'sportization' (not the most elegant of terms, and 'sportification' is hardly better), which in the case of handball occurred relatively late, may also involve more 'traditional' cultures, as demonstrated, for instance, by what happened, relatively recently, to games like the Afghan buzkashi, or the Japanese sumo. In this type of case, we generally also find patterns of resistance, because, as traditional games, they fulfil complex and deeply entrenched cultural functions. Finally, the attempt to impose the sports system on athletic activities that originally had nothing to do with it can be observed in those newly emergent activities commonly referred to as 'Californian sports': such as surfing, skateboarding, kite-surfing, snowboarding, and so on. There, one finds conflicts between those who

4   For instance, there was an 'offside' rule as in soccer. However, this was abandoned after some years, for it had the effect of interrupting the flow of the game.

accept the transformation of their games into sports (with competition, rules, federations, and all the constraints that accompany them) and those who refuse such interference, preferring to stress the freedom of taking part and the absence of regulation.

As regards the diffusion process itself, the usefulness of marking the difference between specific sports and the sports system also becomes apparent. There is the extreme case where a particular sport is adopted with enthusiasm, but the sports system itself is radically rejected. This is exemplified by the way the Trobriand Islanders of Papua New Guinea have transformed cricket, leading to a 'de-sportization' of the game.[5] However, most of the time, it works the other way round: the sports system itself is fully accepted, while, as part of this general acceptance, a specific sport may be rejected – this was the case, for example, with rugby in India, as we shall see.

In trying to understand the diffusion process, it is common to distinguish between two main ways of dealing with the phenomenon. The first could be termed the 'extrinsic approach', and would be represented by many authors, especially Marxist commentators. It stresses the importance of factors which are clearly independent of the specificities of each sport and which concern economic conditions and development, political conflicts, and so forth. The analysis of diffusion through the study of significant historical events might also, perhaps, be regarded as a form of extrinsic approach. The majority of historical approaches to the process of sporting diffusion focus on the role of individuals or institutions. The second method, the 'intrinsic approach', stresses the importance of what may be termed the formal properties of each sport in its acceptance or rejection by the communities within which it is diffused. This theory, developed by Pierre Bourdieu, and brilliantly picked up by Maarten Van Bottenburg,[6] is clearly an interesting attempt to analyse the links between

5   See, for example, A. B. Weiner, 'Trobriand Cricket: An Ingenious Response to Colonialism', *American Anthropology*, vol. 79, no. 2 (1977), pp.506–7.
6   M. Van Bottenburg, *Global Games* (trans. B. Jackson; Urbana, IL: University of Illinois Press, 2001).

the formal properties of a given sport and the social dimensions of a given community; but to my mind, the real heart of the matter lies in the kind of social dimensions that we choose to consider.

For Bourdieu, and the many scholars who have followed him, the diffusion process has to be analysed in terms of social hierarchy: in any society, some sports are fit solely for the membership of the upper classes (according to their possession of capital, both economic and cultural), while other sports can only be appreciated by members of the lower classes. I simplify somewhat, but that is the general idea. The problem is that we cannot draw any general conclusions from this conception, for it has no universal applicability. I recall Pierre Bourdieu, many years ago, trying to explain that rugby – and he was a rugby player himself – was too physically violent to be adopted by members of the upper classes, who favoured other varieties of sport, such as tennis or golf. It was easy to reply that, except in a very limited number of countries like Wales,[7] in the great majority of cases rugby union was (and still is) a sport practised by members of the middle or upper classes, and that, in addition, relations of this kind were open to modifications, sometimes of a very radical kind. It seems reasonable to conclude that there is no necessary or structural link between the formal properties of a sport and the social classes involved in its practice.

I will now try to present my own approach, beginning with some observations about the notion of culture as applied to sports activities. It is not useful to refer to an all-encompassing 'culture' that could be applied to sports as a whole: this would be far too general. In contrast, it is more productive to acknowledge the fact that each sport has its own culture: the culture of basketball is not the culture of rugby, which is not that of tennis, and so on. Although one may identify many things that they have in common, there are also important factors that are different; they thus constitute cultural 'sets' that are only partially connected. Where do these differences come from? They mainly derive from differences in the rules of the games themselves.

---

7   In the Irish context, Limerick city provides a similar example of a working-class rugby union tradition, underpinning the modern professional success of the province of Munster in the European Rugby Cup (winners in 2006 and 2008).

The rules of a game create a framework that is extremely precise and restrictive, effectively constraining the participants; they are the roots of what can be termed the formal properties of a sport. What does it mean exactly to speak of the 'formal properties of a sport'? Let us take some examples, in order to be less abstract. If we consider ball games, a primary distinction has to be made between them with regard to the way the opposing players interact when they are competing to win the ball. In the great majority of such sports, teams endeavour to get (and maintain) possession of the ball: this is the case in soccer, basketball, handball, the different forms of hockey, water polo, and so on.[8] However, in a small number of sports, if the players want to get the ball, they must catch the opposing players first: this is the case in rugby union, rugby league and American football. The significant thing here is the contrast between the first category of sports and those where bodies are in regular contact (often heavily), as in the second category.

This distinction is very important from an anthropological point of view, because it implies two very different ways of using one's body. As regards the second category of ball games, the most striking consequence is the authorization of tackling provided for by the rules. One can assume, for instance, that if a cricket player were allowed to tackle one of his opponents on the pitch, then the culture of cricket would be markedly different from what it is currently.

I would certainly not wish to claim that, within this second category, the culture of rugby union is equivalent to that of American football or even rugby league. For there is something that rugby union does not share with any of the other ball games: that is the specific way the players group together both in static and dynamic phases of the game – such as mauls, rucks and, especially, scrums. There is no equivalent of the scrum in any

8   In this category, it is also possible to make the distinction between sports like soccer or basketball, where players can be present in any part of the field of play, with the ball circulating everywhere, and sports like tennis or volleyball, where players are supposed to stay in their own part of the court (in squash and related games, they do share all parts of the court, apart from at service). But cricket and baseball are interesting cases implying something of a mixed model.

other collective sport or ball game,[9] and what is perhaps more important than anything else is the extraordinary intimacy between the players. First, between the forwards of the same team: for instance, the way the hooker is squeezed by the two props, but also the way a lock's head is inserted between two sets of buttocks, while he is linked with the prop by putting his arm from behind between the player's legs and grabbing the waistband of his shorts. Second, we must not forget what happens in a scrum when one front row is competing against the other, and notably that the head of a tight-head prop (no. 3) is squeezed between the heads of the opposing prop and hooker. I have focused here on the situation in rugby union, but clearly each sport has its own combination of formal properties.

The hypothesis I am presenting is that the formal properties of a given sport have, by themselves, the power to construct a set of behaviours, practical experiences and mental representations of the world: that is, systems of values. Moreover, and this is very important because we are analysing physical activities, these same properties structure a set of relations to the body. By this, I mean that as a player of a given sport, you have a special relationship with your own body, as well as with the bodies of both your team-mates and your opponents. We have seen how this has a dramatic applicability in the case of the forwards involved in a rugby union scrum. These parameters together define what one may call a culture, and specifically a sports culture. It follows that because the rules of, say, handball, rugby union and basketball are not the same, their formal properties are not the same, and their cultures are consequently not the same.

Let us conduct a small empirical test. In doing some fieldwork on rugby union and rugby league clubs,[10] I was fascinated by the discrepancy between the two cultures that they represent, and specifically by the differences in the respective value-systems of their players: while rugby league players were very individualistic and openly claimed to be so, rugby union

9   It does still exist in the rugby league version of the game, but it is not contested in quite the same way. This point is developed below.

10   See, for instance, S. Darbon, *Rugby mode de vie – Ethnographie d'un club: Saint-Vincent-de-Tyrosse* (Paris: Jean-Michel Place, 1995); S. Darbon (ed.), *Rugby d'ici: Une manière d'être au monde* (Paris: Autrement, 1999).

players permanently invoked collective action, and collective behaviour, whether on or off the pitch. Now, the two sports may superficially seem to be very similar from the point of view of their formal properties; but in fact, apart from the difference in the number of players, which I consider relatively unimportant, you have two essential rules which are very different and which mean very different formal properties. The first rule is that, in rugby league, the scrum is not a real scrum; rather it is an enactment or performance. In consequence, there is no need for a collective struggle within a framework of physical intimacy of the kind that you find in rugby union. In rugby union, the decision not to allow contested scrums when regular front-row players are unavailable because of injury or sending off during a match is criticized by many players, who see it as a way of profoundly transforming (for the worse) the spirit of the game. The second distinctive rule in rugby league is that if you run with the ball in hand and are tackled, your team retains possession of the ball five times; there is consequently no need for your team-mates to come to your assistance in keeping the ball, which is an intensely collective action. In short, in rugby league the accent is much less on the collective struggle and much more on the individual one.

This is not intended as a hard and fast explanation, but rather as a kind of general framework for reflection – and it certainly requires refinement. Let us try to go a little further. As the rules of a given sport have to be the same everywhere, in any country, then the formal properties of that sport are also supposed to be the same everywhere, and we may expect the cultural dimensions of that sport similarly to be the same everywhere. There is a tendency towards a kind of invariance, or universality. However, needless to say, it is not as simple as that, for at least two reasons. Firstly, as is the case for all other cultural forms, sports cultures evolve over time, and this may be due to intrinsic factors (for instance, a change in the rules),[11] but also to extrinsic ones (for example, the advent of professionalism in rugby union has certainly had important consequences for the behaviours and

---

11   What would happen, for instance, if the scrum was outlawed in rugby union, as was once considered in the Southern Hemisphere (especially in Australia, where rugby league is dominant)?

the representation of its players). Secondly, in the process of diffusion, a given sports culture is imagined to be similarly embedded in what are, in fact, entirely different societies and cultures. Thus, when Indians play in test matches against England or Australia, they may respect the same rules, but from a cultural point of view Indian cricket is not exactly the same as its English or Australian counterparts; just as Japanese baseball is undoubtedly different from American or Dominican baseball – even if the rules are the same. What I am describing here is what we commonly call *globalization*. So I would like to insist on the following proposition: *What is at stake in the diffusion process is the dialectical play between the universal dimensions and the contextual dimensions of sports cultures*. This approach insists on the importance of reaching *local* solutions, and of investigating *local* situations. It is precisely the meeting of a *given* sport and a *given* cultural configuration.

As an application of that approach, I have tried to show how the formal properties of cricket seem to be in harmony with important cultural features widely represented in Indian society, and how the formal properties of rugby are at odds with at least one fundamental principle of the caste system – namely the principle of separation between members of different castes (along with the two other basic principles, which are the division of labour and the hierarchy between the different caste segments).[12] As regards cricket, and following the very subtle analysis of Ashis Nandy in his fine book, *The Tao of Cricket* (2000),[13] the way time flows during a cricket match, along with the importance of chance – or fate, or destiny – which are direct consequences of various formal properties of the game (for instance, the fact that you never have a situation where the twenty-two players are on the field at the same time), fit very well with the general understanding of Hinduism as it expressed in everyday life. Like Hinduism, cricket is full of numerous options, of solutions that are difficult to rationalize, and which refer more to qualitative rather than quantitative conceptions

---

12   S. Darbon, *Diffusion des sports et impérialisme anglo-saxon: de l'histoire événementielle à l'anthropologie* (Paris: Maison des Sciences de l'Homme, 2008), pp.167–82 and 324–39.

13   A. Nandy, *The Tao of Cricket: On Games of Destiny and the Destiny of Games* (New Delhi: OUP India, 2000).

of the world – this being part of the archaic dimension of cricket, which I have analysed elsewhere.[14] The importance of ritual, of moral attitudes (self-control, style, respect for the law and for one's opponents), elegance of attire, and so on, seem to put the accent on the notion of purity and on timeless or immaterial conceptions of life, similar to those developed for instance in the great warrior epics of India, such as the *Mahabarahta*.

In contrast, the laws of rugby build a combination of formal properties (especially in relation to the bodily proximity imposed by those rules) that are at odds with deep-rooted Indian cultural conceptions (especially the principle of separation within the caste system). Here, of course, we need to be careful not to 'essentialize' cultures: it is impossible to refer to 'Indian culture', or to 'Japanese culture', that would not make any sense. But at certain periods, one can find in given societies very widespread behaviours or systems of values, whether religious or otherwise, which can lead to a rejection of different cultural forms that are externally imposed. Moreover, if there is, for anybody, the possibility, which sometimes becomes a necessity, of sharing different cultures (as, for instance, is certainly the case of an Indian computer specialist working for IBM who finds himself obliged to share his lunch at the office with members of different castes), we must remember that there is no obligation to do so in sport, and that if you have chosen to play a game, you are not obliged to choose rugby instead of tennis, squash, cricket or, if you have enough money, polo.

If we adopt this kind of analysis, there seems to be a problem with wrestling, which is very popular especially in the northern parts of India, and whose formal properties strangely resemble the way rugby forwards, in the scrum, tussle with their opponents or touch very intimately the bodies of their team-mates. In his book *The Wrestler's Body* (1992),[15] Joseph Alter has shown that the ideology shared by the wrestlers is not developed in opposition to the caste system: rather, it is separate from it. And the crucial point is probably that wrestling has deep roots in a complex cultural past, which is not at all the case for rugby. This kind of reflection leads me

14   Darbon, *Diffusion des sports et impérialisme anglo-saxon*, pp.167–82 and 324–39.
15   J. S. Alter, *The Wrestler's Body: Identity and Ideology in North India* (Berkeley, CA: University of California Press, 1992).

to propose Diagram 1.1, opposing two features that appear essential in the Indian case, from a cultural point of view: tradition on the one hand, and physical proximity (or closeness) on the other. Tradition is represented on the vertical axis, proximity on the horizontal axis.

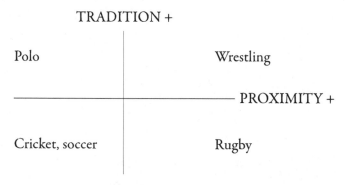

TRADITION +

Polo   Wrestling

———————————————————————— PROXIMITY +

Cricket, soccer   Rugby

Diagram 1.1 Cultural factors in sporting diffusion in India

When physical proximity is absent, the absence of tradition (as in cricket and soccer) is of no importance; while there is no problem for polo, of course, which is deeply rooted in Indian tradition. However, where physical closeness is important, the adoption of a sport is possible only if it is embedded in a cultural tradition that can deal with it (this is the case for wrestling), and it becomes impossible if there is no cultural tradition to refer to, as with rugby.

As regards rugby, we can offer empirical test cases, in countries where there is an important part of the population which comes from India; in Fiji, Mauritius, Trinidad and Tobago or Guyana, where the extensive application of the indenture system encouraged significant migration by Indian workers, the sports that are generally practised are essentially soccer and cricket, but never rugby.[16]

16   For the Fijian case, see S. Darbon, 'Pourquoi les Indo-Fidjiens ne jouent-ils pas au rugby?', *Études rurales*, nos. 165–6 (Jan.–June 2003), pp.103–21.

From the point of view of diffusion, in fact, an insistence on the formal properties of each sport (that is to say, a focus on its intrinsic characteristics) may help us to understand why some sports have had such striking success in certain countries, while others have been rejected. However, as with any anthropological proposition, this proposed explanation remains to be validated by extensive empirical investigation, within a general approach linking it as closely as possible to the historical perspective.[17]

Bibliography

Alter, J. S. *The Wrestler's Body: Identity and Ideology in North India* (Berkeley, CA: University of California Press, 1992).

Darbon, S. *Rugby mode de vie – Ethnographie d'un club: Saint-Vincent-de-Tyrosse* (Paris: Jean-Michel Place, 1995).

——(ed.) *Rugby d'ici: Une manière d'être au monde* (Paris: Autrement, 1999).

——.'Pourquoi les Indo-Fidjiens ne jouent-ils pas au rugby?', *Études rurales*, nos. 165–6 (Jan.–June 2003), pp.103–21.

——.*Diffusion des sports et impérialisme anglo-saxon: de l'histoire événementielle à l'anthropologie* (Paris: Maison des Sciences de l'Homme, 2008).

Guttmann, A. *From Ritual to Record: The Nature of Modern Sport* (New York: Columbia University Press, 1978).

Nandy, A. *The Tao of Cricket: On Games of Destiny and the Destiny of Games* (New Delhi: OUP India, 2000).

Van Bottenburg, M. *Global Games* (Urbana, IL: University of Illinois Press, 2001).

Weiner, Annette B. 'Trobriand Cricket: An Ingenious Response to Colonialism', *American Anthropology*, vol. 79, no. 2 (1977), pp.506–7.

17   For further development of this and related points, see Darbon, *Diffusion des sports et impérialisme anglo-saxon*, passim.

BORJA GARCÍA

Chapter 2
The Governance of European Sport

Introduction

Governance has become one of the most fashionable topics in European sport in recent years, although this interest in sport governance is relatively new. It took high profile scandals for the sporting movement and public authorities[1] alike to question the credentials and the effectiveness of the structures organizing sport in Europe. The bribing of International Olympic Committee (IOC) members around the election of Salt Lake City to host the 2002 Winter Olympic Games and other subsequent accusations of corruption within the IOC put the issue firmly in the headlines. Approximately at the same time, the doping scandal of the Festina team in the 1998 *Tour de France* questioned the willingness of governing bodies to tackle widespread doping practices in sport. Governments and sponsors around the world demanded reforms if the IOC and the sporting movement were to regain their credibility. But more importantly, this generated a renewed interest in the governance of sport. Questions were raised not just about corruption, but also more generally about the structures of European sport, the role of non-governmental sports organizations, the need for the involvement of public authorities and the transformation of European sport in the last decades as a result of commercialization and massive professionalization. Certainly, there is a growing interest in sport

---

1   We will use the expression 'public authorities' throughout this chapter as a general term to refer to governmental institutions and authorities across different levels of governance, including national, supra-national (EU) and sub-national (regional or local authorities).

governance developing among academics, public authorities, sport governing bodies and sport stakeholders.

However, it is not easy to delineate the main components of this debate
because there are too many intervening variables: contrasting opinions
among stakeholders, diverging definitions of governance and a large variety of structures in European sport do not make it easy to analyse. This
chapter aims to present a survey of the current state of the political and
regulatory debates on European sport governance. It will focus mainly on
two elements: (a) the organizational structures of European sport; and
(b) the relationship between public authorities, especially the European
Union (EU) and sports non-governmental organizations in the governance of European sport.

It is argued that professionalization and commercialization have put
under strain the traditional structures of sport in Europe, which the Commission labelled in 1998 the 'European model of sport'.[2] Governing bodies
have been challenged by converging demands from public authorities and
sport stakeholders to increase their levels of legal scrutiny, democracy
and transparency. This chapter describes the structural transformations
in European sport to cope with the challenges of modernization. Vertical,
top-down structures of governance are being replaced by more representative horizontal networks where stakeholders and public authorities claim
their role alongside governing bodies. It is also argued that, underlying the
debate on sport governance, there is a tension between the professional
and amateur dimensions of sport. The question is whether or not further
liberalization to take full advantage of the economic development of sport
may have negative consequences for the socio-cultural aspects of sport. In
the end, there is a political choice to be made: is sport in need of liberalization to realize its economic potential or, on the contrary, is it in need
of protection to fulfil its social functions at grass-roots level? The answer
given to this question conditions the strategy adopted towards sport governance. At present, it seems that there is a fragile consensus in Europe to
protect the social values of sport while trying to maximize its economic

2   European Commission, *The European Model of Sport: Consultation Document of DG
     X* (Brussels: European Commission, 1998).

potential. Despite the diversity of opinions, it is safe to affirm that, at least at the political level, there is an understanding that economic activities in sport should be a means to an end. However, this is a political and ideological choice and, as such, it is prone to change at any moment because there is no real right or wrong in that choice. The current global financial crisis could challenge any protectionist approach towards sport when the European economy is in need of reactivation. On the other hand, it may also be argued that the economic crisis is a perfect example, demonstrating that over-liberalization can have negative consequences and, therefore, sport should not follow the failed route of the financial services sector.

This discussion will proceed in four steps. It will begin by looking at theoretical approaches to governance in order to understand the basics of the concept that will then feature in the rest of the chapter. Second, we will proceed to define briefly the different dimensions of sport in order to understand the complexities underlying the debate on governance. The third section moves on to empirical analysis with a description of the traditional European model of sport and the recent challenges to the governance of sport. Finally, the chapter explains the new structures emerging as a result of the interest in good governance in Europe.

What is Governance?

Probably one of the reasons behind the complexity of the debates on sport governance is the nature of the concept itself. Roderick Rhodes has pointed out that the term governance is perhaps used in too many contexts and with different meanings. For our discussion here, though, the focus will be on two main elements: (a) governance as a network to structure the relationships among a large number of stakeholders;[3] and (b) governance as 'good governance', which is defined as involving the principles of effective,

---

3   R. Rhodes, *Understanding Governance: Policy Networks, Governance, Reflexivity and Accountability* (Buckingham: Open University Press, 1997), p.53.

transparent and democratic management.[4] Thus, as Matthew Holt points out, these definitions of governance can be seen as both analytical (or descriptive) and normative.[5] Applied to sport, this means that we can use this concept to analyse how sport is governed structurally and to comment on how well it is or should be governed.

Network Governance

Network governance is an analytical concept. It refers to a systemic structure where both state and non-state actors interact continuously in networks because they need to exchange resources and negotiate shared purposes.[6] This definition of governance refers to the management of a structure with a large number of stakeholders where power, authority and resources are diffused and distributed across the system.[7] It is difficult, therefore, to single out a focus of power because policies are negotiated among stakeholders in the network. In the area of sport, André-Noël Chaker has defined sports governance as 'the creation of effective networks of sport-related state agencies, sport non-governmental organizations and processes that operate jointly and independently under specific legislation, policies and private regulations to promote ethical, democratic, efficient and accountable sports activities'.[8] Chaker's understanding of governance in the field of sport is, therefore, quite similar to Rhodes' abstract and general definition. In both cases there are three important components: a network structure, the role of non-governmental organizations with a degree of self-regulation and the participation of public authorities in the networks. The purpose of

---

4   Ibid., pp.49–50.
5   M. Holt, *UEFA, Governance and the Control of Club Competition in European Football* (Football Governance Research Centre, Birkbeck College, University of London, 2006), p.4.
6   Rhodes, *Understanding Governance*, p.50.
7   Ibid., p.53.
8   A. N. Chaker, *Good Governance in Sport, a European Survey* (Strasbourg: Council of Europe, 2004), p.5.

this chapter is to investigate the evolution of European sport's governance structures. This relates to questions about the role and responsibilities of governing bodies (e.g. IOC, European sports federations); the level of power and representation of stakeholders (e.g. athletes, supporters or professional clubs); and the relations between public authorities (EU institutions in this case, since the chapter deals with the wider European level) and all those other sports non-governmental actors.

Good Governance

Those who study governance are also interested in the notion of 'good governance'. Rhodes describes good governance as involving the principles of effective, transparent and democratic management, and we can certainly examine these in the context of sport.[9] Good governance refers to the extent to which organizations observe principles of good management, transparency, democracy and/or accountability. Certainly, the notions of good governance and network governance are complementary, as one would expect those involved in network governance to observe good governance principles. In the case of sport, the necessity to observe good governance principles is applied to governing bodies and their policies,[10] but it is also applicable to other stakeholders, such as clubs, in their management of economic and human resources.[11]

---

9   Rhodes, *Understanding Governance*, pp.49–50.
10 For example, in football FIFA, UEFA and the national FAs adopt rules for the regulation of the game that are later implemented at club level. Therefore, it is legitimate to expect that these governing bodies observe good governance standards in their decision-making procedures, such as transparency, wide consultation, representation of stakeholders or accountability. It is also legitimate to expect that the governing bodies manage their economic and human resources in a transparent and effective manner. See for example J. Michie and C. Oughton, *The FA: Fit for Purpose?* (London: The Sports Nexus, 2005).
11 See, for example, S. Hamil, M. Holt, J. Michie, C. Oughton and L. Shailer, 'The Corporate Governance of Professional Football Clubs', *Corporate Governance*, vol.

What is Sport?

Having outlined a definition of governance, it is necessary now to high-
light the complex nature of sport. The only official definition of sport in
Europe is to be found in the European Sports Charter, adopted by the
Council of Europe in 1992. This definition is also used by the European
Commission in its recently adopted *White Paper on Sport*.[12] The Council
of Europe defines sport as:

> All form of physical activity which, through casual or organized participation, aims
> at expressing or improving physical fitness and mental well-being, forming social
> relationships or obtaining results in competition at all levels.[13]

In the Council of Europe's definition one can find a twofold role for sport.
On the one hand, sport has a social function. This approach is consistent
with the Olympic Charter's fundamental principles, which state that sport,
'combining in a balanced whole the qualities of body, will and mind', should
be 'at the service of the harmonious development of man, with a view to
encouraging the establishment of a peaceful society concerned with the
preservation of human dignity'.[14] This view considers sport as an objective
in itself and it is better identified with amateur sport, where economic
wealth is not the primary objective. On the other hand, the Council of
Europe's definition also emphasizes that sport is a competitive activity
aimed at obtaining the best possible results at all levels. This reference can

4, no. 2 (2004), pp.44–51; S. Gardiner, M. James, J. O'Leary and R. Welch, *Sports
Law* (3rd edn; London: Cavendish, 2006), pp.153–5.

12   European Commission, *White Paper on Sport* (2007). COM (2007) 391 final, 11 July
2007, <http://ec.europa.eu/sport/whitepaper/wp_on_sport_en.pdf> (accessed 13
July 2007), p.1.

13   Council of Europe, *European Sports Charter* (1992). Adopted by the Committee
of Ministers at the 480th meeting of the Ministers' Deputies, 24 September 1992,
<http://cm.coe.int/ta/rec/1992/92r13rev.htm> (accessed 15 March 2006), Article
2.1.

14   International Olympic Committee, *Olympic Charter: Fundamental Principles of
Olympism* (2004), <http://multimedia.olympic.org/pdf/en_report_122.pdf>
(accessed 13 March 2006), p.9.

be best identified with the professional side of sport or, as Lincoln Allison puts it, the 'institutionalization of skill and prowess'.[15] Allison distinguishes between the 'commercial-professional' ethos and the 'amateur-elite ethos of sport',[16] the former aiming at maximizing revenue and the latter aimed at maximizing sporting results in competition.

In light of these distinctions, it can be argued that there are four different dimensions of sport: sport for all, amateur sport, elite-amateur sport and professional sport. These four dimensions are embedded in the very nature of sport. They are not mutually exclusive, but rather points in a continuum. Almost every sport has a vertical axis that goes from sport for all to the professional level. This complicates decision-making in the area of sport, for the problems of sport for all are not necessarily those of professional sport. Moreover, sport and public authorities need to strike a balance in the relationship between the amateur and professional dimensions of sport: does professional sport have a duty of care towards the grass roots? Should they be independent of each other? In other words: which type of sport do we want? Again, to a large extent this is mostly a political and ideological choice. It will probably be guided by wider considerations of market and social reality, not only by a particular analysis of sport. The decision made in this regard is paramount, because it will condition the governing structures of sport.

The European Model of Sport

The discussion so far has remained at a more abstract and theoretical level. This section starts now with a description of the traditional structures that have organized European sport for a long time. The institutionalization of sport has been a long process whereby athletes joined clubs that

---

15   L. Allison, 'Sport and Politics', in L. Allison (ed.), *The Politics of Sport* (Manchester: Manchester University Press, 1986), pp.1–26, p.5.
16   Ibid., p.6.

formed leagues or federations, which, in turn, founded governing bodies
at national, continental and global level to structure the administration
of sport.[17] This multi-level structure was labelled in 1998 by the European
Commission the 'European model of sport'.[18] The Commission argues
that European sport has developed certain structures and characteristics
as a result of the very particular cultural, social and historical development
of Europe. Those features are intrinsically linked to sport in Europe and
some of them have been exported to other sports systems in the world.
The argument, to that extent, is similar to Sébastien Darbon's elsewhere
in this volume (Chapter 1).

The concept of the European model of sport outlines what the Commission considers to be the features and the organizational structures of
sport in Europe. In other words, it is a model of European sport's governance. In 1998, following the European Council's Amsterdam Declaration
on Sport,[19] the European Commission drafted an internal working paper
that was only intended to serve as a background paper for the Commission's
internal reflection on how to approach sport.[20] However, the document
has gained relevance over the years because it created the European model
of sport as a policy concept. The document contains a descriptive section
outlining the 'features and recent developments' of European sport.[21] It is
in that description that the Commission first introduced the concept of a
European model of sport:

17   See, for example, M. Marples, *A History of Football* (London: Secker and Warburg,
      1954); B. Murray, *Football, a History of the World Game* (Aldershot: Scholar, 1994);
      L. Allison, 'Sport and Civil Society', *Political Studies*, vol. 46 (1998), pp.709–26.
18   European Commission, *The European Model of Sport*; see also European Commission,
      The Helsinki Report on Sport (1999). Report from the European Commission to the
      European Council with a view to safeguarding current sports structures and main-
      taining the social function of sport within the Community framework. COM (1999)
      644 final, 10 December 1999.
19   European Council, *Declaration No. 29, on Sport* (1997). Attached to the Treaty of
      Amsterdam amending the Treaty on European Union, the Treaties establishing the
      European Communities and certain related acts.
20   European Commission, *The Development and Prospects for Community Action in the
      Field of Sport* (Commission staff working paper, 29 September 1998).
21   European Commission, *The European Model of Sport*, p.1.

> There is a European model of sport with its own characteristics. This model has been exported to almost all other continents and countries, with the exception of North America. Sport in Europe has a unique structure. For the future development of sport in Europe these special features should be taken into account.[22]

Having established the alleged existence of the European model of sport, the document outlines its main features by focusing on two different aspects: the organizational structures of sport and the features of sport in Europe.

The Organizational Structures of the European Model

The first characteristic of European sport highlighted by the Commission is the pyramidal structure in which it is organized.[23] Sport is organized in a system of national federations, which are affiliated to European and international federations: 'Basically the structure resembles a pyramid with a hierarchy'.[24] From the bottom-up, this structure is formed by clubs, regional federations, national federations and European federations.[25] It is important to note that the Commission acknowledges not only the vertical dimension of this structure, but also its hierarchical nature, hence recognizing the authority channels that come from the top (international and European federations) to the lower levels of the pyramid (clubs). The Commission explains that national and European federations have a 'monopolistic' position and that by using their regulatory power 'these organizations try to maintain their position'.[26]

The second organizational characteristic of the European model of sport is a system of promotion and relegation. The Commission explains

22 Ibid., p.5.
23 Ibid., p.2.
24 Ibid.
25 Ibid., pp.2–3.
26 Ibid., p.3.

that the pyramid structure 'implies interdependence between levels, not only on the organizational side but also on the competitive side'.[27] In other words, European sport is an open system of competition whereby low-level clubs can hypothetically earn promotion to the top tiers of their respective sport. This system is identified as 'one of the key features of the European model of sport'.[28]

The Features of Sport in Europe

Further to the organizational characteristics outlined above, the Commission completes its depiction of the European model of sport with a look at three different features that are considered paramount: a grass-roots approach, commitment to national identity and the existence of international competitions.

First, the Commission considers that one of the most important features of sport in Europe is that it is 'based on a grass-roots approach'.[29] The Commission considers that the development of sport originates from the level of the local clubs and that, unlike in the US, it has not been traditionally linked to business.[30] If the grass-roots approach to sport is accepted, together with the system of promotion and relegation, this creates a strong link between the top and lower levels of sport and, in consequence, between the amateur and professional levels of sport. Thus, the European model of sport could be said to have an element of solidarity, according to which the objective of professional sport is not only profit-maximization but also support for amateur sport. Whether real or illusory, the notion of vertical solidarity in sport appears to underpin the Commission's thinking.

27   Ibid., p.4.
28   European Commission, *The European Model of Sport*, p.4.
29   Ibid.
30   Ibid.

The second feature of the European model of sport highlighted by the Commission was the 'commitment to national identity or even regional identity', because it gives 'people a sense of belonging to a group'.[31] The third feature is the existence of international competitions where different countries compete against each other, demonstrating their different cultures and traditions and, thus, 'safeguarding Europe's cultural diversity'.[32] The Commission does not devote much discussion to this, but the sociological and identity aspects are certainly important features of sport.[33] As the Commission suggests, sport, on the one hand, can be a vehicle for individuals to feel included in a group. This sense of belonging can be generated at the more amateur level by participating in sport clubs in various roles (coach, administrator, player, and so forth) or at the professional level by following and supporting a particular team. On the other hand, sport is also a symbol of identities and, quite often, a reflection of clashing identities. National teams are a good example of the former, while the case of FC Barcelona, which is a symbol of Catalan identity as opposed to a Spanish national identity, would be a good example of the latter.

Therefore, to summarize the European model of sport, it is a systemic configuration characterized by a multi-level, pyramidal and hierarchical structure of governance that runs from the international federations down to the national federations and the clubs. This features a top-down, vertical channel of authority where the federations, holding a monopolistic power within their sport, attempt to retain their hierarchical position. Furthermore, sport in Europe is characterized by a grass-roots approach and a system of promotion and relegation, which implies a close link between the professional and amateur levels in sport.

31 Ibid.
32 Ibid., p.5.
33 These sociological aspects have been treated at length elsewhere. See for example A. Tomlinson and C. Young (eds), *National Identity and Global Sports Events: Culture, Politics and Spectacle in the Olympics and the Football World Cup* (Albany, NY: State University of New York Press, 2006); J. Magee, A. Bairner and A. Tomlinson (eds), *The Bountiful Game: Football Identities and Finances* (Oxford: Meyer and Meyer Sport, 2005); A. King, 'Football Fandom and Post-National Identity in the New Europe', *British Journal of Sociology*, vol. 51, no. 3 (2000), pp.419–42.

The European model of sport is to a certain extent an accurate account of European sport's traditional system of governance. For many years, the pyramidal configuration of governance has structured the organization of sport in the continent. This was a system that emerged within sport from the bottom-up, without much regulatory intervention from the public authorities; as Lincoln Allison has put it, it was civil society at its best.[34]

On the other hand, the European model is a generalization and, as such, it is prone to miss specific details. Although most sports presented the characteristics outlined above, it is also true that others differed from the European model to various extents. In some individual sports, such as tennis and golf, the relevance of federations was greatly reduced in favour of associations of professional athletes.[35] Other sports, such as snooker, darts or boxing, never really conformed to the European model. Yet, it is fair to say that the governance of European sport until approximately the 1980s is well encapsulated by the concept of the European model of sport outlined by the Commission.

The 1980s marked the starting point of the commercialization and professionalization of European sport. In the same document, the Commission recognized that sport was undergoing major changes. The Commission referred mainly to the globalization and commercialization of sport, best exemplified by the decision of the IOC to abolish the distinction between amateur and professional sport for the Olympic Games.[36] Other symbolic moments in European sport could be the proclamation of rugby union's professional status, the creation of the Golden League in athletics, the transformation of football's European Cup into the Champions League or the breakaway of First Division football clubs in England to create the Premier League. A clear gap emerged between top professional members and grass-roots members of the sporting movement, with important consequences for sport governance.

34   Allison, 'Sport and Civil Society', p.710.
35   For example the Women's Tennis Association (WTA) or the Professional Golfers' Association (PGA).
36   European Commission, *The European Model of Sport*, p.6.

The 'New Governance' of European Sport

The reality of European sport was transformed during the 1980s and 1990s, and the governance structures have been subject to similar changes. Commercialization principally questioned the relationship between professional and amateur sport. The professionalization of sport opened opportunities for those ready to invest in sport, but the pyramidal structure of the European model largely favoured governing bodies (at the top) over other stakeholders, such as leagues, clubs and athletes (at the bottom). Therefore, athletes or clubs faced systemic barriers if they wanted to benefit from the new commercial opportunities. The decisions of the governing bodies can influence the revenue streams of clubs and players. For example, governing bodies in tennis and snooker regulate the maximum surface of the players' attire where sponsorship can be situated. Thus, it is not difficult to understand that stakeholders disfavoured by the traditional structures of the European model have fought in the last decade for a transformation in the governance of European sport. Furthermore, the incapacity of some governing bodies to manage the new reality of sport strengthened the case for reform, as pointed out earlier in this chapter. New structures and new divisions of power and responsibilities are emerging. This is still an ongoing process that could be categorized as the new governance of European sport.

The European Commission, in its recently adopted *White Paper on Sport*, has recognized that the structures of European sport have changed in recent years. The Commission acknowledges that there is a departure from the characteristics defined in the European model of sport:

> The Commission considers that certain values and traditions of European sport should be promoted. In view of the diversity and complexities of European sport structures it considers, however, that it is unrealistic to try to define a unified model of organization of sport in Europe. Moreover, economic and social developments that are common to the majority of the Member States have resulted in new challenges for the organization of sport in Europe. The emergence of new stakeholders

(participants outside the organized disciplines, professional sports clubs, and so on) is posing new questions as regards governance, democracy and representation of interests within the sport movement.[37]

The Commission explains that it is now 'unrealistic' to define a single model of European sport. This implies a reluctance to endorse the pyramidal structure at the core of the European model. Similarly, the Commission is also flagging the fact that there are new stakeholders gaining power and importance, whose existence must be acknowledged and taken into account in the governance of sport.

Network Governance

The Commission's willingness to highlight the importance of new stakeholders in European sport can be linked to Rhodes' notion of network governance. European sport is organized now in a structure where power and authority are diffused across the network, rather than in the hands of a single actor. This analysis clearly questions the regulatory powers of federations. The new reality of European sport means that decisions cannot be taken by governing bodies in a vacuum and, certainly, their decisions are now much more scrutinized. At the very least, there is a demand for more representation in the federations' decision-making bodies. As the Commission points out, the vertical channels of authority of the European model of sport are losing importance:

> The relevance of the pyramid structure for the organization of competitions (and of the sport itself) is thus greatly reduced. It should be noted that the organization of competitions also largely diverges from the pyramid structure in other sports, such as golf or tennis.[38]

---

37   European Commission, *White Paper on Sport*, p.12.
38   European Commission, *The EU and Sport: Background and* Context (2007), p.41. Accompanying document to the *White Paper on Sport*. SEC (2007) 935, 11 July 2007, <http://ec.europa.eu/sport/whitepaper/dts935_en.pdf> (accessed 13 July 2007).

The Commission acknowledges that sport's governance is now far more complex. New stakeholders are challenging the legitimacy and authority of governing bodies.[39] Thus, the new governance of European sport features a complex horizontal dimension of stakeholder networks,[40] which is replacing the traditional vertical channels of authority defined in the European model of sport. Professional football is probably the best example of this transformation. Stakeholders such as the professional players' trade union (FIFPro), the association of top football clubs (European Club Association, ECA) and the European Professional Football Leagues (EPFL) have now been recognized by FIFA and UEFA and incorporated into their consultation and decision-making procedures (see Diagram 2.1).[41]

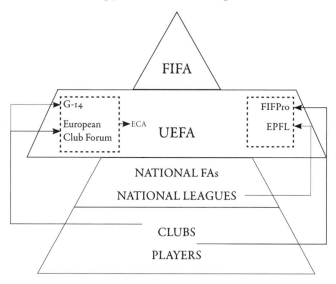

Diagram 2.1 The transformation of football's governance

39   European Commission, *The EU and Sport*, pp.41–2.
40   B. García, 'UEFA and the European Union, from Confrontation to Co-Operation?', *Journal of Contemporary European Research*, vol. 3, no. 3 (2007), pp.202–23, p.221.
41   B. García, 'The New Governance of Sport: What Role for the EU?', in R. Parrish, S. Gardiner and R. Siekmann (eds), *EU, Sport, Law and Policy: Regulation, Re-Regulation and Representation* (The Hague: TMC Asser, 2009), pp.115–36, p.119ff.

The federations have incorporated representatives of the players, clubs and leagues to reduce the threat of breakaway competitions or litigation in the European courts. This is especially visible in UEFA's Professional Football Strategy Council, a consultative but highly influential body comprising four representatives each of UEFA, EPFL, FIFPro and ECA. The Professional Football Strategy Council discusses issues relating to professional football, such as the reform of European club competitions or the introduction of rules to promote the training of home-grown players. The decisions reached in the Strategy Council are then passed to the UEFA Executive Committee for formal adoption.

Football's governance structures are adapting to new realities, but this has not been an easy process. Governing bodies have resisted the transformations of the European model of sport, where they had a prominent role.[42] Only the combined pressure of stakeholders, public authorities and sponsors has forced governing bodies to accept the necessity of opening up the system. In football, for example, the challenge of the G-14 to FIFA's rules on the mandatory release of players for national team duty (known as the Oulmers case) may be considered a significant turning point in the relations between the governing bodies and the professional clubs. In *Oulmers*, the G-14 and the Belgian club Sporting Charleroi started legal action under EU competition law against the aforementioned FIFA rules. When the issue was referred for a preliminary ruling to the European Court of Justice, the G-14, FIFA and UEFA reached an out-of-court agreement in early 2008.

---

42   See, as an example of that resistance, G. Infantino, *Meca-Medina: A Step Backwards for the European Sports Model and the Specificity of Sport?* (Nyon, Switzerland: UEFA, 2006); UEFA, *Sport Should Not Be Ruled by Judges: European Basketball, Football, Handball and Volleyball Are United in Defending the European Sports Model* (2007), Media Release no. 70, 9 May 2007, <http://www.uefa.com/newsfiles/536655.pdf> (accessed 11 May 2007).

New Governance Structures in Partnership

The new governance of European sport is characterized by a network structure of stakeholders. But André-Noël Chaker's definition of sports governance also calls our attention to another important variable: the effective co-operation in the network of what he calls 'sport-related state agencies' with 'sports non-governmental organizations'.[43] This last section focuses on this relationship by covering two issues that deserve further analysis: (a) the specific nature of the responsibilities of EU institutions in sport governance; and (b) the consequences of all the changes for the role of governing bodies.

The Role of Governing Bodies

In the new governance of European sport there is certainly an element that questions the role of federations. Yet, questioning does not necessarily mean denying. Despite the empowerment of new stakeholders, is there still a significant role for federations? The answer to this question, at the present moment, seems to be affirmative. There is a consensus that federations and Olympic committees need more democratic, transparent and representative structures, but their existence is not called into question. The European Commission's *White Paper on Sport* suggests that the transformation of the European model of sport does not necessarily mean a decrease in the relevance of governing bodies in sports governance, but simply realignment:

43 Chaker, *Good Governance in Sport*, p.5.

> The Commission acknowledges the autonomy of sporting organizations and repre-
> sentative structures (such as leagues). Furthermore, it recognizes that governance is
> mainly the responsibility of sports governing bodies and, to some extent, the Member
> States and social partners [...] The Commission considers that most challenges can
> be addressed through self-regulation respectful of good governance principles, pro-
> vided that EU law is respected.[44]

In this paragraph the Commission makes explicit mention of the governing bodies and their responsibilities in sports governance. Certainly, there
is not a firm defence of their hierarchical and monopolistic position in
the pyramid, but there is not a dismissal either. The *White Paper* does not
endorse the federations' primacy in sports governance as other documents
such as the *Independent European Sport Review* have done,[45] but it still
considers federations have a role to play.

The message of the White Paper is twofold. First, that there are alternative models to organize sport and it is up to each sport to decide which
one to use, providing EU law and good governance principles are observed.
Second, there are some features that were included in the definition of the
European model which were acknowledged as both legitimate and important. One of those is the role of sports federations in sports governance.
In the White Paper the Commission, for example, endorses club licensing
systems operated by federations, such as UEFA's club licensing system in
football. The Commission also reiterates that it is happy to assist governing bodies in promoting good governance practices in sport by creating a
catalogue of good governance principles and funding conferences to explore
the implementation of licensing systems.[46]

Thus, the European Commission considers that governing bodies
can still play a role in the new network governance of European sport. In
his conceptualization of network governance, Rhodes pointed out the
diffusion of power and authority among stakeholders. But he also explained
that there may be some actors playing a 'steering role' to provide gentle

---

44   European Commission, *White Paper on Sport*, p.13.
45   J. L. Arnaut, *Independent European Sport Review* (2006). Report by José Luis Arnaut,
     <http://www.independentfootballreview.com/doc/A3619.pdf> (accessed 17 January
     2007).
46   European Commission, *White Paper on Sport*, p.12.

direction and purpose to the network. These steering actors do not have absolute authority but they still perform as a focal point in the network because they have resources for the other stakeholders.[47] That concept of a steering actor within the network encapsulates relatively well the European Commission's view of the governing bodies' role in sports governance.

The Commission's recognition of the governing bodies is conditional upon the latter implementing new standards of democracy and representation. In this respect, the concept of good governance encapsulates perfectly the demands of the new governance of European sport. The Commission, like other public authorities, requires that governing bodies apply effectively principles of good governance. Sports federations have to adapt their organizational structures implementing principles of democracy, transparency, representation, accountability and effective management. Only if governing bodies apply principles of good governance will they be legitimized to perform the steering role in the new network of sport governance.

EU Institutions in Sports Governance: 'Supervised Autonomy'

The *White Paper on Sport* shows a European Commission that is aware of its limitations to intervene in the sports sector, pointing towards good governance and self-regulation as the possible way forward in the organization of sport. However, at the same time the Commission also affirms there is an area where the EU has full powers to scrutinize the actions of sports organizations: the application of EU law to their activities.[48] The Commission's reluctance to surrender this role has considerable implications because sports governing bodies have historically tried to minimize the application of EU law to their activities.

---

47   Rhodes, *Understanding Governance.*
48   European Commission, *White Paper on Sport*, p.13.

To explain the implications of the intervention of EU institutions for the governance of sport in a holistic manner, it may be useful to use the work of Ken Foster on the regulation of sport by the EU.[49] Foster analysed three alternative models of sports regulation by the European Union.[50] First, the enforcement of private rights through the European Court of Justice.[51] Second, the regulation of sport by the Commission through competition policy, which allows for exemptions to be granted in particular cases (Article 101.3, Treaty on the Functioning of the European Union). This was conceptualized as 'supervised autonomy'.[52] Third, a more political approach that would accept sports self-regulation without the intervention of EU law.[53] Building on Foster's argument one can adapt that threefold typology to suggest three alternative visions of sports governance and, consequently, three different roles for EU institutions in those systems of governance.

First, a direct or regulatory approach, where EU institutions would be an essential part of sports governance formulating policies about structures in sport. This approach would see an active role for the EU institutions in sports matters and would also imply that governing bodies' autonomy could be reduced, perhaps to the level of being considered merely *implementing agencies*. In this model the role of the EU could be characterized as a regulator.

Second, a level of 'supervised autonomy',[54] where the sporting movement recognizes the fundamental principles of EU law, but EU institutions do not have a proactive role in directly regulating sports governance, which is left to self-regulation. In this model, however, EU law adds a further layer of complexity because it is recognized that it applies to the activities of sports organizations. Here EU institutions would play a supervisory role to ensure sports organizations behave within the limits of EU law.

---

49   K. Foster, 'Can Sport Be Regulated by Europe? An Analysis of Alternative Models', in
     A. Caiger and S. Gardiner (eds), *Professional Sport in the European Union: Regulation
     and Re-Regulation* (The Hague: TMC Asser, 2000), pp.43–64.
50   Ibid., p.43.
51   Ibid., p.46.
52   Ibid., p.58.
53   Ibid., p.60.
54   Ibid., p.58.

The third model would recognize the total autonomy of sport and sport would be granted an exemption from the application of EU law. In this approach EU institutions would have no regulatory role in sports governance, but ideally they would endorse, support and facilitate sports governing bodies' initiatives (e.g. giving them political recognition or creating funding initiatives). In this model the role of EU institutions could be categorized as partner. For many sports governing bodies that would be an ideal outcome: to be exempted from the application of EU law, but being able to receive funding through EU sports programmes. However, there is a basic contradiction in that. The EU can only allocate funds to sports-related programmes if it has the legal competence to do so.[55] In the absence of such a competence, the Commission is unable to set up major sports-related funding initiatives. Yet, the creation of such a competence might risk evolving into further regulatory functions for the EU in the area of sport if one is to believe traditional neo-functionalist arguments.[56]

It is contended here that the European Commission, in the White Paper, suggests a 'supervised autonomy' to delineate the relationship between EU institutions and sports non-governmental organizations. Supervised autonomy implies that governing bodies and sport stakeholders alike are responsible for the organization and good governance of their respective sport and EU institutions will be supervising to ensure that they all fulfil their duties in respect of EU law. This reinforces the idea that governing bodies have responsibilities that we have conceptualised as a steering role using Rhodes model of network governance. From the governing bodies' point of view, this should be seen as a lifeline at a time when their legitimacy and authority were heavily questioned by other stakeholders and was also subject to the legal scrutiny of the ECJ and the Commission.

---

55 As acknowledged by the European Court of Justice in the ruling of UK v. Commission, case C-106/96, ECR [1998] I-0729. For an analysis of this case see R. Parrish and S. Miettinen, *The Sporting Exception in European Union Law* (The Hague: TMC Asser, 2008), pp.31–2.

56 E. Haas, *The Uniting of Europe: Political, Social and Economic Forces, 1950–1957* (2nd edn; Stanford, CA: Stanford University Press, 1968); P. C. Schmitter, 'Ernst B. Haas and the Legacy of Neofunctionalism', *Journal of European Public Policy*, vol. 12, no. 2 (2005), pp.255–72.

In the new governance of sport, EU institutions are likely to have a twofold role in the years to come. Firstly, EU institutions (especially the ECJ and the Commission) will be ensuring the application of EU law to sport. They will be supervisors. This is a powerful role because EU law might have considerable effects on the activities of sport organizations. In this respect, EU institutions would be located within the network at a superior level to the governing bodies and other sport stakeholders due to the primacy of the law. Secondly, the Commission is happy to identify concrete areas in which its actions can add value to the work of federations and other stakeholders. This role can be characterized as partnership. The main objective of these partnerships will be to ensure high standards of governance and a healthy development of sport. In this respect, the White Paper was accompanied by an action plan, called 'Pierre de Coubertin', which detailed a series of very concrete actions where the Commission can act to the benefit of sport within its current competencies.[57] As a whole, this dual role of supervisor and partner in concrete areas is relatively well encapsulated by the concept of supervised autonomy. The debate is open, however, as to where to put the stress, on the supervision or on the partnership.

Conclusion

The organizational structures of European sport developed through history to conform with what the European Commission labelled in 1998 the European model of sport. This model featured a pyramidal structure with a primary role for sports federations and a hierarchical component that structured the whole system. This implied a vertical channel of authority from the federations down to the clubs and athletes at the bottom. The European model of sport was also defined by a close link between

---

57   European Commission, *Action Plan Pierre de Coubertin* (2007). Accompanying
       document to the *White Paper on Sport*. SEC (2007) 934, 11 July 2007, <http://
       ec.europa.eu/sport/whitepaper/sec934_en.pdf> (accessed 13 July 2007).

professional and amateur sport. However, the economic development of European sport since the 1980s put the structures of the European model of sport under strain. There were converging pressures from stakeholders, public authorities and even sponsors aimed at reducing the power of governing bodies.

As a result of all these converging pressures, a new organizing structure of European sport is emerging, which we have termed the new governance of European sport. Building on theoretical models of governance developed by Rhodes, the new governance of European sport can be characterized by four elements: (a) a horizontal network structure that diffuses the influence of governing bodies and empowers new stakeholders such as clubs, leagues or athletes; (b) the transformation of governing bodies to perform a steering role within the network; (c) the implementation of principles of good governance by governing bodies and other stakeholders in the network; and (d) the participation of public authorities in the network to ensure that governing bodies do, indeed, act in full respect of the law of the land and the principles of good governance.

Building on Ken Foster's work, we can use the concept of supervised autonomy to categorize the role of European Union institutions in the new governance of sport. There is a consensus that sport should self-govern through the network structure. EU institutions, at the moment, do not want to regulate directly the governance of sport, but they are ready to perform a supervisory role to ensure that EU law is respected.

Following more than ten years of debates and legal challenges from stakeholders, EU institutions, national governments, governing bodies and even economic actors such as television operators, it is fair to say that a fragile consensus about the governance of sport is emerging. This chapter has outlined the main elements of that compromise: network governance with governing bodies in a steering role as long as they implement principles of good governance and public authorities acting as supervisors and partners. This has implications for the relationship between amateur and professional sport. Whilst the economic development of sport is not considered detrimental, the political case for a controlled commercialization of sport seems to be winning the debate. This means that, in general, there is an interest in maintaining a link between professional sport and the grass-roots, although protectionist measures to maintain the connection are not accepted blindly. Thus, sport policies need to be proportionate to their objective, not discriminatory, to promote economic competition as much as possible and, needless to say, they ought to respect principles of good governance. Yet, as we pointed out from the outset, this is very much a political choice and, as such, it can easily change. Only time will tell.

Bibliography

Allison, L. 'Sport and Politics', in L. Allison (ed.), *The Politics of Sport* (Manchester: Manchester University Press, 1986), pp.1–26.

——. 'The Changing Context of Sporting Life', in L. Allison (ed.) *The Changing Politics of Sport* (Manchester: Manchester University Press, 1993), pp.1–14.

——. 'Sport and Civil Society', *Political Studies*, vol. 46 (1998), pp.709–26.

Arnaut, J. L. *Independent European Sport Review* (2006). Report by José Luis Arnaut, <http://www.independentfootballreview.com/doc/A3619.pdf> (accessed 17 January 2007).

Council of Europe. *European Sports Charter* (1992). Adopted by the Committee of Ministers at the 480th meeting of the Ministers' Deputies, 24 September 1992, <http://cm.coe.int/ta/rec/1992/92r13rev.htm> (accessed 15 March 2006).

Chaker, A.-N. *Good Governance in Sport, a European Survey* (Strasbourg: Council of Europe, 2004).

European Commission. *The European Model of Sport: Consultation Document of DG X* (Brussels: European Commission, 1998).

——. *The Development and Prospects for Community Action in the Field of Sport* (Commission staff working paper, 29 September 1998).

——. *The Helsinki Report on* Sport (1999). Report from the European Commission to the European Council with a view to safeguarding current sports structures and maintaining the social function of sport within the Community framework. COM (1999) 644 final, 10 December 1999.

——. *The EU and Sport: Background and* Context (2007). Accompanying document to the *White Paper on Sport*. SEC (2007) 935, 11 July 2007, <http://ec.europa.eu/sport/whitepaper/dts935_en.pdf> (accessed 13 July 2007).

——. *Action Plan Pierre de Coubertin* (2007). Accompanying document to the *White Paper on Sport*. SEC (2007) 934, 11 July 2007, <http://ec.europa.eu/sport/ whitepaper/sec934_en.pdf> (accessed 13 July 2007).

——. *White Paper on Sport* (2007). COM (2007) 391 final, 11 July 2007, <http:// ec.europa.eu/sport/whitepaper/wp_on_sport_en.pdf> (accessed 13 July 2007).

European Council. *Declaration No. 29, on Sport* (1997). Attached to the Treaty of Amsterdam amending the Treaty on European Union, the Treaties establishing the European Communities and certain related acts.

European Parliament. *Resolution of the European Parliament on the Future of Professional Football in Europe* (2007). Rapporteur: Ivo Belet (A6–0036/2007, 29 March 2007), <http://www.europarl.europa.eu/sides/getDoc.do?type=TA&reference=P6-TA-2007–0100&language=EN&ring=A6–2007-0036> (accessed 12 January 2008).

Foster, K. 'Can Sport Be Regulated by Europe? An Analysis of Alternative Models', in A. Caiger and S. Gardiner (eds), *Professional Sport in the European Union: Regulation and Re-Regulation* (The Hague: TMC Asser, 2000), pp.43–64.

García, B. 'UEFA and the European Union, from Confrontation to Co-Operation?', *Journal of Contemporary European Research*, vol. 3, no. 3 (2007), pp.202–23.

——. 'The New Governance of Sport: What Role for the EU?' in R. Parrish, S. Gardiner and R. Siekmann (eds), *EU, Sport, Law and Policy: Regulation, Re-Regulation and Representation* (The Hague: TMC Asser, 2009), pp.115–36.

Gardiner, S., M. James, J. O'Leary and R. Welch. *Sports Law* (3rd edn; London: Cavendish, 2006).

Haas, E. *The Uniting of Europe: Political, Social and Economic Forces, 1950–1957* (2nd edn; Stanford, CA: Stanford University Press, 1968).

Hamil, S., M. Holt, J. Michie, C. Oughton and L. Shailer. 'The Corporate Governance of Professional Football Clubs', *Corporate Governance*, vol. 4, no. 2 (2004), pp.44–51.

Holt, M. *UEFA, Governance and the Control of Club Competition in European Football* (Football Governance Research Centre, Birkbeck College, University of London, 2006).

Infantino, G. *Meca-Medina: A Step Backwards for the European Sports Model and the Specificity of Sport?* (Nyon, Switzerland: UEFA, 2006).

International Olympic Committee. *Olympic Charter: Fundamental Principles of Olympism* (2004), <http://multimedia.olympic.org/pdf/en_report_122.pdf> (accessed 13 March 2006).

King, A. 'Football Fandom and Post-National Identity in the New Europe', *British Journal of Sociology*, vol. 51, no. 3 (2000), pp.419–42.

Magee, J., A. Bairner and A. Tomlinson (eds). *The Bountiful Game: Football Identities and Finances* (Oxford: Meyer and Meyer Sport, 2005).

Marples, M. *A History of Football* (London: Secker and Warburg, 1954).

Michie, J. and C. Oughton. *The FA: Fit for Purpose?* (London: The Sports Nexus, 2005).

Murray, B. *Football, a History of the World Game* (Aldershot: Scholar, 1994).

Parrish, R. 'The Politics of Sports Regulation in the EU', *Journal of European Public Policy*, vol. 10, no. 2 (2003), pp.246–62.

Parrish, R. and S. Miettinen. *The Sporting Exception in European Union Law* (The Hague: TMC Asser, 2008).

Rhodes, R. 'The New Governance without Government', *Political Studies*, vol. 44, no. 3 (1996), pp.652–7.

——. *Understanding Governance: Policy Networks, Governance, Reflexivity and Accountability* (Buckingham: Open University Press, 1997).

Schmitter, P. C. 'Ernst B. Haas and the Legacy of Neofunctionalism', *Journal of European Public Policy*, vol. 12, no. 2 (2005), pp.255–72.

Tomlinson, A. and C. Young (eds). *National Identity and Global Sports Events: Culture, Politics and Spectacle in the Olympics and the Football World Cup* (Albany, NY: State University of New York Press, 2006).

UEFA. *Sport Should Not Be Ruled by Judges: European Basketball, Football, Handball and Volleyball Are United in Defending the European Sports Model* (2007), Media Release no. 70, 9 May 2007, <http://www.uefa.com/newsfiles/536655.pdf> (accessed 11 May 2007).

ELENI THEODORAKI

Chapter 3
Expressions of National Identity through Impact Assessments of the Athens 2004 Olympic Games[1]

A careful consideration of the literature on mega sports events reveals that there can be no single 'best' model of capturing the impact of a mega-event the size of the Olympics.[2] Researchers shape their research by their onto-logical and epistemological assumptions, their presuppositions and even social prejudices and political purposes. Whilst considering the plurality of views on what constitutes impact, researchers are also mindful of the particular nature of the various sectors in the host county's community and economy.[3] It could be argued that, like most other social phenomena,

1   An earlier version of this paper that omits the link to Greek identity has been pub-lished as E. Theodoraki, 'Organizational Communication on the Impacts of the Athens Olympic Games', *Journal of Policy Research in Tourism, Leisure and Events*, vol. 1, no. 2 (2009), pp.141–55.
2   C. M. Hall, 'The Effects of Hallmark Events on Cities', *Journal of Tourism Research*, vol. 26, no. 2 (1987), pp.44–5; M. K. Dunn and M. P. McGuirk, 'Hallmark Events', in R. Cashman and A. Hughes (eds), *Staging the Olympics: The Event and its Impacts* (Sydney: Centre for Olympic Studies, UNSW, 1999), pp.19–32; T. Kitchen, 'Cities and the "World Events" Process', *Town and Country Planning*, vol. 65, no. 11 (1996), pp.314–17.
3   M. De Moragas and M. Botela, *The Keys to Success* (Barcelona: Centre d'Estudis Olimpics i de l'Esport, Universitat Autonoma de Barcelona, 1995); S. Essex and B. Chalkley, 'Olympic Games – Catalyst of Urban Change', *Leisure Studies*, vol. 17, no. 3 (1998), pp.187–206; C. Hill, *Olympic Politics* (Manchester: Manchester University Press, 1992); H. Lenskyj, *The Best Olympics Ever? Social Impacts of Sydney 2000* (Albany, NY: State University of New York Press, 2002); M. Roche, *Mega-Events and Modernity: Olympics, Expos and the Growth of Global Culture* (London: Routledge, 2000); K. Toohey and A. J. Veal, *The Olympic Games: A Social Science*

impact means different things to different people, with innumerable and often incompatible ways of measuring its forms, each with its antecedents and ideological orientation. The stakeholders in what can be described as an 'epic' Olympic project include politicians, private, profit-driven companies, the media, journalists, sponsors, the International Olympic Committee (IOC), Organizing Committees (OC), the International Olympic Sport Federations, athletes, National Olympic Committees, citizens, spectators, governments, pressure groups like environmentalists and human rights activists, to name but a few.[4] Such groups bring their own interests to the negotiating table when planning decisions are made, and the outcomes of their jostling for power invariably affect, if not dictate, impacts. Perhaps those who commission impact studies such as ministries or government departments may also affect the parameters of the research design.[5] For example, they may arbitrarily decide which aspects receive attention and which may conveniently be ignored. This multi-dimensionality of impacts leads to the interesting question of how (that is, by using which perspectives) bid/organizing committees choose to capture impact and communicate meanings and findings to their various audiences.

In the case of the Athens 2004 Olympic Games, related assessments of impact are inextricably linked to (a) the narrative on the Greek origins of the modern Olympic Games (OG) and their revival in Greece in 1896 and (b) the drive by the IOC to purify the movement from over-commer-cialization (that marred the centenary event in Atlanta in 1996) and the voting scandals related to the Salt Lake City 2002 Games. Closer to home, impact assessments are affected by notions of national identity and pride,

    Perspective (Wallingford, Oxon: CABI, 2000); D. Whitson and D. Macintosh, 'The Global Circus: International Sport, Tourism, and the Marketing of Cities', *Journal of Sport and Social Issues*, vol. 20, no. 3 (1996), pp.278–95.

4   A. Guttmann, *The Olympics: A History of the Modern Games* (Urbana, IL: University of Illinois Press, 1992); Roche, *Mega-Events and Modernity*; Toohey and Veal, *The Olympic Games*.

5   Avison and Young, *Olympic Impact: Vancouver 2010 and the Industrial Real Estate Market* (Vancouver: Avison and Young, 2003); Ference Weicker and Co., *Impact of 2010 Olympic Winter Games and Paralympic Games on Vancouver's Inner City Neighbourhoods* (Vancouver: Ference Weicker and Co., 2002).

the idea that the games were a gift to the Western World, and then a burden Greece chose to carry as an opportunity to show its modernity to the rest of the world, via the attention that the event brought: 'The "homecoming" rhetoric presents Athens 2004 as a burden that Greece has to carry under the gaze of powerful judges, such as America.'[6]

This chapter seeks to discuss how impacts of the Athens OG have been assessed and communicated by the OC, to explore their rationales, interests and approaches to measurement, as well as their communication tactics to wider audiences. This research contributes to the evolving literature on and understanding of event impact evaluations by moving beyond prescriptive accounts of how games impact evaluation ought to be done, or descriptive accounts of what the studies found, to an analysis of how games impact evaluation has been conceptualized at various stages, of what the assumptions held and approaches used are, and of what issues or areas are omitted or underplayed and how such behaviour can be explained. More specifically, the research objectives were to do the following:

(a) Identify defining attributes of the concepts of impact employed: categories, omissions, organizations, individuals included;

(b) Discuss how evaluation was shaped by organizational communication drives, interests and obligations of the authoring companies, to include the IOC, national and city government;

(c) Explore how the Athens OC linked Greek identity to measures of impact such as Greece's position in Europe, level of security, capacity of tourist industry, level of modernization in economy, transport, environment, social values.

6   R. Tzanelli, *Cultural Reciprocity: Greek Counter-Hegemony in Athens 2004* (Canterbury: University of Kent, 2003), <http://www.kent.ac.uk/sspssr/research/papers/polcult.pdf> (accessed on 10 August 2009).

Impact Assessment as Organizational Communication

Although the terms franchisor and franchisee are not used in the official
Olympic literature generated by bidders, hosts and the IOC, the relationship has been described as such,[7] and the bid/organizing committees are
under considerable pressure, institutional as well as contractual, to conform
to franchisor-led norms, values and guidance notes.[8] Organizational communication from bid and organizing committees is not immune to such
pressure, which is compounded by pressure from local and host-city-based
urban elites (politicians as well as entrepreneurs) with stakes in the event's
perceived successful hosting.

The Athens OG bidders and organizers engaged with the concept of
impact before and after the event in ways that are understandably affected
by the company's public relations and image creation activities, nationally
as well as internationally. To better understand the actions of the local
agents first in the successful bid committee and then in the newly formed
organizing committee, named ATHENS 2004, it is possible to employ
metaphors that identify different ways in which one can view organizations.
Tietze highlights the 'generative function' of a metaphor in its inherent
potential to create new ways of seeing the world.[9] This plurality notwithstanding, the very creation of new connections is often accompanied by
the constraining of a particular view, because attention becomes focused
on specific features at the expense of others. As ATHENS 2004 tried to
communicate to wider audiences the impact of the Olympic Games, it is
relevant to consider research in communication and organization brand
management and stakeholder theory. Putnam et al. claim that the 'ubiquitous nature of the term communication contributes to its elusiveness and
to the difficulty in distinguishing it from related terms such as informa-

---

7   E. Theodoraki, *Olympic Event Organization* (Oxford: Elsevier Butterworth
     Heinemann, 2007).
8   J. L. Bradach, *Franchise Organizations* (Boston, MA: Harvard Business School Press,
     1998).
9   S. Tietze, *Understanding Organizations through Language* (London: Sage, 2003),
     p.35.

tion, channel and media'.[10] An early metaphor employed in the literature on communication and organization was the metaphor of communication as a 'conduit'. The above authors suggest that this encompasses orientations of communication that treat organizations as containers or channels for the amount, type, direction and structure of information flows, with the focus being on transmission. The related metaphor of communication as a 'lens' is a variation of the conduit; this centres on the literature that treats organizations as perceptual systems or eyes that scan the environment, filter data, distort and delay information, screen or gate-keep and route messages. Related studies[11] concentrate on how certain messages are suppressed or distorted and on analyses of what senders believe that receivers want to hear. The existence of a multitude of impact studies that often only focus on a single aspect of the overall event impact (such as, effects on tourism, urban regeneration or civic morale) highlights the variety of lenses and their use as they are employed to investigate impact. The communication as lens metaphor can therefore be used to analyse how communication on impact by the local organizers is linked to organizational image making, public relations, and stakeholder interaction. In so doing, explanations of the selectivity in approaches to impact evaluation are more revealing.

Ancient Glory, Modern Messages

Modern Greece was formed as a nation in 1824, when the leaders gathered on the island of Hydra to form a constitution after the war of independence from Turkey. In defining who was Greek, they agreed that:

10   L. L. Putnam, N. Phillips and P. Chapman, 'Metaphors of Communication and Organization', in S. R. Clegg, C. Hardy and W. R. Norad (eds), *Handbook of Organization Studies* (Thousand Oaks, CA: Sage, 1996), p.375.
11   F. M. Jablin and L. L. Putnam, *The New Handbook of Organizational Communication: Advances in Theory, Research, and Methods* (London: Sage, 2001).

Those that reside in Greece and believe in Christ are Greeks and enjoy all political
rights. Those that come from abroad, have Greek as their paternal tongue and believe
in Christ are also Greeks and can enjoy the same rights. By presenting themselves to
the authorities they can ask to become Greek Citizens.[12]

Cultural identity defined the new nation and the grand vision was for a
modern Greece that links directly back to Byzantium and Ancient Greece
to claim its roots, origins and defining features. However, not all audiences
were prepared for that claim:

That vision was Hellas – the achievements of the ancient Greeks in knowledge,
morality, and art, summed up in one evocative word. What was more, the new Greek
revolutionaries went one step further than their forebears had ever managed to do:
they proposed to embody their entire vision in a unified, independent polity. This
unique nation-state would represent the ultimate achievement of the Hellenic ideal,
and as such would lead all Europe to the highest level of culture yet known.

[…] Europeans in other lands, though largely receptive to the attractions of Classical Greek culture, were not uniformly impressed by the modern Greeks' claim to
represent it. By what token could the latter-day Greeks portray themselves as the
true descendants of the ancient Hellenes? […] Greek scholars constructed cultural
continuity in defence of their national identity. […] they assembled what they considered to be the relevant cultural materials and used them to state their case.

[…] the Greeks were acting no differently than the representatives of other older
European scholarly traditions. […] The concept of Hellas was already a quicksand
of shifting perceptions when the modern Greeks came to it in their turn, bringing
with them their specialized nationalistic concerns.[13]

The Greek war of independence was supported by many 'Philhellenes'
abroad, who mounted expeditions to offer support. Greeks abroad, Byron
and European Romanticism helped construct an image that attracted considerable focus on the Greek cause.[14]

---

12   National Congress, *Law of Epidaurus: Temporary Constitution of Greece* (Hydra:
     National Congress, 1824).
13   M. Herzfeld, *Ours Once More: Folklore, Ideology and the Making of Modern Greece*
     (New York: Athens Printing Company, 1986) pp.3–4.
14   W. St. Clair, *That Greece Might Still Be Free: The Philhellenes in the War of Independence*
     (Cambridge: Open Book, 2008).

The obliteration of any trace of Ottoman rule appeared to be a priority for the identity of the newly defined Greek nation. Within Greece's cosmopolitan cities, where Christians, Muslims and Jews had co-existed for centuries, tensions eventually were created and slowly people moved or were forced to move along ethnic and religious lines. At the same time, the Greek language was being reconsidered, again with significant implications:

> [...] a tension that one meets repeatedly in Greece. The existence of a Greek nation-state was reluctantly predicated by the so-called Great Powers on the Greeks' presumed intellectual ancestry of European civilization; yet this genealogy was itself largely invented by Enlightenment philologists and historians, and the Greeks were constantly told, in the established tradition of imperial paternalism, to let their political elders and betters decide what parts of their present-day culture could legitimately be classified as 'Greek'. In one of the most colossal pieces of global chutzpah ever perpetrated, the Greeks were effectively taught that whatever was most familiar in their everyday lives was probably of Turkish origin and therefore by definition 'foreign'.[15]

The idea that modern Greeks were obsessed with proving their link to antiquity is also aired by others in the literature that considers what happened to language:

> [I see] history as a developing, dialectical continuity, existent everywhere but more deeply felt in some countries than in others. Nowhere have I found it felt as it is felt in Greece, where the past (Ancient Greece – Byzantium – 1821) seems to be vividly present to ordinary people in their daily lives [...].
> 	[...] but it will be enough to mention the exploitation of history to foster right-wing 'Greater Greece' chauvinism and the state of *progonoplixia* (being 'ancestor-struck') which reached its ridiculous apogee under the Helleno-Christian Junta. The most damaging result of this exploitation was probably the imposition of the purist *(katharevousa)* language in an attempt to bring about a return towards Ancient Greek, ignoring the development of the vernacular *dimotiki* over the intervening centuries.[16]

---

15   M. Herzfeld, 'Hellenism and Occidentalism: The Permutations of Performance in Greek Bourgeois Identity', in J. Carrier (ed.), *Occidentalism: Images of the West* (Oxford: Clarendon, 1995), p.218.

16   M. Sarafis, 'Byron and Greek History: A Reply to Emmanuel Sarides', *History Workshop Journal*, vol. 16, no. 1 (1983), pp.129–30.

Having considered modern Greek identity and some of the conditions in which it was shaped, attention now turns to the link to the Olympic Games and their representation by Greeks and others in the contemporary context. Physical activity and athletic competition were very important for Ancient Greeks, and the Olympic Games in particular held a significant role in cultural and religious terms. The Games were an opportunity to gather together from the various colonies in peace and worship, as well as to exchange ideas and plans for the future. The Games continued for a number of years until, in Byzantine times, they were deemed pagan and ceased. When excavations started in the North West Peloponnese, the ancient Olympic Stadium and numerous related sporting, religious and civil buildings were found.

The excavations coincided with a period of continued international interest by Hellenophiles in Western Europe, and Baron Pierre de Coubertin saw the opportunity to connect his sporting aspirations with the ancient Olympic Games, as these were described by the rediscovered Ancient Greek historians. In 1896, the revival of the Olympic Games in Athens showed the significance of the Greek connection, not least because Greece was prepared to finance the project, but also as, for Coubertin, Greece was 'the' place to gain the right allure.

Connecting modern Greek identity to the Olympic Games was natural and authors agree that:

> Greece has experienced a 'dual identity, as heir to the classical tradition, and as a modern European state' (more precisely, in the earlier parts of the story, an aspiring modern European state, the Olympics being seen as a means of achieving modernity). Extending this aim, Kitroeff argues that Greece maintained a privileged place in the Olympics movement because it saw its role as both the affirmation of the ancient heritage and a means to gain international recognition – which implied efficiency, modernity and the civilized values attributed to more advanced European states. Seen in this light, the Olympic Games, whether of 1896 or 2004, were a challenge which Greece could not refuse, whatever the cost to the taxpayer – though Harilaos Trikoupis came near to refusing it in 1895![17]

17   S. M. Llewellyn, 'Wrestling with the Ancients: Modern Greek Identity and the Olympics', *Journal of Modern Greek Studies*, vol. 23, no. 1 (2005), pp.199–201.

Tzanelli examined the Greek genealogy of the modern Olympics at length, because it shed light on the construction of Neohellenic identity:

> Henceforth I will maintain that every time Greeks invoke the Olympic discourse they resurrect their 'ancient modernity' – a peculiar modernity that came to mirror their cultural identity. The Greek metaphor of the nation 'risen from the phoenix's ashes' applies here: Hellenism is not simply resurrected every time the Olympics take place, it is also revered as a universal Neohellenic heritage.
>
> The 'fragments' of Western Orientalism, economic dependence, and political contingencies used by Greek actors define the past of their nation's relationship with Europe and the West. However, the way they are pieced together highlights the manner in which Greeks define the future of this relationship. The rhetoric that official Greek actors use, depicting the Olympic Games as both heritage and as a universal value that changes hands in a system of reciprocal services, is the best possible example of this process.[18]

In retrospect, it is evident that the backdrop of the formation of the Greek nation and the reassertion of the links to Ancient Greece across Europe, as well as in Greece itself, formed fertile ground for Pierre de Coubertin's vision of reviving the Games as a means of achieving his own aims, which were also deeply connected to French nationalism. For the 2004 OG the scene was set for the ideas to be presented and projected once more in numerous ideological expressions and image constructs. Such expressions, as they relate to the impacts, anticipated in the build-up period and perceived as achieved after the event, are the focus of the discussion that follows.

Communications on Perceptions of Impact (ex ante and ex post)

Understandably, the concept of impact first emerged during the bidding phase. Statements of what the ATHENS 2004 Bid Committee envisaged as regards the Games' impact can be traced in the bid documents. These

18   Tzanelli, *Cultural Reciprocity*.

were primarily produced as an IOC requirement to showcase the strength of a given candidacy and to address the IOC's interests, in particular aspects of the Games additionally focusing on a unique selling-point of the candidature (the Green Games, the Games for the Athletes, and so on). They typically comprise sections providing various state guarantees, descriptions of facilities, economic, environmental and political profiles of the host city's country, plans for the cultural dimension of the OG, marketing plans and detailed descriptions of budgets (specific to the event as well as non-Games related, such as general infrastructure). As the Olympic Charter also specifies, bid documents are analysed by an IOC Evaluation Commission, which provides a report, and IOC members, who are expected to select a host city on the strength of its bid.[19] IOC members' visits to candidate cities were banned as a measure to combat corruption,[20] but at the time of the Athens bid remained common practice, and the experiences of the IOC members in the host cities (had they chosen to visit them) would also have helped them to reach a decision on how to vote in the host city selection process.

As expected, the historical continuity with the ancient Olympic Games was strongly emphasized in bid documents:

> The Greeks had kept alive in their memories both the recollection of the 'Pan-Hellenic Games' and the name 'Olympic Games', as we can see from references in the theological and literary texts which survive from the period 393 AD, when the Byzantine Emperor Theodosius suppressed the Games, and the late nineteenth century, when the Games were revived as an international institution. Evidence to prove that the tradition of the Games was kept alive through the Byzantine period is to be found in the vernacular saga *The Epic of King Digenes Akritas*, composed in the eleventh century AD, and in the folk songs generated and sung in all the places where the people spoke Greek. Indeed, the Medieval Greek Digenes Akritas can be identified with Hercules, the feat-performing hero of antiquity. Many of the features

19   International Olympic Committee, *Olympic Charter* (Lausanne: International Olympic Committee, 1999).

20   International Olympic Committee, *Intermediary Report by the IOC 2000 Commission* (Lausanne: International Olympic Committee, 1999), <http://Olympic.org/ioc/e/facts/reports/pdf_reports/cio200_report_e.PDF> (accessed 1 August 2004).

of the ancient tradition of the Olympic Games were preserved in the places where the Greek nation lived and worked, and especially in the feasts and festivals of the people. In the early nineteenth century, the Greeks were dispersed throughout the Eastern Mediterranean and the Balkans, while many more lived in communities of varying degrees of cohesion in the rest of Europe. In those communities, the Greeks kept their cultural identity, and now a few of them became wealthy. It was against this background that the Greek Enlightenment was born and grew to maturity in the second half of the eighteenth century and the early decades of the nineteenth. Following the example set by the Renaissance, it strove to detect the Greek roots in folk traditions and the vernacular heritage.[21]

The intended legacy of the Athens 2004 OG was stated, albeit very briefly, in one of the Athens 2004 Bid volumes: 'For Greece, the birthplace of the Olympic spirit and the Olympic idea, the Athens Games will be a matter of supreme national and cultural significance'.[22]

The approximately 300-word narrative started with a reference to antiquity and how the strength of tradition and the potential of the modern country could contribute to the promotion of the Olympic ideal. Here, the anticipated legacy transcended Greek boundaries and was expected to contribute to the 'modern age', and, by implication, the IOC and the world of sport. Passing reference was made to the significance of the Games for the economy, reducing unemployment and tourism development (the Greek economy being heavily reliant on tourism). There was also an inference that the momentum of the Games would aid the completion of a number of major infrastructure projects that were funded by the European Union (EU) and allow rapid implementation of other projects that were being planned. In its concluding passage, the section referred to the potential for the creation of an enhanced image of modern Greece, improved sporting performance, creativity and the promotion of the collective identity of young Greeks. Following its successful bid, the city of Athens was awarded

21 General Secretariat of Sports, Ministry of Culture, *Athens 2008 ... being crowned victor in Athens* (Athens: General Secretariat of Sports, Ministry of Culture, 1995), p.66.
22 ATHENS 2004 Bid Committee, *ATHENS 2004 Bid Dossiers* (Athens: ATHENS 2004 Bid Committee, 1997).

the OG in 1997, and numerous games preparation projects began, albeit slowly, mainly in the Greek capital. As the date of the opening ceremony neared, the rhetoric on impact in the ATHENS 2004 communications was further developed along with the activities of the company's Image and Communications Department, which aimed to ensure a positive games image abroad and at home.

The values that ATHENS 2004 claimed to have espoused to deliver the Games were: celebration, human scale, heritage and participation. Linked to this were statements of ATHENS 2004's mission to:

> Organize a technically excellent Olympic Games.
> Provide the athletes, spectators, viewers and volunteers with a unique Olympic experience, thus leaving behind a legacy for the Olympic Movement.
> Display the Olympic ideals in a contemporary setting through their traditional Greek symbols.
> Promote and implement the Olympic Truce through the Torch Relay.
> Control the commercial aspect of the Olympic Games. Promote the cultural and natural heritage of Greece and its potential for the future. Protect and enhance the natural environment and promote environmental awareness.
> Promote the benefits of the Games throughout the country.[23]

Some statements of impact maintained the link to antiquity as well as the role played by philhellenes, but now in terms of sponsorship and business development:

> The timeless values of the Olympic spirit are comprised of noble ideas, such as fair play and spirited competition and are transported down through history from the ancient Olympia of 776 BC to modern-day Athens of 2004. For four consecutive years (2001–2004), the interest of the whole world will be focused on Greece. For the 17 days of the Games, Greece will be the centre of the world. It will show that it is a developed country responding to the challenges of today. Athens will become a modern-day metropolis, a source of culture and values. The organization of the Olympic Games in Athens in the year 2004 opens up new horizons to the economy of our country, offering new perspectives to Greek enterprises. The distinguished Greek companies that will play a more direct and active role as sponsors of the

---

23   ATHENS 2004, *Mission* (Athens: ATHENS 2004, 2000), <http://Olympic.org/ ioc/e/facts/reports/pdf_reports/cio200_report_e.PDF> (accessed 18 May 2003).

Athens 2004 Olympic Games become associated with the values of Olympism as partners in this great national effort, continuing the tradition of the Great Benefactors of our country.[24]

Other statements went even further to claim the geopolitical importance of Greece in the Balkans, in addition to the statements of Greece's physical and cultural environmental assets:

[...] Athens, which is also the economic and cultural capital of South-Eastern Europe... One hundred and eight years after the Games were revived in 1896, when they were held at the Panathinaiko Stadium, Athens is preparing to host the Games once more. With a population of four million inhabitants Athens is one of the most popular destinations of the world, since her unique contribution to history and culture down the ages is widely acknowledged and recognized. Spreading out from the sacred rock of the acropolis and the Parthenon, the Greek capital inspires respect and awe, its hundreds of monuments laying their fascination on the visitor. Athens has undergone many changes – from its infrastructure to its environment as has the entire country, vastly improving the quality of life for all Greeks. The 2004 Games will enhance and broaden these improvements. Organizing the Games of 2004 is speeding up the completion of large infrastructure works, making Athens one of the most modern cities and hospitable in the world.'[25]

Pre-Games ATHENS 2004 statements on the Games' legacy were available in its annual reports and website. In them, it was claimed that hosting the Games would have the following lasting impacts:

The Athens 2004 Olympic Games will leave a legacy for Athens, Greece and the world, which will remain for generations to come. As Sydney, Atlanta and Barcelona have shown, there are many tangible, long-term benefits to hosting the Olympic Games. For the people of Greece, the legacy of the 2004 Olympic Games will begin with the economic benefits of investing in upgrades to the transportation infrastructure, telecommunications system, and the environment. These investments will benefit Greece for years to come.[26]

---

24 ATHENS 2004, *Sponsorship Programme: Greece, Focus of the World* (Athens: ATHENS 2004, 2000), p.1.
25 ATHENS 2004, *Athens: Capital of New Greece* (ATHENS 2004 Olympic News 2, 2000), p.36.
26 ATHENS 2004, *Legacy* (Athens: ATHENS 2004, 2000), <http://www.athens2004.com/athens2004/page/legacy> (accessed 18 May 2003).

The descriptions of the event's benefits added below suggest that these are all positive, quantifiable, and quite specific and narrow in scope:

> Economic benefits (65,000 new permanent jobs, an increase in tourism, $1.3 billion boost in public sector revenues)
> Benefits to the Athens Transportation Infrastructure (120 kilometres of new road, new international airport, expanded metro system, new Traffic Management Centre
> Environmental benefits (290,000 new trees, 11 million new shrubs, 35 per cent improvement of the quality of the environment)
> Developmental benefits (in terms of human skills and expertise) and
> Social benefits (in terms of civic pride increase and a surge in volunteerism).[27]

In order to analyse the various statements on intended impact, it is prudent to consider their context by examining the authors, intended audiences and purposes of those documents where references to impact are made. As explained previously, the bid document was an IOC requirement. Obviously the bid document had to be professionally developed and convincing to make a good impression on the IOC Evaluation Commission and voting IOC members.

A positive spin on the impacts of the OG can surely be anticipated as: (a) the IOC expects Organizing Committees for the Olympic Games (OCOGs) to protect and enhance the Olympic brand, and (b) OCOGs need to rally community support for the games' preparations and this is also nourished through the dissemination of certain company messages to its various stakeholders and audiences. The types of impact anticipated are predominantly economic and social. Discussions of the effects on the environment, the political landscape, technological spheres, or even sports participation itself, are conspicuous by their absence. As ATHENS 2004 approached the date of the event, statements of impacts appear to be more clearly articulated.

After the OG came to a close, ATHENS 2004 orchestrated a last major campaign to showcase certain evidence of 'perceived' success in the organization of the event and, by extension, its manifold positive impacts. This evidence was made available by ATHENS 2004 one month after the

27   Ibid.

closing of the Games, in the form of two market survey reports. The first of these reported opinion surveys on perceptions of the success and benefits of the Games held by the people of Greece nation-wide. The method used was a quantitative survey with personal, face-to-face, structured interviews in the households of respondents with a geographically layered sample of 2000 persons.

The survey focused on whether the success of the Olympic Games enhanced the position of Greece on the international scene and whether people felt that the successful organization was of benefit to the country. To the question 'Compared with one year before, the place of our country in the world became more powerful, weaker, or remained the same?', over half of the respondents expressed the view that the place of Greece on an international level was more powerful. This view was complemented by the opinion that the successful organization of the Olympic Games was of benefit to the country, an opinion shared by 72.3 per cent of the citizens who participated in the survey. A significant 79.2 per cent of the respondents also expressed the view that 'undertaking to host the Games was the right choice for Greece', with only one in ten respondents holding the opposite view (10.9 per cent).

The survey also showed that the majority of citizens (at 92 per cent) rated as exceptional or very good the overall work implemented in Greece in connection with the organization of the Games, while for 89 per cent of the participants in the survey, the concepts of the 'International Olympic Committee' and of the 'Olympic Games in Greece' elicited a positive response on an emotional scale of 0 to 100. Finally, roughly eight out of ten respondents (81.6 per cent) rated the work of ATHENS 2004 during the preparation and the organization of the Games as exceptional or good.[28]

The second opinion survey referred to a new Greek identity. Greece is a 'safe destination', a 'modern European Country' that organized 'technically excellent' Olympic Games with a 'human dimension'. This is the new 'Greek identity' that emerges after the successful hosting of the Games, as

---

28 MRB –VPRC Research International, *Nation-wide Survey Conducted in Greece Concerning the Olympic Games* (Athens: ATHENS 2004 Press Office, 2004).

perceived by citizens in five major countries.'²⁹ The survey reported on the
perceptions of Greece held by people in the USA, Spain, Germany, France
and the UK. These sets of perceptions were elicited through a quantitative
telephone survey following a random calling process. The sample size was a
little over 500 respondents in each of the following countries: Spain, Germany, France and the UK and a little over 1,000 in the USA. The survey
considered whether respondents felt positive before and after the OG, given
what they saw or heard during the Games period. US respondents were
asked to comment on the likelihood of them visiting Greece for holidays
in comparison to other countries. The level of association with certain
statements was also explored. For example, respondents were asked their
opinions on the extent to which the Athens Games united nations of the
world, justified Greece as a European country, were technically excellent,
encouraged tourists to visit Greece as a summer destination, showed that
Greece is a modern country, and attracted foreign investment.

    In both surveys, the audience and intended recipients of the reports
were primarily domestic, together with the IOC, but material was also
strategically relayed to media and the press via the ATHENS 2004 website. The surveys aimed to provide quantitative market research in order
to substantiate claims of change in (a) the nature of Greece's image, (b)
the ability of the authorities and systems to handle complex events, and
(c) the perceptions of OG success and its attractiveness to tourists. Some
questions had a temporal dimension with pre- and post-Games data collection points.

    As regards the themes of impact investigated in the survey, some politi-
cal impact was implied in the reference to the justification for being considered a European Union country. Organizational and economic impact
was also documented, along with socio-cultural aspects (in the form of
the perceived changes in the image of Greece), and finally technological
impact. There was no discussion of domestic politics, environmental impact
or the impact on the availability of sports facilities in attracting future

29   MRB –VPRC Research International, *How Greece is perceived by the citizens of five
      major countries* (Athens: ATHENS 2004 Press Office, 2004).

event-related projects. There were no questions related to perceptions of overspending, stretching the budgets or the perception of the cost of these OG. The quantitative method employed allowed for no open-ended questions that could reveal other perceptions of impact. It is important also to consider the geographical scope of the surveys. The nation-wide survey did not produce any results per region that might reveal differences of perceptions on, for example, how beneficial the Games were for Greece. No justification was given for the choice of the USA, the UK, Spain, Germany and France as the sample for the international survey, apart from the description that these are five major countries. Tourists from Germany and the UK account for about 40 per cent of the country's annual visits, and this may be one of the reasons why these two countries were chosen. Spain and the USA, however, account for a much smaller number of visitors in comparison with countries like Italy.[30]

Conclusion

The data presented earlier revealed a number of interesting viewpoints about the Athens 2004 bid: namely, the ways in which the link of the modern games to the ancient Olympic Games was presented to build support; how the notion of a debt to Greece was presented to cultivate a sense of responsibility to persuade the IOC members to vote for Athens; the nature of the linkage between the games and the modernization of Greece made at bid and planning stages to build support by domestic audiences; and, most importantly, the key communication messages on the event's success immediately after the events were hosted and what they reveal about modern Greek identity and the interests of the organizers and the IOC.

---

30 Hellenic Organization of Tourism, *Annual Report* (Athens: Hellenic Organization of Tourism, 2004).

For Tzanelli, 'official Greek discourse on Athens 2004 articulates a version of identity that keeps the "Neohellenic" imagined community alive'.[31] Ex post statements on the impacts of the Athens 2004 Olympic Games were expressed by stakeholders in organizational communications, on the basis of Games impact surveys, to produce two key messages: (a) that the Games rightly returned to the Olympic roots for nourishment – which is what the IOC wanted; and (b) that Greece successfully showcased its modernity – which is what the Greek state wanted. It is important to consider the narratives present in the survey results, and to evaluate the ways in which the Organizing Committee of the Athens 2004 Olympic Games linked perceptions of the event's impacts to Greek identity and how these were communicated to various audiences post-Games. By drawing on the data, comments are also made on the selectivity of the evaluation indicators used to suit particular interests and how Greek identity is linked to such measures.

Relevant literature that allows the consideration of organizational communication activity as seeking to create certain meaning(s), as well as brand management literature, has aided the interpretation of these findings, and the communication on impacts of the Athens 2004 OG is seen to be part of the image-building exercises undertaken. The analysis also identifies how domestic cultural identity, as well as the institutional and contractual obligations of the bid committee and the organizing committee, at different times affected the ideology and conceptualization of impact communication data and reports.

In retrospect, it is clear to see how the bid committee and OC engaged with the concept of the OG impact in an attempt to create an image of productivity to various audiences and to protect, maintain and enhance a particular image of Olympism as per their contractual responsibilities.[32] In such a context, the franchisor behaved in ways endorsed by the franchisee and both the bid committee and OC conceptualized the event's legacy/

---

31   Tzanelli, *Cultural Reciprocity*.

32   International Olympic Committee, *Athens Host City Contract* (Lausanne: International Olympic Committee, 1998).

impacts in ways that suited their interests in achieving legitimacy and maintaining a positive image. It is important to highlight the relative lack of discussion of sporting and political impacts of the Athens OG and the lack of extensive research on these types of impacts.

The use of the two opinion surveys to substantiate claims of impact illustrates the priorities of the organizers to present perceptions of impact rather than attempt to capture actual impact in a concerted manner. Finally, in the light of the lens metaphor proposed by Putnam et al.,[33] the organizational communication on the event's impacts to the various audiences can be viewed as a concerted effort to create particular viewpoints, and also create a certain reputation for the overall administrative work of the organizations involved.

Bibliography

ATHENS 2004 Bid Committee. *ATHENS 2004 Bid Dossiers* (Athens: ATHENS 2004 Bid Committee, 1997).

ATHENS 2004. *Mission* (Athens: ATHENS 2004, 2000), <http://Olympic.org/ioc/e/facts/reports/pdf_reports/cio200_report_e.PDF> (accessed 18 May 18 2003).

——. *Sponsorship Programme: Greece, Focus of the World* (Athens: ATHENS 2004, 2000).

——. *Athens: Capital of New Greece* (ATHENS 2004 Olympic News 2, 2000).

——. *Legacy* (Athens: ATHENS 2004, 2000), <http://www.athens2004.com/athens2004/page/legacy> (accessed 18 May 2003).

Avison and Young. *Olympic Impact: Vancouver 2010 and the Industrial Real Estate Market* (Vancouver: Avison and Young, 2003).

Bradach, J. L. *Franchise Organizations* (Boston, MA: Harvard Business School Press, 1998).

---

33   L. L. Putnam, N. Phillips and P. Chapman, 'Metaphors of Communication and Organization' in S. R. Clegg et al., *Handbook of Organization Studies*, pp.375–408.

De Moragas, M. and M. Botela. *The Keys to Success* (Barcelona: Centre d'Estudis Olimpics i de l'Esport, Universitat Autonoma de Barcelona, 1995).

Dunn, M. K. and M. P. McGuirk. 'Hallmark Events', in R. Cashman and A. Hughes (eds), *Staging the Olympics: The Event and its Impacts* (Sydney: Centre for Olympic Studies, UNSW, 1999), pp.19–32.

Essex, S. and B. Chalkley. 'Olympic Games – Catalyst of Urban Change', *Leisure Studies*, vol. 17, no. 3 (1998), pp.187–206.

Ference Weicker and Co. *Impact of 2010 Olympic Winter Games and Paralympic Games on Vancouver's Inner City Neighbourhoods* (Vancouver: Ference Weicker and Co., 2002).

General Secretariat of Sports, Ministry of Culture, *Athens 2008 ... being crowned victor in Athens* (Athens: General Secretariat of Sports, Ministry of Culture, 1995).

Guttmann, A. *The Olympics: A History of the Modern Games* (Urbana, IL: University of Illinois Press, 1992).

Hall, C. M. 'The Effects of Hallmark Events on Cities', *Journal of Tourism Research*, vol. 26, no. 2 (1987), pp.44–5.

Hellenic Organization of Tourism. *Annual Report* (Athens: Hellenic Organization of Tourism, 2004).

Herzfeld, M. *Ours Once More: Folklore, Ideology and the Making of Modern Greece* (New York: Athens Printing Company, 1986).

——. 'Hellenism and Occidentalism: The Permutations of Performance in Greek Bourgeois Identity', in J. Carrier (ed.), *Occidentalism: Images of the West* (Oxford: Clarendon, 1995), p.218.

Hill, C. *Olympic Politics* (Manchester: Manchester University Press, 1992).

International Olympic Committee. *Athens Host City Contract* (Lausanne: International Olympic Committee, 1998).

——. *Olympic Charter* (Lausanne: International Olympic Committee, 1999).

——. *Intermediary Report by the IOC 2000 Commission* (Lausanne: International Olympic Committee, 1999), <http://Olympic.org/ioc/e/facts/reports/pdf_reports/cio200_report_e.PDF> (accessed 1 August 2004).

Jablin, F. M. and L. L. Putnam. *The New Handbook of Organizational Communication: Advances in Theory, Research, and Methods,* (London: Sage, 2001).

National Congress. *Law of Epidaurus: Temporary Constitution of Greece* (Hydra: National Congress, 1824).

Kitchen, T. 'Cities and the "World Events" Process', *Town and Country Planning*, vol. 65, no. 11 (1996), pp.314–17.

Lenskyj, H. *The Best Olympics Ever? Social Impacts of Sydney 2000* (Albany, NY: State University of New York Press, 2002).

Llewellyn, S. M. 'Wrestling with the Ancients: Modern Greek Identity and the Olympics', *Journal of Modern Greek Studies*, vol. 23, no. 1 (2005), pp.199–201.

MRB–VPRC Research International. *How Greece is perceived by the citizens of five major countries* (Athens: ATHENS 2004 Press Office, 2004).

——. *Nation-wide Survey Conducted in Greece Concerning the Olympic Games* (Athens: ATHENS 2004 Press Office, 2004).

Putnam, L. L., N. Phillips and P. Chapman. 'Metaphors of Communication and Organization', in S. R. Clegg, C. Hardy and W. R. Norad (eds), *Handbook of Organization Studies* (Thousand Oaks, CA: Sage, 1996), p.375.

Roche, M. *Mega-Events and Modernity: Olympics, Expos and the Growth of Global Culture* (London: Routledge, 2000).

Sarafis, M. 'Byron and Greek History: A Reply to Emmanuel Sarides', *History Workshop Journal*, vol. 16, no. 1 (1983), pp.129–30.

St. Clair, W. *That Greece Might Still Be Free: The Philhellenes in the War of Independence* (Cambridge: Open Book, 2008).

Theodoraki, E. *Olympic Event Organization* (Oxford: Elsevier Butterworth Heinemann, 2007).

Tietze, S. *Understanding Organizations through Language* (London: Sage, 2003).

Toohey, K. and A. J. Veal. *The Olympic Games: A Social Science Perspective* (Wallingford, Oxon: CABI, 2000).

Tzanelli, R. *Cultural Reciprocity: Greek Counter-Hegemony in Athens 2004* (Canterbury: University of Kent, 2003), <http://www.kent.ac.uk/sspssr/research/papers/polcult.pdf> (accessed on 10 August 2009).

Whitson, D. and D. Macintosh, 'The Global Circus: International Sport, Tourism, and the Marketing of Cities', *Journal of Sport and Social Issues*, vol. 20, no. 3 (1996), pp.278–95.

PART 2

National Sporting Narratives

Chapter 4
'I Like to Have a Go at the Swanks':[1]
Alf Tupper and English Society, 1945–1990

From the late 1940s until the early 1990s, Alf Tupper, the 'Tough of the Track', was a popular athlete hero in boys' comics published by the Dundee (Scotland) firm of D. C. Thomson. Although Thomson was well known for its popular Scottish vernacular literature, the firm's output also included many comic books with a broader British appeal.[2] Tupper was part of this market. His stories had a clearly English setting and were aimed at a readership drawn largely from teenage males across a wide geographical and social spread. Alf Tupper had first appeared in the *Rover* in 1949. His early popularity coincided with and was no doubt explained by a period of British successes in middle-distance running that came shortly afterwards. The achievements of Roger Bannister, Chris Chataway, Gordon Pirie and other outstanding runners in the early and mid-1950s gave hope of a British renaissance in athletics and, by implication perhaps, in world affairs generally. Tupper was a top-class middle-distance runner himself. His pinnacle of success was achieved at the summer Olympic Games of 1952 when he won the 1,500 metres title, but for many years afterwards he competed at the highest level. In the early 1960s, he was moved to the mainly comic-strip format of another D. C. Thomson title, the *Victor*, and ran there for another thirty years before eventually disappearing in 1992.

---

1   *Rover*, 29 April 1950.
2   On D. C. Thomson, see <http://www.geo.ed.ac.uk/scotgaz/people/famousfirst437. html> (accessed 9 March 2009); Wikipedia contributors, 'David Coupar Thomson', *Wikipedia: The Free Encyclopedia*, <http://en.wikipedia.org/wiki/David_Coupar_ Thomson> (accessed 9 March 2009).

By this time, with major changes taking place in British life, Tupper had become something of a sporting and social anachronism. Indeed, from the late 1970s, his appearances in the comic had been less and less frequent. His eventual passing marked the end not just of a fictional hero but of a particular post-war cultural discourse. Tupper had occupied a historical role not dissimilar to that of another popular boys' paper, the *Eagle*, of which the author Philip Pullman has noted that it 'lasted roughly as long as the post-war consensus, which in many ways it exemplified'.[3]

Tupper: The Man

Created around the time of the 1948 Olympics by the writer Gilbert Dalton, Tupper was a poor young man, with no family, who denied himself worldly goods and pleasures for the sake of his one true love: running.[4] In keeping with the prevailing orthodoxy in British athletics, he was a devoted amateur but unlike many of his rivals had no independent means to sustain him in

3   P. Pullman, 'Picture Stories and Graphic Novels', in K. Reynolds and N. Tucker (eds), *Children's Book Publishing in Britain Since 1945* (Aldershot: Scholar, 1998), p.123. The *Eagle* was published from 1950 until 1969. The total circulation of the *Rover* in the mid-1950s was just under 300,000, but by 1960 this had dropped to 196,000. The *Victor* began with almost half a million sales in 1961, falling to 384,000 in 1970 and 135,000 in 1980. Approximately half of the *Rover*'s sales were in London, Lancashire and Yorkshire, with London accounting for roughly a quarter of total sales. London's share of the *Victor*'s sales was rather more – around a third (38,000 in 1980). (I am indebted to Mr Bill McLoughlin of D. C. Thomson for providing this information.)

4   Dalton (1903–63) was born in Kidderminster, the son of a journalist. He had worked as a sports reporter for various national newspapers, but after the Second World War seems to have devoted most of his time to writing stories for D. C. Thomson. He contributed an immense number, being responsible for both Tupper and the equally popular Wilson stories, written often under the name W. S. K. Webb. See I. R. Smith, 'The Truth about W. S. K. Webb', *Track Stats*, vol. 36, no. 3 (1998), pp.54–7. I am grateful to both Ian Smith and Peter Lovesey for information on Dalton.

his sport. The header for the second story tells us: 'No track suits or training aids for Alf Tupper. All he has to help him reach the top in athletics
is – DETERMINATION'.[5] He was dependent on a manual job (Alf was
a welder by trade), and the twin features of work and sport provide the
core plot elements in the Tupper stories. In essence, however, they have
a moral thrust, dealing with a man's struggle to succeed in a world where
the odds are against him.

Alf's popularity is intriguing. His exploits and his philosophy of life
and athletics seem to have had a particular resonance for the young reader.
The stories drew much from the growing interest in athletics and its heroes,
and a variety of literary conventions ensured that the comics offered a 'good
read'. There was the social realism of the setting, in which familiar, everyday
situations were encountered; the demotic portrayal of Alf himself – gruff,
plain spoken, down-to-earth and 'ordinary'; the character's independence,
with Alf stripped of both family and broader domestic associations; and
his success on the athletics track, which forms the dramatic climax of the
stories and is presented as the just reward for hard work and self-discipline.
Such literary features reinforce the distinct phase of British society in which
the character of Alf made its appearance. In many ways Tupper personi-
fies a period of history, lasting for roughly the quarter-century from 1945,
when it seemed that the nation was on a trajectory of modernization and
social improvement, intended among other things to bring benefits to
those who had previously been among the more disadvantaged sections of
society. Tupper, a definite 'have-not' himself, stands almost as an 'everyman'
of this era, his own struggles representing the grander social and political
quest for 'fair shares for all'.

Comic-book heroes in commercial publications, though often inscribed
with (and within) a latent conservative ethos, have rarely voiced an explicit
political message. George Orwell, in a celebrated essay on boys' weeklies,
noted this implicit conservatism in publications of the earlier twentieth
century.[6] Tupper is exceptional in this respect for the inescapable political

5   *Rover*, 7 May 1949.
6   G. Orwell, 'Boys' Weeklies', in *The Penguin Essays of George Orwell* (Harmondsworth:
     Penguin, 1984), pp.84–106. See also Michael Oriard, *Dreaming of Heroes: American
     Sports Fiction, 1868–1980* (Chicago: Nelson Hall, 1982), Ch. 2.

dimension to his stories, and for this reason a 'political' situating of the character is important if its significance for English post-war identities is to be grasped. Even the most cursory reader could not have been unaware of the place occupied in the stories by social conflict. Alf's contests on the athletics track are most often against runners whose personal wealth and family resources place them at an advantage; they are unambiguously symbolic of the unequal distribution of wealth and opportunity in society. What is more, they all too often display an air of contempt towards Alf and people like him – in brief, they are *snobs*. Their very names often underline the point: Clifford Bellamy, Louis Marchant, Second-Lieutenant Rex Glider, the Hon. Piers Mornington, and Jerrard Tarn. Lew Murdoch sounds less superior, until we learn that he has a rich father who has provided him with a motor caravan driven by a personal masseur to take him from one athletics meeting to another. Skimba Ru is another longstanding opponent, no less snooty for being African – his father is a Zulu chief, and Skimba himself behaves with the haughtiness of one born to rule. All are good athletes, fortunate to have the private means that enable them to practise their skills at a high level without the need to work for their living. To Alf they are 'swanks' and 'toffee-nosed types' who, by looking down on working people, reveal their lack of common decency.

The reader is immediately positioned against such people, with the stories exploiting an instinctive animus against the rich. We share Alf's distaste for Clifford Bellamy, who has at his disposal a private running track, built for him by his industrialist father as a present for Clifford's birthday ('The only birthday present I ever had', says Alf, 'was a clip round the ear hole for asking for one'.)[7] Alf asks for an invitation to compete in a special event on the private track, but is rebuffed by Bellamy, who tells him: 'I'd sooner invite an unwashed Hottentot'.[8] Where others might quietly skulk away Alf would never bear such insults with equanimity. Within five hundred words of the opening of the very first story of 1949, for example, we find Alf getting into a fight with a bullying quarter-miler

7   *Rover*, 2 February 1957.
8   *Rover*, 9 February 1957.

who seeks to dominate the athletics club and who is not above cheating to advance his position. Alf will have none of it. He is unafraid to speak his mind and to resort to his fists when necessary to prevail over the obvious wrongdoer. In many of his opponents privilege is accompanied (necessarily, some might infer) by under-handedness. By contrast Alf's main weapons are honesty, self-discipline and natural ability. To readers his demeanour would have seemed righteous. It is neither selfish, nor individualist, nor gratuitously violent. It is firmly a part of that structure of feeling so brilliantly evoked by Richard Hoggart – the culture of 'Us', which is in perpetual tension with the world of 'Them'.[9] Tupper is a champion of 'Us', a man of 'the People'.

The Man and the People

'The People' is a term that largely dropped out of British popular usage at some point in the 1950s, so much so that it is now difficult to imagine the emotional purchase it once had. In some senses a paradoxical concept, it suggested an identity that was simultaneously particular yet indefinable. Its very imprecision, however, gave the term a powerful ability to evoke meanings and relationships. 'The People' were not by any means everybody; they were not the rich, nor were they probably those who exercised authority. They were not confined to the English, nor to the working class, and were not simply men, though they were probably assumed to be white. In the war and the immediate post-war years the term carried something of the idea of 'the masses' – those people encountered in buses and trains, in British restaurants and factory canteens, at football matches, at Woolworth's, in cinemas, and drinking tea in the NAAFI (Navy, Army and Air Force Institutes). They were the audience addressed in Wilfred Pickles's

---

9   R. Hoggart, *The Uses of Literacy: Aspects of Working-Class Life with reference to Publications and Entertainments* (London: Chatto and Windus, 1957), Ch. 3.

immensely popular radio programme *Have A Go* – which, as Wilfred told his listeners every week, 'presented the people to the people'.[10] They were, in short, 'all of us ordinary people'.[11] During the war the term occupied a central place in propaganda designed to boost civilian morale – it was the People for whom the war was being fought, and all the hardships and sacrifices suffered during the war were to be a prelude to improvements in the years to follow. Thus, the 'People's War' came to be perceived not as a conflict to preserve the *status quo ante*, but rather as a social crusade that heralded a new future.[12] This progressive idea had gained political momentum by the closing years of the war, but not without a struggle. It was contested and argued for by a variety of activist groups until, by the war's end, it had become a national narrative accepted by a significant proportion of British society.

One of its clearest wartime articulations came in *Picture Post*'s renowned edition of January 1941 – *A Plan for Britain* – which placed the idea of 'reconstruction' before the British public.[13] From it a groundswell of opinion grew in favour of change. It was registered in the Labour Party's general election manifesto of 1945, *Let Us Face the Future*, and in the spectacular victory for Mr Attlee's party at the polls in the summer of that year.[14] 'So far as Britain's contribution is concerned', the Labour

10   The programme, broadcast by the BBC, ran from the end of the war until 1967. At its peak in the 1950s it had some 20 million listeners.

11   See J. Baxendale, '"You and I – All of Us Ordinary People": Renegotiating "Britishness" in Wartime', in N. Hayes and J. Hill (eds), *'Millions Like Us'?: British Culture in the Second World War* (Liverpool: Liverpool University Press, 1999), pp.295–322.

12   See A. Calder, *The People's War: Britain 1939–45* (London: Jonathan Cape, 1969).

13   *Picture Post*, 4 January 1941. This edition was one of the most influential ever produced by the journal, the overwhelming sentiment in the many letters received from readers being supportive of its content. Fifteen-year-old Michael Dunnett wrote from Winchester College to say 'it is the best thing done here since "Rights of Man"' (*Picture Post*, 25 January 1941).

14   *Let Us Face the Future: A Declaration of Labour Policy for the Consideration of the Nation* (London: Labour Party, 1945). For a recent appreciation of the 1945 election, see David Kynaston, *A World to Build* (London: Bloomsbury, 2007), Ch. 3.

manifesto had declared, 'this war will have been won by its people'.[15] In saying this, Herbert Morrison, the manifesto's principal architect, had taken up and developed a nineteenth-century radical sentiment that spoke not simply to the working class.[16] Like the Chartists of a century earlier, Labour strategists in 1945 sought to augment their political appeal through a coalition of social support. Thus the manifesto spoke to the worthy and productive members of society, who were ranged against those who lived off the labour of others (the 'idle rich' as they were called in former times) and who were characterized in *Let Us Face the Future* as 'sectional interests' and controllers of 'private monopoly'.[17] The Labour manifesto eschewed overt suggestions of class and class conflict in favour of a communitarian spirit of unity among the many, whose military and home front service had made victory possible, and whose continuing willingness to work together would prevent the years of peace from being dominated by the interests of the few. '[W]e appeal to all men and women of progressive outlook, and who believe in constructive change, to support the Labour Party'.[18] It was in this political atmosphere, still vibrant in the late 1940s, despite the economic setbacks experienced in Labour's first term, that Alf Tupper was introduced to his reading public.

Tupper's egalitarian sensibilities chimed perfectly with the times. Alf judges people according to their ability, not by their title or by their perception of themselves. No man is his master: all are addressed as 'mister'. Ability and competence are of paramount importance. Pomposity and pretension are always deflated. In a story where Alf has to deliver metal pipes to the engineering department of the local university, he arrives just as the university sports are about to open amidst a flourish of ritual, with the tutors and athletes, led by their snobbish captain, Louis Marchant, gathered to sing their Latin song. Given wrong directions, Alf takes his load, on a handcart, to the athletics ground and there dumps it in the

---

15   *Let Us Face the Future*, p.1.
16   The text was written by Michael Young, sociologist, social reformer and author of *The Rise of the Meritocracy* (1958).
17   Ibid., p.2.
18   Ibid., p.12.

middle of the ceremony.[19] The incident sums up much of the Alf Tupper mentality. He has no time for display and the trappings of status. What concerns him is inner worth. Alf himself is a skilled worker whose astuteness on many occasions saves his employers from grave errors. He takes pride in his skills and, as in his running, sees a job well done rather than money payment as being the chief reward for labour. Material gain is of no consequence to him. He works for his living, but only to provide himself with the basics that enable him to devote time to his running. He has no interest in the excrescences of the 'affluent society', and quickly abandons a well-paid sinecure given to him as a reward for his Olympic victory. There is something ascetic – monkish almost – about Alf.

Athletics provides fertile terrain for the Tupperian morality. Historically, British athletics was strongly imprinted with the amateur ethos of the public schools and the ancient universities. It was, on the whole, a sport with its centre of gravity in the south of England.[20] Whereas association football could with accuracy be described as the 'people's game',[21] athletics, along with rugby union, was perceived as middle-class, run by voluntary officials and with star performers who, as often as not, had a university background. Roger Bannister, the first athlete to break the four-minute barrier for the mile, was the exemplar of this type, though during the 1950s athletes from far humbler backgrounds were beginning to establish leading positions.[22] In spite of this, however, sport's governing body – the Amateur Athletics Association – banned any competition for money, and even the payment

---

19 *Rover*, 22 April 1950.

20 See R. McKibbin, *Classes and Culture: England 1918–50* (Oxford: Oxford University Press, 1998), p.358.

21 It was so described in one of the first academic studies of the game, James Walvin's *The People's Game: A Social History of British Football* (London: Allen Lane, 1975).

22 Among them were some who recorded their experiences; for example, Gordon Pirie, *Running Wild* (London: W. H. Allen, 1961); Derek Ibbotson, *Four-Minute Smiler* (London: Stanley Paul, 1960); Ron Hill, *The Long Hard Road: An Autobiography*, Part 1 (Hyde: Ron Hill Sports, 1981); Fred Norris had no autobiography, but his obituary appeared in *The Guardian*, 17 January 2007. On Bannister see: R. Bannister, *First Four Minutes* (London: Putnam's, 1955); J. Bale, *Roger Bannister and the Four-Minute Mile* (London; Routledge, 2004).

of expenses was strictly limited; it was not until the later 1950s that a fund was set up to give athletes pocket money when competing for Great Britain in international events.[23] The uncompromising stance of amateurism in relation to money payment was summed up in the quasi-legal language adopted by two leading officials in a coaching manual aimed at youngsters in the early 1950s: 'no amateur should at any time take part in contests for which money prizes are offered, and he (*sic*) should not compete against others whom he knows, or has good cause to believe, have been in the habit of participating in competitions for money'.[24] Amateurism has been seen by many historians as a code devised in the nineteenth century by men who possessed the personal resources and leisure time to perform sport for the love of the game rather than as a means of earning a living.[25] Sport as work – 'professionalism' – was regarded as an unseemly activity for a gentleman, further soiled by its associations with gambling. It was outlawed in many sports until the very last years of the twentieth century.[26] Tupper the athlete is thus placed in a sporting arena that gives ample scope for developing the dramatic tensions between the social classes. His triumphing against his upper-class opponents is seen as not only a fair outcome in personal terms but as the vindication of a philosophy seeking social justice.[27]

23   J. Crump, 'Athletics', in T. Mason (ed.), *Sport in Britain: A Social History* (Cambridge: Cambridge University Press, 1989), pp.44–77, p.64.

24   H. Abrahams and J. Crump (eds), *Athletics* (London: Naldrett, 1951), p.15.

25   For a recent and somewhat 'revisionist' view of this, see R. Holt, 'The Amateur Body and the Middle-Class Man: Work, Health and Style in Victorian Britain', *Sport in History*, vol. 26, no. 3 (December, 2006), pp.352–69.

26   See R. Holt and T. Mason, *Sport in Britain, 1945–2000* (Oxford: Blackwell, 2000), Chs 3 and 4, esp. pp.43–9. Professional coaches were, on occasion, accepted in athletics and swimming, though many sought work overseas on account of hostile attitudes in Britain. D. Day, 'Steak, Stout and Strychnine: the development of a thesis', unpublished paper to International Centre for Sport History and Culture, Research Seminar, 30 April 2009, De Montfort University, Leicester, UK.

27   For a fuller discussion of Tupper and amateurism see J. Hill, "'I'll Run Him": Alf Tupper, Social Class and British Amateurism', *Sport in History*, vol. 26, no. 3 (December 2006), pp.502–19.

However, in spite of its associations with social privilege the amateur principle is one that Alf, surprisingly perhaps, accepts. He is a working-class amateur. In one very obvious sense almost everyone involved in sport was an amateur since few were good enough to earn money from it. Alf Tupper's steadfast belief in the idea of sport for sport's sake can be understood as an act of solidarity with all those ordinary men and women who run for the love of it. It seals his populist authenticity. There are several instances in the stories of his refusing offers of money. 'I've nothing to say against professional running', he remarks on one occasion (perhaps in tacit acknowledgement of what in the 1950s was a sporting occupation for some working men), 'except that I ain't going to be a professional. Running is my sport, mister, I'm not making a job of it'.[28] After winning a race sponsored by a local businessman for a £50 prize, Alf declines the money: 'running's me sport. I don't need no money for it'.[29] Thus, while Tupper was clearly a very businesslike amateur – he could not have achieved the level of performance he did without a 'professional' approach to training – work nonetheless remained the central part of his life. Alf, we are told, 'worked for his living, and lived for his running'.[30]

Running is simply an expression of natural ability. Tupper's success on the track is accounted for by the marriage of innate gifts and sheer determination. Spontaneity and intuition are his watchwords; anything that suggests formal learning or science is shunned.[31] Style, too, is secondary. In contrast to the easy loping strides of the upper-class amateur, typified by Bannister, Alf is depicted as an inelegant runner who 'always looked as if he were fighting his way along'.[32] Shrewd observers, however, will note that

28   *Rover*, 7 June 1958.
29   *Victor*, 2 February 1963.
30   *Rover*, 24 April 1952.
31   There are several stories in which Tupper is confronted by science, usually in the shape of coaches with new methods of training involving dietary regimes. In none is an approach based upon technical knowledge successfully adopted, and in many cases the scientific method is specifically rejected in favour of doing what comes naturally.
32   *Rover*, 24 April 1954.

'between every stride he has momentarily relaxed, with all tension gone from his big thigh muscles'.[33] This happens naturally; Alf is not aware that he is running in this way. It is part of the sheer enjoyment he finds in athletics – 'running's fun' he says, and we are told Alf is 'crazy about running'.[34] It is coupled with his immense will to win, which is enough to spur him along. He rejects the complex training routines favoured by athletes such as Pirie and Ibbotson.[35] Asked about his method his response is: 'I ain't got one … I just run as fast as my legs will carry me'.[36]

Tupper and Modernization

As a fictional contribution to the debate on 'modernization' in post-war British life the Tupper stories had both national and international significance. Domestically, a broadly agreed set of priorities in economic and social policy was contained within the notion of a 'social-democratic consensus';[37] in international terms, there was a recognition of Britain's changed great-power status, aptly expressed in Harold Macmillan's 'winds

33 *Rover*, 12 January 1957.
34 *Rover*, 22 April 1950; *Victor*, 5 January 1980.
35 Set out in some detail in their autobiographies. See Pirie, *Running Wild*, pp.24–6, and Ibbotson, *Four-Minute Smiler*, p.153ff.
36 *Rover*, 8 June 1957.
37 The notion is not without its critics and there is considerable debate as to its validity. Calder's *People's War* is an early critique; C. Barnett, *The Audit of War* (London: Macmillan, 1986) another; P. Hennessy, *Never Again: Britain, 1945–51* (London: Jonathan Cape, 1992) returns to the original idea of wartime consensus put forward by, for example, P. Addison, *The Road to 1945* (London: Jonathan Cape, 1975). David Marquand, in *Britain Since 1918: the Strange Career of British Democracy* (London: Weidenfeld and Nicolson, 2008), provides a slightly different slant, drawing attention to the competing but also overlapping traditions that shaped political discourse in nineteenth- and twentieth-century Britain.

of change' rhetoric of 1960 in relation to imperial and colonial questions.[38] In this context, the Tupper stories can be read as narratives about national improvement and change, arguing for a more cohesive society equipped with the skills and competences necessary to deal with the challenges facing Britain. In sport these were considerable. It was an area in which airy optimism about a 'new Elizabethan age' was viewed with scepticism, if usually on the back rather than the front pages of the national dailies.[39] In the decade or so following the end of the war there were numerous examples, especially in the Olympic Games, of the loss of British sporting status, and in 1957 these prompted a broad-ranging review of the condition of British sport by the one body at this time with an overarching role, the Central Council of Physical Recreation.[40]

The public resourcing of sport became a fundamental issue, and the Tupper stories had drawn attention to it almost from their beginning. The clearest example is a series set in the USA that ran from the winter of 1952 into the following summer. It offers critical reactions to the poor performance of British athletes in the Olympic Games of 1952 as well as some wry asides on Anglo-American relations. The relative poverty of resources in British athletics is contrasted with the apparent plenty to be found in America. Alf visits the USA as a member of a team of workers maintaining a locomotive exhibited in a British Railways publicity tour. The idea is that he will also have the opportunity to see indoor running tracks, virtually unknown at that time in Britain. The Americans 'have their

---

38   See C. Williams, *Harold Macmillan* (London: Weidenfeld and Nicholson, 2009), pp.358–9.

39   See, for example, reactions to the association football matches between England and Hungary in 1953 and 1954. J. Hill, 'Narratives of the Nation: The Newspaper Press and England v. Hungary, 1953', *Sport in History*, vol. 23, no. 2 (Winter 2003–04), pp.47–60.

40   The Committee (usually known as the Wolfenden Committee on Sport because chaired by Sir John Wolfenden, Vice-Chancellor of Reading University) made a number of critical points about the state of British sport (and the sporting press) at this time, but was ambivalent about amateurism. The Committee's papers (now in the possession of Sport England) reveal members to have been divided over the relevance of the amateur principle and this came through in its final report, *Sport and the Community* (Central Council of Physical Recreation: London, 1960).

indoor tracks and can keep going throughout the year ... it's time we had some changes here'.[41] In preparation for the novelty of indoor running Alf has to improvise; he trains first in a local dance hall that has a sprung floor, and then on the deck of the *Queen Mary*. His arrival in New York is made the occasion for a blank refusal on Alf's part to be impressed by things American, and aside from his welding Alf concentrates on running, in which his chief rival is 'Killer' Ginnis. 'Killer' is an American 'swank', a braggart who deliberately knocks Alf over at the start of a major indoor mile race at Madison Square Gardens. Alf nonetheless goes on to win, in spite of becoming confused by the unusual number of indoor laps. In all, Alf's successes (and some failures) in America, and his defiance in the face of unjust treatment, provide readers with a glow of British pride, reassuring them that Britain still has a presence in the world. But the resources available to the Americans present a serious challenge that will have to be met if that place is to be maintained. We are left, however, with a reminder that one outstanding attribute still relevant in overcoming overseas competition will be British pluck. When an American press reporter praises Alf for his fortitude – 'He wouldn't be licked'[42] – readers might have concluded that the same quality will also see the old country through its difficulties.

Ambiguous Alf

It makes some sense to superimpose Alf's story on to the narratives of war, reconstruction and modernization that had become prevalent by the late 1940s. But to see him simply as a fictional characterization of the social-democratic consensus would be misleading. The text is an elusive one, by no means without its contradictions. The character presents a number of ambiguities, with storylines that move in different directions, pointing up vexing problems of both authorial intent and reader reception. Just as

41   *Rover*, 20 December 1952.
42   *Rover*, 17 January 1953.

political ideologies at this time were fluid, never neatly aligned with party political labels,[43] so the 'meanings' of Tupper were subject to a variety of possible readings.

From the perspective of what is encoded in the text we should note that neither the publishers nor the original author of the Tupper stories, Gilbert Dalton, seem to have had a polemical intention. Dalton's aim was simply to arouse an interest in athletics among young readers after the disappointing performance of Great Britain in the 1948 Olympics,[44] while Thomson's aim was fundamentally commercial. The firm had published a number of leading newspaper titles in Scotland from the beginning of the twentieth century, including the *Dundee Courier* and the widely read *Sunday Post*. To be sure, all were conservative in tone (if not always strictly Conservative in party politics), and the company was opposed to trade unionism. Some have claimed that it was also anti-Catholic.[45] By the late 1930s, however, it had become known in the rest of Britain chiefly for its output of children's comics. Those for pre- and early-teen readers, the *Beano* and the *Dandy*, enjoyed much success. The *Rover* (started in 1922) and the *Victor* (which replaced it in 1961) also had a strong appeal; together with their companion titles the *Adventure* and the *Wizard* they circulated among youngsters at secondary school and, quite possibly, those in industrial apprenticeships. A regular feature of the *Rover's* front page in the 1950s was a display of school badges from around the country, though school stories were never the comic's staple copy. Heroism in war or sport predominated, with characters who were either adults or, like Tupper, at a transitional adolescent-adult stage.[46] In spite of an age difference, Tupper's demeanour is little different from that of another *Rover* hero, the wartime

43   See Marquand, *Britain Since 1918*, Ch. 3 and pp.117–53.

44   I am grateful to Peter Lovesey, author of *The Official History of the Amateur Athletics Association* (Enfield: Guinness Superlatives, 1979) for bringing to my attention material from Dalton's diaries (private correspondence, P. Lovesey to J. Hill, 8 April 2008).

45   See Tam Dalyell's obituary of Brian Thomson (1918–2006) in *The Independent*, 10 November 2006.

46   In his opening story, Alf is described as being 'nearly 19', an age at which he remains for the next 40 years (*Rover*, 30 April 1949).

pilot Matt Braddock, whose stories represent the same kind of challenge to conventional officer-class heroism that Tupper did to sporting heroes. Braddock (a name bringing to readers' minds both a tough American boxer of the 1930s and a truculent husband and wife Labour political team from Liverpool) was appropriately a sergeant; his enemies, apart from the Germans, were incompetent or snobbish members of the officer class, whose pig-headedness had to be brushed aside in the interests of victory. Braddock was not the customary, well-mannered, gentleman hero found in contemporary war films, and Tupper shared with him a similarly 'difficult' disposition. Within this fictional frame the publishers were able to reach into popular mentalities, maintaining the commercial viability of their products while at the same time offering a text that undeniably subverted conventional narratives.

Subversion, however, was never allowed to transgress fairly clear limits. These were set in accordance with tried and tested fictional, often comedic, conventions that had a long history in British popular culture. They underscore Nicholas Tucker's claim that children's literature of the immediate post-1945 period retained a number of older conservative themes alongside newer forms of social awareness that had grown during the war.[47] Cocking a snook at authority was a well-established feature of much popular cultural consumption, evident in forms such as seaside postcards, music-hall repertoire, and particularly the comedy films of Gracie Fields, George Formby and Will Hay.[48] But none of this was intended seriously to question the social order. Authority that was palpably just and efficient was not challenged. Alf Tupper showed no antipathy towards the good works foreman and manager, or, in his National Service stories, the fair-minded NCO; in athletics there is nothing but praise for the hard-working voluntary official. In fact, it is by emphasizing the virtuous qualities in leadership figures that we come to understand why working men despise the incompetents.

---

47 Nicholas Tucker, 'Setting the Scene', in Reynolds and Tucker, *Children's Book Publishing*, Ch. 1.

48 Hay's stage and film act mocked incompetent authority and often upset accepted notions of the work ethic. For example, *Oh! Mr Porter* (M. Varnel, UK, 1937).

In other ways too the Tupper stories inherit this conservative fictional legacy. Though never stridently jingoistic Alf's national identity is plainly expressed through an Anglo-centric perspective on the world; readers are drawn into knowing nods at the foibles of the French and Americans, or East Europeans and their rigid communist bureaucracy; even Skimba Ru, though a member of the Commonwealth and English-educated, is placed outside Alf's circle of decent people, perhaps as much for his social as his ethnic background. In the story sequence that features Alf's Olympic gold medal victory of 1952 there is a very hostile portrayal of his main opponent, the Moroccan El Jebel, who conforms to many of the stereotypes found in contemporary 'orientalism': he is devious, dishonest, prone to arrogance, and has a coach who cheats.[49] All these features contrast with Alf's honesty. There is more than a hint in the characterization of El Jebel of the contemporary attitudes towards Arabs that came to the fore during the long-running Suez crisis culminating in the Anglo-French invasion of 1956.

Changing Alf

Elusive and ambiguous though the text might be, the Tupper stories nonetheless endured commercially because they continued to deliver a plausible form of social realism to successive generations of readers. Alf himself was ageless, and so to a degree was his narrative. It proved adaptable to a variety of historical situations. Nor, when necessary, were the publishers above subverting their own text to keep up with the times. In a lengthy series in the *Victor* of the early 1970s, for example, D. C. Thomson came out with a new story, 'The Boyhood of Tupper', which demanded a radical shift in readers' perception of Alf. In refashioning the character it reached out to new social paradigms. A fictional time never previously explored in the stories is created, one which undermines much of the existing 'truths' about the character. Readers had always known a young man of about nineteen or twenty, but were now introduced to an eleven-year-old Alf; and having

49   *Rover*, 9 August 1952.

assumed that his background was working-class, they find now that it was petty-bourgeois. Alf is the son of a respectable shopkeeper and his wife, and is placed on the wrong side of the educational and social divide established by the 1944 Education Act. He attends the local grammar school where he is a promising pupil with aspirations to study for a future in engineering. Ironically (in view of what readers already know about Alf), he is the subject of hostility from boys at the secondary-modern school, who regard him as 'snooty'.[50] Alf's social position is thus reversed. He is, however, propelled into a life of poverty in his teenage years by the sudden deaths of both parents and his being taken into care by Aunt Meg, the only developed female character in the entire Tupper canon. She is a harridan whose meanness ensures Alf's downward slide. He leaves the grammar school for a grim secondary-modern – appropriately named Mudd Lane – from which he is expelled after being wrongly accused of violent behaviour, and sent to an Industrial School until the age of 15. At this point the history of Alf as formerly understood is resumed. In comparison with some of the bland stories that had appeared in the previous decade, this is a dark tale, incorporating an episode where the usually spirited Alf sinks into depression: 'Alf's lost heart' comments one of his teachers.[51] The stories target several objects of criticism: lazy workers, cynical teachers, inept liberal headmasters, athletics clubs who favour grammar-school boys over others, and above all the institution of the secondary-modern school itself, which by the early 1970s was on the point of being replaced in most parts of the country by the less divisive comprehensive system. Alf survives in this environment because he remains strong-willed, ready in the last resort to use his fists. The education provided is contemptible, its ethos summed up in the warnings given by a pupil charged with inducting Alf into the system:

> Now listen Tupper. Nobody works here, get it. No swots. No doing homework. Not that we get any. No neat exercises. No carrying home books. No nothing. And we don't want you breaking the code, Tupper. So watch it.[52]

---

50   The series began on 17 February 1973 and ran for several months.
51   *Victor*, 9 June 1973.
52   *Victor*, 7 April 1973.

His escape from this environment into the world of work and sport brings no material success, but his achievements in both fields are enough to bestow a sense of self-esteem.

Changing Times

In the long run, however, the moulding of Alf to his social surroundings had its limitations. Eventually he came to seem 'out of time'. This occurred, perhaps, more because of changes in sport than in politics. With the emergence in the 1980s of a more confrontational political ideology to challenge the 'social-democratic consensus', it is conceivable that the Tupper character might have undergone a refashioning as a hero of the radical right. After all, some of the hallmarks of Thatcherism – individual responsibility, private enterprise, market forces, and the 'level playing field' – had long been present in Tupper's make-up. Despite his proletarian truculence Alf's had been essentially an *individual* struggle against injustice. His world lacked any sense of collective endeavour. There was no trace, for example, of trade-unionism in Alf's workshop relationships. Nor had Alf ever been swayed by the idea of consumerism, the very practice upon which much of economic growth and modernization had depended. He was the antithesis of the teenage consumer, completely resistant to clothes, music, coffee bars, motor scooters, sex and all the other paraphernalia of the sub-culture.[53] He might well have suited an era of mass unemployment. But, as against this, the changes of the late twentieth century in sport, and especially in British athletics, were immense. With the final rejection of the amateur principle and the surge towards commercial sport, top athletes could earn very large sums of money.[54] Alf's 'sport for sport's sake' philosophy now seemed part

---

53   M. Abrams, *The Teenage Consumer* (London: London Press Exchange, 1959). See also D. Hebdige, *Sub-Culture: the Meaning of Style* (London: Routledge, 1979).

54   See Holt and Mason, *Sport in Britain*, pp.43–9 and p.86.

of a bygone age. The image of an impoverished gold-medal winner living in a welding shop and eating fish and chips simply defied belief. In this new social and political environment, then, the values that for some forty years had exercised an enduring fascination for young readers could no longer so easily claim their attention.

Tupper's success had stemmed in large part from the purveying of simple moral precepts through a strong textual stereotype. Michael Oriard's research has identified much of this in American sports fiction over the course of the late-nineteenth and twentieth centuries.[55] It is frequently based upon 'good' boys in a school environment, who succeed by dint of diligence and decent citizenship. Frank Merriwell is perhaps the archetypal hero of the genre, though there are several others.[56] Alf Tupper shares many characteristics with them. His story is one of ultimate success in the face of adversity (bad luck – of which Alf suffers plenty – and the dirty tricks played by unprincipled opponents). The basic plot in the Tupper stories involves a *test* – a key literary device in all such fiction – that had to be faced to prove one's mettle. In Alf's case, the test is usually a double one, bringing into operation both work and sport; work, as Alf avers, always takes priority, and there is often a 'rush job' to be completed, typically involving long shifts and sleepless nights, before Alf can race on a Saturday. He will arrive at the stadium worn out but uncomplaining, and compete. If he loses, there is an explanation (though not, in Alf's moral universe, an *excuse*); if victorious, the achievement is all the more astounding, a tribute to persistence. Running, says Alf, demands self-discipline, that you 'stick at it'.[57] In this sense, the stories promote the idea of perseverance and fortitude in the face of whatever life might throw at you. To prevail in a life beset by manifold problems is a mark of character. It brings Alf personal success in tasks he has set himself. But he does not grow rich, he exercises no more power at the end of his story than he did at the beginning, and the same

55   Oriard, *Dreaming of Heroes*, esp. Ch. 2.
56   The creation of Gilbert Patton (pen-name 'Burt L. Standish'), 1866–1945. See C. K. Messenger, *Sport and the Spirit of Play in American Sports Fiction: Hawthorne to Faulkner* (New York: Columbia University Press, 1981), pp.165–71.
57   *Victor*, 10 February 1968.

obstacles are still there to be overcome in the next day's work and sport. The stories contain no sense of a journey. The absence of a beckoning 'career' is, we might suppose, an experience shared by many readers.

What Tupper adds to such stories (and what American versions often lack) is a clear historical context. For at least twenty years after its first appearance the Tupper character was a sounding board for a number of prominent issues in British politics and society. Of these, class antagonisms are possibly the most striking. But the relationships and structures of class conflict are displaced into personal stories that encourage readers to dislike unpleasant individuals who are also rich. Moreover, Tupper's fight against the injustices and snobbery represented by 'the swanks' draws upon sentiments that were part of the British radical tradition of the nineteenth century. They do not always sit easily alongside later twentieth-century perceptions of society in which notions of 'embourgeoisement', the 'end of ideology', and the decline of social class suggest the possibility of a more consensual social order. Thus Tupper often seems old-fashioned, out-of-tune with the new political vocabulary.[58] However, the times themselves change. It may be that in the early twenty-first century, with a realization that the inequalities post-war social democracy had sought to eliminate are still with us, and with a growing popular anger at the conspicuous consumption of the rich and its 'bonus culture', we are ready for the return of Alf Tupper.

58   Many of the new ideas about 'embourgeoisement' and the 'end of ideology' appeared in the discipline of sociology in the 1950s and early 1960s. For a contemporary critical appraisal see J. H. Westergaard, 'The Withering Away of Class: A Contemporary Myth', in P. Anderson and R. Blackburn, *Towards Socialism* (London: Fontana, 1965), pp.77–113.

Bibliography

Abrahams, H. and J. Crump (eds). *Athletics* (London: Naldrett, 1951).

Abrams, M. *The Teenage Consumer* (London: London Press Exchange, 1959).

Bale, J. *Roger Bannister and the Four-Minute Mile* (London: Routledge, 2004).

Bannister, R. *First Four Minutes* (London: Putnam's, 1955).

Baxendale, J. '"You and I: All of Us Ordinary People": Renegotiating Britishness in Wartime', in N. Hayes and J. Hill (eds), *'Millions Like Us?' British Culture in the Second World War* (Liverpool: Liverpool University Press, 1999).

Calder, A. *The People's War 1939–45* (London: Jonathan Cape, 1969).

Central Council of Physical Recreation (CCPR). *Sport and the Community* (London: CCPR, 1960).

Crump, J. 'Athletics', in T. Mason, (ed.), *Sport in Britain: A Social History* (Cambridge: Cambridge University Press, 1989), pp.44–77.

Hill, J. 'Narratives of the Nation: The Newspaper Press and England v. Hungary 1953', *Sport in History*, vol. 23, no. 2 (Winter 2003/4), pp.47–60.

——. '"I'll Run Him": Alf Tupper, Social Class, and British Amateurism', *Sport in History*, vol. 26, no. 3 (December 2006), pp.502–19.

Hoggart, R. *The Uses of Literacy: Aspects of Working-Class Life with Reference to Publications and Entertainments* (London: Chatto and Windus, 1957).

Holt, R. 'The Amateur Body and the Middle-Class Man: Health and Style in Victorian Britain', *Sport in History*, vol. 26, no. 3 (December 2006), pp.352–69.

—— and T. Mason. *Sport in Britain 1945–2000* (Oxford: Blackwell, 2000).

Ibbotson, D. *Four-Minute Smiler* (London: Stanley Paul, 1960).

Kynaston, D. *A World to Build* (London: Bloomsbury, 2007).

Labour Party, *Let Us Face the Future: A Declaration of Labour Policy for the Consideration of the Nation* (London: Labour Party, 1945).

Lovesey, P. *The Official History of the Amateur Athletics Association* (Enfield: Guinness Superlatives, 1979).

Marquand, D. *Britain Since 1918: The Strange Career of British Democracy* (London: Weidenfeld and Nicolson, 2009).

McKibbin, R. *Classes and Cultures: England 1918–50* (Oxford: Oxford University Press, 1998).

Messenger, C. K. *Sport and the Spirit of Play in American Sports Fiction: Hawthorne to Faulkner* (New York: Columbia University Press, 1981).

Oriard, M. *Dreaming of Heroes: American Sports Fiction 1868–1980* (Chicago: Nelson Hall, 1982).

Orwell, G. 'Boys' Weeklies', in *The Penguin Essays of George Orwell* (Harmondsworth: Penguin, 1984), pp.84–106.

Pirie, G. *Running Wild* (London: W. H. Allen, 1961).

Reynolds, K. and N. Tucker, *Children's Book Publishing in Britain Since 1945* (Aldershot: Scholar Press, 1998).

Smith, I. R. 'The Truth About W. S. K. Webb', *Track Stats*, vol. 36, no. 3 (1998), pp.54–7.

Westergaard, J. H. 'The Withering Away of Class: A Contemporary Myth', in P. Anderson and R. Blackburn (eds), *Towards Socialism* (London: Fontana, 1965).

Williams, C. *Harold Macmillan* (London: Weidenfeld and Nicolson, 2009).

PAUL DIETSCHY

Chapter 5
From 'Sports Arditism' to Consensus-Building:
The Ambivalences of the Italian Sporting Press
under Fascism[1]

In common with all other authoritarian and totalitarian regimes, the Fascist regime in Italy made use of the press for the purpose of shaping public opinion and specifically to establish a consensus on the part of a majority of the population around the person of Benito Mussolini. In this editorial construction of the so-called *consenso*, the pages of the sporting press played a role that should not be underestimated by historians of the *Ventennio*, the twenty years of Fascist rule, 1922 to 1943. In fact, as part of a broader European expansion of the sporting press, both specialized and generalist Italian periodicals communicated, from the later 1920s until the summer of 1943, multiple representations of the *homo sportivus*, perceived as the outstanding exemplar of the new Italy. The relevant publications thereby established themselves as unprecedented and powerful vectors for the mobilization and nationalization of the Italian masses, thanks to the exploits of the *Azzurri* (the Blues, as the nation's representative athletes are still known, especially the national football team), in the process imparting a vision of a modern Italy in which futuristic stadiums, together with Fascism's other architectural projects, were added to the architectural treasures of the Renaissance.

1   A version of this chapter was first published in French as 'De l'"arditisme sportif" à la fabrique du consensus: les ambivalences de la presse sportive italienne sous le Fascisme', *Le Temps des Médias*, no. 9 (2nd semester, 2007), pp.63–78. It is included here by kind permission of the original publishers. The English translation is by Philip Dine.

If Italian sports journalists were, like the rest of their profession, undoubtedly acting under orders, it would nevertheless be reductive to imagine the sporting press of the Fascist period as merely one of the means employed for the communication of the regime's values. In fact, the editorial space given over to sport was also able to serve as a site for the expression of relatively neutral information, and even for the display of ideological deviations that were encouraged by professional sports and by a sporting passion that was at some distance from the tenets of authentically Fascist physical activities. The discussion that follows will consequently seek to explore the forms of ambivalence and even the contradictions that resulted from the conjunction of the strong constraints imposed on the press in the Fascist era and the marginal autonomy that sport continued to offer to its various actors. These journalistic reactions will be considered as a set of 'elective affinities', which very early on united the nationalist movement and then its Fascist successor, and which were maintained until the painful reassessments of the summers of 1943 and 1945.

The Sporting Press and Fascism: Elective Affinities?

At the time of Mussolini's March on Rome (28 October 1922), Italy had already developed a sporting press consisting notably of fourteen publications that had survived the trauma of the Great War. As in France, the first sports papers had been devoted to cycling, such as *La Gazzetta dello Sport*, established in Milan in 1896. Initially published twice weekly, *La Rosea*, a nickname derived from the pink paper on which the paper was printed, followed the lead of the French paper *L'Auto* (which in 1903 had launched the Tour de France cycle race) by organizing, from 1909 onwards, an Italian equivalent, the *Giro d'Italia*, the success of which allowed the newspaper's publishers to turn it into a daily in 1913.[2] Similarly, cycling

2   See D. Marchesini, *L'Italia del Giro d'Italia* (Bologna: Il Mulino, 1996), pp.37–8.

and then other sports made their appearance in the generalist press: thus, the Milan daily *Il Corriere della Sera* had created the weekly *Il Ciclo* in 1894, while in Turin, *La Stampa* launched an illustrated supplement in 1901 called *La Stampa Sportiva*.

Even if newspapers in the major southern cities were similarly interested in the activities of cyclists, gymnasts and other athletes, it is clear that the appearance of a specialist sporting press was initially a product of the northern 'industrial triangle', and more particularly of middle-class curiosity regarding fashionable activities in Britain and France. The eulogizing by the Italian press of mobility and speed, and the accompanying promotion of a new cult of the sporting body and the sporting hero, should consequently be understood as part of the broader cultural dynamism of the early twentieth century. Indeed, the rise of sport is closely linked to the advent of modernity in Italy, and particularly its most aggressive intellectual expressions, such as the futurism of F. T. Marinetti and the nationalism of Gabriele D'Annunzio. In fact, at grassroots level, prompted by the military triumphs in Cyrenaica and Tripolitania in 1911–12,[3] Italian gymnastic associations and their press organs, such as *Il Ginnasta* and *La Palestra*, had idealized the virtues of soldier-gymnasts who were 'perfectly prepared' to combat an adversary well adapted to a hostile North African environment. Later, in the spring of 1915, as the kingdom swung from neutrality to war, *La Gazzetta dello Sport* followed the *Corriere della Sera* and other dailies in unhesitatingly reproducing the incendiary declarations of D'Annunzio, who had by then returned from France, and other interventionists. As early as 17 May 1915, an editorial in *La Gazzetta dello Sport* celebrated 'the mysterious energies which, throughout twenty years of sporting propaganda, [had] animated two generations of young people', and who were now being called upon to serve their country or were actually volunteering for duty themselves. Just like Henri Desgrange, who, in *L'Auto* on 3 August 1914, had encouraged sportsmen to join in the 'great game' of the First World War, the Milan daily preached its belligerent message, urging its readers to do their 'sporting'

---

3   These were two of the three constituent provinces of the Italian colony of Libya that was established in 1934.

duty: 'Brothers who have known, practised and loved sport, take up your arms for the sport that is the most ancient, the most strong and the most true: war; and in that never-ending phalanx make up the units providing the best possible example, because sport has endowed you with physical force, moral strength and discipline, which are the supreme virtues at the present time'.[4] Like its French counterpart, and in spite of the economic difficulties brought about by the conflict, the Italian sporting press placed itself on a war footing, launching public appeals to pay for the sending of 'balls and boxing gloves' to the troops, and vaunting the sacrifice of mobilized sportsmen. After the disastrous Italian defeat at the battle of Caporetto in late 1917, this discourse was combined with the myth of the *Ardito* (storm trooper) a new type of combatant, conceived as a 'rapid and effective attacker, completely devoted to offence and victory, and capable of imposing himself on the attention of the public'[5].

Thus, the spirit of sacrifice of the *Arditi* should, according to Vittorio Varale, one of the editors of *La Gazzetta dello Sport*, both inspire sport after the war and bring about its purification.[6] Moreover, despite the return to peace, the figures of the aviator, the machine-gunner and the soldier were maintained as archetypal men of action, as exemplified at the heroic Italian defence at the battle of the Piave River in the summer of 1918, and would become staple objects of fascination for a section of the sporting press in the post-war period. The support of industrialists combined with the patriotic, and even nationalist, tone of periodicals published by sports associations, as well as the intervention of the public authorities in the sporting sphere, quickly led those in charge of the sporting press to support nationalist candidates, and then the first initiatives by the Mussolini

---

4   'Il dovere', *La Gazzetta dello Sport*, 24 May 1915.

5   G. Rochat, *Gli arditi della Grande Guerra: Origini, battaglie e miti* (Gorizia: Libreria Editrice Goriziana, 2006), p.75.

6   'L'avvenire agli "Arditi"!', *La Gazzetta dello Sport*, 16 December 1918. The *Arditi* were elite Italian troops during the 1914–1918 conflict. On the Italian sporting press and the First World War, see especially S. Giuntini, *Lo sport e la grande Guerra: Forze armate e Movimento sportivo in Italia di fronte al primo conflitto mondiale* (Rome: Stato Maggiore dell'Esercito, 2000).

government in the field of sport and physical education. Thus, from October 1919, Guido Verona, the director of *La Stampa Sportiva*, was pleading the cause of the party that 'has no opponents, and that can have no contradictors', that of sport;[7] going on to hail the establishment of a 'parliamentary sports group', whose members were linked to industrial employers and the nationalist movement.[8]

These 'elective affinities' with the nationalist and military matrix of a Fascist order then in the process of construction were also encouraged by the apathy of a liberal regime that had done little to encourage either physical education or sport, in spite of the De Sanctis law of 1878, which had introduced the teaching of gymnastics in the school system of what was by then a unified Italy. They were also reinforced by the aversion to sport expressed by a section of the leadership of the Italian Socialist Party (PSI), which saw in these new practices an 'instrument of the bourgeois class' designed to divert the proletariat from its 'revolutionary objectives'. Even if Antonio Gramsci's paper *Ordine Nuovo* devoted a significant amount of space to sport when it became a daily in 1922, and if the Maximalist leader Giacinto Serrati founded the review *Sport e proletariato* in the post-war period, the opinions of both publications were opposed in principle to 'bourgeois' sport, favouring a class-based approach that could never meet with the approval of the established titles of the sporting press.

In contrast, those periodicals were delighted by the early initiatives of the Mussolini government, and particularly its Minister of Public Instruction, the philosopher Giovanni Gentile, who, in March 1923, announced a reform of physical education through the creation of a National Board for Physical Education (*Ente Nazionale per l'Educazione Fisica*, ENEF), also reacting well to the government's organization of prime-ministerial receptions for sporting champions.[9] Moreover, despite its proclaimed political

---

7   'Lo Sport e le Elezioni', *La Stampa sportiva*, 12 October 1919.
8   'Formiano il Gruppo Parlamentare Sportivo', *La Stampa sportiva*, 7 December 1919.
9   Thus, the boxer Erminio Spalla and the cyclist Ottavio Bottechia were received by Mussolini in August 1923. See 'Come il Governo di Mussolini incoraggia e premia i nostri campioni dello sport', *La Stampa Sportiva*, 26 August 1923.

neutrality, the sporting press also supported the *listone*, the list of candidates established by Mussolini, with his conservative and nationalist allies, and presented for the legislative elections of April 1924. Moreover, these same publications would go on to applaud the authoritarian establishment of control over Italian sport in 1925. Indeed, this response amounted to nothing less than social revenge. For in liberal Italy, sports correspondents had actually been considered by their peers to be failed journalists. Against this backdrop, the interest in sport expressed by the Fascists allowed the regime to mobilize 'without difficulty a troop of allies who were both valuable and appreciative'.[10]

The 'Sportization' of the Major Dailies under the Fascist Regime: Between Political Control and Economic Strategy

By the end of 1925, the press had lost all freedom of expression. This had become increasingly obvious since the signing by King Victor-Emmanuel III of the decree of 15 July 1923, which gave the government the power to suppress or sequester any newspaper judged to be 'a threat to national interests'. Whether they liked it or not, sport and the sporting press were equally obliged to conform to the projects of the regime. Soon to become known as *il primo sportivo d'Italia* (Italy's foremost sportsman), Benito Mussolini was perceived as the epitome of Italy's 'new man', and was depicted as such in the pages of the press and for the cameras of the LUCE Institute, perfectly embodying '"everything that is manly", including a passion for sport and physical fitness, the love of risk-taking and challenges'.[11] As for the regime's policy on sport, it was as much one of concrete development in favour of the masses, through the building of stadiums, swimming pools and gym-

10   F. Fabrizio, *Sport e Fascismo: La politica sportive del regime 1924–1936* (Florence: Guaraldi, 1976), pp.152–3.
11   L. Passerini, *Mussolini immaginario: Storia di una biografia 1915–1939* (Rome: Einaudi, 1991), p.100.

nasiums, together with a 'moralizing' of elite sport under the auspices of the Italian National Olympic Committee (*Comitato Olimpico Nazionale Italiano*, CONI), as an image-based campaign depicting, through the print media, the cinema and the radio, a powerful, modern and long dreamed of Italy, as a metaphor of the 'eternal youth of Fascism'.

In this respect, the generalist press, under state control, quite quickly discovered – or rediscovered – the charms and the usages of sporting information. In fact, influential dailies such as *Il Corriere della Sera* and *La Stampa* had adopted a policy of open opposition to the Fascists in July 1924, in response to the assassination of the socialist deputy Giacomo Matteotti. However, following the establishment of the dictatorship, the most critical figures in the press were obliged to give up their positions. Yet the departure of those journalists opposed to Fascism, or judged to be so, did not only mean a change of political line, but also left the field open for a radical transformation of 'the form and content of Italian newspapers. The rhetoric, images and tenets that characterized official cultural theories were thus, for the first time, imposed on the country in a systematic and generalized fashion'.[12] Sport, with its chronicles and imagery, thus arrived to brighten up a daily press whose approach to page design was characterized, on the one hand, by a mode of presentation that failed to discriminate adequately between the significance of individual items, and on the other, by a lack of photographic illustrations. Henceforth, in the more easily readable and better illustrated layouts that appeared after 1925, sporting champions were more visible on the front pages, while the space devoted to sport grew, both in the dedicated sports pages, which increased in number, and in the photo-journals that began to appear in the late 1920s. It is true that as a combined result of the suppression of democratic debate and the peaceful diplomatic situation that prevailed until 1934–1935, the space given over to sporting news could be increased relatively easily. However, from 1935 onwards, when Italian ambitions in Ethiopia came to the fore, significantly less space was to be available.

---

12   P. V. Cannistraro, *La fabbrica del consenso: Fascismo e mass media* (Rome: Laterza, 1975), p.181.

The Turin daily press of the first half of the 1930s provides a clear illustration of the 'sportization' of the generalist press in the Fascist period. It was the writer Curzio Malaparte who, as editor-in-chief of *La Stampa* from March 1929 to January 1931 was the first to transform the hitherto austere daily, which had been acquired by Giovanni Agnelli, the founding president of the Fiat automobile company. Seeking to enlarge his readership by publishing each week for 'less culturally ambitious readers [...] a whole page given over to photos which, on the model of the weeklies, replaced an article by short, attention-grabbing captions,'[13] Malaparte also devoted at least a page of the newspaper each day to sport, which dealt in minute detail with the activities of the leading figures in Italian sport, from their triumphs in international competitions to their vacations on the beaches of the Tyrrhenian coast. Under his management, the sports pages of *La Stampa* took on a spectacular, eye-catching cast: not only did the paper take delight in grand panoramic shots showing the 'choreographic spectacle' of massed crowds in stadiums, but it was also prone to sensationalism, for instance reproducing at actual size the right footprint of the heavyweight boxer Primo Carnera.[14]

In order to compete with *La Stampa*, Giangiacomo Ponti, the Turin industrialist who owned *La Gazzetta del Popolo* (see Figure 5.1) followed the same route, with its increased attention to sporting news giving his daily a more popular feel intended to allow it to gain access to 'working-class audiences which had thus far remained closed to Fascism.'[15] The sports desk was run by the southern-born journalist Renato Casalbore, and was entitled to a full page on weekdays, with at least two each Monday, all backed up by abundant photographic illustrations. However, whereas the more middle-class readership of *La Stampa* was primarily interested in high-level sport, *La Gazzetta del Popolo* also reported on amateur competitions, in order to maintain close relations with its target readership. Above and beyond these

---

13   G. B. Guerri, *Malaparte* (Paris: Denoël, 1981), p.110.

14   *La Stampa*, 10 November 1929.

15   N. Tranfaglia, P. Murialdi and M. Legnani, *La Stampa Italiana nell'età fascista* (Rome: Laterza, 1980), p.117.

differences, both Turin dailies organized sports tipster competitions right through the 1930s, designed to encourage the loyalty of their readers. In the case of the competition organized by *La Stampa* in 1931, participants were required to predict the results 'not only [of] first-division football matches, but also [of] all the games that the national team [was] required to play over the course of the season'.[16] Those with the requisite foresight, or luck, were hoping to win a Fiat 515 motor car, a Moto Guzzi 500 motorcycle, or a Marelli radio, all products that remained inaccessible to the great majority of Turin citizens, and thus, by extension, to most Italians.

In this way, supported by these demonstrations of largesse, the development between 1929 et 1935 of *cronaca sportiva* (dedicated sports reporting), and its spin-offs in the generalist press, was an integral part of the period identified as that of 'the Consensus' by Renzo De Felice.[17] In fact, the rise of sport and its editorial success contributed to the leisure policy put in place to seduce the masses, and which included everything from cinema and radio to sport. This process also helped create the illusion of the very first consumer society, the Latin ancestor of later Anglo-Saxon models, which Fascism intended to offer, at least on the level of rhetoric, to the Italian masses. However, the increase in the quantity and quality of sports reporting also reflected a broader European tendency, exemplified in France by the rise in the 1930s of the newspaper *Paris-Soir*, the sales of which were given a notable boost by its photographs and the dynamism of its sports pages, under the direction of Gaston Bénac.

16 'Grande concorso pronostici de La Stampa. Le linee generali del regolamento', *La Stampa*, 8 September 1931.
17 R. De Felice, *Mussolini il duce: Gli anni del consenso, 1929–1936* (Turin: Einaudi Tascabili, 1996), p.55.

The Editorial Ambiguities of the Sporting Consensus

This said, the 'sportization' of the press during the *Ventennio* was not neutral. Whether it was political, literary, or sporting, journalistic writing had, in fact, been obliged to follow the directives and other 'orders of the day' issued from 1928 onwards by the Minister of the Interior, Luigi Federzoni, and by the CONI and its president, the Fascist literary and sporting journalist, Lando Ferretti. The task at hand was to offer 'serious' news through the prudent and concise use of the Italian language, in a way that was intended to break with the verbose and grandiloquent tone of the country's liberal publications. The sporting press was thus obliged to conform to these demands, both in the dedicated columns of the daily newspapers and in the specialist periodicals contributing, according to the secretary of the CONI, Enrico Beretta, 'to the moralization of sport'.[18] In the short term, sports journalists invented Italian equivalents of existing sporting vocabulary, whereas a few years earlier they had been happy to pepper their articles with foreign terms, borrowed principally from English and French. 'Football' was definitively transformed into *calcio*, players previously known as 'halves' became *mediani* (mid-fielders), and 'backs' became *terzini*, while the *mêlée* (scrum in French) became the *mischia*. In November 1929, the Fascist national union of journalists decided to formalize these translations in an 'Italian sporting dictionary'.

As part of the same process, sports news sometimes became difficult to distinguish from the official communiqués, statements of 'norms' and other 'orders' emanating from the CONI; even when the directives did not actually come directly from the office of the Under-Secretary of State for Propaganda. Thus, the holder of that office in May 1934, Galeazzo Ciano, urged newspaper editors, just before the start of the competition, to give 'the maximum possible visibility to [world] championship football games, by giving over a part of the front page to match reports so as to attract the interest and attention of the public'. The press was also liable to be incited to

18   See Fabrizio, *Sport e Fascismo*, pp.153–4.

ignore the disappointing performances of the regime's sporting champions, as in June 1935 when the order went out to 'not publish the photographs of Carnera lying on the ground',[19] following the unexpected knock-out of the boxer, who hailed from the northern region of Friuli, in his match against the 'negro' Joe Louis. In other words, the press was destined to serve not only as a lever for sporting mobilization, and thus for the diffusion of the cult of the body among the masses, but also to contribute to the exaltation of the 'Italic race', specifically on the eve of a military expedition against a 'dark' and 'savage' Ethiopia.

To this end, a sporting press financially controlled by the regime came into being in the later 1920s. Thus, in December 1927, Leandro Arpinati, the *ras* (local fascist chief) of Bologna, and additionally president from 1926 to 1933 of the Italian football federation (*Federazione Italiana Giuoco Calcio*, FIGC), had taken control in that city of the *Corriere dello Sport*, which he transformed into *Littoriale*, a sports daily which also doubled as the official organ of the CONI. Similarly, in June 1928, Landro Ferretti had created a richly illustrated monthly titled *Lo Sport fascista* (see Figure 5.2) which featured contributions from such leading figures of the Fascist regime as Augusto Turati, Italo Balbo and Alessandro Pavolini. Ferretti's aim was to defend a conception of sport's purity, both in its values and its practices, and thus to present 'sport as a theatre of combat and propaganda'.

Nevertheless, it would be reductive merely to focus on these 'Black-shirt' periodicals in offering a survey of the sporting press under Fascism. In fact, the period 1924–34 was marked by a genuine flowering of the specialist press: more than fifty-eight such titles may consequently be identified in Italy in 1928.[20] If a majority of these were either short-lived or restricted to regional distribution, the most important ones, such as *Il Guerin Sportivo* and *La Gazzetta dello Sport*, achieved circulations of more than 100,000 copies, as did *Calcio Illustrato*, launched in 1931 and printed on the presses of the *Popolo d'Italia*. The content of such publications perfectly illustrates

---

19   D. Marchesini, *Carnera* (Bologna: Il Mulino, 2006), p.148.
20   A. Ghirelli, 'La stampa sportiva', in V. Castronovo and N. Tranfaglia (eds), *La Stampa italiana del neocapitalismo* (Rome: Laterza, 1976), pp.313–76, p.334.

the contradictions of the use of sport made by the regime's propagandists, and, more generally, of Italian sport itself during the *Ventennio*. There can be no doubt that sporting periodicals served as a channel for the transmission of orders issued by the CONI, together with national federations that were now controlled by administrators loyal to the regime. By the same token, they undoubtedly celebrated the triumphs of the *Azzurri* at the 1932 Olympic Games in Los Angeles, and in the 1934 and 1938 football World Cup competitions (see Figure 5.3), as so many successes for Mussolini. However, professional sports spectacles such as football, cycling and boxing continued to function as tools in the sporting conquest of the masses, to the detriment of 'elementary' sports such as athletics and swimming, which were additionally valued as training for soldiers and, by extension, the new Fascist man.

Thus, from 1932, the publication by *La Gazzetta dello Sport* of the first volume in a series devoted to *Campioni e Avvenimenti del giorno* (Champions and Events of the Day) marked the launch of a collection which, three years later, numbered 'sixty-five biographies of athletes, making available to sport a set of documents of high and sure quality', and offering its readership as many *exempla* to follow.[21] However, the life stories on offer typically presented essentially petit-bourgeois models of behaviour, such as the number devoted to Virginio Rosetta, a defender for the Juventus club (of Turin) and the national football team, which described the player as the 'wise administrator of his twenty years', who went on at the end of his career to manage 'the fruits of his savings with the same wisdom that he takes care of his thirty-three years of athleticism'.[22] While middle-class conformism and dreams of wealth may have been elements in the seductive power of the regime's propaganda, as evidenced by the success of so-called 'white telephone' films,[23] they were nevertheless out of step with the images of youth and power that 'Blackshirt' sport was designed to promote.

---

21   'Io Campioni a L. 4', *La Gazzetta dello Sport*, 1 August 1935.
22   E. Levi, *Viri* (Milan: Biblioteca della Gazzetta dello Sport, 1935), p.91 and p.200.
23   These were glossy dramas and comedies in which the eponymous telephone apparatus served as a symbol of glamour and luxury.

At the same time, the sporting press continued to blow on the embers of a regionalism that the regime itself wished to overcome. In June 1927, for instance, a 'sporting and satirical' weekly, *Il Tifone*, had been created in Rome. As its first editorial pointed out, the paper's aim was to represent and defend the interests of southern sportsmen: 'We are men of the south. We challenge anybody not to be southern. When it's 36 degrees in the shade'.[24] In the event, by engaging in an early form of sporting investigative journalism, the *Tifone* team actually exposed a case of corruption involving the Juventus defender, Luigi Allemandi, which cost the club's Turin rival, Torino, a first national championship in November 1927. However, in the 1930s, while *Il Tifone* continued its struggle against the competitive and financial hegemony of the northern football clubs, other periodicals based in Turin and Milan railed against the centralization of sporting power in Rome, where the national sports federations had been relocated. They also criticized the political and sporting favouritism that had been shown to the capital's teams, AS Roma and Lazio. Thus, in 1931–1933, the Turin journalist Giorgio Tonelli had attempted to re-launch *La Stampa Sportiva*, which had previously ceased publication in the mid-1920s, establishing the paper's editorial line as the 'defence of Piedmont sport'. As he explained, in somewhat contradictory fashion, in its edition of 23 February 1932, defending Savoy's sportsmen was not proof of parochialism: 'The parish-pump mentality no longer exists, a new wind of Italian-ness is blowing through our beautiful peninsula, wonderfully united by the will of a Man'. The man in question, Mussolini, in common with several other members of the Fascist hierarchy, had no real taste for the oratorical outbursts prompted by regionalist antagonisms. This was made apparent by the call to order issued by *Littoriale*, the organ of the CONI, which served as the vehicle, in the sporting sphere, for the thoughts of *Il Duce* on the damage done by regionalism: 'The continual harping on about rivalries between region or towns, the raising of doubts either openly or by insinuation about clubs and people who are completely above suspicion, and the egging on of supporters who by their very nature are impressionable and excited, as are

24   *Il Tifone*, 23 June 1927.

sportsmen and the young, are all deplorable and unwise things; moreover, nine times out of ten, they are not justified and lead to reprisals which are just as regrettable'.[25]

In addition to public order problems, the representations of the *tifo* (fan) communicated by the press could, in fact, be considered a form of depoliticization. The portraits of *tifosi* presented by journalists insisted on the almost pathological passion that structured the sporting week and made them venerate the 'zebra' or the 'bull', the symbols of Turin's Juventus and Torino clubs, or made them fill trains to travel in support of the Naples team when it played away in Rome. The 'middle-class' passion for football thus proved impossible to contain within the regime's project of 'modelling' crowds: the 'Sunday battles' described by the Italian press, without the metaphor being specific to the *Ventennio* period, could not plausibly be depicted as authentically Fascist. Led by footballers easily represented as mercenaries of South-American origin, and recruited at enormous expense by 'sponsors' from the worlds of industry and finance, these encounters came over as the distant echoes of clashes between the *condottieri* of the Renaissance and their armies, rather than the desired demonstrations of force of the regime's youth.

Nevertheless, the coverage of competitions was on occasion liable to take on a subtly political character, as in the case of the rivalry between the cyclists, Learco Guerra and Alfredo Binda.[26] Guerra, whose family name – meaning 'war' – was itself highly evocative, was viewed as 'the cyclist of the regime' by the press, which lauded as an example to be emulated his volunteering for service in the wars in Ethiopia and Spain, while his attack-minded and aggressive approach to race-riding was perceived as an illustration of his fidelity to the regime. The cold, calculating and 'scientific' style of Binda, who had begun his career over the border in Nice, marked his distance from the journalistic tenets of the Fascist champion, even if the press hailed his three titles as world road-racing champion in 1927, 1930 and 1932. Much the same could be said of Gino Bartali: the image of 'pious

25   'Dopo la parola del Duce: Basta coi regionalismi!', *Il Littoriale*, 28 July 1932.
26   Marchesini, *L'Italia del Giro d'Italia*, p.120.

Gino', the disciple of Saint Francis of Assisi and a devotee of the Virgin Mary, was the polar opposite of the consciously 'brutal' and even 'bestial' representations of the boxer Primo Carnera, of whom he was held to be the antithesis. His successes, even if inaccurately reported, served to mark the revenge of the Italian Catholic Action movement (*Azione Cattolica Italiana*, ACI), which had seen all its physical and sporting activities banned in the 1931 crisis that occurred between the Fascist regime and the Vatican.[27]

Epilogue: Ideological Orthodoxy and Repositioning – the Press and Italian Journalists at the End of the *Ventennio*

Nevertheless, and such is the plasticity of sport, the victory of Bartali in the 1938 Tour de France made it possible temporarily to absolve him of clericalism (see Figure 5.4). A month after the success of the *Azzurri* in front of a hostile French crowd in the football World Cup, and just over a fortnight after the publication of the racial laws collectively known as *Il Manifesto della razza* (the Manifesto/Charter of Race), the success of the Tuscan rider on the roads of a 'decadent' France was taken to confirm, in the eyes of the zealots in the sporting press, the dynamism of Fascism. By applauding Bartali, in the view of Bruno Roghi, editor of *La Gazzetta dello Sport*, the spectators at the Parc des Princes stadium in Paris 'were hailing the athletic and moral virtue of an exemplar of [the Italic] race'.[28] For its part, and in common with the rest of the Italian press, the Milan sports daily *Il Littoriale*, now under the ownership of Count Alberto Bonacossa, a chemical engineer and Olympic administrator, relayed the decisions of the Italian government on the so-called 'Jewish question' and applauded the stance of Mussolini as 'the peace-marker of Munich'. In the same way, the harden-

27   On Bartali and Catholic sport in Italy, see S. Pivato, *Sia lodato Bartali: Ideologia, cultura e miti dello sport cattolico (1936–1948)* (Rome: Edizioni Lavoro, 1985).
28   'Nel clima dell'Italia di Mussolini', *La Gazzetta dello Sport*, 1 August 1938.

ing attitudes of the regime rendered obligatory a doctrinal orthodoxy that henceforth was to colour sports reporting, for instance through praising the proletarian origin of certain athletes or footballers in order to conform to the anti-bourgeois turn taken by the regime, or by ever more regularly likening the sporting struggle to war. The fact of the matter, as is made clear by the archives of the Ministry of Popular Culture (now conserved in the *Archivio Centrale dello Stato* in Rome), is that sports news, even if its volume was being reduced in the generalist press, continued to have an important political function. Right up to 1943, in fact, requests for financial support by newspaper publishers to the *Minculpop* were granted, notably those of Bonacossa, who, in the summer of 1940, obtained from *Il Duce* a monthly grant of 10,000 lira, to compensate for the fall in sales by *La Gazzetta dello Sport*, in exchange for the newspaper's support for soldiers who had left for the front, for the Fascist youth organization, the *Gioventù Italiana del Littorio*, and for the organization of military sports on the model of Italy's ally, Germany. By the same token, the sporting press might slip into its accounts of military sports competitions the claim that the maintenance of the football championship was proof that life was going on as normal in Italy. However, from the summer of 1943, the first renunciations began to be made: three days after the ousting of Mussolini by the Fascist Grand Council, Bruno Roghi was stating that 'sport is freedom itself for the youth that devotes itself to the Fatherland to make it more beautiful and more noble'.[29] It now only remained for the editors and publishers of the sporting press to wait for the end of the war, while the tragic interlude of the Italian Social Republic (the German puppet state that was headed by a fatally weakened Mussolini and based at Salò, on Lake Garda), would see a dramatic reduction in both competitions and sports reporting.

Having failed to come out on 23 April 1945, *La Rosea* reappeared on Italian newsstands on 2 July 1945 in a provisionally twice-weekly format under the new tutelary figures of 'the Partisan and the Patriot', but still under the editorship of Bruno Roghi.[30] It is true that henceforth what counted more were the choices made after September 1943 than prior allegiance to

29   'Lo sport per la patria', *La Gazzetta dello Sport*, 28 July 1943.
30   'Rinascita', *La Gazzetta dello Sport*, 2 July 1945.

the regime during the *Ventennio*. Moreover, sporting infrastructures and successes were a part of the Fascist heritage that could be preserved. Just as the *Littoriali*, the sporting and cultural competitions instituted by the regime in the early 1930s, had allowed the emergence of a generation of film-makers and writers who would be considered masters of neo-realism, the development of sports reporting under Fascism had helped to train talented journalists who, like Renato Casalbore, the founder of *Tuttosport* in July 1945, would go on to establish high-quality sporting periodicals. Following the death of Casalbore in the Superga air crash of 1949 (in which almost the entire Torino squad also perished), the Italian sporting press would nevertheless return to the sensationalism and sporting nationalism that had characterized the Fascist period, embarking on a monoculture of *calcio* that would only be varied by the highlights of the cycling season and the motor sport calendar.[31]

Bibliography

Cannistraro, P. V. *La fabbrica del consenso: Fascismo e mass media* (Rome: Laterza, 1975).

De Felice, R. *Mussolini il duce: Gli anni del consenso 1929–1936* (Turin: Einaudi Tascabili, 1996).

Dietschy, P. 'Sport, éducation physique et fascisme sous le regard de l'historien', *Revue d'histoire moderne et contemporaine*, vol. 55–3, July–September 2008, pp.61–84.

Fabrizio, F. *Sport e Fascismo: La politica sportive del regime, 1924–1936* (Florence: Guaraldi, 1976).

Foot, J. *Calcio: A History of Italian Football* (London: Fourth Estate, 2006).

Ghirelli, A. 'La stampa sportiva', in V. Castronovo and N. Tranfaglia (eds), *La Stampa italiana del neocapitalismo* (Rome: Laterza, 1976), pp.313–76.

---

31   On football's development more generally, see J. Foot, *Calcio: A History of Italian Football* (London: Fourth Estate, 2006); also A. Papa and G. Panico, *Storia sociale del calcio in Italia* (Bologna: Il Mulino, 2002).

Giuntini, S. *Lo sport e la grande Guerra: Forze armate e Movimento sportivo in Italia di fronte al primo conflitto mondiale* (Rome: Stato Maggiore dell'Esercito, 2000).

Guerri, G. B. *Malaparte* (Paris: Denoël, 1981).

Levi, E. *Viri* (Milan: Biblioteca della Gazzetta dello Sport, 1935).

Marchesini, D. *L'Italia del Giro d'Italia* (Bologna: Il Mulino, 1996).

——. *Carnera* (Bologna: Il Mulino, 2006).

Martin, S. *Football and Fascism: The National Game under Mussolini* (Oxford: Berg, 2004).

Papa, A. and G. Panico. *Storia sociale del calcio in Italia* (Bologna: Il Mulino, 2002).

Passerini, L. *Mussolini immaginario: Storia di una biografia, 1915–1939* (Rome: Einaudi, 1991).

Pivato, S. *Sia lodato Bartali: Ideologia, cultura e miti dello sport cattolico (1936–1948)* (Rome: Edizioni Lavoro, 1985).

ÁLVARO RODRÍGUEZ DÍAZ

Chapter 6
Spain's Social Values through Film: Films about Sports

Introduction

Film and sport are two activities ostensibly isolated from one another; two systems that only coincide when a film includes sport as an essential part of the storyline. But they also coincide indirectly when social practices, be they artistic or sporting, are determined by a single system of values within a specific society. The way in which a film is made links in with the social context surrounding the director, scriptwriter or actors, which cannot be separated from their own socialization. In turn, sport within a given country, the way it is played and its specific forms, may also be seen to coincide with the character of its communities, its dominant morality, and the specific identities of its members. Sport in national cinema is an excuse to tell a story, with characters, dialogues and images chosen to connect easily with that country's citizens. This chapter looks at the social identity of the Spanish through their films about sport. It encompasses all the official sports that appear in fictional films. Bullfighting has been excluded from the analysis because, although it is considered a sport by many Spaniards, it is a differentiated activity, with highly ritualized and pre-modern connotations, and hence merits its own analysis elsewhere.

A nation's sporting victories, through a team or an athlete, can unite its citizens even further. These triumphs have also been remembered and represented on film, which acts as a sounding board to transmit that spirit of national solidarity and collective pride. For example, one of the elements that have strengthened Germany's identity as a nation is its World Cup victories (as Arnd Krüger describes in Chapter 13). The 1952 win coincided with the start of its economic recovery and is commemorated in the film *Das Wunder von Bern* (*The Miracle of Bern*, Sönke Wortmann, 2003), while the national side's victory in the 1990 championship coincided with German reunification, reflected in the film *Good Bye, Lenin!* (Wolfgang Becker, 2003). This situation has occurred in many countries: the film *Invictus* (Clint Eastwood, United States, 2009) follows the interest of Nelson Mandela in using South Africa's victory in the 1995 Rugby World Cup to unite the nation after he was released from prison. In Castro's Cuba, the film *El Juego de Cuba* (*The Cuban Game*, Manuel Martín, Spain, 2001) looked at the country's victories in the Baseball World Cup. However, the use of sports films to feed into nationalism is not a common phenomenon, since most countries have rarely won major world sporting championships. Hence, almost all Spanish films about sport present local situations and discourses, which are almost familial in nature, and thus are a far cry from nationalistic pride.

The Spanish Nation: History, Identity, Life Typology

The origins of a collective 'Spanish' identity may be traced to the union of Catholic kingdoms achieved at the end of the fifteenth century, creating a political conglomerate whose borders have basically remained stable over the intervening five centuries. The coordinated resistance to the Napoleonic army that invaded the country during the Peninsular War (1807–1814) proved that some kind of 'Spanish' identity existed at the beginning of the modern period.

National identities are typically defined by foreigners, who usually choose the symbols used to define 'others'. If we were to ask any European about the symbols of Spain, most would say bullfighting, flamenco, tapas bars, sangria, sun and sand. However, many Spaniards do not identify with these symbols, especially citizens who belong to regional communities looking to gain independence, such as the Basques and the Catalans. Most of the aforementioned symbols are more characteristic of Andalusia, which is the region of Spain most visited by foreign visitors. Such clichéd representations as bullfighting and flamenco – and the closely associated fiery temperament of the Spanish people – were first spread in the eighteenth and nineteenth centuries by Romantic travellers and artists, typically from northern Europe and America, who considered Spain to be the last bastion of spirituality and oriental exoticism in Europe, but also of backwardness and poverty. Other artists did not travel around Spain but created influential works that shaped a stereotype of Spain, such as Georges Bizet's opera *Carmen*, first performed in Paris in 1875.

Modern-day Spanish identity has been strongly influenced by key events throughout the twentieth century. In 1931, the Republic was constituted and the royal family exiled. The tensions that resulted would contribute to the most traumatic event in Spain's modern collective memory: the Civil War of 1936–1939. This conflict radically divided the Spanish, polarizing them in ways which, still today, continue to inform diametrically opposed belief-systems and political agendas. The Franco dictatorship lasted from 1939 until 1978, the year in which a democratic constitution was approved.

Spain is divided into seventeen territories or autonomous regions with their own regional governments, as well as their own laws, and even tax systems and police. This decentralization has been very positive economically and socially for the country, and has also created new social identities. Ferrán Requejo (2005) has defined Spain as a 'multinational federalist state'.[1] In fact, it grants more independence and autonomy to its regional governments than any other European country and it could be called a nation of nations.

Spain is one of the countries in Europe with the least nationalist feeling. The flying of the national flag is relatively rare and remains associated with traditionalism, in marked contrast to the regularly seen emblems of autonomous territories. Revealingly, the national anthem remains without

---

[1]   F. Requejo, *Multinational Federalism and Value Pluralism: The Spanish Case* (New York: Routledge, 2005).

lyrics, while recent competitions to provide the same have been abandoned due to the serious controversy generated. As the British historian Henry Kamen has observed, Spain 'does not impart the feeling of nationhood, and that makes it impossible to agree on a text for the anthem'.[2]

Surveys targeting Spanish attitudes to current life situations and future expectations reveal two characteristic national types: those who, like Cervantes' Don Quixote, combine present unhappiness with future optimism; and those who, like his faithful companion, Sancho Panza, combine present happiness with future pessimism. Here too, Spanish society is divided along distinctive lines. The largest percentage of Spaniards are 'Sancho Panzas', happy in the present but sceptical about what the future will bring (62 per cent). The smallest percentage are Don Quixote types, whose unhappiness in the present is combined with the conviction that the future will be brighter (3 per cent).[3] This rarely considered aspect of social identity is clearly reflected in Spanish sports films.

Spanish Films as an Expression of Identity Values

Since the invention of cinema in the late nineteenth century, the history of the movies in Spain has been connected with the economic, social and political evolution of the country. Since the 1980s, this link has become more visible internationally, due to the greater exposure abroad of the work of Spanish film-makers. One of the most internationally famous Spanish directors is Luis Buñuel, who directed *Viridiana* (1961), one of his most highly acclaimed films. However, the definitive boost for cinema came with films that won the Oscar for best foreign language film, awarded to directors such as José Luis Garci (*Begin the Beguine*, 1982), Fernando

2   H. Kamen, 'Debería tener letra el himno nacional?', <http://www.elmundo.es> (accessed 18 June 2007).
3   J. de Miguel, 'Transformations of politics and society in Spain', European Sociological Association Conference (Murcia, 2003; unpublished paper).

Trueba (*Belle Époque*, 1992), Pedro Almodóvar (*All About My Mother*, 2001) and Alejandro Amenábar *The Sea Inside*, 2006). In the 1990s, over the decade, Spanish productions reached nearly three hundred titles. Spain is today the seventh largest film-producing country in the world, and has 4,140 screens.[4]

Like other European countries, Spanish cinematographic production increased steadily over the course of the twentieth century, with the exception of the 1940s. Films rooted in folklore dominated production, taking advantage of the singers and dancers of the day. These films portrayed a typical Spain, with a strongly rural and traditional mentality. During the Civil War, many films of this kind, which can be classed as nationalist, were made in Nazi Germany. The content reflected local clichés, which were used to build a national identity from the 1930s to the 1950s. They reproduced the traditional values of certain Spanish myths: the *bandolero*, flamenco and the fiery world of the *gitanos*. They were termed *españoladas*, referring to a kind of cinema with social and domestic roots aimed at the working classes, whose tradition was grounded in a popular form of musical theatre known as *Zarzuela*.[5] The film *La Niña de tus Ojos* (*The Girl of Your Dreams*, Fernando Trueba, 1998) looks at the filming of an *españolada* in Berlin in 1938. Anne Hardcastle has claimed that this film suggested 'a subversive appropriation of the traditional icons of Spanish identity seen in the *españolada* and their redeployment in a liberal, contemporary construction of Spanishness'.[6] However, the *españoladas* made in Fascist Germany were propaganda films with latent political messages.

---

4   Instituto de la Cinematografía y de las Artes Audiovisuales, 'Boletín Informativo 2008' (Madrid: Ministerio de Cultura, 2009).

5   Luis Navarrete has recently recognized a new kind of *españolada*, characterized by 'nationalist, vanguardist, artistic and reflexive euphemisms'. Although the conceptual development of such categories is still in its early stages, as Navarrete has chosen for his analysis specific directors and films without offering a historical perspective, the starting point is suggestive. L. Navarrete, 'La españolada en el cine', in P. Poyato (ed.), *Historia(s), motivos y formas del cine español* (Cordoba: Plurabelle, 2005), pp.23–31.

6   A. Hardcastle, 'Representing Spanish Identity through *españolada* in Fernando Trueba's *The Girl of Your Dreams* (La Niña de tus Ojos)', *Film Criticism*, vol. 31, no. 3 (2007), pp.7–15.

This theme continued in the early years of Franco's dictatorship. It was not until the 1960s that Spain modernized thanks to different development plans and its increasingly open attitude to other countries. This was also when more liberal and open cinema productions appeared, but they were still subject to a significant element of political censorship. The country entered a consumer decade thanks to the appearance of the middle classes, through industrial investment and the growth of the service sector. This was also the start of mass foreign tourism, largely from northern Europe, the presence of which also enabled many Spaniards to discover and assimilate new cultural values more fitting to modernity.

It was not until the Democratic Constitution was passed in 1978 that social, political and cultural freedom was officially enshrined. But society was divided between two identities, the past and the present, between peripheral nationalities and the central state, between the political left and right, between religion and atheism. According to Barry Jordan and Mark Allinson, the rapid and important changes in values that developed in the post-Franco era meant that there was no clear, characteristic and symbolic Spanish identity; hence Spanish cinema also represented this concern and the ongoing search for identity.[7] Some of the legislative transformations that have taken place in Spain have been highly advanced, even ahead of other countries, and normally in spite of the opposition of the Catholic authorities, such as, for example, the legalization of same-sex marriages in 2005. However, traditional institutions such as the family have also broken down: in 2007 there were 201,579 same-sex marriages, and there were also 137,510 divorces and separations.[8] These social statistics are reflected in Spanish films in the first decade of the twenty-first century.

Several authors have pointed to postmodernity as a combination of tradition and modernity, creating a hybrid, different and special identity.[9] In this respect, the novelty and success of films by Pedro Almodóvar, for

---

7   B. Jordan and M. Allinson, *Spanish Cinema: A Student's Guide* (London: Hodder Arnold, 2005).

8   Instituto Nacional de Estadística (National Statistics Institute, Spain), <http://www.ine.es/prodyser/pubweb/espcif/poblo9.pdf> (accessed 17 October 2009).

9   D. Harvey, *The Condition of Postmodernity*, (Oxford: Blackwell, 1990); J. Urry, *Consuming Places* (London: Routledge, 1995).

example, are based on characters and situations that can be understood as an ironic and at the same time nostalgic version of traditional Spanish values, while adding new social identities and elements to include not only religion, bull fights and flamenco, but drugs, sex and the police as well.

Films about Sport

Sport is in society and society is in sport; both spheres share the same values, which are values pertaining to modernity and the process of social pacification: union, betterment and the collective effort to achieve victory without the use of violent methods and under conditions of equality.[10] Howard Becker has argued that sociologists should be interested not in *what* people do but in *how* they do it.[11] In our case, the Spanish approach sport differently from Americans, for example, because different ways of being are represented in their 'game'. Similarly, the cinema of each country is a form of collective expression for its inhabitants. One can talk of American, European or Indian cinema. There are films made in Spain that are only aimed at Spaniards; it is a domestic form of cinema, which exists in almost all countries. One can also talk of films about sport as a specialist genre, conveying images and content in which sport is the main thread running through the script.

Between 1900 and 1999, 902 productions were made featuring sport: the majority (454) were documentaries, 244 were videos and 204 were feature films.[12] With a few exceptions, most Spanish sports films have historically been about football and boxing. Between 1900 and 1999,

10 E. Dunning, *Sport Matters: Sociological Studies of Sport, Violence, and Civilization* (London: Routledge, 1999), pp.52–61.
11 H. Becker, *Doing Things Together* (Evanston, IL: Northwestern University Press, 1986).
12 Source for statistics: J. Romaguera, *Presencia del deporte en el cine español, un primer inventario* (Seville: Fundación Andalucía Olímpica and Consejo Superior de Deportes, 2003), supplemented by my own research.

sixty films were produced focusing on football, and fifty-three on boxing (Diagram 6.1):[13]

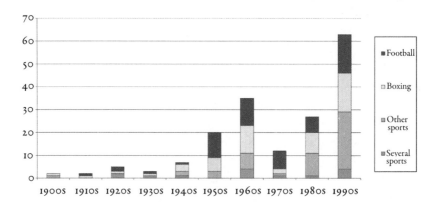

Diagram 6.1 The evolution of films about sport in Spain, 1900–1999

Football is the most played sport in Spain, and is practised almost exclusively by males. Boxing appears in a higher proportion of films than it does in society, insofar as it is a minority sport in Spain. Interest in boxing in film owes more to the cinematic tradition behind this individual and universal sport, brimming with metaphors, making it easier to relate to the drama of the loser and the triumph of the winner.

Mention should also be made of cinema referring to hunting, about which eleven films were made in the last century. In Spain there has long been a great hunting tradition, and until the 1980s it was the sport with the highest number of registered club members. One of the most prestigious films is entitled *La Caza* (*The Hunt*, Carlos Saura, 1965). It centres on four men, three older and one younger, who decide to spend the day hunting. As they fire their first shots, the sun hardens the land, making it barren and difficult. We learn that the area in which they are hunting was the scene of clashes during the Civil War, and echoes from that national

13   Ibid.

trauma inform the rest of the action. Made in the era of censorship, the film's violence may thus be read as a metaphor for that of the Civil War. Another important film is *La Escopeta Nacional* (*The National Shotgun*, Luis García Berlanga, 1978). This is a comedy and is very significant because a range of Spanish social identities appear represented as different topical figures of society: the ruined Marquis, the Catalan trader, the Andalusian freeloader, and the clergyman. The film denounces corruption in public life, and strives for genuine democratic change.

Another issue to consider, if briefly, is nationalist cinema, especially Basque film, since the production of sporting cinema in Catalonia, whether national in character or devoted to regional sports, is much less prolific, although an abundance of documentaries have been made. The Basque Regional Government fervently supports the production of its own domestic cinema, and some of the films made have been linked with sport, the most famous being *La Pelota Vasca* (*The Basque Ball*, Julio Medem, 2002). This is a Basque film which met with great interest from the public. It is a documentary on the conflict in the Basque country in which the filmmakers interview people representing all sectors of society and politics. It uses the playing of the traditional game of *pelota* as a motif, with the hardness of the impact of the ball striking the wall representing the intractable nature of the Basque problem. Another pelota-themed film is *Lokarri* (Jean-Pierre Grasset, 2001), a Basque-French production, which examines the connections that people have with their land: *Lokarri* in Basque means 'that which unites us'.

Focusing on the specific case of Spain, the following sections provide individual brief analyses of the films made about football and boxing, and of the social message they respectively produce.

Football: Comedies of Customs and Manners

The first professionally made films about football appeared in the 1940s. During this decade and until the late 1950s, the actors who worked on these films were also leading figures in Spanish football. They celebrated values relating to male camaraderie, loyalty and team effort. These films presented a lot of supporting characters, but there was always a leading role for a famous football player. As the protagonist, he represented very positive social values. Thus, his character was honest and he helped the poor. These were also films in which women appeared in three stereotypical roles: firstly, the homemaker, who was a good wife, cautious, sincere and simple, usually the perfect partner to the protagonist. Secondly, there was the moral woman, older, austere, a spinster, very Catholic and devoted to charitable works. The third and final role was that of the *femme fatale*, characterized as a gold-digger, attractive, provocative, seductive, false and disloyal. The protagonist usually suffered a certain degree of tension, being tied to the homely woman but tempted by the *femme fatale*.

The first film about football worthy of consideration is *Campeones!* (Champions!, Ramón Torrado, 1943), an epic feature about the positive values of sport. Other films included highly ideological aspects such as *Los ases buscan la paz* (The Aces are Seeking Peace, Arturo Ruiz, 1955), which told the story of the footballer Ladislao Kubala, an actor in the film, who was exiled from communist Hungary and played in Franco's Spain, an issue alluded to in the title itself. A comic parody of this film was *El fenómeno* (The Phenomenon, José Elorrieta, 1956), a screwball comedy in which the figure of the anti-hero appeared for the first time. But the most important film was *Once pares de botas* (Eleven Pairs of Boots, Francisco Rovira, 1955), which tells the story of a player from his arrival in the first division to when he makes it internationally. The legendary player Alfredo Di Stéfano starred in two films, *La Saeta rubia* (Blonde Arrowhead, Javier Setó, 1956; see Figure 6.1) and *La batalla del domingo* (Sunday Battle, Luis Marquina, 1963), films in which, once again, all the football greats of the day appeared. In almost all the films made up until the 1950s, the protagonist was identified with the role of the hero, not only on the playing field, for his talent and courage, but also outside of sport, displaying humanitarian values by helping marginalized children in the slums, teaching them to play football as a means of achieving social integration. According to sociologist Pierre Bourdieu, for young lower-class men, sport is the only means of moving up in society: 'The sports market is to the physical capital of these boys, what the system of beauty contests and related occupations – hostesses, etc. – is to the physical capital of girls; and working-class worship of sportsmen of their same social origin undoubtedly explains why these "triumphal stories" symbolize the only recognized path to money and fame'.[14]

From the 1960s on, footballers no longer appear as actors, while films about football are more professional, showing local customs and manners. *Los económicamente débiles* (The Economically Weak, Pedro Lazaga, 1960) was a comedy based around a regional team. *Volver a vivir* (Back to Life, Mario Camus, 1968) tells of the second chance given to a former football star when he gets a job coaching a second division team. These two films are representative of the twelve made about football in the 1960s, which presented aspects of the organization of local communities in which sport was a functional means to achieve social cohesion.

In the 1970s, football moved into the background and few films dealt with this topic.[15] *Las Ibéricas F.C.* (The Iberians FC, Pedro Masó, 1971) was a comic tale about a women's football team, although the script was

14   P. Bourdieu, 'Deporte y clase social', in J. Barbero (ed.), *Materiales de sociología del deporte* (Madrid: La Piqueta, 1993), pp.57–82, p.73. All translations are my own, A. R. D.

15   Duncan Shaw claims that Francoism used football for its own party political interests, manipulating public opinion particularly through coverage of sporting events. However, Richard Holt points out that this manipulation was not used exclusively by authoritarian regimes, since European liberal democracies have also fostered the use of sport for their national interests. D. Shaw, *Fútbol y franquismo* (Madrid: Alianza, 1987); R. Holt, 'El deporte durante el periodo de entreguerras y las relaciones internacionales: algunas conclusiones', in T. González Aja (ed.), *Sport y autoritarismos: la utilización del deporte en el comunismo y el fascismo* (Madrid: Alianza, 2002), pp.50–79.

threaded through with sexist overtones, since the actresses were popular singers of the day, and their scantily clad images were directed at the male gaze of the audience. *Jenaro el de los 14* (Jenaro, the Football Pools Winner, Mariano Ozores, 1974) is also a comedy about how one lucky man's life was changed when he won the football pools.

In the 1980s, the production of films about sport doubled, but the numbers centred on football stayed at the same level as in the 1970s. In 1982, the World Cup was held in Spain and the Spanish side delivered a miserable performance. Perhaps for that reason, in the 1980s only seven films were made about football, none of which dealt with the sport as its main theme. In the 1990s, football was portrayed in a comedy entitled *Matías, juez de línea* (Matías the Linesman, La Cuadrilla, 1995) which showed the problems faced by a linesman in spite of his honesty and ethics. At the start of the twenty-first century, Gonzalo Suárez (2000) filmed *El portero* (*The Goalkeeper*), a tragicomedy set in post-war Spain in which a goalkeeper is reduced to hustling money from strangers who think they can get a penalty kick past him. The film was a critique of the political power of the Franco dictatorship. *Días de fútbol* (*Football Days*, David Serrano, 2003; see Figure 6.2) tells a comic story involving a group of friends, each about thirty years of age, who are unsuccessful in their career plans. They also have problems with their wives. They reunite to form a football team. This gives them a brief illusion of success, while escaping some of their social problems. Football becomes a kind of male refuge from the power of feminism in their everyday and emotional lives, similar to the findings of Eric Dunning and Kenneth Sheard in relation to rugby in England during the birth of militant feminism.[16] *El penalti más largo del mundo* (*The Longest Penalty in the World*, Roberto Santiago, 2005) was another hit comedy that used football as a premise for comic situations and amorous entanglements. Within what could be termed the subgenre of 'football comedy', we also have *Salir Pitando* (Going Out Whistling, Álvaro Fernández, 2007), a story where the best referee in Spain is set to referee a 'home game', which brings big problems and the referee has to set aside refereeing for a while.

---

16   E. Dunning and K. Sheard, *Barbarians, Gentleman and Players: A Sociological Study of the Development of Rugby Football* (Oxford: Martin Robertson, 1979).

He returns, however, for a decisive match. The situation is further complicated when he learns that his ex-wife is living with his match assistant, the linesman, who also happens to be his best friend. In general, football comedy in the 2000s is based on the everyday life of the middle classes and, above all, the working classes, in which social relations are reflected through sport. Normally, these films feature the figure of the anti-hero, or Sancho Panza type, with a main character who is fairly insignificant and lacking in ambition, and who, almost by chance or against his will, becomes an unexpected hero, stopping a penalty during a key match for his local team, for example. Most commonly, these films depict the transition to hero as fortuitous, providing a metaphor for modern democratic Spain, a society of equal, but not necessarily predictable, opportunities.

The first decade of the twenty-first century saw the emergence of football films that could be classed as an exception to the rule, since they do not portray local communities or working-class neighbourhoods; rather, these films have a more global intention to go beyond national borders. They include *Real, la película, (Real, the Movie*, Borja Manso, Eloy González and Goyo Villasevil, 2005), a recreation of Real Madrid and its mega-stars, such as Beckham, Ronaldo, Zidane and Raúl. It was filmed all over the world and is actually a promotional vehicle for the famous club, mainly aimed at children. There was also a comedy titled *La Gran Final* (The Grand Final, Gerardo Olivares, 2007; see Figure 6.3), which also takes place in different locations around the world, telling the story of how people of different ethnic backgrounds, from the Mongolian desert to the Amazonian jungle, get ready to watch the final of the 2002 World Cup, between Brazil and Germany on television.[17] Global football films contrast with local football films, showing this dual sense of belonging, termed 'glocalization', where

17 David Rowe points out that *La Gran Final* is a film that affirms the importance of 'liveness' in sport, indicating the need for sports spectacles to use time in order to conquer space. He concludes that the film presents high-level televised football competitions as a way of uniting local and global time. D. Rowe, 'Time and Timelessness in Sport Film', *Sport in Society*, vol. 11, nos. 2–3 (2008), pp.146–58.

universalism merges with tribalism,[18] and which is represented by characters who support both their local and global team, making it clear that sport is part of an international language, a shared code of understanding.

There has been an evolution in the social content of Spanish films about football, starting with the fact that up until the 1950s the protagonists were professional footballers and portrayed as heroes. From the 1960s and particularly the 1990s onwards, scripts focused more on real people, who could be your next-door neighbour, in comedies of customs and manners (*costumbrista*) offering characters with whom the Spanish public could identify. In this social context, the main roles were no longer heroes like Don Quixote, but rather anti-heroes like Sancho Panza, which is why almost all the films are comic in tone. Once democracy had been established, from the 1980s onwards, women took on a more significant role on screen, moving out of their background, supporting roles as mother or wife, to become lead characters in line with the reality in Spain, in which women have been integrated into positions of responsibility under equal conditions with men. In any case, football films under Franco's regime and during the democratic era have highlighted the value of friendship, and particularly of friends sticking together, thus reaffirming the values of loyalty in the male population. Finally, and in summary, there are two contrasting identities presented for men, according to the ethical status of their behaviour: the incorruptible figures, normally sportsmen, and the corruptible ones, who are looking for easy money, which includes the club owners, politicians, managers and even journalists.

18   J. Naisbitt, *Global Paradox: The Bigger the World Economy, the More Powerful its Smallest Players* (New York: William Morrow, 1994).

Boxing: the Hero's Drama

Boxing is one of the great cinematographic sports. In Spain, just as with films about football, there are many comedies, although dramatic scripts are proportionally more significant. One of the first representative films was the comedy *El Tigre de Chamberí* (The Tiger of Chamberi, Pedro Ramírez, 1957), a tale of a bad boxer who has difficult relationships with his girlfriend, his friend, manager and coach. Boxing shows the harshness of life in a humorous manner. The 1960s were the golden decade of Spanish boxing. Several boxers, all former international champions, made the leap to the big screen, starring in films about boxing. The most famous was *El marino de los puños de oro*, (The Sailor with the Fists of Gold, Rafael Gil, 1968) starring the world champion Pedro Carrasco. These are upbeat films, but with a few dramatic twists and turns, showing the values of sacrifice and discipline, coinciding with the decade of development and modernization in Spain, which also entailed a change in social values. In this subgenre, the fame of the boxer at that time was used to launch the film. Among the most notable titles were *Escuela de periodismo* (School of Journalism, Jesús Pascual, 1959), *Cuadrilátero*, (Ring, Eloy de la Iglesia, 1969) and *Urtain, el rey de la selva* (*Urtain, King of the Mountains*, Manuel Summers, 1969). An exception to this group of films about famous boxers triumphing is *Young Sánchez* (1963) by Mario Camus, a drama that had considerable success, even at an international level. In this film, the leading roles are played by actors, and the story looks at a man of humble origins who becomes a boxing star. He discovers the dark side of the sport, something which he opposes. He represents the archetype of Don Quixote, an aspiring hero faced with impossible situations.

In the 1970s, the volume of production fell for all kinds of films, including those about boxing, and there were no significant titles. The genre presented one grotesque film: *Yo hice a Roque III* (I made Roque III, Mariano Ozores, 1980), which was a parody of Stallone's *Rocky* (1976) about three rogues who want to earn quick money through boxing. The film reflected elements of Spain's picaresque tradition. In the 1990s, there

was a public debate about the violence of this sport, to such an extent
that several media organizations, including Spain's leading newspaper, *El
País*, refused to report on boxing. Its popularity fell, but this did not have
a great impact on the production of new films. Since 2000, several films
have been made, almost all dramatic in tone and focusing on the margins
of society. Titles include *Cravan versus Cravan*[19] (Isaki Lacuesta, 2002),
Segundo Asalto (*Second Round*, Daniel Cebrián, 2005) and *La Distancia*
(*The Distance*, Inaki Dorronsoro, *2005*). *A golpes* (The Beatings, Juan Vicente
Córdoba, 2005; see Figure 6.4) is a different kind of drama, insofar as the
lead character is a young woman boxer living in a poor neighbourhood of
Madrid. To some degree it reveals the integration of Spanish women into
all facets of society, including boxing, but also into the world of crime.[20]
Dramatic films about boxing highlight the tension between the positive
values defined by the rules of this sport and the negative social values
that surround it, especially through the business side of things. These are
films which, unlike those focusing on football, offer greater possibilities
for looking at dramatic and even tragic scenarios, as an individual sport
in which the subject delivers and receives physical blows and, ultimately,
has to conduct his own inner struggle. In short, we could say that boxing,
in the Fordist production era of the 1960s, presented professional boxers
as actors in lightweight comedies, whereas, since the 1990s, films focusing
on the sport have presented professional actors in dramatic roles which
examine its negative and stigmatized aspects. The sociological analysis of
Richard Sennett is particularly apposite when talking about the transition
from Fordism to Post-Fordism as a process in which the subject moves from

19   This film refers to the Dadaist poet Arthur Cravan's match in Barcelona in 1916 against
     the first African-American heavyweight champion of the world, Jack Johnson.
20   In this respect, Jayne Caudwell analysed the film *Girlfight* (Karyn Kusama, United
     States, 2000) which tells the story of a young woman from New York City who
     trains at a boxing gym. However, the story focuses on the protagonist's tensions in
     her school, family and love life. For Caudwell, the film is not about boxing but rather
     a woman boxer, which allows it to open the door to new interpretations regarding
     the concepts of masculinity and femininity. J. Caudwell, '*Girlfight*: Boxing Women',
     Sport in Society, vol. 11, nos. 2–3 (2008), pp.227–39.

relatively entrenched community cohesion to the 'corrosion of the personal character' typical of the current Post-Fordist era.[21] The first boxing films were choral and featured collective protagonists, whereas nowadays they focus on the psychological aspects of the individual boxer. To an extent, in the early years of democracy, Spanish society moved towards defending and promoting collective rights, above all through left-wing governments, whereas in the twenty-first century individual rights have begun to dominate, particularly through right-wing governments, within the framework of neo-liberal policies.

Culture and Identity: Sport and Cinema

It is common knowledge that national identities are closely linked with sports competitions to the extent that the achievement and representation of victories and defeats are signs that strengthen or diminish the national spirit. This fact is linked to the specificity of each nation-state, to the 'national' character of its citizens, as well as to broader issues of social identity. Even the manner of playing a particular sport is part of a way of being linked to each territory. Janet Lever highlights the fact that Brazilian players are usually virtuosos at dodging in a one-on-one situation, at feinting and dribbling around their opponents. According to this author, the same strategy is applied by many lower-class Brazilians in their everyday life, where the need to survive obliges them to haggle and hustle in the street, to dodge and feint, just so they can make it through the day.[22] That is not to say, however, that the Brazilians necessarily agree with this external analysis. Along these same lines, Joseph (Sepp) Blatter, president of FIFA,

21   R. Sennett, *The Corrosion of Character: The Personal Consequences of Work in the New Capital* (New York: W. W. Norton, 2000).

22   J. Lever, *Soccer Madness: Brazil's Passion for the World's Most Popular Sport* (Long Grove, IL: Wavelan Press, 1983).

coined another metaphor, claiming that 'the Spanish game of football is like flamenco, not only technical but also attractive, elegant'.[23] He made this statement when the Spanish team beat the world record number of straight wins (thirty-five) in 2009, just a few days before a weak US side, not as technically accomplished or attractive, managed to beat Spain 2–0.

In fact, films about sport in Spain can be analysed on the basis of various dichotomies or binary identities. Firstly, there is the eminently cinematographic distinction to be made between good and bad, in which the sportsmen are normally the 'goodies', ethically upstanding, and also young, handsome and athletic, whereas others who surround them such as club owners, bankers, managers, politicians and journalists are the 'baddies', who are also typically older, fat, ugly and immoral. This paradigm is clearly Manichean, at once universal and 'real', and offers a simplistic but reassuring option in the choice of values. The social values of the athlete are positive and represented by fair play, whereas the social values of the financial or political system appear to be negative, insofar as Spanish society tends to link them with corruption.

Another identity is that of gender, illustrated in the roles assigned to men and women. There are goodies and baddies, both in the male and female characters, although the role of women is still secondary, supporting the male protagonists, a basic distinction characteristic of the inherent gender inequalities in films about sport. However, women play leading roles in some films towards the end of Franco's dictatorship, but they were used essentially as an erotic 'hook' to attract male audiences; whereas in the democratic era, from the 1980s onwards, women have started to appear as the athlete, the protagonist, and thus as independent subjects. They even acquire elements of the sexist character, especially in boxing films. In some regards they act like men by usurping traditionally masculine roles. This also reveals a certain crisis of masculinity among men themselves. At the same time, the traditional roles of the homely woman and the *femme fatale* have gradually disappeared from film scripts, as Spanish women have become more integrated into society, to the extent that, for example, Spanish MPs are divided almost equally between the two sexes.

23   Orfeo Suárez, 'El fútbol de España es como el flamenco', <http://www.elmundo.es/elmundodeporte/2009/06/05/futbol/1244223415.html> (accessed 6 June 2009).

Another dichotomy is the contrast between the global and local. Both aspects feature in many films about football, although Basque and Catalan nationalist cinemas focus more on local and folkloric sports and issues. But there are global Spanish films that focus on teams or sports stars that are almost commercial brands, such as Real Madrid and David Beckham. In fact, films about sport are not among the most popular with cinema audiences, even though initially, both in football and boxing, the athletes of the day were given the starring roles. As for boxing, the settings are very local, although the projection of their message is effectively sociological, insofar as it reflects a marginal world, in line with the observations made by Loïc Wacquant in a revealing study about the black ghetto of Chicago, analysing the Afro-Americans who went to one of the city's boxing gyms.[24]

One important issue to emphasize is that football and, especially, boxing are sports in which there is a great deal of physical contact. The French sociologist Christian Pociello (1997) pointed out the social difference between sports reserved for the lower classes like football and boxing, where there is physical contact and hardly any equipment used, and those practised by the upper classes, where there is a greater use of instruments and physical contact is avoided, such as sailing or golf.[25] Physical contact is more linked with the possibility of using bodily and physical violence. In the terms proposed by the theory of the 'civilizing process', developed by Norbert Elias and also noted by Eric Dunning (1999), the evolutionary nature of sport has entailed the attenuation of violence, as part of a historical process of pacification.[26] Perhaps for that reason, the number of films about boxing and their popularity in Spain has fallen in recent decades, although films about football have remained fairly stable, but without showing as much aggression as the early films in the 1940s and 1950s; where violence is featured it is now usually portrayed comically. A similar conclusion is reached by Demetrius Pearson et al. (2003) in their analysis of films about sport in the US since 1930, detecting a decrease in scenes and sports with

24 L. Wacquant, *Body and Soul: Ethnographic Notebooks of an Apprentice-Boxer* (New York: Oxford University Press, 2004).

25 C. Pociello, *Les Cultures sportives* (Paris: Presses Universitaires de France, 1997), p.22.

26 Dunning, *Sport Matters*, pp.52–61.

physical contact.[27] In this context, in Spain, a steadily increasing number of films have appeared referring to sports other than football or boxing. In total, there were ten in the 1980s and this rose to twenty-five in the 1990s. Most are about sports such as pool, athletics, tennis or skiing, in which there is no physical contact between competitors, reflecting a tendency of the new Spanish middle classes in the 'Consumer Years' (1994–2008).

Furthermore, there is the dichotomy between comedy (football) and drama (boxing), which at the same time represents two ways of being, two characters: Sancho Panza, the pessimist who wins; and Don Quixote, the optimist who loses. The opposite is true of American cinema, which commonly shows the image of the winner as a solitary hero. The figure of the *hero* is not as Spanish as the figure of the *victim*. The level of national pride in Spain is not as pronounced as it is in the US or other European countries. Hence, there are few films which show a vocational hero who thinks of an optimistic future for which he fights tenaciously. Even the few heroes that appear in some Spanish boxing films end up as martyrs or, at best, survivors. The role of the victim, which makes the narration more dramatic, is strongly present in Basque nationalist cinema, where at times sacrifice is identified as an effort to combat the lack of an established homeland, like a Quixotism that turns into melancholy. However, the classification of a film as a comedy or a drama is relative, since it is subject to socio-cultural reference points. For example, the melodramas of Pedro Almodóvar are, for many Spaniards, comic films because they break with the stereotypes of certain Spanish taboos related to tradition. The *españolada*, understood as a *costumbrista* comedy, reflects the upbeat and open character of the Spanish, and also represents national flaws, such as typically Iberian individualism and a certain degree of apathy. However, new *españoladas* move away from traditional archetypes such as flamenco and bullfighting in search of new defining features through universal factors, such as sport, and through perspectives on the Spanish character aimed at domestic consumption. Films about sport in Spain are usually a form of comic entertainment that

---

27   D. Pearson, R. Curtis, A. Haney and J. Zhang, 'Sport Films: Social Dimensions over Time, 1930–1995', *Journal of Sport & Social Issues*, vol. 27, no. 2 (2003), pp.145–61.

celebrates the unity of the local community and the genuine friendship that finally, and with difficulty, overcomes the forces of 'evil', represented by greed and selfish individualism.

Bibliography

Becker, H. *Doing Things Together* (Evanston, IL: Northwestern University Press, 1986).

Bourdieu, P. 'Deporte y clase social', in J. Barbero (ed.), *Materiales de sociología del deporte* (Madrid: La Piqueta, 1993), pp.57–82.

Caudwell, J. '*Girlfight*: Boxing Women', *Sport in Society*, vol. 11, nos. 2–3 (2008), pp.227–39.

De Miguel, J. 'Transformations of Politics and Society in Spain', European Sociological Association Conference (Murcia, 2003; unpublished paper).

Dunning, E. *Sport Matters: Sociological Studies of Sport, Violence, and Civilization* (London: Routledge, 1999).

—— and K. Sheard *Barbarians, Gentleman and Players: a Sociological Study of the Development of Rugby Football* (Oxford: Martin Robertson, 1979).

Hardcastle, A. 'Representing Spanish Identity through *españolada* in Fernando Trueba's *The Girl of Your Dreams* (La Niña de tus Ojos)', *Film Criticism*, vol. 31, no. 3 (2007), pp.15–35.

Harvey, D. *The Condition of Postmodernity* (Oxford: Blackwell, 1990).

Holt, R. 'El deporte durante el periodo de entreguerras y las relaciones internacionales: algunas conclusiones', in T. González Aja (ed.), *Sport y autoritarismos: la utilización del deporte en el comunismo y el fascismo* (Madrid: Alianza, 2002), pp.50–79.

Jordan, B. and M. Allinson, *Spanish Cinema: A Student's Guide* (London: Hodder Arnold, 2005).

Lever, J. *Soccer Madness: Brazil's Passion for the World's Most Popular Sport* (Long Grove, IL: Wavelan Press, 1983).

Naisbitt, J. *Global Paradox: The Bigger the World Economy, the More Powerful its Smallest Players* (New York: William Morrow, 1994).

Navarrete, L. 'La españolada en el cine', in P. Poyato (ed.), *Historia(s), motivos y formas del cine español* (Cordoba: Plurabelle, 2005), pp.23–31.

Pearson, D., R. Curtis, A. Haney and J. Zhang, 'Sport Films: Social Dimensions over Time, 1930–1995', *Journal of Sport & Social Issues*, vol. 27, no. 2 (2003), pp.145–61.

Pociello, C. *Les Cultures sportives* (Paris: Presses Universitaires de France, 1997).

Requejo, F. *Multinational Federalism and Value Pluralism: The Spanish Case* (New York: Routledge, 2005).

Romaguera, J. *Presencia del deporte en el cine español, un primer inventario* (Sevilla: Fundación Andalucía Olímpica and Consejo Superior de Deportes, 2003).

Rowe, D. 'Time and Timelessness in Sport Film', *Sport in Society*, vol. 11, nos. 2–3 (2008), pp.146–58.

Sennett, R. *The Corrosion of Character: The Personal Consequences of Work in the New Capital* (New York: W. W. Norton, 2000).

Shaw, D. *Fútbol y franquismo* (Madrid: Alianza, 1987).

Urry, J. *Consuming Places* (London: Routledge, 1995).

Wacquant, L. *Body and Soul: Ethnographic Notebooks of an Apprentice-Boxer* (New York: Oxford University Press, 2004).

PART 3

Gendered Representations

DAVID SCOTT

Chapter 7
Boxing and Masculine Identity

> Boxing tempts writers. It bids them to riff on the contained savagery
> of the prizefight. It entices them to explore the endeavour in terms of
> masculinity, race and class.
>
> —JAMES ELLROY[1]

Introduction – What Is Masculinity?

Within the western tradition from the Greeks onward, masculine identity
seems, much more so than feminine identity, something that had to be
constructed. As Elisabeth Badinter convincingly argues in *XY: De l'identité
masculine* (1992),[2] the exhortation 'Sois un homme' is one that continues to
haunt modern man, the onset of feminism over the last few decades exac-
erbating the male plight. Monique Schneider, in *Généalogie du masculin*
(2000),[3] traces the necessity for men to define themselves against the feminine or other as part of the Greek ideal of the male as warrior and defender
of the city (*civis*) or state. Whereas the Female relatively effortlessly could
incarnate life, the body and sexuality, the Male was associated with death,
soul or spirit and gender. The woman represented (Mother) nature, while
the man exemplified culture or civilization. Nature was given, culture and
civilization had to be fought for. Boxing commentators and historians such

---

1   Preface to F. X. Toole's *Pound for Pound* (London: Vintage, 2006), p.ix.
2   E. Badinter, *XY: De l'identité masculine* (Paris: Livre de Poche, 1992), p.13.
3   M. Schneider, *Généalogie du masculin* (Paris: Flammarion, 2000).

as Grombach (1977)[4] have noted that boxing as a sport began to develop (with the Greeks and possibly before them with the Egyptians) as western or Mediterranean civilization began to establish itself fully. It became, in effect, as I shall argue further below, a *sign of civilization*. Boxing was taught to Greek youths as an important part of their education, just as over 2,500 years later, it was taught to British schoolboys. For the Greeks, the Olympic Games were in part a symbolic re-enactment of martial skills, just as British imperialist battles were later supposedly to be won on the playing fields of Eton.

The later nineteenth- and early twentieth-century revival of concern in the West with masculinity or manliness is in part symptomatic of a need to answer the question: how is male identity to be constructed in a post-heroic, post-Christian, post-evolutionary age? As we shall see, Maurice Maeterlinck's essay *Éloge de la boxe* (c.1900) discusses boxing in the context of Darwin's theory of natural selection, while Robert Musil, in *The Man without Qualities* (c.1930) argues that boxing is a 'modern theology', answering to the needs of twentieth-century man in a secular and industrialized age.[5] At the same time, a nostalgia for a model of masculinity untainted by the horrors of the First World War was increasingly to find expression in avant-garde art and literature of the 1920s. In the same period in America, the work of American boxing painters such as George Bellows, famous for such pictures as *Stag at Sharkey's* (1909), should be viewed against the background of ideas of 'masculinity' or 'manhood' which were very much at issue in America at the time of the end of the Last Frontier and the beginning of women's rights movements. At the same time in America, boxing was establishing itself as a model for black male identification, offering a heroic route out of the ghetto into a world in which respect, as well as fortune and celebrity, were the prizes to be won. Finally, in the later twentieth century, boxing as a model of masculinity was to be re-appropriated by women as part of a strategy of ultimate feminist liberation.

4   J. V. Grombach, *The Saga of the Fist: The 9,000 Year Story of Boxing in Text and Pictures* (London: Thomas Yoseloff, 1977 [first published 1949]).
5   M. Maeterlinck, *Éloge de la boxe*, in *Morceaux choisis* (Paris: Nelson, n. d. [first published c.1900]); R. Musil, *The Man without Qualities*, vol. I, trans. E. Wilkins and E. Kaiser (London: Picador [Pan], 1983 [1930]).

It will be the aim of this chapter to trace the relation between boxing and masculinity from the later nineteenth century through to the present day, focusing in particular on the way that the tensions and paradoxes of their interaction are expressed in both writing and visual representation.

Boxing and Violence

> [I]n boxing, as in many other fields, there is very little new under the sun, and millions of fists over thousands of years have developed the art and science of boxing to what it is today.
>
> — JOHN V. GROMBACH[6]

> It is a great thrill to feel that all that separates you from the early Victorians is a series of punches on the nose.
>
> — A. J. LIEBLING[7]

Violence is an intrinsic potentiality of most forms of human and animal life. What *civilizes* violence in human societies is not so much its elimination as its regulation and control through communally agreed conventions. Thus actions such as killing, unthinkable in peacetime, become tolerable within the conventions of war, while fighting between individuals, frowned upon in regular society, becomes acceptable, is actually promoted, if it takes the form of boxing or other recognized martial arts. Indeed it has been argued that the elaboration of forms of regulated and codified violence such as boxing are closely related to the development of civilization.[8] Such controlled forms of violence are optimally *public*, because it is important that they should be viewed by a representative section of the community and thus serve their purpose as a controlled enactment of the violence that

6   Grombach, *Saga of the Fist*, p.201.
7   A. J. Liebling, *The Sweet Science* (London: Gollancz, 1989 [1951]), p.1.
8   See Grombach, *Saga of the Fist*, p.147; A. Rauch, *Boxe, violence du XXe siècle* (Paris: Aubier [coll. Histoires], 1992), pp.117–18.

might otherwise erupt in other, uncontrolled, ways. It is for this reason that today as much as at any time in the past, sports and games perform a necessary function in civil society in that they provide, as well as entertainment and amusement, an outlet for violent impulses.

The evolution of boxing as more or less recorded in history over the last three thousand years reflects the gradual civilization or formalization of the lethal and chaotic potentiality of fighting. First and foremost, boxing became, with the Greeks, a general spectacle, viewed in a public arena, within a defined space. The performance of the combatants became open to public approbation and judgment within a certain ethos. Ethical principles such as fairness and the reduction of unnecessary brutality were natural corollaries and although differences of weight (and therefore power) between boxers only began to be regularized at the beginning of the modern period (from the late eighteenth century), the sense of the match being even was always an important part of the spectator's pleasure. If it was males rather than females who were chosen to re-enact violence within the controlled space, first of the sports arena, later of the boxing ring, this would seem to have been (until the late twentieth century at any rate) because, as Monique Schneider argues,[9] within early Greek culture, the male was permitted to exercise violence as warrior and defender of the city. In the Olympic arena or in the boxing ring, the male therefore re-enacts what is at stake in such a role for the social and ethical approval of the community gathered as witnesses. For the woman, representing (consciously or unconsciously) in the classical world the principle of life, the body and sexuality, it would have been inappropriate, indeed unethical, even obscene, to participate in such a display. The boxing ring has come therefore to be acknowledged as a primarily *masculine* space, though the dominant presence of the male within it has not, as we shall see, totally eliminated – despite its conspicuous absence – traces of feminine presence.

9   Schneider, *Généalogie du masculin*, pp.12–13.

The Boxing Ring as Feminine Space of Masculine Domination

> The boxer's attempt is to obliterate all other objects and take up exclusive residence of the ring.
> — SHELLEY G. MACDONALD[10]

> The ring is a place of order in an otherwise shifting social milieu.
> — JOHN SUGDEN[11]

The boxing ring is one of the most alluring and perturbing spaces in modern civilization. This allure is no doubt in part a function of the many dualities the ring encompasses. Some of this allure and anxiety is a function of projection: for the combatant, the ring is a theatre of potential pain, exhaustion and danger while at the same time it offers the possibility of victory and correspondingly (and in varying degrees) fame and fortune. It is a blank sheet on which a chapter in a sporting career, a destiny or even a life may be about to be written. For the audience, it is a theatre in which an unscripted play will be enacted, within conventional rules, and yet with an outcome nobody can predict with certainty. It is a contest in which either combatant may have invested in him monetary, ethnic, national, cultural or other symbolic values, yet in which at the same time allegiances may change as a function of the match's progression. A particular paradox of the space is that it is both a place of order and of potentially chaotic action. Although from a sociological perspective, the boxing ring, like the gym, provides a site for the controlled release of aggression that might otherwise irrupt into the street, it also offers, from a psychological point of view, an outlet for a display of violent and aggressive action. The interaction of these two tendencies – controlling on the one hand, releasing on the other – creates the special tension and excitement that is inseparable from the boxing experience.

---

10 S. G. MacDonald, *Observations on Boxing: A Psychoanalytic Study* (Dagenham: University of East London, 2000), p.6.

11 J. Sugden, *Boxing and Society: An International Analysis* (Manchester: Manchester University Press, 1996), p.121.

As a psychological space, the boxing ring is particularly rich in tensions. The setting up of the ropes, at the end of the nineteenth century, as a kind of elasticated trapezoid suspended a short distance inside the four corner posts maximized this potential: the confined space was now moving and flexible, adding a new dynamic to ring movement. The ropes, having a certain degree of 'give', could be bounced off or backed into; more than just a line of demarcation, they became a dynamic element within ring strategy and could be used in a variety of attacking and defensive ploys. Both a potential trap – having one's 'back against the ropes' has become a general term for finding oneself in a difficult situation – and a possible aid to counter-attack, the flexible ropes of the modern ring express both the containing and the expansive potential of the boxing encounter.

While it has been male writers (very often former boxers) who have written about the ring most eloquently in terms of spatial relations, ring-craft and tactics, it is women writers who have been more attracted by the psychological or psychoanalytical implications of the space of the boxing encounter, a space to which their response is often profoundly ambivalent. Shelley MacDonald, fascinated by what she sees to be the 'male' world of boxing as practised by her grandfather, analyses the sport in terms of a 'phallic' male desire, acted out unconsciously by the boxer, to re-appropriate a feminine or even maternal space – that of the boxing ring – by asserting the law of his dominance over other male opposition. This is undoubtedly a suggestive thesis, supported by numerous unconscious features of boxing that have never been rationally accounted for – the boxer's underwear-like apparel of satin (which counts as a 'feminine' fabric), the reference to the 'apron' of the boxing ring, the hovering white-clad figure of the Law in the form of the referee, not to mention the final aim of sending at least one participant in the scene back to a position of foetal unconsciousness. In this view, the ring becomes the theatre of quasi-psychotic action, a regression into a sphere of impossible desire for possession, the psychic motivation of which perhaps fuels the exceptional energy expended in close-fought boxing encounters.

A complementary take on boxing from a woman's perspective is that of Joyce Carol Oates, to whom, as with MacDonald, the sport was introduced by a dominant male figure, in this case the father, a boxing correspondent who frequently took his daughter with him to boxing matches, and for whom, once again, the sport is a model of irresolvable ambivalence. Oates is particularly sensitive to the strong (homo-)erotic charge implicit in the male encounter in the boxing ring with its quasi-nudity, sustained and systematic violence, and elaborate ritual. Rather than the Mother or the Father (or Phallus), for Oates the boxing ring is a space of encounter with the Self in which the boxer meets a dream (or nightmare) distortion of himself in which his weaknesses become the strengths of the other. In this way, the ring, in its geometrical symmetry with its matched opponents, becomes a mirror-like structure in which, for the duration of the bout, the boxer is trapped in a confrontation of self and other that can only be resolved by extreme violence. The shattering of the glass, the dispelling of the shadow-self, comes as the knock-out blow, temporarily restoring the split consciousness to one as opposed to two centres, as one figure's phallic verticality triumphs over the flattened horizontality of the other.

More recent insights into contemporary female attitudes towards boxing, from the point of view of active participation as opposed to passive observation, are provided by a growing corpus of female writing.[12] What these insights in part reveal is that, despite the significance of gender difference, women's anxieties and elation in relation to boxing are remarkably similar to those of men: 'masculinity' as a quality or a potentiality is not synonymous with 'male' and is therefore as open to exploration from a female as from a male point of view. So, for example, Rene Denfeld is able, through boxing, to refine her conception of aggression and see that, far from being a purely (male-)gendered category, 'it is a human condition, not confined to one sex'.[13] Kate Sekules observes that the hunger to box is

---

12   R. Denfeld, *Kill the Body, the Head Will Fall: A Closer Look at Women, Violence and Aggression* (London: Vintage, 1997); K. Sekules, *The Boxer's Heart: How I Fell in Love with the Ring* (New York: Villard, 2000; London: Aurum, 2001); also C. Rotella, *Good with Their Hands: Boxers, Bluesmen, and Other Characters from the Rust Belt* (Berkeley, CA: University of California Press, 2002), pp.13–50.

13   Denfeld, *Kill the Body*, p.11.

related to the drive found in all athletes but that it has a distinctive flavour, and that it may not be so different in a man, except that women share discrete areas of additional pressure in this culture.[14]

She goes on to write of the thrill of sparring: 'It doesn't strike me as violent. I see it as an abstruse language that I know slightly as if I were in Tokyo after a year of Japanese lessons'.[15] For women writers who are also boxers, the theoretical issues raised by boxing (psychological, social) addressed by Oates and MacDonald become thus complicated and nuanced by the emotional and visceral involvement of the sparring or fighting situation, leading to a more complex understanding of what is at stake in boxing and necessitating a productive re-think of categories such as aggression and masculinity. Participation in boxing also enables them to develop a more nuanced understanding than that offered by Oates of the erotic aspect of the sport. For Denfeld, contact sports such as boxing promote a heightened physical awareness, a sensuality that is physically intense without necessarily being sexual, a 'form of eroticism that can occur without sexual arousal'.[16] She adds that 'The glow of warm pleasure from exercise is akin to the suffused relaxation following sex'.[17] Similarly, Sekules observes how the physical contact between male boxers and their trainers is one of 'easy familiarity, even intimacy', one which now 'without fanfare or special training' becomes the norm also for women boxers, one in which 'There is no sexual content'.[18]

14   Sekules, *The Boxer's Heart*, p.17.
15   Ibid., p.50.
16   Denfeld, *Kill the Body*, p.155.
17   Ibid., p.157.
18   Sekules, *The Boxer's Heart*, p.108.

Boxing and Masculinity

> Three punches, 1–2–3, the fruit of centuries of practice, mathematically
> exhaust the thousand useless alternative possibilities risked by the inex-
> perienced. Three punches – complete, irresistible, indisputable.
> — MAURICE MAETERLINCK[19]

At the same time – around the turn of the nineteenth and twentieth centuries – that the modern conventions and practice of boxing, both amateur
and professional, were codified and perfected, so also were the techniques
and equipment related to boxing training. Punch bags and weights were
already used by the ancient Greeks who regularly trained in purpose-built
gymnasiums. The revival of boxing in England in the eighteenth century
brought with it further refinements in training methods and equipment.
Broughton introduced the use of mufflers or gloves in boxing training and
set up properly organized training routines in a purpose-built gymnastic
space. It is interesting to see how quickly the punch ball and boxing gloves
as signs of masculinity make their appearance in autobiography and fiction from the early twentieth century onwards. So, for example, the young
Vladimir Nabokov (1899–1977) in his autobiographical text *Speak, Memory*
(1967) fondly evokes his father's library at the turn of the century in which
regular training in fencing and boxing took place:

> The place combined pleasantly the scholarly and the athletic, the leather of books
> and the leather of boxing gloves. Fat armchairs stood along the book-lined walls. An
> elaborate 'punching ball' affair purchased in England – four steel posts supporting
> the board from which the pear-shaped striking bag hung – gleamed at the end of
> the spacious room.[20]

Here, the leather smell of books and boxing gloves is a visceral sign of the
father's presence as master of language and the law, as well as of the manly
arts. Another aspect of boxing as masculine discipline is evoked by Nabokov

19   Maeterlinck, *Éloge de la boxe*, p.197.
20   V. Nabokov, *Speak, Memory: An Autobiography Revisited* (Harmondsworth: Penguin,
       2000 [1967]), p.141.

in his description of the disciplinary measures of one of his tutors who, as a punishment, would engage him in rounds of sparring, in which he would be punched in the face 'with stinging accuracy'.[21] Meanwhile, we discover about the same time in the dressing room of Robert Musil's *The Man without Qualities* a ceiling-suspended punch-bag similar to the one in Nabokov's father's library. In Musil, the eponymous hero would strike the punch-bag with a strength, speed and accuracy that he prided himself on as fully as his equivalent intellectual qualities, thereby testifying in modern terms to the Greek conception whereby the masculine expresses itself through physical as well as intellectual mastery of objects.[22]

The paradoxical relation between fighting and boxing, modern military aggression with its explosive weapons and the more humanized forms of physical struggle, is also explored at the turn of the twentieth century by the Belgian Symbolist poet and dramatist, Maurice Maeterlinck (1862–1949), Nobel Prize winner in 1911. In the light of Darwinian and other evolutionary theories, Maeterlinck argues in his essay *Éloge de la boxe* for the appropriateness of living forms adapting by intelligent selection to their circumstances and environment. Just as animals use the appropriate strengths or attributes of their bodies – the horse's hoof, the bull's horns – to defend themselves, so the principal form of human self-protection should be the fist and all conflict between men should be resolved using such a weapon. In other words, men should defend themselves and settle differences, as many members of the English pro-boxing fraternity were already suggesting in the eighteenth century, through the manly art of boxing, where the word 'manly' is understood to embrace all its connotations (virile, virtuous, courageous, decent). So in promoting boxing as a general solution to human problems, Maeterlinck argues that:

> On the pain of committing an unpardonable crime against the fundamental laws of the human species, a wiser race would prohibit any other form of combat. After several generations would be established a sort of awe-inspired respect for human life. And what a prompt selection, perfectly in tune with the will of nature, would

21   Ibid., p.123.
22   Musil, *The Man without Qualities*, p.8.

the intensive practice of boxing bring, in which all the hopes of military glory would be invested! For selection is, after all, the only really important thing we should be preoccupied by: it is the first, the vastest and the most eternal of our duties to the species.[23]

In a way similar to that proposed by Maeterlinck, boxing is singled out by Robert Musil (1880–1942) who also practised the sport himself, at least on the level of training, until his death, as being an activity representative of modern life and modern manliness. Combining as it does swiftness of reflex and logic of actions, boxing, as the following passage makes clear, enables man to experience the full potentiality of his being as an intellectual animal:

> [L]ife had to look for some other image of manliness. [...] If one were to analyse a powerful mind and a champion boxer from the psycho-technical point of view, it would in fact turn out that their cunning, their courage, their precision and their combinatory ability, as well as the quickness of their reactions on the territory that they have made their own, are approximately equal [...] But apart from this there is one other advantage that [...] a boxer [has] over a great mind, and that is that their achievement and importance can be indisputably assessed and that the best among them is really acknowledged as the best. In this way, sport and functionalism have deservedly come into their own, displacing the out-of-date conception of genius and human greatness.[24]

In this way, boxing also provides, in a post-religious, post-heroic, post-World War One world, a system of values adequate to the demands of purpose, exhilaration and challenge experienced as fully by twentieth-century as by earlier man. So, the casual violence of the punch-up can be rationalized and rendered socially and aesthetically decorous by boxing, and the wilder masculine impulses regulated into socially acceptable and enjoyable channels. In the process, participant and spectator can come to feel, in different ways, some of the ecstasy formerly supplied by religious or other highly charged ritual observances, phenomena that can be theorized, as Musil suggests in the passage below, as a kind of modern theology:

---

23 Maeterlinck, *Éloge de la boxe*, pp.194–5.
24 Musil, *The Man without Qualities*, p.47.

[...] this experience of almost complete ecstasy or transcending of the conscious personality – was related to a now lost kind of experience that had been known to the mystics of all religions, and hence it was, in a way, a contemporary substitute answering to eternal needs; even if a poor one, still, at least, it was one. Boxing, or similar forms of sport that put all into a rational system, was therefore a kind of theology [...].[25]

Picking up from their modernist forbears, a number of contemporary European artists have focused on the inner, psychological dimension of the boxing experience. This poses a particular challenge for a number of reasons. Firstly, because in boxing things happen so fast: a high degree of concentration is needed simply to follow the rapid succession of movements compressed into the three minutes of a round. Secondly, the intense visual excitement of boxing tends fully to absorb the viewer's attention, drastically reducing his or her time to reflect on the competing boxers' mental processes. And, thirdly, from the point of view of the boxer, since boxing is a sport in which reflection and action are of necessity so closely and intensely coordinated, it is difficult to separate visceral experience (energy, pain, shock) from psychological reaction. In the light of this, the procedure adopted by the artists examined here – Philippe Perrin (b. 1964), Miguel Rio Branco (b. 1946) and James Coleman (b. 1941) – is essentially that of exploring the various means of slowing down and projecting key moments of the action and the various peripheral or preparatory rituals associated with the boxing match. In doing so, they offer insight into the 'psyching-up' process as well as the psychological experience of the boxing encounter in both its real and its mythical dimensions.

The Grenoble-based French installation artist Philippe Perrin, between 1983 and 1990, explored what to him was at stake in the champion boxer by elaborating an imaginary or mythical identity. He began by constructing this persona from the outside, using, like any actor, the props and costumes that would help to shape the role. He produced posters advertising his imaginary fights, reconstructed a training gym, released booklets listing various boxing accessories such as gum-shields and gloves. Then, in an installation titled *My Last Fight* (1990), he produced a series of life-size head and shoulders black and white portrait photographs in which the boxer persona is shown in the ritual and delicate act of binding his hands before leaving the dressing room to enter the ring. Most significant of all in *My Last Fight*, however, is the way the theatre of the boxing encounter – the ring – is transformed by the artist (Figure 7.1): for the *canvas* that traditionally covers the surface of the boxing ring becomes the support of a giant self-portrait of the artist. It is painted in black and white, not only because it is adapted from one of the hand-bandaging photo images, but also because this restricted palette perhaps expresses a certain objectivity on the part of the artist – the painting is ostensibly the work of 'an official Soviet political painter', executed in the 'socialist realist' style. The frame provided by the boxing ring, scene in the fight itself of an unarticulated psychological though physically fully apparent drama, is thus finally put to specifically artistic use as it frames the artist's portrait. The very size of the latter emphasizes the vulnerability of both boxer and artist as they literally and metaphorically lay themselves open to the scrutiny of the viewer. The ropes enclosing the ring express not only the tensions implicit in the boxing encounter, but also the imprisoning of the portrait in its frame, the trapping of the combatant in his encounter with his opponent and the obligation of boxer and artist to perform within bounds that ensure the maximum visibility and scrutiny of their actions by the viewer. In this way, the metaphor of the boxing ring as site of heroic masculine self-confrontation in a very public sphere, a potentiality, as we have seen, hinted at implicitly in some earlier artistic representations of it, is here made clearly manifest.

In *Saint Sebastian* (Figure 7.2), Rio Branco reveals what is at stake in the inner mental life of the boxer by presenting him as a martyr figure whose physical sufferings have a spiritual motivation. Saint Sebastian was a Roman officer at the time of Diocletian in the third century AD, born in Narbonne, France, and put to death in Rome. Secretly a Christian, he was ordered to be shot with arrows and left for dead. Miraculously, none of the arrows pierced any vital organs and he was nursed back to health. When he confronted the Roman emperor with a fresh avowal of faith, he was beaten to death with clubs and dumped into the Cloaca Maxima, the main Roman sewer. As a Christian icon (and as a theme for the portrayal of the male nude), he became popular in Italian painting from the fourteenth century. In re-interpreting Saint Sebastian as a boxer, Rio Branco had merely to change the context of his martyrdom from an execution ground to the boxing ring. Bare-chested and perspiring, head raised heavenwards, this Sebastian awaits not the piercing arrows, but the heavy blows of his second chastisement, the Roman clubs being re-interpreted in terms of his opponents' fists, the bundle of boxing gloves hanging just behind his head metonymically expressing the flurry of punches he is about to suffer. The insight into the internal turmoil of the boxer is given in particular through the figure's beseeching, up-turned eyes, by the flawless but vulnerable torso and by the half-open mouth in which the gum-shield provides an original artistic expression of both the torment and the ecstasy of the boxer. The effect of chiaroscuro, light and dark, reproduces the painterly technique of an Italian artist such as Caravaggio, expressing in the process the emotional and physical as well as the more purely visual reverberations of the situation.

But what precisely are these associations? The boxer, is after all, not a Christian saint. To whom or to what is his martyrdom dedicated? To a heroic vision of himself? To a certain image of masculinity? To an experience of the mind-body relationship in which pleasure and pain, resistance and release exist in symbiotic contiguity? To living momentarily (the duration of a match or a round or two of sparring) on an edge in which excitement and danger create a sense of the primeval vitality of life unmatched perhaps by any other experience? No doubt there is an element of all these factors at play in this image, which, as it is not straightforwardly allegorical, does not invite a specific interpretation. That Saint Sebastian survived his first death sentence to live, as it were, to fight another day, is a feature shared of course by many boxers, for whom a defeat is often only the prelude to a further, hopefully more successful, combat. In the same way, Rio Branco's image may also suggest repeated and not necessarily identical interpretations.

Another, and no doubt better known incarnation of the boxer as Saint Sebastian is that of 'The Passion of Muhammad Ali' as presented on the cover of *Esquire* magazine in April 1968 (Figure 7.3). The context of this remarkable image, as all boxing fans know, is the travails of the former Cassius Clay who, on refusing to accept his conscription into the US army to fight in Vietnam, was threatened with imprisonment and disqualified from his claim to the World Heavyweight Boxing Championship. In hindsight, and probably even at the time, depending on the viewer's response, the image works more generally as an archetype of the boxer as saint, shouldering the pain and anxiety of the male condition and representing his 'passion' as an icon to others of his sex. There is little doubt that the image, in the light of the arrows piercing the immaculate flesh of this perfect specimen of manhood, is also one of homoerotic desire.

Perhaps the most complete recent synthesis of takes on the boxing experience, in both internal/psychological and external/visual terms is that contrived by the Irish artist James Coleman in his 1977 installation *Box (Ahhareturnabout)*. This piece consists of a film-loop of short fragments of original film footage of the famous Jack Dempsey/Gene Tunney heavyweight championship bout of 1927 (Figure 7.4) accompanied by a voice-over in which the obsessive thoughts of Tunney are breathlessly articulated. From the observer's point of view, the continual play-back of a few instants of the fight (this was the match of the famous 'long count' of the seventh round, which in effect saved the day for Tunney) gives the viewer an opportunity to savour, despite the flickering movement of the screen, specific moments of the combat. The circling of the boxers expresses their entrapment not only in the match, not only in the ring, but also in the narcissistic mirror-image of two Irish Americans battling to defeat both each other and, perhaps, something in themselves. Tunney needs Dempsey to prove himself (his existence, his authenticity as a man, as a complete being, his hero-status as world-champion boxer) but risks certain pain and possible death in the process. The same holds for Dempsey.

The voice-over that forms an essential part of this piece manages to convey, through its use of pauses, silences and semi-articulate sighs, as well as a sophisticated repertory of articulatory strategies, a sense of the confused but motivated mental processes of the boxer under stress. Combining conscious observations and self-instructions with quasi-mythical associations or imprecations surfacing from a less conscious level, it provides a kind of mental choreography of the boxing event. Simultaneously strategic and emotional, images of beer, wood, leather; limbs, blows, moves, operate as metonyms of the boxer's body and mind, somehow combining to connect the action to a larger picture in which the embattled Tunney can perhaps find the mythical strength he requires to sustain him in his awesome task. The effort will, of course, only ever be partially successful: the unity of self, of body and mind, of energy and determination, can only be sustained under the pressure of combat. After the match, after the adrenaline high has abated, the body will fall back into its old mental/physical duality and the boxer will soon be yearning again for a new challenge, for a fresh opportunity to experience that ecstasy of pain and danger that for some, it seems, only boxing can provide.

Competing Models of Boxing as Masculinity

> [Boxing] permits a man to behave in a way that is beyond and above his normal capacity.
>
> — VERNON SCANNELL[26]

> Boxing is a form of kitsch, which explains why so many intellectuals have been attracted to it.
>
> — GERALD EARLY[27]

The writers in the post-World War Two era who have attempted to rationalize Musil's concept of boxing as a 'theology' can be divided broadly into two camps roughly coinciding with two different general views of boxing. On the American side, writers such as Oates and Early explore boxing in later twentieth-century America – in particular in its professional form – in terms of the problematic issues of race and masculinity, while on the other side, European writers and boxers such as Musil and Vernon Scannell (b.

26   V. Scannell, 'Why I Enjoy Boxing', *The Boxing Companion* (London: Eyre and Spottiswood, 1964 [1963]), pp.39–44, p.43.
27   G. Early, *The Culture of Bruising: Essays on Prizefighting, Literature and Modern American Culture* (Hopewell, NJ: Ecco, 1994), p.xiv.

1922) focus more on the general and positive aspects of boxing as a lyrical expression of male potentiality. A brief analysis of these contrasting but complementary perspectives on boxing is offered here by way of conclusion.

Boxing in the later twentieth century undoubtedly seems to have loomed larger in the popular construction of masculinity in America than in Europe, and has been deeply affected by the major contribution of black American athletes to the sport – of whom, as Gerald Early convincingly argues,[28] Floyd Patterson, Sonny Liston and Muhammed Ali constitute the three main types. For Early, like Rauch, boxing is a metaphor for the philosophical and social condition of modern man in mass society,[29] providing a theatre in which his insecurity on the level of identity may be acted out – an insecurity complicated further by racial and economic factors. Even white writers such as Norman Mailer, Early argues, have to factor blackness into their account of boxing, in view both of the massive input of black fighters into the sport and what this input symbolizes in social and philosophical terms. So for Early, modern, industrialized man is marginalized and isolated, having little control over his destiny and living a life of increasingly vicarious satisfactions. Boxing expresses the neurosis of his condition in its melodramatic, even kitsch, dramatization of violence and rebellion, one that is controlled precisely by the forces (social and economic) against which the boxers are, if not always consciously, expressing their resistance through fighting. Jean-Paul Sartre develops this argument in Part Two of his *Critique de la raison dialectique* (1985)[30] to show how the tensions inherent in modern capitalist society find their incarnation in professional boxing in which the (generally) proletarian boxer, instead of identifying in solidarity with his own class (the working class), is alienated both from it and from the bourgeois world he is obliged to enter as a professional fighter.[31]

28   Ibid., pp.46–65.
29   Rauch, *Boxe, violence du XXe siècle*, p.252; Early, *Culture of Bruising*, p.xiv.
30   J.-P. Sartre, 'Rapports du conflit singulier avec les conflits fondamentaux de l'ensemble social', in *Critique de la raison dialectique*, vol. II, 'L'Intelligence de l'histoire' (Paris: Gallimard, 1985), pp.26–60.
31   For a succinct account of Sartre's argument, see R. Aronson, 'Boxing and Incarnation', in *Sartre's Second Critique* (Chicago: University of Chicago Press, 1987), pp.51–75.

While plainly democratic, professional boxing in America is primarily a sport for the underdog, more particularly the black or ethnic underdog, one offering the chance of a narrow, dangerous yet relatively glamorous passage out of a dead-end position in a racially and economically unequal society. Boxing offers the illusion of the possibility of male assertion through courage, discipline and strength, even if these heroic qualities, ultimately directed only toward a form of mass entertainment, no longer relate in any real sense to the values underlying modern mass society. As Early argues in his chapter 'The Romance of Toughness: LaMotta and Graziano' (1994),[32] boxing becomes an increasingly popular but also vicarious response to the undirected male energies at play in an egalitarian consumer society. Sport, and in particular boxing, thus becomes a 'traumatic romance where complete rationality of aspiration meets the utter irrationality of act' or vice versa.[33] The psychotic or, at least, anarchic, potentiality of boxing – or, more properly bare-knuckle fighting – in this respect is explored in Chuck Palahniuk's *Fight Club* (1997), in which male combat not only brings contemporary man squarely back into confrontation with the real, but also proposes, if only on a fantasy level, the illusion of the possibility of changing the world.[34]

In contrast, Vernon Scannell's take on modern boxing is more in line with a white, European and sportsmanlike tradition, in which, although many of the issues of neurotic masculinity as explored by Early and Palahniuk are still present, they are compensated or mitigated by other factors. For Scannell, boxing is more of a *game* in the aesthetic as well as the social sense and, perhaps because less entrammelled in the modern European tradition with racial and economic issues, can offer a less complicated form of enjoyment, on the part both of boxer and spectator. Scannell thus emphasizes the physical excitement and pleasure as well as the dread and pain associated with the sport, and stresses its potential as a measure of individual male destiny perhaps less fraught with wider social resonances than is the case with Early in the black, American context. Like Nabokov

32   Early, *Culture of Bruising*, pp.86–109.
33   Ibid., p.92.
34   C. Palahniuk, *Fight Club* (London: Vintage, 1997).

and Musil, Scannell is attuned to the sensuous aspect of the boxing gym, of which he gives an evocative account in his novel *Ring of Truth*.[35]

In his essay 'Why I enjoy boxing' of 1963, Scannell links in a more concentrated form the appeal of boxing, in all its paradoxes, to the equally contradictory make-up of modern man. Like Musil, Scannell evokes the ecstatic nature of the boxing experience, whether that of the nervous antici-pation before the event or the exhilaration, both mental and physical, of the combat itself. Like Musil, he emphasizes the synthesizing dynamic of boxing in which 'the contest is so totally absorbing of all faculties, physical and mental, that it seems no part of the mind, conscious or sub-conscious, is free to record details of sensation'.[36] So, like Musil, Scannell is deeply sensitive to the aesthetic appeal of boxing, to the way it organizes into a harmonious event sensations, actions, fantasies and impulses that would otherwise remain unfocused. He compares the 'functional economy' of boxing as a sport[37] to that of poetry as a form of literary creation, sug-gesting that 'both the fighter and the poet should have mastered all the orthodox manoeuvres yet be able to modify and adapt them as new and surprising problems are presented'.[38] He is also aware of the paradoxical impulses of love and aggression inherent to boxing, the 'feeling of remark-able well-being and [...] glow of affection for the opponent'.[39] Dismissing commanding officer or headmaster claptrap of the 'boxing makes a man of you' kind, Scannell asserts rather that boxing permits a man 'to behave in a way that is beyond and above his normal capacity. [...] He may be stupid, vain, ignorant, and brutish [...] but in the exercise of his art he becomes the embodiment of transcendental courage, strength and chivalry'.[40] In other words, for Scannell, despite its neurotic components, boxing still enables, in an alluringly concentrated and aesthetic form, access to a heightened experience of the complexity and vitality of human life.

35   V. Scannell, *Ring of Truth* (London: Robson, 1983), p.193.
36   Scannell, 'Why I Enjoy Boxing', p.42.
37   Ibid., p.43.
38   Ibid.
39   Ibid., p.44.
40   Ibid.

Conclusion

> Bruising is a kind of dumb play of the human crisis of identity in the
> modern society.
>
> — GERALD EARLY[41]

> It takes constant effort to keep the slippery, naked, near-formless fact
> of hitting swaddled in layers of sense and form. Because hitting wants
> to shake off all encumbering import and just be hitting, because boxing
> incompletely frames elemental chaos, the capacity for the fights to mean
> is rivalled by their incapacity to mean anything at all.
>
> — CARLO ROTELLA[42]

Boxing is a paradoxical sport, bringing together positive and negative – even
pathological – tendencies. As we have seen, the social aspect of boxing,
with the deep questions it raises in relation to masculinity, identity and
racism, finds its fullest expression in American professional boxing as analysed by Early, Oates and others. The problematic of neurotic masculinity,
what Early refers to as 'the most metaphorical drama of male neurosis ever
imagined in the modern bourgeois-dominated world',[43] is revealed in the
tensions and violence that characterize the sport and the fascination it exerts
on a public which finds itself, in today's post-industrial world, further and
further removed from the visceral reality of objects. The way this neurosis
can be made meaningful in a positive sense, as a metaphor or lesson for
life, has recently been interestingly explored by Carlo Rotella[44] but, as the
second epigraph to this section suggests, Rotella is far from underestimating
the fineness of the line dividing boxing from chaos. The positive aspect of
boxing – its promotion of fitness, friendship and sportsmanship – seems
to have been more consistently advocated by European writers, and more

---

41   Early, *Culture of Bruising*, p.xiv.
42   C. Rotella, *Cut Time: An Education at the Fights* (New York: Houghton Mifflin,
      2003), p.14.
43   Early, *Culture of Bruising*, p.10.
44   Rotella, *Good with their Hands*; Rotella, *Cut Time*.

often in the context of amateur boxing, according to a model explored by Musil, Scannell, and others.[45] Here the role of boxing is seen as that of taming violence, of freeing and glorifying atavistic impulses while it excites without brutalizing a mass audience. This aspect of the sport represents a positive model of masculinity in which in more recent times women as well as men are able to explore aggressive potentialities without losing dignity.[46] The English concept of sportsmanship, with its implications of stalwartness and decency, plays a significant part in this exploration of the positive aspects of a masculine ethos.

Through these two tendencies – neurotic masculinity and positive masculinity – boxing is also concerned to confront the real and the visceral whether encountered in social or physical terms. Here it is a question of interrogating the meaning of what it is to be human in a modern, post-industrial society, and of exploring the strength, energy and durability of the body. The eloquent exposition of the problematic aspects of boxing as social expression have tended however to make us lose sight of the positive aspect of the sport. For as a sport, boxing is also capable of deepening and celebrating human relations, especially between men, relations characterized (in particular at club level) as much by friendship as by rivalry or hatred. To a certain extent, boxing can become the purest expression of masculine friendship, implying mutual respect and knowledge, a desire better to understand the other, to test resistance, and in the process to understand oneself through the other. Viewed in this way, pleasure, excitement (or 'buzz') and a certain spirit of adventure make up part of the intrinsic charm of the sport.

45   Musil, *Man without Qualities*; Scannell, 'Why I Enjoy Boxing'.
46   Denfeld, *Kill the Body*; Sekules, *The Boxer's Heart*.

Bibliography

Anasi, R. *The Gloves* (Edinburgh: Mainstream, 2002).

Aronson, R. 'Boxing and Incarnation', in *Sartre's Second Critique* (Chicago: University of Chicago Press, 1987), pp.51–75.

Badinter, E. *XY: De l'identité masculine* (Paris: Livre de Poche, 1992).

Chandler, D., J. Gill, T. Guha and G. Tawadros (eds). *Boxer: An Anthology of Writing on Boxing and Visual Culture* (London: Institute of International Visual Arts; Cambridge, MA: MIT Press, 1996).

Denfeld, R. *Kill the Body, the Head Will Fall: A Closer Look at Women, Violence and Aggression* (London: Vintage, 1997).

Early, G. *The Culture of Bruising: Essays on Prizefighting, Literature and Modern American Culture* (Hopewell, NJ: Ecco, 1994).

Egan, P. *Boxiana: Or, Sketches of Ancient and Modern Pugilism* (Leicester: Vance Harvey, 1971 [1812]).

Fleischer, N. *The Heavyweight Championship: An Informal History of Heavyweight Boxing from 1719 to the Present Day* (New York: Putnam, 1961).

Grombach, J. V. *The Saga of the Fist: The 9,000 Year Story of Boxing in Text and Pictures* (London: Thomas Yoseloff, 1977 [1949]).

Hoff, C. *The Fights*, ed. Richard Ford (San Francisco, CA: Chronicle Books, 1996).

Holt, R. *Sport and the British: A Modern History* (Oxford: Oxford University Press, 1990), see esp. pp.20–2 and 301–3.

Liebling, A. J. *The Sweet Science* (London: Gollancz, 1989 [1951]).

MacDonald, S. G. *Observations on Boxing: A Psychoanalytic Study* (Dagenham: University of East London, 2000).

Maeterlinck, M. *Éloge de la boxe*, in *Morceaux choisis* (Paris: Nelson, n. d. [c. 1900]).

Mailer, N. *The Fight: The True Story of the Greatest Heavyweight Championship of All Time* (London: Hart-Davis McGibbon, 1976).

Musil, R. *The Man without Qualities*, vol. I, trans. E. Wilkins and E. Kaiser (London: Picador [Pan], 1983 [1930]).

Nabokov, V. *Speak, Memory: An Autobiography Revisited* (Harmondsworth: Penguin, 2000 [1967]).

Oates, J. C. *On Boxing* (London: Bloomsbury, 1987).

Palahniuk, C. *Fight Club* (London: Vintage, 1997).

Rauch, A. *Boxe, violence du XXe siècle* (Paris: Aubier [coll. Histoires], 1992).

Rio Branco, M. (1992–1993) 'São Sebastio', *Santa Rosa Series* in *Museu de Arte de São Paulo: Coleção Pirelli* (Sao Paulo: MASP, 1997), pp.74–5.

Rotella, C. *Good with Their Hands. Boxers, Bluesmen, and Other Characters from the Rust Belt* (Berkeley, CA: University of California Press, 2002).

———. *Cut Time: An Education at the Fights* (New York: Houghton Mifflin, 2003).

Sartre, J.-P. 'Rapports du conflit singulier avec les conflits fondamentaux de l'ensemble social', in *Critique de la raison dialectique*, vol. II, 'L'Intelligence de l'histoire' (Paris: Gallimard, 1985), pp.26–60.

Scannell, V. 'Why I Enjoy Boxing', *The Boxing Companion* (London: Eyre and Spottiswood, 1964 [1963]), pp.39–44.

———. *Ring of Truth* (London: Robson, 1983).

Schneider, M. *Généalogie du masculin* (Paris: Flammarion, 2000).

Scott, D. *The Art and Aesthetics of Boxing* (Lincoln, NE: University of Nebraska Press, 2009).

Sekules, K. *The Boxer's Heart: How I Fell in Love with the Ring* (New York: Villard, 2000; London: Aurum, 2001).

Shipley, S. *Boxing*, in T. Mason (ed.), *Sport in Britain: A Social History* (Cambridge: Cambridge University Press, 1989), pp.78–115.

Sugden, J. *Boxing and Society: An International Analysis* (Manchester: Manchester University Press, 1996).

Toole, F. X. *Rope Burns* (London: Secker & Warburg, 2000).

———. *Pound for Pound* (London: Vintage, 2006).

Wacquant, L. *Corps et âme: Carnets ethnographiques d'un apprenti boxeur* (Marseille: Agone, 2000).

———. *Body and Soul: Notes of an Apprentice Boxer* (Oxford: Oxford University Press, 2004).

CATHAL KILCLINE

Chapter 8
California Dreaming: Surfing Culture in Mediterranean France

This paper takes a cultural studies approach to the analysis of a range of texts and other cultural production, focusing specifically on representations of surfing and its derivatives on France's Mediterranean coast. The representations studied range from both documentary and fictional film to the local press and specialized publications, with this cultural production placed within the context of the socio-historical development of body cultures both in France and internationally. Jean Baudrillard's work on the interrelationship between representation and fact in consumer society, and particularly his notion of the 'precession of simulacra', guides the discussion of the myths and realities of French surfing culture.[1] Deleuze's and Guattari's influential nomadic epistemology and their concept of deterritorialization will facilitate the discussion of the relationships between sportspeople and the places in which they practise their sport.[2] This study of surfing and windsurfing in the French Mediterranean thus serves to elucidate the relationship between what could be classed as individualistic or ephemeral sporting practices and the locations in which they are conducted.

1   J. Baudrillard, *The Consumer Society: Myths and Structures* (London: Sage, 1998) and *Simulacra and Simulation*, trans. by S. F. Glaser (Ann Arbor, MI: University of Michigan Press, 1995).
2   G. Deleuze and F. Guattari, *A Thousand Plateaus: Capitalism and Schizophrenia*, trans. by B. Massumi (London: Athlone, 1988 [1987]).

Surfin' USA, *surf en Méditerranée*

In the mid-1970s, among the most prominent of the raft of new body
cultures to become popular in France were those sports generated by the
surfing culture imported from California. The sport had taken root in
California in the 1950s, following its importation from Polynesia, where
its long heritage as a tribal practice was documented as early as Captain
Cook's voyages of the eighteenth century.[3] These activities differed and
ran counter to traditional sports by emphasizing ecological, non-compet-
itive, individual and unregulated ideals, in short, by proposing alternatives
to traditional sports. These new sports were particularly well received by
the post-1968 generation of French youth. For this 'génération glisse', the
counter-cultural appeal of the sports – which Alain Loret characterizes
variously as counter-cultural, 'fun', 'underground', or 'alternative' – lay in
the fact that they were characterized by little or no associative element and
hence had little interaction with state organizations.[4] This dynamic was
particularly potent in France, where sport is marked by strong intervention
on the part of both the state and local authorities.[5]

---

3   One of the earliest records of surfing dates back to 1777 and William Anderson, a
      naturalist on Captain Cook's third voyage (1767–1780), who observed a local practice
      while in Tahiti. See W. Anderson, 'Surf', in J.-J. Scemla (ed.), *Le Voyage en Polynésie:
      Anthologie des voyageurs occidentaux de Cook à Segalen* (Paris: Robert Laffont, 1994),
      pp.876–7.
4   A. Loret, *Génération glisse* (Paris: Autrement, 2003). Translations unless otherwise
      indicated are my own, C. K.
5   In the French model of sports administration, the state, in the guise of the Ministry of
      Youth and Sports, plays a particularly interventionist role, especially since 1960 and
      the poor French performance at the Rome Olympics of that year. The state formally
      recognizes the public service mission of the sports federations, who are the only
      organizations authorized to promote, develop and organize physical and sporting
      activities and grant official sport 'licences'. This organizational model has led to a
      symbiotic relationship between the state and the sport federations that has proven
      highly productive, yet has also been criticized for failing to adapt to contemporary
      shifts in French society. See P. Dine, 'Sport and the State in Contemporary France:

Described variously as Californian sports, 'sports libres' (free sports), or 'sports de glisse' (sliding sports), these practices, as their name suggests, generally involve a moving, rolling, sliding or gliding instrument that exploits energies exterior to the body and extracted from nature, such as wave, wind and slope. The notion of 'sport libre' or footloose sport resonates with multiple meanings. They are considered freedom-loving activities: free in relation to time and risk – respecting climactic conditions, disdaining over-regulated timetables, overcoming institutional constraints and learning by experience among a group of peers, rather than via any institutional element.

Surfer magazine, dating from 1961 and which was to become the 'surfer's bible', was influential in establishing and propagating the defining myths of Californian surf culture. In 1965, the magazine wrote that: 'Surfing is a release from exploding tensions of twentieth-century living, escape from the hustling, bustling city world of steel and concrete, a return to nature's reality'.[6] Texts of this kind, promoting a Californian notion of the fantasy surfing lifestyle with psychedelic covers, articles about travel and high-quality surfing photography, were influential in the development of the sport internationally. The notion of surfing as an escape from civilization means that travel and surfing have become inexorably linked, the two activities coalescing in the notion of the 'surfari'. Bruce Brown's seminal 1964 film *Endless Summer* – following two Californian surfers around the globe in search of the perfect wave – constitutes an early and fully formed expression of two underlying myths of surfing culture: the search for the perfect wave and the notion of surfing as an escape from civilization.[7] The pair visit Senegal, Ghana, South Africa, Australia, Tahiti and Hawaii, with each destination stereotyped in a particular way via Bruce Brown's voice-over.

From *la Charte des Sports* to decentralization', *Modern & Contemporary France*, vol. 6, no. 3 (1998), pp.301–11, and P. Chifflet, 'The Sport Supply in France: From Centralization to Segmentation', *Sociology of Sport Journal*, vol. 12, no. 2 (1995), pp.180–94.
6   Cited in S. George, *The Perfect Day: 40 years of Surfer Magazine* (San Francisco, CA: Chronicle, 2001), p.15.
7   *Endless Summer* (B. Brown, USA, 1964).

In Africa, they demonstrate their sport to the locals, in other destinations they meet up with fellow surfers, and everywhere they listen to American pop music on their transistor radio.[8] This pop music also played its part in broadcasting the message of Californian surf culture. In the 1960s, the Beach Boys were marketed as clean-cut youths who, with songs like 'Fun, Fun, Fun', 'Surfing Safari', 'California Girls' and 'Surfin' USA', evidently cared for nothing more than cars, girls and, of course, surfing. The Beach Boys thus added a musical element to a wave of cultural production emanating from California that spread the good news of surfing as sport and lifestyle across the globe.

After the sport's first arrival in France, surfing resorts soon emerged on the Atlantic coast, and particularly in and around the traditional seaside resort of Biarritz in the region of Aquitaine.[9] In the more placid waters of the Mediterranean coast, meanwhile, a derivative of surfing, in the form of windsurfing, grew rapidly in popularity. For the likes of Manu Bertin, the pioneering windsurfer and native of the city of Toulon on France's Mediterranean coast, chance encounters with manifestations of Californian surfing culture, such as those mentioned above, proved the stimulus for a life dedicated to these new sports. In his case, it was the chance discovery of an edition of *Surfer* magazine in a local shop that set him on course for a life dedicated to various forms of physical expression capturing the kinetic and aesthetic potential of wind and waves. He describes this chance encounter with California surfing as follows:

> How did that publication get there? I'll never understand why, but, knowing nothing about this sport, and coming from Toulon and a Mediterranean not renowned for its big waves or breaks, I nonetheless bought the magazine.[10]

Bertin's sporting exploits reflect the adoption of the central values of Californian surfing culture by Mediterranean aficionados. For example, in the 1980s Bertin was one of the leaders of a desert 'surfari' called the

8   For more on *Endless Summer*, see J. Ormrod, '*Endless Summer* (1964): Consuming Waves and Surfing the Frontier', *Film & History*, vol. 35, no. 1 (2005), pp.39–51.

9   See J.-P. Augustin, 'Emergence of Surfing Resorts on the Aquitaine Littoral', *Geographical Review*, vol. 88, no. 4 (1998), pp.587–95.

10 M. Bertin and R. Fière, *De la mer jusqu'au ciel* (Paris: Arthaud, 2003), p.18.

'Défi multiglisse' – an expedition to the Sahara by a group of surfing and windsurfing enthusiasts. In a convoy of Peugeot 504s, they crossed Spain and Morocco to the desert in Southern Algeria.[11] Armed with paragliders, speedsails and snowboards, they 'surfed' the dunes, sailed the sands and were towed across the desert by the Peugeots. As a publicity stunt by the clothing companies that sponsored these professional sportspeople, the expedition failed miserably, but it succeeded in indelibly marking the romantic soul of the Toulonnais windsurfer. On his adventure in the desert, Bertin realized the surfing dream of an escape from civilization, finding there only 'virgin spaces and endless plains'.[12]

Inspired by the influential early representations of the sport, the quest for such 'virgin' or 'boundless' sites is endemic in surfing discourse. Moreover, surfing is seen as independent of the location in which it is practised: a notion that has been perpetuated in French *sports de glisse*. As indicated by the subtitle of Jean-Pierre Augustin's seminal work on surfing in the Atlantic, *Les territoires de l'éphèmere* (1994), these activities attract a footloose, international audience and participants who do not necessarily have any lasting attachment to the places in which they practise their sport, wishing solely to profit from the natural elements and climactic conditions the area has to offer.[13] Conversely, and inevitably, these new practices have been influential in the evolution of the spaces in which they take place. As Augustin states: 'The way of life in seaside resorts has been altered by new sports activities, new images, and new resorts that contrast with and complement those already in existence'.[14] Given the underlying imagining of surfing culture as existing outside the norms of civil society, it is necessary to interrogate the interaction – and, equally significantly, the absence of interaction – between the participants in these sports and the spaces and cultures in which the sports are practised.

11   Ibid., p.44.
12   Ibid.
13   J.-P. Augustin (ed.), *Surf Atlantique: les territoires de l'éphémère* (Bordeaux: MSHA, 1994).
14   Augustin, 'Emergence of Surfing Resorts', p.587.

Augustin's references to 'territories' and the emergence of 'new territorialities' are significant: new meanings are mapped on to coastal spaces by surfing communities in order to make sense of this 'new' space, in line with the sport's underlying values.[15] The concept of *territorialization*, or, more specifically, *deterritorialization*, is informed by the work of Deleuze and Guattari. In their poststructuralist epistemology:

> Every rhizome contains lines of segmentarity according to which it is stratified, territorialized, organized, signified, attributed, etc., as well as lines of deterritorialization down which it constantly flees.[16]

Deterritorialization occurs when a movement or evolution, an 'event of becoming', 'escapes or detaches itself from its original territory'.[17] This concept has itself been appropriated in the field of anthropology to refer to the weakening of ties between culture and place. In political geography, it refers to the taking away of control and order from a land or place that is already established and replacing the traditional structures with different beliefs and rituals. In particular, globalization and cross-cultural links, of which sports such as surfing can be considered catalysts, are seen as a force of deterritorialization, leading to the erosion of traditional boundaries.[18] In most of these cases, deterritorialization fits with Deleuze's and Guattari's fundamental idea of a break with established structures of representa-

---

15   J.-P. Augustin, 'Les pratiques de plaisance en Languedoc-Roussillon: nautisme et sports de glisse,' in J. Rieucau and G. Cholvy (eds), *Le Languedoc, le Roussillon et la mer: des origines à la fin du XXe siècle, 1960–1990*, vol. 2 (Paris: L'Harmattan, 1992), pp.217–35, p.228.
16   Deleuze and Guattari, *A Thousand Plateaus*, p.9.
17   C. Colebrook, *Gilles Deleuze* (New York: Routledge, 2002), p.59.
18   Anssi Paasi, referencing Deleuze and Guattari in his discussion of boundaries and deterritorialization, writes that: 'It is now increasingly being argued that capitalism and the processes of globalization will give rise to new global geographies and increase all manner of links (cultural, political, economic, international) across boundaries. This will detract from the role of state boundaries and lead to the deterritorialization and reterritorialization of the territorial system'. A. Paasi, 'Boundaries as Social Processes: Territoriality in the World of Flows,' *Geopolitics*, vol. 3, no. 1 (1998), pp.69–88, p.70.

tion. For Deleuze and Guattari, this break with established structures of representation is made by the postmodern figure of the nomad. Nomads are 'vectors of deterritorialization': 'The nomad distributes himself in a smooth space: he occupies, inhabits, holds that space; that is his territorial principle.'[19]

Nomads of the Mediterranean

Following Deleuze and Guattari, the proudly peripatetic windsurfers can be considered sporting examples of postmodern nomads, with their deterritorialization of maritime spaces traced in their cultural production. In the case of Manu Bertin, a pioneer of 'surfaris' from the sands of the Sahara to the icebergs of Greenland, deserts and seas are deterritorialized as empty, culture-free zones and reterritorialized as the perfect space for the practice of a sport advocating personal freedom and promoting an escapist philosophy. The Sahara is deterritorialized as 'virgin spaces and endless plains' and reterritorialized as the perfect space for the practice of his sport.[20] The tracks left by the boards and Peugeot 504s mark the desert with a culture spawned in Hawaii and cultivated in California.[21] The desert, here playing its Braudelian role as 'the second face of the Mediterranean', is, like the sea, conceived as a wilderness space, void of inhabitants, on to which can

19   Deleuze and Guattari, *A Thousand Plateaus*, pp.381–2.
20   Bertin and Fière, *De la mer jusqu'au ciel*, p.44.
21   An interesting parallel narrative is found in Michel Tournier's novel *La Goutte d'Or*, in which the traces made in the sand of the Sahara by the Land-Rover of French tourists ultimately leave a profound imprint on the life of a young oasis-dweller by the name of Idriss. The tyre tracks lead to an encounter between Idriss and the tourists that ultimately results in the protagonist travelling to Paris to retrieve the photograph taken of him in the desert. In Paris, he encounters representations of Africa and the Sahara that do not correspond to the homeland he remembers. See M. Tournier, *La Goutte d'Or* (Paris: Gallimard, 1986), pp.12–14.

be mapped individual desires, imaginations and liberties.[22] This concept of the wide-open wilderness is itself imbued with colonial connotations: the local population is typically absent or relegated to the status of exotic decor.[23]

Similar lacunae are projected on to spaces in Mediterranean France as can be traced in the foremost windsurfing publication in France, *Wind Magazine*. In a 1991 article, the correspondents' report from Corsica leads with the evocative banner headline (in English, as is frequently the case): 'In the middle of nowhere'.[24] Despite the fact that the reporters themselves were natives of the south of France (and thus allude to some implicit affinity with the island), they are delighted to find themselves in what they describe as a 'quasi-desert, boasting heat worthy of the tropics'.[25] Corsica is represented as the windsurfer's dream destination, insofar as 'nature reigns supreme' and thanks to its 'empty and virgin' land- and seascapes. Even local windsurfers, typically the only locals identified in such articles, agree that the foremost appeal of the island lies in the fact that 'there's nobody here'.[26] A 'funboarder' from Marseille, seduced by this windsurfers' paradise comments that: 'Corsica isn't an island, it's a continent'.[27] *Wind Magazine* concurs: for their windsurfers, Corsica is a continent, a desert, a tropical paradise, everything they want it to be, everything except Corsica. It is above all another empty space on to which they can map their desires.

22   F. Braudel, *The Mediterranean and the Mediterranean World in the Age of Philip II*, trans. by S. Reynolds (London: Collins, 1972), p.169.

23   See E. W. Said, *Orientalism* (New York: Pantheon, 1978; repr., London: Penguin, 1991), p.1.

24   B. Franceschi, 'La Corse: destination obligatoire!', *Wind Magazine*, no. 135 (August 1991), pp.31–2. The headline is in English, reflecting the widespread use of the language generally among surfing and windsurfing enthusiasts. *Wind Magazine* is a French publication dedicated exclusively to windsurfing and is the most popular of its kind in France.

25   Ibid., p.31.

26   Ibid., p.32.

27   Ibid. 'Funboard' is a spectacular version of windsurfing that is closer in form to surfing than sailing. Using a smaller board, with no rudders, the emphasis is on the tricks and stunts the sailors perform, rather than the speed at which they can travel.

Particularly significant is the exclamation that, in Corsica, 'nature reigns supreme'. Corsican culture is absent, however: the people and their history are effaced in favour of clear skies, deserted beaches and strong winds. The only mention of people, outside of the windsurfing community, is the ubiquitous 'caravan full of Germans', whom the windsurfers resent for slowing them down on the roads on the way to their favourite 'spots'.[28]

A year later, another *Wind Magazine* reporter on a 'Corsica Trip' is similarly discommoded: 'The Germans are omnipresent and easily recognizable thanks to their equipment-packed caravans and their backsides tanning on the deserted beaches'.[29] This kind of disdain is symptomatic of the attitude of windsurfers towards the holidaymakers with whom they share the otherwise 'deserted' beach. Rather than the 'banal and hegemonic model of the tourist or traveller', the windsurfers-as-nomads see themselves as a form of resistance, a way of 'preserving ideas that may otherwise have been condemned to wilful obliteration or to collectively produced amnesia' and protectors of a way of life and practice that is inherently more worthy than that of the banal and indulgent behaviour of the tourists.[30] The windsurfers self-consciously distance themselves from the vulgarity of the holidaymakers, who are represented as foreign not only to Corsica, but also to the lofty ideals of the windsurfer on his implicitly noble quest for wind and waves.

Despite the irritating 'foreign' presence, Corsica remains 'the paradise of the French windsurfer'.[31] In particular, we are told that, in Corsica, windsurfing has preserved its soul: 'Conviviality among windsurfers, which is rapidly disappearing in the busier French spots, is still vibrant here'.[32] Windsurfing discourse thus constructs a (largely imagined) heritage of the sport on the island and describes the island as a purist's refuge from the disillusionment experienced on more populated shores. This conviviality among

---

28 Ibid.
29 O. Lafleur, 'Corsica Trip', *Wind Magazine*, no. 144 (June 1992), pp.40–4.
30 R. Braidotti, *Nomadic Subjects: Embodiment and Social Difference in Contemporary Feminist Theory* (New York: Columbia University Press, 1994), p.24.
31 Lafleur, 'Corsica Trip', p.43.
32 Ibid., p.42.

windsurfers – on an island famously noted for its hospitality – seemingly does not extend to the non-windsurfing community, however. Again the only reference to Corsican culture to be conjured up depicts 'old men sitting in the shade waiting for chestnuts to fall' and other tired clichés and familiar stereotypes associated with the Mediterranean island. The reporters themselves even reference Asterix's trip to Corsica to help conjure up some kind of 'authentic' Corsican ambiance for their readers.[33]

Typically, in the discourse of surfing and windsurfing, stereotypes and essentialist characteristics of the local population are recited before the windsurfer retreats into the 'cocoon' of his sporting peers and attendant sub-culture. The local populations, if they are recognized at all, are evoked only in static, eternalized form. They are thus disempowered, their lived identity obscured by stereotypes, their places emptied of meaning and thus ripe for appropriation by the dynamic, nomadic surfers. For example, as a professional windsurfer sponsored by clothing company *Gaastra*, Manu Bertin returned to live with his grandmother in Pradet near Toulon, in 'a *Pagnolesque* ambiance, under the sun of the Midi', with the only cloud on the horizon being that coastal development had blocked his cross-country passage from his grandmother's house to the sea: 'Too many buildings and hasty constructions – concrete scars of a deadly urbanization'.[34] Likewise, an article in *Wind* vaunting the special attributes of the famous Mistral prevailing wind is accompanied by a cartoon depicting a stereotypical Marseille fisherman 'with cap on head and *pastis* in hand', pitching a *boule* and balancing drunkenly with one foot on a surfboard.[35] Presumably windsurfing is not for fishermen. Neither is the Mistral, according to *Wind*: 'For most of

---

33   R. Goscinny and A. Uderzo, *Astérix en Corse* (Neuilly-sur-Seine: Dargaud, 1973).

34   Bertin and Fière, *De la mer jusqu'au ciel*, p.43. *Pagnolesque* refers to the writings and films of Marcel Pagnol. Though originally composed in the 1930s and 1940s, these representations of southern French ways of life have maintained a firm hold on the public imagination. Typical scenes *à la Pagnol*, such as men sharing a *pastis* in the shade, or gathering for a *partie de boules* at the village square, became the clichéd images of the *Midi*, with the consumption of the aniseed-flavoured spirit and the playing of the game of *pétanque* enshrined as the totemic signifiers of meridional culture.

35   B. Franceschi, 'Mistral: le maître', *Wind Magazine*, no. 135 (August 1991), pp.52–3.

the year in the ports around Marseille, the fishermen are unemployed. On these days, on the Mediterranean, the Mistral reigns supreme.'[36] So, when the Mistral blows, and the fishermen are left to their *pastis* and *pétanque*, the windsurfers take over.

The windsurfer, by positioning his sport in opposition to the totemic meridional rituals of *pastis* and *pétanque*, thus self-consciously opposes his cultural identity to that of the city-dweller. To refer to Deleuze and Guattari again, according to their nomadic epistemology, metropolitan space opposes nomadic trajectories: *nomos* confronts the *polis*, open nomadic space contests the sedentary power of the city.[37] Windsurfers typically position themselves as nomadic outsiders vis-à-vis civic society. In the case of Marseille, the nomadic windsurfers are contrasted with the football fans rooted in the culture of the city. *Wind* magazine tells us:

> In Marseille, when you're 16 years old, you are expected to read *France Football*, hate the referee and venerate *Olympique de Marseille* football club. But Renaud Daron, a young windsurfer from the city, reads *Wind*, doesn't hate anyone and is a fan only of windsurfers like Robby Naish.[38]

The city of Marseille and its emblematic football club are seen as having a symbiotic relationship – the rejection of one necessitating the rejection of the other, a phenomenon that was particularly robust in the early 1990s as Olympique de Marseille became the first French club to win the European

36 Ibid, p.52.
37 Deleuze and Guattari use the metaphor of board games: 'The "smooth" space of Go, against the striated space of chess. The *nomos* of Go, against the State of chess. *Nomos* against *polis*. The difference is that chess codes and decodes space, whereas Go proceeds altogether differently, territorializing or deterritorializing it', Deleuze and Guattari, *A Thousand Plateaus*, p.353.
38 S. Arfi, 'Robby the Kid,' *Wind Magazine*, no. 144 (June 1992), p.84. Robby Naish, son of a Californian competitive surfer and surfboard shaper, was one of the leading proponents of the fledgling sport of windsurfing on Hawaii in the 1970s. He has since developed his own line of clothing and equipment and followed Manu Bertin into kite-surfing in the late 1990s. Unlike Bertin and Laird Hamilton, fellow pioneers in surfing forms, Naish surfed competitively, winning numerous world championships in windsurfing and kite-surfing.

championship.[39] Instead, however, the young windsurfer creates his own Marseille, 'mon Marseille à moi' as he calls it. Like all windsurfers, Daron detests the crowds, pollution and stress of city life: 'I'm not really a city-boy' comments Daron himself.[40] His life is that of the coast: 'Myself and my mates', he says, 'we never stray more than 500 yards from the shore'.[41] They hang out at the *Yacht Club de la Pointe Rouge*, where they store their equipment, drink a *pastis* or a *mauresque* and mix with other sailors and windsurfers. They are aware of the 'negative image' of Marseille, but care little about it: 'We couldn't care less about the city, we stick to the wind and the waves'.[42]

The Legend of 'Flat Country'

By the mid 1990s, windsurfing on the Mediterranean had reached its zenith, with Augustin, for example, describing the windsurfers' 'annexation' of the Languedoc coastline.[43] However, with the majority of windsurfers now affiliated with elite sailing clubs – which had established windsurfing sections to cater for the new individualistic maritime desires – for many of the pioneers of the sport, the counter-cultural appeal of windsurfing had already been and gone. Thus disillusioned with his favourite activity, which had become burdened by the expense, the overly complicated techniques and the sheer weight of equipment, Manu Bertin, for example, quit windsurfing in the mid-1990s to concentrate on perfecting a new form of

39   For more on the relationship between Marseille and its football club, see Christian Bromberger's influential ethnographic study of the football cultures of Marseille, Turin and Naples. C. Bromberger, *Le match de football: Ethnologie d'une passion partisane à Marseille, Naples et Turin* (Paris: Éditions de la Maison des Sciences de l'Homme, 1995).
40   Arfi, 'Robby the Kid', p.84.
41   Ibid.
42   Ibid.
43   Augustin, 'Les pratiques de plaisance', p.227.

surfing, namely kite-surfing, which he pioneered in Hawaii in the company of surfing legend Laird Hamilton.[44]

As windsurfing lost its counter-cultural cachet, due to the increasingly important associative element and increasing regulation of popular 'spots', it nonetheless contributed to the deterritorialization of the French Mediterranean coastline, mapping a synthetic Americana on to fishing villages and port towns from Nice to Perpignan. As André Rauch describes, at the end of the 1970s, devotees of sea and sun on the *Côte d'Azur* changed their look: 'sailboards ... wetsuits ... flowered Bermuda shorts ... coloured T-shirts printed front and back in colours with the English words *Fun, California* or *Don't worry* [and] the slogan *we find the perfect wave*' became rallying points for a new kind of maritime identity.[45]

This appropriation of the markers of Californian surfing culture is the subject of James Huth's 2005 hit comedy *Brice de Nice*, with the eponymous hero a parody of the kitsch and absurd nature of French surfing culture in general, and on the Mediterranean littoral in particular.[46] For Jean Baudrillard, kitsch is a cultural category associated with the sociological reality of consumer society, whereby 'broad swathes of the population are moving up the social ladder, reaching a higher status and, at the same time, acceding to cultural demand, which is simply the need to manifest that status in signs'.[47] Baudrillard defines kitsch as the following:

> [...] a pseudo-object or, in other words, as a simulation, a copy, an imitation, a stereotype, as a dearth of real signification and a superabundance of signs, of allegorical references, disparate connotations, as a glorification of the detail and a saturation by details.[48]

---

44   Bertin and Fière, *De la mer jusqu'au ciel*, p.61. Bertin was also the first person to kite-surf across the Atlantic and the Mediterranean (from France to Corsica). Laird Hamilton is the star of documentary surfing films including Stacey Peralta's *Riding Giants* (USA/France, 2004).

45   A. Rauch, 'Vacationing on France's Côte d'Azur, 1950–2000', in S. C. Anderson and B. H. Tabb (eds), *Water, Leisure and Culture: European Historical Perspectives* (Oxford: Berg, 2002), pp.223–39, p.233.

46   *Brice de Nice* (J. Huth, France, 2005).

47   J. Baudrillard, *The Consumer Society*, p.110.

48   Ibid.

Brice de Nice self-consciously parodies these simulations, documenting the superabundance of signs consumed by the hapless hero in his quest to pioneer the Californian surfing dream in his hometown. Every day, Brice, or 'Braïce de Naïce', as he prefers to be known, takes his surfboard out on to the placid waters of the Baie des Anges in the hope of catching a 'méga-tube' ('big wave'). Inevitably, though, he returns disappointed: the Mediterranean at Nice is always 'mort' ('dead' or 'glassy'). Not only does he fail to catch the perfect wave, he fails to catch any wave at all. Brice explains to his mates that 'there wasn't any swell, the wind was blowing off-shore'.

Despite being critically panned, the film was the most popular French film in 2005, attracting almost 4.5 million cinema-goers.[49] Jean Dujardin, who plays Brice in the film, originally invented the character ten years previously as part of a series of sketches by the *Nous C Nous* comedy group and on the *Graines de Star* programme on the M6 television channel. Thanks to these sketches and other amateur *courts-métrages* reprising the character, Brice developed such a significant cult following on the internet that Dujardin became convinced of the viability of a full-length feature film featuring the incompetent *Niçois*.[50] Brice is thus the quintessential postmodern sporting hero in the sense that he is effectively the product of internet communication – a simulation composed of anonymous contributions brought together via information technology.

Dujardin lampoons the defining myths of Californian surf culture: the search for the 'perfect wave', the rejection of official structures and institutions, and the oriental mysticism favoured by many surfers. Brice himself worships at a temple dedicated to Bodhi – Patrick Swayze's character in the 1991 surfing movie *Point Break*.[51] When Brice's father is arrested for laundering funds and collusion with the Sicilian mafia (an allusion to the Médecin controversies that have dogged contemporary local politics in Nice), the younger Agostini – inspired by Bodhi's fictional gang, which robs banks dressed as the Presidents of the USA – decides to raid the local

---

49   N. Vulser, 'En France, la fréquentation des salles de cinéma a baissé de 10% en 2005,' *Le Monde*, 8 January 2006 (online edition).

50   T. Sotinel and P. Wagner, 'Comment la Toile a propagé le virus *Brice de Nice*,' *Le Monde*, 16 April 2005 (online edition).

51   *Point Break* (K. Bigelow, USA, 1991).

Caisse de Nice disguised as Jacques Chirac.[52] After this failed attempt, Brice travels to the French surfing capital of Hossegor on the Atlantic coast to compete in the 'World Underground Surf Cup' – a parody of surfing's desire to retain counter-cultural status despite the growing popularity of competitions and organizations that contradict this ideal.

Remarkably, there are many real-life Brices, intent on defying geographical and climactic limitations in a Sisyphean mission to create and live a Mediterranean surfing culture. A documentary, appropriately entitled *Flat Country: 100% Méditerranée*, by Sandrine Fiacre and Jessica Rossigneux, members of the 'Mediterranean Surf Community' based at Sausset-les-Pins, chronicles some of the rare moments of Mediterranean surf and interviews a number of those dedicated to this often thankless pursuit.[53] These surfers tell us that 'our desire to surf is such that we are willing to surf whatever the sea gives us … the long wait for waves only sharpens our sensations, and our willingness to prove our status as committed surfers'.[54] Most frequently, this means surfing small or weak waves, and using larger, more cumbersome boards in order to stay afloat on slow-moving waves that lack the aesthetic spectacle and sensory thrill of their Atlantic counterparts. Often, the surfers' quest is entirely futile. Patrick, for example, regularly takes time off from his work as a mechanic to 'surf the Marseille waves'. Unfortunately for Patrick, the day he is interviewed by the journalist for the regional newspaper, *Le Provençal*, is what he calls a 'jour sans' – that is to say, another wave-less day on the Mediterranean: 'there is wind alright, enough for the windsurfers … but we need waves'.[55]

---

52 Jacques Médecin, five times mayor of Nice, was indicted for misuse of public funds in 1990. Eight years earlier, he had been accused of corruption following an exposé of judicial and police malpractice by the celebrated British novelist, Graham Greene, entitled *J'accuse: The Dark Side of Nice* (London: Bodley Head, 1982). Brice's escape on a motorcycle following his failed bank robbery is also an allusion to the Albert Spaggiari case of 1976, involving a Nice-based photographer and Médecin 'hanger-on', who became a local hero when he stole over 46 million francs from the *Société Générale* bank. For more on *Niçois* politics see M. Blume, *Côte d'Azur: Inventing the French Riviera* (New York: Thames and Hudson, 1992), in particular pp.14–21.

53 *Flat Country: 100% Méditerranée* (S. Fiacre and J. Rossigneux, France, 2006).

54 Ibid.

55 O. Biblioni, 'Le sport est une fête', *Le Provençal*, 17 May 1993, p.3.

The potential Mediterranean surfer is thus advised by the Mediterranean surfing community to 'remain humble', but also to be prepared to travel in search of 'the wave that works best'.[56] These surfers often travel two to three hundred kilometres in a day crisscrossing the same area in search of surf-able waves (the car, we are told, is a crucial element of Mediterranean surfing: 'the more you drive, the more you surf') whilst any Mediterranean surfer worth his (or her) salt must be ready to leave any other pursuit in an instant in order to follow news of a potential swell.[57] As is typical of surfing ideologies generally, total commitment to the sport, and its associated lifestyle, is expected by those at Sausset-les-Pins. The Mediterranean Surfing Community is distinctive, however, in the inevitable frustration experienced by its members in their doomed struggle to live a fulfilled surfing lifestyle in spite of insurmountable geographical and climactic barriers. Like Brice waiting for his 'méga-tube' in the Baie des Anges, the members of this community speak of 'the legend of the Flat Country ... where there aren't any waves, but one day, you'll see ...'[58] On the Atlantic, meanwhile, we discover that Brice cannot surf at all – his only real ability is his capacity to cut down his opponents in verbal jousts. His jibes are typically word-plays on the French adoption of surfing culture or pronunciation of American surfing terminology. As Brice recognizes, for many, himself included, surfing 'is not a sport, it's a dream.'[59]

For Jean Baudrillard, California was a model for his notion of the 'hyperreal order', a place where dreams, legends and myths are constantly recycled to produce a simulation that determines human action and interaction and subsumes any notion of objective reality. The adoption of Californian values and myths by surfers across the world can be seen to prove – in sometimes comical fashion given the Mediterranean example – the truth of Baudrillard's thesis that in contemporary society the image precedes, and ultimately subsumes any rational or objective claims to reality. To quote Baudrillard:

56   Fiacre and Rossigneux, *Flat Country*.
57   Ibid.
58   Ibid.
59   Ibid.

It is no longer a question of imitation, nor duplication, nor even parody. It is a question of substituting the signs of the real for the real, that is to say of an operation of deterring every real process via its operational double, a programmatic, metastable, perfectly descriptive machine that offers all the signs of the real and short-circuits all its vicissitudes.[60]

Mediterranean surfing belongs to Baudrillard's hyperreal order, whereby the myths and mannerisms of surfing culture are consumed by those for whom the actual sport is a practical near-impossibility.[61] Freed from the constraints of rationality, the Californian Mediterranean exists in hyperreal form; it is 'operational' as Baudrillard might say and is acted out by Brice and his 'real-life' acolytes.

For Baudrillard, the superabundance of signs that he associates with kitsch is especially prevalent in the case of holidaymakers:

Sisyphus, Tantalus, Prometheus: all the existential myths of 'absurd freedom' are reasonably accurate representations of the holiday-maker in his setting, with all his desperate efforts to imitate 'vacation', gratuitousness, a total dispossession, a void, a loss of himself and of his time which he cannot achieve.[62]

Similarly, Mediterranean surfers continue on their quest for 'absurd freedom', chasing receding waves in a similar fashion to the way in which Sisyphus was condemned by the gods of Greek mythology to ceaselessly roll a rock to the top of a mountain, only for it always to roll back down. In the attempt to understand the surfers' ill-fated predicament, perhaps it is best to leave the last word on their seemingly futile plight to another great Mediterranean sportsman, namely Albert Camus, who once stated: 'the struggle itself towards the heights is enough to fill a man's heart. One must imagine Sisyphus happy'.[63] As a celebrated advocate of the sun, sea and sport he enjoyed on the Mediterranean beaches of his youth, Camus

60   Baudrillard, *Simulacra and Simulation*, p.2.
61   Ibid.
62   Baudrillard, *The Consumer Society*, p.154.
63   A. Camus, *The Myth of Sisyphus*, trans. by J. O'Brien (1955; repr., London and New York: Penguin, 1975), p.111.

can be considered a particularly apt figure from which to draw conclusions on Brice and the Mediterranean surfing communities, happily California dreaming on the Côte d'Azur.[64]

Conclusion

The first conclusion to be drawn from Mediterranean surfing culture pertains to the perennial and robust nature of myths, and their capacity to influence lived experience in the form of affiliation and commitment to a body culture. Surfing is often described as a way of life, or a vocation, rather than a hobby or pastime, and this essay proposes that this way of life is determined as much by the myths and morals communicated through a range of cultural production, as it is determined by the climactic, physical and geographical demands of the practice itself. The profound and pronounced influence of discourses and representations on behaviours and attitudes is thus fundamental to the understanding of such a self-consciously constructed sub-culture.

The second central issue here is the notion of an individual's or a community's identification with place through the medium of sporting practices. As Nancy Midol sets out:

> When a sociologically circumscribed group has no other aim in life but to live in a world of waves or snow, when an entire life is devoted to one moment of ecstasy, it is time to consider the most intimate ways by which human beings build their own cultural landmarks and make them meaningful.[65]

64   For more on references to sport, especially football, boxing and gambling, in Camus's work see I. H. Walker, 'Camus, Sport and Literature,' *French Studies*, vol. XXX, no. 2 (1976), pp.173–80.

65   N. Midol, 'Cultural Dissents and Technical Innovations in the *Whiz* Sports,' *International Review for the Sociology of Sport*, vol. 28, no. 1 (1993), pp.204–12, p.207.

The tracing of sporting developments via what could be described, in the terms adopted by Deleuze and Guattari, as *arborescent* (or tree-like) structures – be they national, municipal, religious or educational institutions – has proven eminently fruitful for the study of modern sports.[66] Surfing and its derivatives develop in a fundamentally different fashion however, growing in what Deleuze and Guattari would describe as *rhizomatic* forms via the making and breaking of connections through a variety of media.[67] A surfer's identification with a place is not then mediated through the history and heritage of a club, parish or municipality but rather through the cultural production of a nomadic peer group. As we have seen, places are thus deterritorialized and reterritorialized in line with the founding myths of a sporting sub-culture and according to the desires of nomadic surfers.

The final point concerns the potential value of the study of liminal spaces in the examination of a sporting culture. The work of Sébastien Darbon, and his study of rugby in the football heartland of Marseille, is pioneering in this regard.[68] In a similar vein, the Mediterranean, which is at the extreme margins of the surfing world, could possibly be regarded as a privileged site to study the essence of surfing culture. Surfers revel in the extremity of their sport, but perhaps the most extreme conditions for a surfer, and thus the most fruitful terrain for the study of distinct behaviours and attitudes, is not *Riding Giants* with Laird Hamilton off the coast of Hawaii, but rather waiting in vain for the perfect wave in the placid waters of the Baie des Anges.[69]

66   Deleuze and Guattari, *A Thousand Plateaus*, p.16.
67   Ibid., p.20.
68   S. Darbon, *Du rugby dans une ville de foot: Le cas singulier du Rugby Club de Marseille – ASPTT* (Paris: L'Harmattan, 1997).
69   Peralta, *Riding Giants*.

Bibliography

Anderson, W. 'Surf,' in J.-J. Scemla (ed.), *Le Voyage en Polynésie: Anthologie des voyageurs occidentaux de Cook à Segalen* (Paris: Robert Laffont, 1994), pp.876–7.

Arfi, S. 'Robby the Kid', *Wind Magazine*, no.144 (June 1992), p.84.

Augustin, J.-P. (ed.) 'Les pratiques de plaisance en Languedoc-Roussillon: nautisme et sports de glisse,' in J. Rieucau and G. Cholvy (eds), *Le Languedoc, le Roussillon et la mer: des origines à la fin du XXe siècle, 1960–1990*, vol. 2 (Paris: L'Harmattan, 1992), pp.217–35.

———. *Surf Atlantique: les territoires de l'éphémère* (Bordeaux: MSHA, 1994).

———. 'Emergence of Surfing Resorts on the Aquitaine Littoral', *Geographical Review*, vol. 88, no. 4 (1998), pp.587–95.

Baudrillard, J. *Simulacra and Simulation*, trans. by S. F. Glaser (Ann Arbor, MI: University of Michigan Press, 1995).

———. *The Consumer Society: Myths and Structures* (London: Sage, 1998).

Bertin, M. and R. Fière. *De la mer jusqu'au ciel* (Paris: Arthaud, 2003).

Biblioni, O. 'Le sport est une fête', *Le Provençal*, 17 May 1993, p.3.

Blume, M. *Côte d'Azur: Inventing the French Riviera* (New York: Thames and Hudson, 1992).

Braidotti, R. *Nomadic Subjects: Embodiment and Social Difference in Contemporary Feminist Theory* (New York: Columbia University Press, 1994).

Braudel, F. *The Mediterranean and the Mediterranean World in the Age of Philip II*, trans. by S. Reynolds (London: Collins, 1972).

Bromberger, C. *Le match de football: Ethnologie d'une passion partisane à Marseille, Naples et Turin* (Paris: Éditions de la Maison des Sciences de l'Homme, 1995).

Camus, A. *The Myth of Sisyphus*, trans. by J. O'Brien (London: Penguin, 1975 [1955]).

Chifflet, P. 'The Sport Supply in France: From Centralization to Segmentation', *Sociology of Sport Journal*, vol. 12, no. 2 (1995), pp.180–94.

Colebrook, C. *Gilles Deleuze* (New York: Routledge, 2002).

Darbon, S. *Du rugby dans une ville de foot: Le cas singulier du Rugby Club de Marseille – ASPTT* (Paris: L'Harmattan, 1997).

Deleuze, G. and F. Guattari. *A Thousand Plateaus: Capitalism and Schizophrenia*, trans. by B. Massumi (London: Athlone, 1988 [1987]).

Dine, P. 'Sport and the State in Contemporary France: From *la Charte des Sports* to decentralization', *Modern & Contemporary France*, vol. 6, no. 3 (1998), pp.301–11.

Franceschi, B. 'La Corse: destination obligatoire!', *Wind Magazine*, no. 135 (August 1991), pp.31–2.

——. 'Mistral: le maître', *Wind Magazine*, no. 135 (August 1991), pp.52–3.

George, S. *The Perfect Day: 40 years of Surfer Magazine* (San Francisco: Chronicle, 2001).

Goscinny, R. and A. Uderzo. *Astérix en Corse* (Neuilly-sur-Seine: Dargaud, 1973).

Greene, G. *J'accuse: The Dark Side of Nice* (London: Bodley Head, 1982).

Lafleur, O. 'Corsica Trip', *Wind Magazine*, no. 144 (June 1992), pp.40–4.

Loret, A. *Génération glisse* (Paris: Autrement, 2003).

Midol, N. 'Cultural Dissents and Technical Innovations in the *Whiz* Sports', *International Review for the Sociology of Sport*, vol. 28, no. 1 (1993), pp.204–12.

Ormrod, J. '*Endless Summer* (1964): Consuming Waves and Surfing the Frontier', *Film & History*, vol. 35, no. 1 (2005), pp.39–51.

Paasi, A. 'Boundaries as Social Processes: Territoriality in the World of Flows', *Geopolitics*, vol. 3, no. 1 (1998), pp.69–88.

Rauch, A. 'Vacationing on France's Côte d'Azur, 1950–2000', in S. C. Anderson and B. H. Tabb (eds), *Water, Leisure and Culture: European Historical Perspectives* (Oxford: Berg, 2002), pp.223–39.

Said, E. W. *Orientalism* (New York: Pantheon, 1978; repr., London: Penguin, 1991).

Sotinel, T. and P. Wagner. 'Comment la Toile a propagé le virus *Brice de Nice*', *Le Monde*, 16 April 2005 (online edition).

Tournier, M. *La Goutte d'Or* (Paris: Gallimard, 1986).

Vulser, N. 'En France, la fréquentation des salles de cinéma a baissé de 10% en 2005', *Le Monde*, 8 January 2006 (online edition).

Walker, I. H. 'Camus, Sport and Literature', *French Studies*, vol. XXX, no. 2 (1976), pp.173–80.

Filmography

Bigelow, K. *Point Break* (USA, 1991).

Brown, B. *Endless Summer* (USA, 1964).

Fiacre, S. and J. Rossigneux. *Flat Country: 100% Méditerranée* (France, 2006).

Huth, J. *Brice de Nice* (France, 2005).

Peralta, S. *Riding Giants* (USA/France, 2004).

MARCUS FREE

Chapter 9
Antihero as National Icon? The Contrariness of Roy Keane as Fantasy Embodiment of the 'New Ireland'

Roy Keane's career as Republic of Ireland international soccer player and captain included many controversial episodes, most famously his expulsion prior to the 2002 World Cup following outspoken criticisms of manager Mick McCarthy's squad preparation in Saipan. Previously, in 1996, he was sent off following a dangerous tackle in his first game as captain and missed a post-season international tournament for a family holiday. He subsequently missed numerous internationals due to injury, an explanation that when challenged by McCarthy prompted the outburst that precipitated his dismissal in Saipan. His Manchester United club career was also blighted by controversy, foremost being a horrific tackle on Alfie Haaland, compounded in its seriousness by the later apparent admission of intent to cause injury and punishment by the English Football Association for bringing the game into disrepute.[1]

However, as a successful Manchester United captain in the 1990s and early 2000s, Keane was also an exemplar of successful Irish emigration to Britain, still a key gauge of personal and collective Irish achievement internationally. He was voted Irish player of the tournament in the USA '94 World Cup by Irish public service broadcaster RTÉ's viewers,[2] the man who 'dragged Ireland to the World Cup in 2002 by using the engine of his

1   R. Keane and E. Dunphy, *Keane: The Autobiography* (London: Michael Joseph, 2002), p.231.
2   S. Hildred and T. Ewbank, *Captain Fantastic: Roy Keane, the Biography* (London: John Blake, 2000), p.150.

own fierce willpower and rage' (see Figure 9.1),[3] and voluntarily returned
to the national team in 2004. In 2006 he was appointed Sunderland football club manager by chairman Niall Quinn (former Ireland player and
McCarthy ally in 2002), compounding the impression of an 'Irish' club
takeover by the Quinn-led 'Drumaville' consortium. He won the English
Championship and promotion to the Premiership in his first season, and
became an amusing commentator on British football for a British, but more
particularly an Irish audience deeply ambivalent towards British football,
having a huge British club fan base, regularly monitoring Irish footballers
in Britain, but somewhat sceptical of the media 'hype' surrounding leading players and clubs.

Many soccer supporters and professional commentators questioned his
apparent pursuit of individual over collective interests,[4] seemingly extended

3   J. Doyle, 'Goal, The New York Times Soccer Blog: Roy Keane, the Celtic Tiger
     Tamed', *The New York Times*, 10 December 2008, <http://goal.blogs.nytimes.
     com/2008/12/10/roy-keane-the-celtic-tiger-tamed/?> (accessed 23 January 2009).
     Such hyperbole in Irish journalism abounded. Vincent Hogan wrote of Keane's per-
     formance against Holland (in a crucial World Cup qualifier) that 'Holland seemed
     to fear the force of his character as much as his legs. His greatness [...] bears the
     simple mark of efficiency and unrelenting manliness'. 'Dutch transfixed by glare of
     "The Stranger"', *Irish Independent*, 4 September 2001, <http://www.independent.
     ie/sport/soccer/dutch-transfixed-by-glare-of-the-stranger-331465.html> (accessed
     16 January 2009). Likewise marvelling at his 'hard' masculine quality, Jonathan O'
     Brien remarked: 'Without Keane, the Irish team is a bit like the weakling schoolkid
     whose strongly-built elder brother, normally his protector and guardian in the vicious
     maelstrom of the playground, is sick at home'. 'About a Roy', *Hotpress*, 8 November
     2001, <http://www.hotpress.com/archive/1571590.html> (accessed 10 November
     2008).

4   The *Irish Independent* editorial, for example, opined that Ireland's reaching the 2002
     World Cup second round 'was a victory over [his] selfishness, ego and begrudgery'.
     'Triumph for a true team', *Irish Independent*, 12 June 2002, <http://www.independ-
     ent.ie/opinion/analysis/triumph-for-a-true-team-302628.html> (accessed 18 January
     2009). Another commentator deemed him 'the perfect national hero for Celtic
     Tiger Ireland: 100 grand a week for acting the prick and throwing strops while no
     one is quite sure what it is you actually do.' 'It's déjà vu once again for Roy', *Sunday
     Independent*, 16 October 2005, <http://www.independent.ie/opinion/analysis/
     its-deja-vu-once-again-for-roy-473286.html> (accessed 20 January 2009).

by his premature resignation from Sunderland in December 2008.[5] For others, however, Keane's contrariness inspired his celebration as an exemplary figurative representative and literal embodiment of a 'new Ireland' of rigorous, uncompromising professionalism – contrasting with an 'old Ireland' of underachievement and routine incompetence – the 'Celtic Tiger' Ireland of the mid-1990s to mid-2000s economic boom:

> He [achieved his success] through talent, force of will, dedication and a winner's attitude – all the things that Irish people were now associated with in the days of the Celtic Tiger. Irish society was now a society of success, of entrepreneurs, of results. So the Roy Keane attitude of 'fail-to-prepare, prepare-to-fail' rang true.[6]

> His departure divided Ireland into two camps, between the new, professional and highly ambitious Irish, who see no Pearsean triumph in failure, and the traditionalist Ireland that thinks: 'It'll do.'[7]

> [Keane] is the perfect exemplar of the new Celtic Tiger Ireland that has taken off since the 1994 World Cup. Like the new Ireland, he is rich, upwardly mobile and driven by a ruthless work ethic.[8]

> As a player he was the best of the Premiership generation, one of the young Celtic cubs who grew up to be Tigers.[9]

5   Again, Keane's alleged hubris, petulance and childish selfishness supposedly precipitated his downfall. See, for example, Aidan Fitzmaurice's comparison of Keane as manager to 'one of the kids in Charlie and the Chocolate Factory, holding the golden ticket, surrounded by goodies but never satisfied with what he got, spitting out something if he didn't like it and getting something else instead'. 'Roy's Golden Ticket Expired', *Evening Herald*, 5 December 2008, <http://www.herald.ie/sport/soccer/roys-golden-ticket-expired-1564855.html> (accessed 8 January 2009).
6   D. Whelan, *Who Stole Our Game?* (Dublin: Gill and Macmillan, 2006), p.221.
7   P. West, 'The New Ireland Kicks Ass', *New Statesman*, 17 June 2002, <http://www.newstatesman.com/200206170012> (accessed 15 January 2009).
8   F. O' Toole, 'The ruthless Celtic Tiger turns his back on the auld sod', *The Guardian*, 24 May 2002, <http://www.guardian.co.uk/football/2002/may/24/worldcupfootball2002.sport6> (accessed 20 November 2009).
9   G. McDermott, 'Football world waits for Keane's next step', *Irish Independent*, 13 June 2006, <http://www.independent.ie/sport/soccer/football-world-waits-for-keanes-next-step-92441.html> (accessed 21 January 2009).

[...] the Celtic tiger, a thrusting European state, young, ambitious, claret-quaffing and Armani-clad. [...] To adherents of the latter idea of Ireland, his steely-eyed professionalism and insistence that the team should give themselves the best possible opportunity of actually winning the [World Cup], however crazy an idea that seemed, make him something of a latter-day saint.[10]

This chapter argues that such claims were individual and collective imaginative fantasies of a homology between Keane's masculine corporeal economy and competitive zeal and the then increasingly competitive Irish economy,[11] illustrating how 'heroic reputations are products of the imaginative labour through which societies and groups define and articulate their values and assumptions, and through which individuals within those societies or groups establish their participation in larger social or cultural identities'.[12]

It additionally argues that such 'native' commentaries, both 'professional' and 'amateur', positive and negative, were discursive 'performances' of national-as-gendered, typically (but not exclusively) masculine identities, in Judith Butler's sense of discourse performatively reproducing the 'phenomenon that it regulates and constrains'.[13] These discursive constructions

10   D. Kelly, 'Keane lost on radio ga ga', *The Times*, 4 September 2006, <http://www.timesonline.co.uk/tol/sport/columnists/article627337.ece> (accessed 20 November 2008).

11   A 1999 OECD Survey typified its celebration: 'the Irish economy has notched up five straight years of stunning economic performance', with output growth averaging 'over 9 per cent on a GDP basis in the period 1994–1998'. In the 1980s, by contrast, 'output was stagnant; the unemployment rate was surging to the record high level of 17%, despite heavy emigration; real investment was sliding by a cumulative 25%; the current balance was on average in deficit to the tune of over 7% of GDP'. OECD, *OECD Economic Surveys: Ireland 1998/1999*, vol. 1999, no. 14, 1999, Paris: OECD, <http://oberon.sourceoecd.org/vl=13622975/cl=13/nw=1/rpsv/ij/oecd-journals/03766438/v1999n14/s1/p1> (accessed 11 January 2009), pp.10–11.

12   G. Cubitt, 'Introduction: heroic reputations and exemplary lives', in Geoffrey Cubitt and Allen Warren (eds), *Heroic Reputations and Exemplary Lives* (Manchester: Manchester University Press, 2000), p.3.

13   J. Butler, *Bodies that Matter: On the Discursive Limits of 'Sex'* (New York: Routledge, 1993), p.2.

reproduced, negotiated and created gendered 'imaginary positions'[14] in relation to existing discourses of national identity, thereby both creating while invoking Keane's figurative and literal embodiment of inexorable economic, social and cultural change and enabling their originators to perform gendered personal-national identities themselves. Such phenomena associating Keane with national economic regeneration and the proliferation of classical analogies to make sense of his behaviour – Philoctetes, Achilles, Coriolanus, etc. – may be seen as means of gendered self- and national aggrandizement on the part of those who coined such analogies, rather than being in any way explanatory of social and cultural change.

Keane additionally became a symbolic means of expressing nuanced, gendered and competing varieties of Irish identity through, for example, his association with Cork (commonly known in Ireland as the 'Rebel County', mainly due to its prominence in the War of Independence) and, as Sunderland manager, his symbolizing Irish success in Britain following emigration. However, the considerable variety in positions taken with respect to such symbolism and the dialogical interactions between proponents and dissenters illustrate the seeming paradox that shared national identity is frequently enhanced through argumentative differences with respect to such controversial figures, giving affective intensity to the imagining of that common identity.

But they also illustrate how his national-hero status has been somewhat tempered by his own 'antiheroic' confounding or refusal of heroic status as an often elusive object of fantasy projections, particularly during his managerial career, whose highlights have been verbal declarations rather than exploits on a par with his achievements as a player, and because his working-class background and career trajectory fit uneasily with 'Celtic Tiger' fantasies. Hence, Keane's has been an uneven and contested career as a national sporting icon in Ireland that nonetheless has inspired the sense of national affinity amongst fans and detractors alike.

14   M. Wetherell and N. Edley, 'Negotiating Hegemonic Masculinity: Imaginary Positions and Psychodiscursive Practices', *Feminism & Psychology*, vol. 9, no. 3 (1999), pp.335–6.

Why Sport, and Why Roy Keane?

As a rich source of metaphors, in discourses ranging from politics to business, warfare and sexual relations,[15] sport offers a 'world of ethical clarity
and functional simplicity', granting 'the possibility of sanctuary from the
complications of the everyday'.[16] Figures like Keane become attractive as
metaphors which help to 'structure how we perceive, how we think, and
what we do',[17] exemplifying popular heroes' incorporation, literally in
their corporeal actions, 'of normative and disruptive tendencies',[18] and
the sporting hero's 'duality', being 'aggressive and officially supported,
anarchist and institutionalized [...] representative and elite, collective and
individual'.[19]

Sports journalists concerned with fellow national competitors are
frequently partisan fans, even in 'quality' broadsheet varieties. For these
Irish commentators, just as Keane 'like[d] to get his retaliation in early'[20]
to dominate opponents, so he simultaneously represented a competitive
Irish economy 'punching above its weight'[21] on the 'world stage'. Even the

---

15   J. O. Segrave, 'The Sports Metaphor in American Cultural Discourse', *Culture, Sport
      and Society*, vol. 3, no. 1 (2000), pp.48–60.

16   J. O. Segrave, 'Sport as a Cultural Hero-System: What Price Glory?', *Quest*, vol. 45,
      no. 2 (1993), pp.182–96.

17   G. Lakoff and M. Johnson, *Metaphors We Live By* (Chicago: University of Chicago
      Press, 1980), p.1.

18   Cubitt, 'Introduction: heroic reputations', p.8.

19   J. Calder, *Heroes: From Byron to Guevara* (London: Hamish Hamilton, 1977),
      p.184.

20   A. McLeod, 'Whither Now Roy Keane?', *Irish Independent*, 1 October 2005, <http://
      www.independent.ie/sport/soccer/whither-now-roy-keane-233657.html> (accessed
      20 January 2009). The paradoxical exhortation, 'get our retaliation in first' has been
      attributed both to former Ireland and Lions rugby captain Willie John McBride and
      former Lions coach Carwyn James.

21   Examples of this common sporting metaphor include its use as a metaphor for the
      'Celtic Tiger' (itself a metaphor) in a 2004 *Economist* survey; J. Peet, 'The Luck of the
      Irish', *The Economist*, 14 October 2004, <http://www.economist.com/PrinterFriendly.

growing tendency towards critical quotation or parody in Ireland ironically reflected the power of the myth:

> [...] was it [the] real fans who hounded Mick McCarthy out of his job? In fact, you'll find it was the Johnny-come-lately prawn-sandwich brigade, the Celtic tigers who see Keane as the embodiment of the new can-do professional Ireland.[22]

And when Keane's departure from Sunderland in 2008 coincided with the Irish economy's rapid decline, comments like John Doyle's completely elided the distinction between psychic projection, metaphor and reality: 'He is us. We are him. As he goes, so do we. The Celtic Tiger is tamed.'[23]

These remarks reflect the growing significance of spectator sports in Irish media and popular culture, from the Gaelic Athletic Association's resurgence, Munster's (2006, 2008) and Leinster's (2009) Heineken Cup rugby successes, Ireland's 2009 Six Nations Rugby 'Grand Slam' victory and Ireland's celebrated but modest achievements in the Euro '88 and 1990 and 1994 World Cup soccer tournaments. They also reflect the repeated association of Irish international sporting success with literal, rather than merely metaphoric national economic regeneration, exemplified by the following:

> As all smart economic historians know, the date of birth of the Celtic Tiger was June 12, 1988 (2.36pm to be precise.) [...] the date and time when Ray Houghton put the ball in the English net at the European Championships in Germany. [...] The debt/

---

cfm?Story_ID=3261071>, p.2 (accessed 11 January 2009); and its use as a metaphor for economic competitiveness by the Director General of Science Foundation Ireland, who directly compared Keane's managerial challenge to 'mov[ing] up the league' with Ireland's research and development prospects: 'Now we need to move to the industries of the future. That's the league to strive for'. John Kennedy, 'Putting Ireland in Premier League', *Irish Independent*, 13 September 2007, <http://www.independent.ie/business/technology/putting-ireland-in-premier-league-1078722.html> (accessed 23 January 2009).

22   B. O' Connor, 'Keane holds to ransom our sporting future', *Sunday Independent*, 10 November 2002, <http://www.independent.ie/opinion/analysis/keane-holds-to-ransom-our-sporting-future-504908.html> (accessed 13 January 2009).

23   J. Doyle, 'Goal, The New York Times soccer blog'.

GNP ratio, then hovering at 130 per cent, immediately went into reverse; exports soared; the level of foreign direct investment grew dramatically. [...] The Stuttgart Effect sustained the economy for the next 14 years.[24]

Keane's disruptive persona linked both favourable and antagonistic commentaries, whether the Ireland he rocked was construed as a staid, rigidly hierarchical and mediocre society or a collective, inclusive, integrative 'community' valuing 'national' over self-interest. His heroic qualities mingled in the popular imagination with the 'antiheroic'. The literary character whose 'personal value system conflicts with that of the powers that be and implies its impoverishment or irrelevance',[25] the antihero is typified by the post-war American 'tired, apathetic, cool, and beat rejection of lofty goals'.[26] But for his proponents, Keane's antiheroic contrariness, criticism and refusal of authority embodied a code of professional excellence exceeding that of his social 'betters'. Yet his belligerent style also repeatedly affirmed conventional, culturally constructed attributes of sporting mas-

24 'Did Roy Keane shoot down the Celtic Tiger?', *Sunday Independent*, 20 October 2002, <http://www.independent.ie/business/irish/did-roy-keane-shoot-down-the-celtic-tiger-504485.html> (accessed 15 January 2009). Journalists in an Irish radio discussion ('What if?', *RTE Radio One*, 29 September 2004) posited that the economic boom 'was all to do with the confidence factor engendered [...] once we qualified for *Euro '88*' (Ronan Furlong) and that 'people began to think [...] we can go out, compete in markets and put people under pressure' (Eoghan Corry). See also Aidan O' Hara's 'Spirit of '88 opened up a sense of unlimited possibilities we hadn't dared to contemplate', *Sunday Independent*, 8 June 2008, <http://www.independent.ie/sport/soccer/spirit-of-88-opened-up-a-sense-of-unlimited-possibilities-we-hadnt-dared-to-contemplate-1401880.html> (accessed 15 January 2009). Later, the 2009 Six Nations (rugby union) Grand Slam was repeatedly cited as a source of direct rather than metaphorical 'lessons' and thus inspiration for surviving the then worsening economic recession. A management consultant on *RTE Radio One*'s 'The Business' (22 March), for example, suggested that the Cabinet would 'have to really, now, start togging out and start training'.
25 R. B. Rollin, 'General Introduction', *Hero/Anti-Hero* (New York: McGraw-Hill, 1973), p.xvii.
26 O. E. Klapp, *Heroes, Villains and Fools: the Changing American Character* (Englewood Cliffs, NJ: Prentice-Hall, 1962), p.157.

culinity: self-reliance, independent-mindedness, physical strength, desire and ability to dominate opponents, and will to win. Thus, his proponents made him a weapon with which imaginarily to beat an 'older' Ireland of complacency, hierarchy and economic stagnation into an economically productive, competitive future, mapping an idealized version of Keane's corporeal achievements on to the nation. These associations gave physical form to the implicitly but often also explicitly masculine hero of neoliberalism, the economic orthodoxy from the mid-70s onwards.[27]

However, the rhetoric often contradictorily evoked an earlier era, with Keane as a 'footballing dinosaur' threatened by a 'morally redundant and relativistic' contemporary world.[28] Central to this impression was Keane's ghost writer, (auto-)biographer Eamon Dunphy. A former professional footballer, Dunphy had championed a 'hard', uncompromising, distinctly 'masculine' football from his classic *Only a Game?* (1976), through his contributions as a newspaper columnist and pundit for RTÉ television's football coverage. His description of football as a 'test' of ability to 'cheat fate and [...] get some sort of result. As opposed to caving in and getting done'[29] underpinned often scathing critiques of stylish but allegedly lazy footballers. Later, as a radio (*Today FM*, 1997–2004) and television chat show host (*The Dunphy Show*, *TV3*, 2003), and as a ubiquitous interviewee himself, he was a populist mouthpiece for the neoliberal economic orthodoxy pervading Irish politics and business. For Dunphy, Keane linked an old-fashioned football embodying 'virtues [...] fundamental to our nature: resilience; determination; physical endurance [...] willingness to battle harder and longer'[30] with 'Celtic Tiger' Ireland. So, typically, following Keane's dismissal in Saipan, he conflated Keane's footballing prowess with his pre-eminence as 'a *man* [stretching the vowel sound] [...] a perfect

27   D. Harvey, *A Brief History of Neoliberalism* (Oxford: Oxford University Press, 2005).

28   C. Brick, 'Boom Boom: Roy Keane and the Footballing Dinosaur', *M/C Reviews: Culture and the Media* (July 2002), <http://reviews.media-culture.org.au/modules. php?name=News&file=article&sid=1853> (accessed 4 January 2003).

29   E. Dunphy and P. Ball, *Only a Game?* (Harmondsworth: Penguin, 1976), p.73.

30   E. Dunphy, 'A law unto himself', *Sunday Independent*, 12 June 1994, p.12.

human being', and equated Keane with 'the financial services area [...] where excellence is achieved and required' (interview on the 'Gerry Ryan Show', 2FM, 24 May 2002), echoing Irish economists' celebration of the 'new self-confidence' and entrepreneurialism of Irish 'business culture'.[31]

Given the financial services sector's role in the current recession,[32] this now seems rather ironic. But why was Keane such an unprecedently symbolic figure at this time? Perhaps it reflected the 'new' Ireland's questionable existence and the absence of any comparable 'hero' in the Irish business world. As O'Hearn[33] has argued, Ireland 'bought economic tiger-hood' by encouraging foreign direct investment through low corporate tax rates, rendering a high proportion of nominal GDP fictional due to multinationals' capital 'repatriation'.[34] Rampant consumerism and debt were fuelled by low EU-set interest rates and income tax reductions despite poor transport, health and social services infrastructural investment and development.[35] Foreign investment progressively shifted to cheaper economic locations from the mid-2000s, and an unsustainable construction boom rapidly declined from 2007 to 2009, directly and indirectly increasing unemployment.[36]

As Whannel maintains, sports stars' images 'constitute rich tools for cultural analysis' as 'thermometers and barometers' by which 'to take the social temperature and to assess the pressures generated by tensions and

31 J. Fitzgerald, 'The story of Ireland's failure – and belated success', in B. Nolan, P. J. O'Connell and C. T. Whelan (eds), *Bust to Boom: the Irish Experience of Growth and Inequality* (Dublin: Institute of Public Administration, 2000), p.55.

32 For analysis, see, for example, Simon Carswell's review of the 2008 financial year, 'Bad dreams become reality', *Irish Times*, 2 January 2009 <http://www.irishtimes. com/newspaper/finance/2009/0102/1230842348874.html> (accessed 10 February 2009).

33 D. O'Hearn, 'Globalization, "New Tigers", and the end of the Developmental State? The Case of the Celtic Tiger', *Politics & Society*, vol. 28, no. 1 (2000), p.74.

34 Fitzgerald, 'The story of Ireland's failure', p.54.

35 P. O'Connell, 'The Dynamics of the Irish labour market in comparative perspective', in Nolan et al., *Bust to Boom*, pp.58–89.

36 For an analysis of the rapid downturn in the Irish economy, see A. Barrett, I. Kearney and J. Goggin, *Quarterly Economic Commentary, Winter 2008* (Dublin: Economic and Social Research Institute, 2008), <http://www.esri.ie/UserFiles/publica-tions/20081218171124/QEC2008Win.pdf> (accessed 10 February 2009).

contradictions'.[37] A visceral 'hard man' with uncompromising drive and ambition was a highly attractive symbol of fantasized collective achievement, a powerful icon because physical competition is corporeal, visible and measurable, generating 'moments when an affective unity can be posited against the grain of structural divisions and bureaucratic taxonomies'.[38] And Keane's asceticism as both player and manager neatly coincided with the neo-liberal managerialist discourses of the 'lean', competitive economy in 'Celtic Tiger' Ireland, local variants of the congruence between the discursive construction of 'male athletic' and '(white) managerial masculinities'.[39]

Keane's supposed historical transitional symbolism was elsewhere formulated by academic commentators who argued that his aggressively masculine challenge to British-born McCarthy was an assertion of postcolonial independence from a history of colonial subordination. For Featherstone, Keane was refusing 'to agree to the maintenance of a subordinate position, social (that is, class-based) and national (colonial)'.[40] Sharkey posited that Keane represented 'the growing power of the post-colonized over the national symbol of the colonizer: the beautiful game. One suspects that the next Irish manager will have an Irish accent, and in a few years his name will be Keane. [...] Meanwhile, this World Cup, Ireland must cope without its Celtic Tiger'.[41] Sharkey's unashamedly partisan reading both constructs and validates a narrative of Keane as embodiment of the 'new Ireland' which it purports to analyse. Indeed the hyperbole here matches

37 G. Whannel, *Media Sport Stars: Masculinities and Moralities* (London: Routledge, 2002), p.46.
38 D. Rowe, J. McKay and T. Miller, 'Come together: sport, nationalism and the media image', in L. A. Wenner (ed.), *MediaSport* (London: Routledge, 1998), pp.119–33, p.120.
39 A. Knoppers and A. Anthonissen, 'Male Athletic and Managerial Masculinities: Congruencies in Discursive Practices?', *Journal of Gender Studies*, vol. 14, no. 2 (2005), pp.123–35, p.123.
40 S. Featherstone, *Postcolonial Cultures* (Edinburgh: Edinburgh University Press, 2005), pp.93–4.
41 R. Sharkey, 'Reading Cultures: Mediating Power', *M/C Reviews: Culture and the Media* (July 2002), <http://reviewmedia.ci.qut.edu.au/modules.php?name=News&file=article&sid=1849> (accessed 4 January 2003).

Fintan O'Toole's classical analogy of Sophocles' Philoctetes[42] for Keane's
abandonment in Saipan, and a contributor to the 2007 television documentary *Red Mist*, who compared Keane to Shakespeare's Coriolanus.[43]
Such classical analogies and historical connections give 'legitimacy' to the
otherwise trivial world of sport and its supposed symbolism of social and
cultural transition.[44]

Central to this 'antihero' persona is a myth of belligerent masculinity as 'authenticity', 'truth' to oneself and contrariness. The contrarian
antihero romantically invokes Aristotelian 'virtue', the achievement of a
'mean' between unreasonable extremes,[45] here complete subservience to
an abstract 'national' cause and utterly self-serving individualism, contrariness being an intermediate rather than an oppositional state. Keane's idi-
osyncratic discursive pattern, exemplified by the interview precipitating his
confrontation with the offended McCarthy in Saipan,[46] fuelled this impression: the repetition of metaphorical ('tip of the iceberg', 'not my scene'),
metaphorical-metonymic ('get my head down') and matter-of-fact ('it's not

42   F. O' Toole, 'Let's get back perspective and recall a true World Cup tragedy',
     Irish Times, 28 May 2002, <http://www.irishtimes.com/newspaper/opin-
     ion/2002/0528/1017357805762.html> (accessed 20 November 2008).

43   Directed by Eamon Little (Wildfire Films), broadcast on Setanta Ireland, 26
     December 2007.

44   Variations on this theme proliferated. Colin Teevan's poem 'The RoyKeaneiad', in
     Missing Persons: Four Tragedies and Roy Keane (London: Oberon Books, 2006),
     pp.57–64, compared him to both Achilles and Philoctetes. A collection of Keane
     quotations, no author (or page numbers), *The Little Book of Roy Keane by the Unknown
     Fan* (Dublin: New Island, 2002), introduced him as 'the Spartan General'. The
     Philoctetes analogy was repeated, additionally gesturing towards Robert Graves's
     I, Claudius (1934) in the musical stage dramatization of the Saipan affair, *I, Keano*
     (2005).

45   Aristotle, *The Ethics of Aristotle: the Nicomachean Ethics Book II*, trans. by J. A. K.
     Thomson (Harmondsworth: Penguin, 1953/1976), pp.101–2. This 'virtuous' mean
     was exemplified by John Wayne's screen personas; see S. Matheson, 'The West–
     Hardboiled: Adaptations of Film Noir Elements, Existentialism, and Ethics in John
     Wayne's Westerns', *Journal of Popular Culture*, vol. 38, no. 5 (2005), pp.888–910.

46   T. Humphries, 'Keane says he will quit Ireland after World Cup', *Irish Times*, 23 May
     2002, <http://www.irishtimes.com/newspaper/frontpage/2002/0523/1017357801
     102.html> (accessed 15 November 2008).

right') phrases and of rhetorical questions ('what was I supposed to do?') in a progressive self-justification, combined with mock humility ('maybe I just don't get it'; 'I want what's best. If it's a crime, fuck it, I'm guilty') and mock self-deprecation (on his own managerial prospects: 'Nobody would play for me but we'd have great facilities'). He later engaged in a typically imaginary, hypothetical conversation with himself concerning his refusal to apologize to McCarthy, concluding with characteristic self-reassurance: (*RTE One Television*, 27 May 2002) 'if there was any doubt in my mind that "Roy, you were a little bit out of order" [...] But I won't accept, I can't accept this.' As Wetherell and Edley highlight, resisting conformity – by 'being his own (and by implication, superior) man', placing himself outside the heavy-drinking, euphemistically labelled 'male-bonding' raucousness of the Irish squad and their acceptance of poor preparation – is a classic means of constructing masculine identity as autonomous individuality.[47] Arguably, too, this asceticism appealed to broadsheet journalistic and other middle-class commentators historically ambivalent towards the undisciplined working-class body.[48]

In a variation apparently propagated by Keane himself, while Sunderland manager, he was cast as an outsider among over-indulged European footballers, representing an Irish tradition of diligence and honesty while British football was dominated by pampered mediocrity. For Keith Duggan, he was a 'conscience for the increasingly manufactured world of the Premier League',[49] typified by his criticism of Manchester United's corporate boxes and growing new middle-class fan base in the 1990s: they 'have a few drinks and probably the prawn sandwiches, and they don't realize what's going on out on the pitch';[50] and, as Sunderland manager, by his retrospective

---

47 Wetherell and Edley, 'Negotiating hegemonic masculinity'.

48 R. Horrocks, *Male Myths and Icons: Masculinity in Popular Culture* (Basingstoke: Macmillan, 1995), p.163.

49 K. Duggan, 'Premier League circus loses a compelling act', *Irish Times*, 6 December 2008, <http://www.irishtimes.com/newspaper/sport/2008/1206/1228494049031.html> (accessed 15 January 2009).

50 Quoted in A. Hooper, 'Keane slams "prawn sandwich" fans', 9 November 2000, <http://soccernet.espn.go.com/archive/england/news/2000/1109/20001109mufckeanefans.html> (accessed 8 January 2009).

acknowledgment of a vocal supporter's 'spot-on' criticism, at a game, of his failing tactics.[51] Keane's unsolicited interview and press conference remarks have continued in this deconstructive vein. Difficulties in attracting players to Sunderland, for example, were attributed to wives preferring London's shopping: 'it's a lifestyle move. It tells me the player is weak and his wife runs his life. [...] The players we're talking about are soft'.[52] Such remarks typify the reiteration of 'symbolic opposition to femininity' and 'inferior' masculinities subject to feminine control 'in order to confirm [men's] own sense of masculinity'.[53] Their wide reporting undoubtedly appealed to the largely male football news readership by validating an 'old fashioned', functionally – and production – orientated working-class sporting body focused on the maximizing of embodied 'physical capital'[54] to justify the rewards of economic capital, but with an ascetic disdain for self-indulgent consumption – by 'supporters', players or female partners.

The Intersubjective Work of National-as-Gendered Fandom

Despite his popularity, Keane's antihero-as-hero status was not uncontested. Nonetheless, as the focus of argumentative differences he may be seen as a vehicle for the creative and constructive intersubjective *work* of fandom and commentary in forging, renewing and transforming individual and collective identities. For detractors and supporters alike, as a fantasy object of identification or dislike, he inspired the imagining of national

51   T. Humphries, 'United still feel the sting of Roy's venom', *Irish Times*, 5 April 2008, <http://www.irishtimes.com/newspaper/sport/2008/0405/1207343051691.html> (accessed 15 November 2008).

52   L. Taylor, 'Roy Keane sees red again with outburst about Wags and their shopping jaunts', *The Guardian*, 15 August 2007, <http://www.guardian.co.uk/uk/2007/aug/15/football.britishidentity> (accessed 15 February 2009).

53   S. Johnson, 'Theorizing Language and Masculinity', in S. Johnson and U. H. Meinhof (eds), *Language and Masculinity* (Oxford: Blackwell, 1997), pp.8–26, p.22.

54   P. Bourdieu, 'Sport and social class', *Social Science Information*, vol. 17, no. 6 (1978), pp.819–40.

community, even through disagreement, by enabling commentators' performative discursive constructions of gendered national identity (largely, but not exclusively masculine) in 'sideline' contests through which he or his opponents were subjected to disciplinary fantasies. These fantasies connected even diametrically opposed commentators as fellow 'national' subjects through their degree of *affective* investment, mapping the boundaries of nation and gender in the process.

I use 'performative' in Butler's[55] sense of gender as a performance (rather than a biological given) 'that enacts or produces that which it names' through discursive and bodily behaviour. Those features of masculine identity mapped on to Keane and in turn mapped on to the collective 'we' of the nation as a masculinized, thrusting, invasive force might be seen as facilitative of varied performative constructions of gender through identification with this symbolic figure. But, for male detractors, Keane's otherwise celebrated contrariness contrasted with their own unswerving national loyalty, implicitly gendered as masculine steadfastness and reliability. Indeed, some accusations explicitly or implicitly questioned his masculinity, his implied fragility indirectly rhetorically confirming their own masculine credentials. Note, for instance, the constructive discourse of masculinity as consistency, self-sacrifice and machine-like reliability in these radio phone-in exchanges ('Liveline', 22 May 2002, *RTE Radio One*, following Keane's initial voluntary withdrawal from the Ireland squad in Saipan; it may usefully be noted in this context that, as 'Liveline' is the second most popular radio show in Ireland, the programme's rating status and role as occasional agenda setter for news media in Ireland is possibly unparalleled in Europe).[56] Caller C, a thirteen-year-old boy, is already schooled and being schooled in the discourse of post-Oedipal submission to masculine authority:[57]

---

55   Butler, *Bodies that Matter*, p.23.
56   See A. Healy and K. Doyle, 'RTE Radio One Remains Most Popular Station', *Irish Times*, 12 February 2009, <http://www.irishtimes.com/newspaper/breaking/2009/0212/breaking77.html> (accessed 8 June 2009).
57   On sport as institutionalized enactment of the resolved Oedipus Complex and acceptance of symbolic 'paternal' authority, see L. E. Peller, 'Libidinal Phases, Ego Development, and Play', *Psychoanalytic Study of the Child*, vol. 9 (1954), pp.178–98.

CALLER A: It's a wheel and he is one of the spokes. He can be replaced. [...] We're a team, and it's a team with 11 men, and not one man.
CALLER B: [...] Niall Quinn, right, he was injured for a period and he went on and played for his country in a number of games.
CALLER A: Exactly.
[...]
CALLER C: I think it's a disgrace [...] that he is the best player on the Irish team and [...] that he's basically saying to 'do what I say or ...'
CALLER A: He's abusing his ability, exactly.
[...]
PRESENTER [Caller C has compared Keane to his own teammate]: And how does he behave?
CALLER C: Like he loves himself. [...] If you're in the spotlight, you eventually just think you're great, you're known to be the best player and then you get too cocky and then you get smacked down. [Keane is] acting like a spoilt child.

Caller B further asserted:

It's about being patriotic for your country, I mean I'd cut off my left arm [to play ...] He's got millions of pounds, right, and I think it's time he gave something back. [He played] against Man City last year and he put in a tackle on [Alfie Haaland] and the guy'll never again play football. [...] There's two million like myself who'd probably give their right arm to be on that squad, and there Roy is and he (sic) abusing it.

The 'left arm'/'right arm'/ money/ tackle comments suggest envious resentment at Keane's remaining physically intact, both undiminished by and financially gaining from international football, but lacking commitment comparable with the supporters'. The corporeal, castration-like metaphor of willing self-sacrifice and the desire for Keane to give 'something back' suggest frustration at Keane's self-serving individualism, corporeal and financial integrity and refusal of self-sacrificial incorporation into the imaginary nation by identifying with a post-Oedipal masculine ideal.

On sport's facilitating of a psychodynamic tension between the post-Oedipal and 'pre-Oedipal fantasy and play', see M. Free, 'Psychoanalytic Perspectives on Sport: A Critical Review', *International Journal of Applied Psychoanalytic Studies*, vol. 5, no. 4 (2008), p.276.

Irish women also engaged in gendered performances of national identity in mediated discursive interactions, typically by eliding the distinction between nation as metaphorical and actual family. Thus, on the same
programme, a female caller performed a form of maternal femininity by
continuing the 'spoilt child' analogy: 'he really should pull his socks up
now, he's not a child. [...] There's no need to throw a wobbly for every
little thing like a child'. And there was considerable variation. Another
used her identification with Keane's masculinity to articulate an aggressive,
geographically specific (Cork as 'Rebel County') but national feminine
identity by invoking her grandmother's memory: 'That man that's criticizing him from Cork, I hope you're run out of Cork. [...] It's because he's a
Cork man he's a fiery man, and that's it. My grandmother's from Kanturk
[in Cork] and I'm the same temperament'.

These gendered performances symbolically constructed shared national
identity ironically both despite and through their differences. The divergences of interpretation might confirm Sandvoss's position that fans project
their own concerns and fantasies on to 'their' team, that 'fan texts' are 'neu-
trosemic', facilitating such divergent readings that 'intersubjectively' they
are meaningless.[58] However, the distinct patterns of support and criticism
suggest that Keane's projected symbolism was specific to a collective sense
of transition, read positively or negatively. The fantasized embodiment of
and individualist threat to national identity were connected, both deriving
from and feeding a sense of national community through shared, distinctively gendered affective investment.

For negative journalistic commentators, too, Keane was a symbolic
vehicle by which they articulated gendered positions regarding football,
sport and Irish society. Indeed some, particularly following his managerial
resignation, and like the examples above, indicated a degree of envy, now
combined with schadenfreude. Eoghan Corry commented that:

---

58   C. Sandvoss, *Fans* (Cambridge: Polity, 2005), p.126.

The Achilles who sulked before the gates of Troy in 2002 has all his vulnerability
on display once more, the arrow of misfortune through his heel. A sports locker
room is no place for a tortured genius. It is where the language is foul and the bully
is king.[59]

Such comments rhetorically claimed a harder-than-thou masculinity, as did
Cormac Murphy's assertion that Keane's wife, 'the rock that has guided her
fragile husband through his turbulent adult life' was 'showing the strain' of
'Roy's exit';[60] the reference to fragility and female dependency suggesting
inferior masculinity. Even former supporter Eamon Dunphy, renowned
for ferocious verbal attacks, now criticized Keane for becoming 'a rent-a-
quote [...] deflecting attention away from his own flawed approach to the
job', his 'failure of humility and people skills'.[61] Such attacks typify the
ambivalent envy afforded celebrities whose commodified (and dispensa-
ble) images make them 'fair game' for both idealizing and denigrating (or
alternating) fantasies.[62]

But whatever their differences or vicissitudes, each position here contributed to reinforcing the status of 'sport as a *masculinizing practice* that
organizes various knowledges about bodies and shapes relations of power
between multiple "subjects".'[63] Whether Keane was deemed right or wrong,
success in football as a (particular type of) *man's* game was reinforced as
a gauge of national achievement in the 'new Ireland'.

---

59   'A locker room is no place for a tortured genius', *Evening Herald*, 5 December 2008,
     <http://www.herald.ie/opinion/comment/a-locker-room-is-no-place-for-a-tor-
     tured-genius-1564842.html> (accessed 8 January 2009).

60   C. Murphy, 'Did Roy's exit become too much for Theresa?', *Evening Herald*, 5
     December 2008, p.12.

61   E. Dunphy, 'I never thought this was a relationship that could work...', *Irish Daily
     Star*, 5 December 2008, p.93.

62   See also S. Wagg, 'Angels of us all? Football Management, Globalization and the
     Politics of Celebrity', *Soccer & Society*, vol. 8, no. 4 (October 2007), pp.440–58;
     Whannel, *Media Sport Stars*, pp.203–6.

63   P. Markula and R. Pringle, *Foucault, Sport and Exercise: Power, Knowledge and
     Transforming the Self* (London: Routledge, 2006), p.102, original emphasis.

Keane as Elusive Object of Fantasy

In the wake of Saipan, Keane, his fans and detractors have inspired various humorous impersonations and parodies in the Irish media, including sketches by a trio of comedians, 'Après-Match' (who commenced their regular post-match spoofing of football punditry on RTE television during the 1998 World Cup), a stage musical, *I Keano* (first performed in 2005), and a series of radio sketches entitled 'Radio Roy'.[64] 'Laughing at ourselves', recognizing shared peculiarities through laughter that may mystify or alienate 'outside' observers, both confirmed shared national identity through lampooned internal differences and rendered Keane a vehicle for the performative construction of a distinctive form of Irish masculinity founded on ironic distance from and identification with their comic referents. These contributions reinforced the masculine world of football as important in itself, symbolic and indicative of national identity and fortunes, and signified a 'mature' collective masculinity sufficiently 'thick-skinned' (using an appropriately corporeal metaphor) to lampoon 'our' absurdities.

Nevertheless, Keane remained a contradiction who eluded straightforward elevation to national iconic status. He repeatedly placed individual conscience and personal commitments above external loyalties; was a committed team-player who led by example and exhorted maximum effort from team-mates; yet, in his public utterances and on-field actions, frequently transgressed both the official code of sportsmanlike conduct and the unofficial euphemism and cliché-ridden code of 'sportspeak' in their verbal bluntness and their rule-stretching (or breaking) physicality respectively. Keane's verbal playfulness was increasingly tinged with serious introspection and anger outwardly directed at his own players. Hence the double-edged, ironic gibe at Nyron Nosworthy: 'Now that Nos has switched to centre-back he's got much less time on the ball, which is best for

---

64 Part of Mario Rosenstock's 'Gift Grub' sketch series on 'The Ian Dempsey Breakfast Show', *Today FM* (2000–present).

all concerned';[65] and (implicitly criticizing his own managerial purchases), following a defeat, 'that's maybe why these footballers are at Sunderland or at other clubs that might be classed as mid-table or bottom half'.[66]

These consistently, perhaps increasingly, attacking and aggressive remarks are suggestive of a masculinity so contingent that it requires reinforcement through repeated discursive reiteration, particularly, perhaps, when the sporting body is no longer active as such. And Keane's deliberate outspokenness attracted accusations of hypocrisy and of representing the style-over-substance world of English football he was otherwise held to oppose. As exemplified by Dunphy's later criticisms, Keane's style was now construed as destructive of younger, more vulnerable men. James Lawton, for example, concluded: 'when [at Sunderland] the hour of crisis called', a man 'stridently judgemental' of others had 'run away'.[67]

As for his playing career, most famously he was accused of breaking a fundamental sporting code by admitting intent to injure Alfie Haaland in an illegal tackle with the 'recalled' words 'take that you cunt',[68] so crudely feminising a male opponent and thus causing him to lose some of his own erstwhile supporters (though Keane was defended by ghostwriter Dunphy – who claimed 'artistic licence' – for his retrospective honesty!)[69] Even

---

65   S. Turnbull, 'The second coming of Roy Keane', *The Independent*, 11 April 2007, <http://www.independent.co.uk/sport/football/football-league/the-second-coming-of-roy-keane-444129.html> (accessed 8 January 2009).

66   M. Walker, 'How the Wearside Messiah lost the plot in just 40 days', *The Independent*, 5 December 2008, <http://www.independent.co.uk/sport/football/premier-league/how-the-wearside-messiah-lost-the-plot-in-just-40-days-1052356.html> (accessed 15 February 2009).

67   J. Lawton, 'Keane – the fighter who quit when most needed', *The Independent*, 5 December 2008, <http://www.independent.co.uk/sport/football/news-and-comment/article1052354.ece> (accessed 15 February 2009).

68   Keane and Dunphy, *Keane*, p.231.

69   M. Walsh, 'The ghost in the machine', *New Statesman*, 16 September 2002, <http://www.newstatesman.com/200209160046> (accessed 10 February 2009). Walsh notes that Keane at times seems no more than a 'ventriloquist's dummy' for Dunphy in the 'autobiography', suggesting an imaginary Keane as Dunphy's own fantasy projection.

the staunchest supporters justified his actions with sometimes strained rhetoric. Hence, following his resignation from Sunderland, Roy Curtis's rescuing of – to others – extreme self-serving individualism as a heroic exercise of conscience: 'he looked in the mirror and posed the hardest questions of all. Am I the right man for the job? Might somebody else be better equipped to move the club on? [...] Does defeat hurt these players as much as it does me? [...] Keane left [...] because he cared too much'.[70] If the humorous parodies signified a 'thick-skinned', self-reflexive nation comfortably 'laughing at itself', perhaps the vehicle for the laughter was altogether more 'thin-skinned'.

Keane also proved problematic as a national symbol by positioning himself somewhere between abstract symbolic representative and self-serving individual, and repeatedly highlighting football *as* a game, maintaining a playful commentary on it, while being a participant in it at the same time. He commented, for example, unusually and very consistently on a key condition of footballers' extraordinary, but temporary wealth and exalted cultural status, the commodification of their labour power, such that they can be moved or discarded against their will: 'to football clubs, players are just expensive pieces of meat. The harsh realities remain and when a club decide they want to sell there is little you can do'.[71]

This directness, combined with his 'value-for-money' consistency and clearly felt need to 'prove' himself as a player is perhaps more explicable in terms of a 'professionalism' cultivated as an *emigrant* at a *British* club, having emigrated from Ireland as an unemployed teenager,[72] than as symptomatic of 'native' virtue. But his appropriation as national representative typifies how Irish twentieth-century emigration has been recast in recent years as a narrative of adventure and success, rather than an index of post-Independence Irish economic failure. As Ken Early argued (though still celebrating Keane's 'heroic' status):

---

70 R. Curtis, 'Roy cared too much – that's why he's gone', *Sunday World*, 7 December 2008, p.143.

71 '10 classic Roy Keane rants', *The Guardian*, 24 August 2006, <http://www.guardian.co.uk/football/2006/aug/24/sport.comment> (accessed 9 January 2009).

72 Keane and Dunphy, *Keane*, pp.10–11.

Keane doesn't really exemplify anything about the new Ireland. You could argue he fits into the tradition of the Irish emigrant made good, like the Kennedys or Ambrose O'Higgins, or at a stretch that of the exiled artist, forging the uncreated conscience of his race ... But the Celtic Tiger? Where is Keane's obsession with excellence, his determination to make the most of every last ounce of his potential, reflected in [its] waste and chaos.[73]

And despite economic success, relying on the sale of his bodily labour power was as, if not more, akin to fellow post-war working-class Irish emigrants than to new middle-class Irish fans and commentators in two respects: the considerable risk of temporary or longer lasting injury through bodily intensive labour;[74] and the lack of control over employment conditions, being 'expensive pieces of meat' vulnerable to sale, possibly internationally.

In this respect, we should, finally, heed Sandvoss's points that sports fandom positions 'the fan within social, cultural, economic and technological macro structures and transformations of contemporary life',[75] and that any critical questioning is 'created through the economic and social forces which already structure the conditions of modern industrial living [so that] fandom cannot function as a space for the creation of new social norms'.[76] If Keane questioned the amateurish, pre-modern governance of Irish soccer and the bourgeoisification of English soccer while being a hero of the Irish diaspora in Britain as a successful Irishman abroad, and if he could be deemed to embody a new post-Independence, postcolonial self-reliant and combative masculinity, he (the imaginary 'he' of fan projections) has also legitimated, by embodying a standard ideological fantasy

73   K. Early, 'Blinded by his light', *Village*, 15 June 2007, <http://www.village.ie/Sports/
      Athletics/Blinded_by_his_light/> (accessed 15 February 2009).
74   D. Hannigan, *The Garrison Game: the State of Irish Football* (Edinburgh:
      Mainstream, 1998) pp.102–18; and Tom Humphries, 'Trapped on fast train to
      Nowheresville', *Irish Times*, 8 February 2003, <http://www.irishtimes.com/news-
      paper/sport/2003/0208/1044549986130.html> (accessed 15 February 2009) have
      traced the exemplary injury-blighted career declines of former Irish full and youth
      internationals, Davy Langan and Liam George, respectively.
75   Sandvoss, *Fans*, pp.112–13.
76   Ibid., p.151.

of neo-liberal economic commentary, the self-motivated, value-for-money economic labour unit striving to maximize his own productivity and that of his colleagues. And although framed by an implicit code of masculine banter, his remarks about players – even his 'pieces of meat' observation – served to reproduce the 'performance principle' whereby the higher an athlete in the 'pyramidal social structure of the feeder system', the more 'expendable' and subject to 'empathic neglect or even empathic abuse'[77] he becomes – irrespective of his substantial financial rewards.

Bibliography

Aristotle. *The Ethics of Aristotle: the Nicomachean Ethics Book II*, trans. by J. A. K. Thomson (Harmondsworth: Penguin, 1953/1976).

Barrett, A., I. Kearney and J. Goggin. *Quarterly Economic Commentary, Winter 2008* (Dublin: Economic and Social Research Institute, 2008), <http://www.esri. ie/UserFiles/publications/20081218171124/QEC2008Win.pdf> (accessed 10 February 2009).

Bourdieu, P. 'Sport and Social Class', *Social Science Information*, vol. 17, no. 6 (1978), pp.819–40.

Brick, C. 'Boom Boom: Roy Keane and the Footballing Dinosaur', *M/C Reviews: Culture and the Media* (July 2002), <http://reviews.media-culture.org.au/modules. php?name=News&file=article&sid=1853> (accessed 4 January 2003).

Butler, J. *Bodies that Matter: On the Discursive Limits of 'Sex'* (New York: Routledge, 1993).

Calder, J. *Heroes: From Byron to Guevara* (London: Hamish Hamilton, 1977).

Cubitt, G. 'Introduction: heroic reputations and exemplary lives', in G. Cubitt and A. Warren (eds), *Heroic Reputations and Exemplary Lives* (Manchester: Manchester University Press, 2000), pp.1–27.

Dunphy, E. and P. Ball. *Only a Game?* (Harmondsworth: Penguin, 1976).

---

77 A. G. Ingham, M. A. Chase and J. Butt, 'From the Performance Principle to the Developmental Principle: Every Kid a Winner?', *Quest*, vol. 54, no. 4 (2002), p.309.

Featherstone, S. *Postcolonial Cultures* (Edinburgh: Edinburgh University Press, 2005).

Fitzgerald, J. 'The story of Ireland's failure – and belated success', in B. Nolan, P. J. O'Connell and C. T. Whelan (eds), *Bust to Boom: the Irish Experience of Growth and Inequality* (Dublin: Institute of Public Administration, 2000), pp.27–57.

Free, M. 'Psychoanalytic Perspectives on Sport: a Critical Review', *International Journal of Applied Psychoanalytic Studies*, vol. 5, no. 4 (2008), pp.273–96.

Hannigan, D. *The Garrison Game: The State of Irish Football* (Edinburgh: Mainstream Publishing, 1998).

Harvey, D. *A Brief History of Neoliberalism* (Oxford: Oxford University Press, 2005).

Hildred, S. and T. Ewbank. *Captain Fantastic: Roy Keane, the Biography* (London: John Blake, 2000).

Horrocks, R. *Male Myths and Icons: Masculinity in Popular Culture* (Basingstoke: Macmillan, 1995).

Ingham, A. G., A. M. Chase and J. Butt. 'From the Performance Principle to the Developmental Principle: Every Kid a Winner?', *Quest*, vol. 54, no. 4 (2002), pp.308–31.

Johnson, S. 'Theorizing Language and Masculinity', in S. Johnson and U. H. Meinhof (eds), *Language and Masculinity* (Oxford: Blackwell, 1997), pp.8–26.

Keane, R. and E. Dunphy. *Keane: the Autobiography* (London: Michael Joseph, 2002).

Klapp, O. E. *Heroes, Villains, and Fools: the Changing American Character* (Englewood Cliffs, NJ: Prentice-Hall, 1962).

Knoppers, A. and A. Anthonissen. 'Male Athletic and Managerial Masculinities: Congruencies in Discursive Practices?', *Journal of Gender Studies*, vol. 14, no. 2 (2005), pp.123–35.

Lakoff, G. and M. Johnson. *Metaphors We Live By* (Chicago: University of Chicago Press, 1980).

The Little Book of Keane by the Unknown Fan (Dublin: New Island, 2002).

Markula, P. and R. Pringle. *Foucault, Sport and Exercise: Power, Knowledge and Transforming the Self* (London: Routledge, 2006).

Matheson, S. 'The West-Hardboiled: Adaptations of Film Noir Elements, Existentialism, and Ethics in John Wayne's Westerns', *Journal of Popular Culture*, vol. 38, no. 5 (2005), pp.888–910.

O'Connell, P. J. 'The dynamics of the Irish labour market in comparative perspective', in B. Nolan, P. J. O'Connell and C. T. Whelan (eds), *Bust to Boom: the Irish Experience of Growth and Inequality* (Dublin: Institute of Public Administration, 2000), pp.58–89.

OECD. *OECD Economic Surveys: Ireland 1998/1999, Volume 1999 (14)* (Paris: OECD), <http://oberon.sourceoecd.org/vl=13622975/cl=13/nw=1/rpsv/ij/oecdjour-nals/03766438/v1999n14/s1/p1> (accessed 11 January 2009).

O'Hearn, D. 'Globalization, "New Tigers", and the end of the Developmental State? The Case of the Celtic Tiger', *Politics & Society*, vol. 28, no. 1 (2000), pp.67–92.

Peet, J. 'The luck of the Irish', *The Economist*, 14 October 2004, <http://www.econo-mist.com/PrinterFriendly.cfm?Story_ID=3261071>, p.2 (accessed 11 January 2009).

Peller, L. E. 'Libidinal phases, ego development, and play', *Psychoanalytic Study of the Child*, vol. 9 (1954), pp.178–98.

Rollin, R. B. 'General Introduction', *Hero/Anti-Hero* (New York: McGraw-Hill, 1973).

Rowe, D., J. McKay and T. Miller. 'Come Together: Sport, Nationalism and the Media Image', in L. A. Wenner (ed.), *MediaSport* (London: Routledge, 1998), pp.119–33.

Sandvoss, C. *Fans* (Cambridge: Polity, 2005).

Segrave, J. O. 'Sport as a Cultural Hero-System: What Price Glory?', *Quest*, vol. 45, no. 2 (1993), pp.182–96.

——. 'The Sports Metaphor in American Cultural Discourse', *Culture, Sport and Society*, vol. 3, no. 1 (2000), pp.48–60.

Sharkey, R. 'Reading Cultures: Mediating Power', *M/C Reviews: Culture and the Media* (July 2002), <http://reviewmedia.ci.qut.edu.au/modules.php?name=News&file=article&sid=1849> (accessed 4 January 2003).

Teevan, C. *Missing Persons: Four Tragedies and Roy Keane* (London: Oberon, 2006).

Wagg, S. 'Angels of us all? Football Management, Globalization and the Politics of Celebrity', *Soccer & Society*, vol. 8, no. 4 (October 2007), pp.440–58.

Wetherell, M. and N. Edley, 'Negotiating Hegemonic Masculinity: Imaginary Posi-tions and Psychodiscursive Practices', *Feminism & Psychology*, vol. 9, no. 3 (1999), pp.335–56.

Whannel, G. *Media Sport Stars: Masculinities and Moralities* (London: Routledge, 2002).

Whelan, D. *Who Stole Our Game?* (Dublin: Gill and Macmillan, 2006).

Worrall, F. *Roy Keane: Red Man Walking* (Edinburgh: Mainstream, 2006).

Figure 5.1 Sport and social commentary are combined in a cartoon from
La Gazzetta del Popolo. Copyright-free.

Figure 5.2 *Lo Sport fascista* reports on a rugby match between the S. S. Ambrosiana club of Milan and the visiting Paris Université Club. Copyright-free.

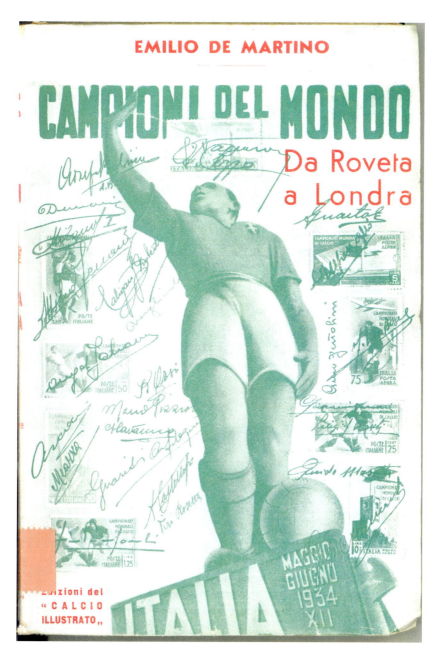

Figure 5.3   Italian success in the 1934 football World Cup as celebrated by a team-signed
copy of Emilio De Martino's book *Campioni del mondo: da Roveta a Londra*
(Milan: Ediz. Del Calcio Illustrato, 1935). Copyright-free.

Figure 6.2 Advertising poster for *Días de fútbol* (*Football Days*, David Serrano, 2003).
Reproduced by permission of Tomás Cimadevilla and Telespan 2000.

Wanda Films presenta

56 Internationale Filmfestspiele Berlin
Berlinale Special

LA GRAN FINAL

UNA PELÍCULA DE **GERARDO OLIVARES**

AHMED ALANSAR   MAHAMADOU ALZOUMA   ESENTAI SAMER KHAN   KHOSHIBAI EDIL KHAN   WIRAPITANG KAAPOR   KINCHIRAN KAAPOR

UNA PRODUCCIÓN DE WANDA FILMS COPRODUCIDA POR GREENLIGHT MEDIA

IDEA ORIGINAL GERARDO OLIVARES GUIÓN CHEMA RODRÍGUEZ DIRECCIÓN DE FOTOGRAFÍA GERARDO OLIVARES GUY GONÇALVES
SONIDO DIRECTO CARLOS DE HITA EDICIÓN DE SONIDO JUAN FERRO MEZCLAS ALFONSO RAPOSO MÚSICA MARTÍN MEISSONNIER MONTAJE RORI SAINZ DE ROZAS
PRODUCTORES EJECUTIVOS MIGUEL MORALES STEFAN BEITEN NIKOLAUS WEIL COPRODUCTORES SOPHOKLES TASIOULIS ANDRÉ SIKOJEV
PRODUCTOR JOSÉ MARÍA MORALES DIRECCIÓN GERARDO OLIVARES

www.wanda.es

Figure 6.3   Advertising poster for *La Gran Final*
(The Grand Final, Gerardo Olivares, 2007).
Reproduced by permission of Wanda Vision S. A.

Figure 6.4 Advertising poster for *A golpes* (The Beatings, Juan Vicente Córdoba, 2005). Reproduced by permission of Video Mercury Films and Enrique Cerezo P. C.

Chapter 7

Figure 7.1 Philippe Perrin / Official Soviet political painter: *My Last Fight*, 1990. Installation. Reproduced by permission of the artist.

Figure 7.2 Miguel Rio Branco: *Saint Sebastian* (Santa Rosa series), 1992. Photograph. Reproduced by permission of the artist.

Figure 7.3 Muhammad Ali as Saint Sebastian, 1968.
Photomontage: *Esquire* magazine cover.

Figure 7.4 James Coleman: *Box* (*Ahhareturnabout*), 1977. Installation voice-over text.
Reproduced by permission of the artist.

Figure 9.1 Roy Keane (left) acknowledges manager Mick McCarthy's gratitude
following Ireland's 1–0 victory over Holland, 1 September 2001.
Copyright InphoPhotography. Reproduced by permission.

Figure 15.1 Typical photograph showing the arrangement of the 'apparatus' for
Rwandan jumping, taken in 1926 by J. W. Roome.
Reproduced by permission of A. and C. Black.

Figure 15.2 Atypical photograph showing signs of German organization (notches in the uprights and German-style rope and sandbags) taken in 1907 by Jan Czekanowski, anthropologist of the Mecklenburg Expedition of that year.

Figure 15.3 Photograph demonstrating 'high jump' technique taken by
the Belgian physical educationalist and anthropologist, Joseph Ghesquière, 1950s.
Reproduced by permission of Joseph Ghesquière.

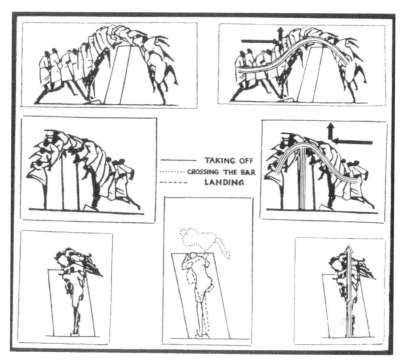

Figure 15.4 'The Tutsi high jump' represented as a docile, techno-athletic object. Diagram by Ernst Jokl showing the athlete as a machine analogue. *Journal of Physical Education and School Hygiene.*

PART 4

Contesting and Reinventing Identities

ALAN BAIRNER

Chapter 10
Representing the North: Reflections on the Life Stories of Northern Ireland's Catholic Footballers

Introduction

In the past few years, a number of young Catholic footballers, born in Northern Ireland, have chosen to represent the Republic of Ireland in international competition. The best known of these is Manchester United's Darron Gibson. At first glance, it might seem odd that this phenomenon has emerged at a time when the constitutional status of Northern Ireland has never been so secure. This chapter explores this development against the backdrop of the evolving constitutional status of Northern Ireland and in relation to questions of identity formation.

The signing of the Good Friday Agreement in 1998 and the subsequent difficult, but at present relatively successful, quest for an acceptable basis upon which to base devolved government, have led to the two more extreme nationalist and unionist political parties entering the mainstream of political life and agreeing to share power. Yet, concerns continue to be expressed about the extent to which the public at large have moved forwards in the same spirit. In particular, to what extent do the new political arrangements either reflect or encourage the emergence of a widely shared sense of Northern Irishness? One might be tempted to call such a phenomenon a 'national identity', but for the time being, and borrowing from the relevant literature relating to another contested place, namely Taiwan, it might be better to talk instead of a 'Northern Ireland consciousness'.[1]

---

1   See M. J. Brown, *Is Taiwan Chinese? The Impact of Culture, Power, and Migration on Changing Identities* (Berkeley, CA: University of California Press, 2004); L. T. S.

Basic ethnographic evidence tells us that Northern Irish people, whether nationalist or unionist, have for many years regarded themselves as different – unionists, of course, as different from 'the Irish' but also, it can be argued, from the British, and especially the English, and nationalists from the British but also, in a more nuanced way, from their compatriots in the Irish Republic. Conversely, a history shared by unionists and northern nationalists, even though interpreted differently, is undeniable. But to what extent, if at all, does this provide a basis upon which to build a shared consciousness?

The main focus of this chapter is on the representation of Northern Ireland, with the word 'representation' being used in two distinct ways. First, the chapter is concerned with association footballers from a Catholic background who have *represented* Northern Ireland in international competition. Second, the chapter examines the published life stories of these players as representations of Northern Ireland as a particular place. Two relatively minor terminological issues are worthy of consideration at the outset. The word 'Catholic' is used here not as a consequence of any insight into the religious beliefs of the players under discussion. In other circumstances, the word 'nationalist' would be preferable to that of 'Catholic' not least insofar as it attests to the fact that the conflict in and about Northern Ireland has been essentially political rather than religious. Given the subject matter of the chapter, however, it is important at the outset not to attach political labels to the players whose life stories are central to the discussion. The words 'football' and 'footballers' are regularly used here despite a recognition that in many parts of Ireland, 'football' refers to Gaelic football and the word 'soccer' is used for association football. Indeed, the players examined in this chapter frequently tend to favour 'soccer' rather than 'football', although in Belfast, the largest city in Northern Ireland, the usual distinction that is made, even in nationalist areas, is between 'Gaelic' and 'football'.

Ching, *Becoming 'Japanese': Colonial Taiwan and the Politics of Identity Formation* (Berkeley, CA: University of California Press, 2001); S. Corcuff (ed.), *Memories of the Future: National Identity Issues and the Search for a New Taiwan* (Armonk, NY: M. E. Sharpe, 2002).

A third terminological issue is far less easy to resolve. Indeed, its prob-lematic nature lies at the heart of the analysis that follows. What should we call 'Northern Ireland'? For many, particularly in the unionist commu-nity, the constitutional term is sufficient. For others, however, especially nationalists and republicans, the term is anathema, representing as it does a political entity which they have never formally supported – hence the use of the term 'the six counties' or more vaguely 'the north of Ireland' which conveniently ignores the fact that Donegal, in the Republic of Ireland, is situated to the north of a number of the six counties that constitute Northern Ireland. Equally misleading is the use of the word 'Ulster' by unionists inasmuch as it is intended to refer not to the nine counties of the province of Ulster but only to the six counties of Northern Ireland. For that same reason, with reference to the political status of Northern Ireland, the word 'province' is inappropriate. But what are the alternatives? Is it a state, a country, a nation or simply a region (and, if so, of what, the United Kingdom or Ireland or, indeed, both)? All of this might help to explain the use of 'the North' in the title of this chapter.

Arguably, not since the formation of the Northern Ireland state in 1921 has there been such a good opportunity to assess the meaning of Northern Ireland in relation to the identity formation of those who live there – to consider what Northern Ireland has been and what it can become, particu-larly in light of the evolving constitutional context of the United Kingdom in general. Ulster unionists can explore to a greater extent than ever before their precise feelings about Northern Ireland vis-à-vis the rest of the United Kingdom. Is the continued constitutional relationship with Britain an end in itself or merely a means to an end – namely, a bulwark against incorpora-tion within the Republic of Ireland, itself no longer a possibility without their consent? As Todd et al. point out, the Agreement 'poses new ques-tions for ordinary Protestants in Northern Ireland, casting into doubt older assumptions, requiring of them new modes of practice and interaction'.[2]

2   J. Todd, N. Rougier, T. O'Keefe and L. C. Bottos, 'Does Being Protestant Matter? Protestants and the Re-making of Ethno-religious Identity after the Good Friday Agreement', *National Identities*, vol. 11, no. 1 (2009), pp.87–99, p.87.

More significant perhaps is the question of where the Peace Process and the re-introduction of institutions of devolved government for Northern Ireland have left nationalism and, more controversially, republicanism. Is former republican prisoner Anthony McIntyre correct to claim that the majority of republicans in the north of Ireland, especially in Belfast, were never fully committed to the idea of a united Ireland, motivated as they were primarily by the desire for social justice which could be, and arguably has been, accommodated through reform within Northern Ireland? As McIntyre reminded his readers in 2004, 'before the Provisional IRA was founded the Unionist prime minister of Northern Ireland, Terence O'Neill, pompously stated that if the Unionist community would only treat Catholics well and allow them some prosperity, they would stop having seventeen children and come to live like Protestants'. According to McIntyre, 'his day has come'.[3]

In relation to sport, one visible signifier of the existence of Northern Ireland as a separate place is participation as a 'national' team in the Commonwealth games. The fact that this puts Northern Ireland on a par with the Isle of Man, Jersey and Guernsey as well as England, Scotland and Wales serves to lessen its significance. More interesting is the manner in which the Gaelic Athletic Association (GAA), that most nationalist of Irish sporting organizations, has acquired two rather different roles since the partition of Ireland. It has even been suggested that the GAA in Northern Ireland has attained a de facto semi-autonomous status.[4] Certainly within the nine counties of Northern Ireland, most Gaelic football rivalries tend to follow the contours established by partition – Tyrone versus Derry, and Down versus Armagh in the north and Cavan versus Monaghan on the other side of the border.

In reality however, it is the Irish Football Association (IFA), the Irish League and, above all, a 'national' football team that attest most stridently

3   A. Macintyre, *Good Friday: The Death of Irish Republicanism* (New York: Ausbo, 2008), p.228.

4   D. Hassan, 'Sport, Identity and Irish Nationalism in Northern Ireland', in A. Bairner (ed.), *Sport and the Irish: Histories, Identities, Issues* (Dublin: UCD Press, 2005), pp.123–39.

to the existence of Northern Ireland as a separate place, at least in terms of sport. So how have Catholic footballers articulated their relationship with Northern Ireland – their football nation? The main catalyst for asking this question was previous work on northern unionists who have represented Ireland in rugby union.[5] But are Catholics who have played for Northern Ireland at football as willing to talk about their experiences? To date, the signs are not encouraging.

Methodological Challenges

There is a marked reluctance on the part of Catholics who have represented Northern Ireland to discuss their experiences with researchers. There are probably two major explanations for their reticence in addition to the general piece of advice so often proffered during the Troubles – 'whatever you say, say nothing'. First, some ex-players maintain close relations with the IFA and are keen to avoid circumstances in which they might appear to be criticizing that organization. Second, playing for Northern Ireland brings into sharp focus the hierarchies of identity that consistently serve to complicate the Northern Irish political scene. To admit that the experience had been largely negative would be controversial. Equally controversial, however, at least in those communities in which the players grew up would be expressions of pride. The latter point is particularly significant given the recent relationship between Northern Ireland's nationalist population and the Northern Ireland football team.

---

5   See A. Bairner, 'Sport, Irishness and Ulster Unionism', in Bairner (ed.), *Sport and the Irish*, pp.157–71; A. Bairner, 'Political Unionism and Sporting Nationalism: An Examination of the Relationship between Sport and National Identity within the Ulster Unionist tradition', *Identities: Global Studies in Culture and Power*, vol. 10, no. 4 (2003), pp.517–35.

As Fulton notes, 'throughout most of the twentieth century Catholic football fans did not experience the expression of a northern nationalist sentiment and support for the north's international team as mutually exclusive practices'.[6] He continues, 'Northern Catholic support for the Republic's football team thus emerges as a relatively recent phenomenon, the product of the last twenty years or so'.[7] Indeed, even during the 1982 World Cup Finals in Spain there was evidence of widespread cross-community support for the 'national' team. There have been vigorous efforts on the part of the Community Relations Department of the IFA to make Northern Ireland games more attractive to nationalists. In addition, the Amalgamation of Official Northern Ireland Supporters' Clubs which was formed in 1998 comprises over 60 clubs and 2500 members and was re-branded in 2007 as 'The Green and White Army' (an interesting choice of name in itself given that in the not too distant past, many Northern Ireland supporters preferred to wear red, white and blue in celebration of their Britishness instead of the green and white of their team's kit).[8] Nevertheless, old habits die hard. As Fulton points out, 'The sense of alienation felt by many northern Catholic supporters certainly must be seen in the context of the broader resonance of Protestant symbolism that came to surround the Northern Ireland team during the recent conflict'.[9] This would include the abuse directed by Northern Ireland fans at two young players Anton Rogan, a Catholic and Allen McKnight, a Protestant, both of whom were playing for Celtic FC when chosen to represent their country, in marked contrast to the treatment of Bertie Peacock, also a Protestant, who had played for Celtic and Northern Ireland in the 1950s.[10]

6   G. Fulton, 'Northern Catholic Fans of the Republic of Ireland Soccer Team', in Bairner (ed.), *Sport and the Irish*, pp.140–56, p.147.
7   Fulton, 'Northern Catholic Fans', p.147.
8   For further information on supporters of the Northern Ireland football team see the following website: <http://www.ourweecountry.co.uk/greenwhitearmy.html> (accessed 1 June 2008).
9   Fulton, 'Northern Catholic fans', p.149.
10   J. Sugden and A. Bairner, *Sport, Sectarianism and Society in a Divided Ireland* (Leicester: Leicester University Press, 1993).

In such circumstances the unwillingness of most players to discuss their experiences is scarcely surprising. For that reason, it has been decided, for present purposes, to concentrate instead on analysing the autobiographies of Catholic players who have 'represented the North', in both meanings of that phrase.

The autobiographies of footballers (many of them ghost-written), like celebrity autobiographies more generally, have a poor reputation. Widely regarded as poorly written, they are also dismissed for the vacuous quality of their contents. Many such works consist either of boring accounts of goals scored and saves made, or of a racy celebration of various extra-curricular activities. In large part, what is involved is the presentation of self[11] and the author presents himself 'in accordance with his audience's presumed expectations'.[12] This explains the emphases on on-field exploits and off-field indiscretions. On the other hand, 'he must also cope with the audience's growing demands for authenticity; he is summoned to display his intimate self. In other words, he is asked to remove the masks of social roles and show the flesh and blood character under the [...] stereotyped parts'.[13] Often, however, it is in those passages of an autobiography that neither the author nor the audience might consider important that the researcher finds the most useful data – asides that keep the narrative moving along but which offer, almost certainly unintended, insights. Such data figure prominently in this discussion.

In addition, it should be noted that autobiography has been described as 'the medium for a variety of present day writers under siege, and particularly those writing from a postcolonial standpoint'.[14] It is 'particularly valuable to individuals and groups whose perspectives and experiences have

---

11   E. Goffman, *The Presentation of Self in Everyday Life* (New York: Harper, 1959).
12   R. Amossy, 'Autobiographies of Movie Stars: Presentation of Self and its Strategies', *Poetics Today*, vol. 7, no. 4 (1986), pp.673–703, p.675.
13   Ibid.
14   G. Weiner, 'Disrupting autobiographical narratives: method, interpretation, and the role of gender', <http://www.educ.umu.se/~gaby/autobiography.html> (accessed 12 May 2008), p.2.

been hitherto hidden or absent from history'[15] – hence, its importance in relation to postcolonial experience.[16] The precise nature of Ireland's colonial past is complex.[17] We can state with some degree of certainty, however, that the autobiographies that are central to this study were written by, or ghost-written on behalf of, men whose experience of being part of a distrusted minority inevitably coloured their perspectives. Findings to date based on four autobiographies and one biography suggest three major themes – the relationship between Gaelic games and soccer, the influence of a Catholic/nationalist habitus in the stories that are told, and the attitudes of the players involved to international football and, specifically, to 'representing the North'.

Association Football and Gaelic Games

Charlie Tully (1924–1971) made ten appearances for Ireland/Northern Ireland. He notes in his autobiography that at his school, St Kevin's, Belfast, the preferred game was hurling. 'Most of us', he recalls, 'didn't fancy it at all, but the lads accepted it. Which didn't suit me'.[18] Indeed, 'realizing, even as a youngster that life is too short to do something you don't want to do, I organized my pals into a soccer team so that when we should have been "hurling" we were away out of the road practising how to become

15   Ibid.
16   A. Hornung and E. Ruhe, *Postcolonialism and Autobiography* (Amsterdam: Rodopi, 1994).
17   See D. Kiberd, 'Modern Ireland: Postcolonial or European?', in S. Murray (ed.), *Not on Any Map: Essays on Postcoloniality and Cultural Nationalism* (Exeter: University of Exeter Press, 1997), pp.81–100; S. Howe, *Ireland and Empire: Colonial Legacies in Irish History and Culture* (Oxford: Oxford University Press, 2000); A. Bairner, 'Sport, Nationality and Postcolonialism in Ireland', in J. Bale and M. Cronin (eds), *Sport and Postcolonialism* (Oxford: Berg, 2003), pp.159–74.
18   C. Tully, *Passed to You* (London: The Soccer Book Club, 1958), p.10.

footballers'.[19] Tully tells his readers that, one Saturday morning, he 'turned up at a public park where some of the Protestant schoolboys were playing a match. How I used to envy them, because this was the sport they were encouraged to play'.[20]

Peter McParland (b.1934) played 34 times for Northern Ireland including appearing in the 1958 World Cup finals in Sweden. He grew up in Newry where football is a popular sport, but Catholic grammar schools for boys are noted for Gaelic football. 'Peter McParland suspended sine die [i.e. indefinitely]', he writes, '...yet when I heard the news, I roared with laughter and became more determined than ever to become a professional footballer!'.[21] 'Mad Irishman?', he exclaims, 'Not a bit'. So how had he come to be suspended? In fact, 'the suspension came from the local Gaelic Athletic Association at Newry, and the reason for the "sine die" verdict was that I had been playing soccer'.[22] 'Unlike most English stars', McParland continues, 'I played no schoolboy soccer. At the Christian Brothers' School (Newry), you played Gaelic football whether you liked it or not and soccer was a forbidden word'.[23]

He then goes on to make a rather more contentious point:

> There's no doubt soccer would be a far more popular game among the Irish youngsters. I can remember my own school days only too well. I was skipper of the school's Gaelic team, yet as soon as we were out of sight, handling would be taboo and the ball would be kept where it belongs – on the floor.[24]

Whether or not soccer or Gaelic football is the more popular sport amongst nationalists in towns such as Newry today is virtually impossible to answer. The two sports serve very different functions. Unlike in the past, choice is no longer a matter of 'either/or'. But ten years after McParland had attended school, little had changed.

19   Ibid., p.11.
20   Ibid., pp.11–12.
21   P. McParland, *Going for Goal* (London: The Soccer Book Club, 1960), p.10.
22   Ibid., p.10.
23   Ibid., p.11.
24   Ibid., p.11.

Another Newry man, Pat Jennings (b.1945) made 119 appearances for Northern Ireland. 'Soccer', he recalls, 'was banned at my school, but the local league was always the big topic of conversation.'[25] An academic who also grew up in the town explains the implications of the emphasis on Gaelic football in Newry's Catholic schools:

> [...] I was taken aback to learn that a good Catholic school like Clongowes – indeed, a rather superior Catholic school – could encourage decent Irish Catholics to play such a notoriously British game as cricket. Growing up as I did in Northern Ireland (in Newry), I had in my own time (the forties and fifties) only a remote sense of what Clongowes College might be like: but I knew that some of the prominent citizens of Newry (like, for example, our own family doctor) sent their sons there. Some of us, however, had to stay in Newry; and taught as I was there by a very different religious order from the Jesuits at Clongowes – the Christian Brothers – it was simply inconceivable that we would be allowed to play cricket.[26]

Soccer, 'we were informed in the most caustic tones, was a game for "corner boys", for effete and pasty-faced city dwellers who were deficient in the manly athleticism of our own Gaelic footballers...'[27]

Newry was by no means alone in this respect. Martin O'Neill (b.1952), who played 64 times for Northern Ireland, spent his early years in County Derry before subsequently attending school in Belfast. According to his biographer, 'it was simply accepted among the O'Neill boys that sport was for you, an essential part of life, particularly because of their father's love of Gaelic football'.[28] But an increasingly familiar dilemma now presented itself: 'The nationalism in his family introduced him to the Gaelic game, but he knew the money and the glory would come from his mastery of the

25   P. Jennings, *Pat Jennings: An Autobiography* (London: Panther, 1983), p.8.

26   B. Cosgrove, 'Not Cricket?', in E. Longley, E. Hughes and D. O'Rawe (eds), *Ireland (Ulster) Scotland: Concepts, Contexts, Comparisons*, Belfast Studies in Language, Culture and Politics, no. 7 (Belfast: Cló Ollscoil na Banríona, 2003), pp.61–4, p.61.

27   Ibid., p.62.

28   A. Montgomery, *Martin O'Neill: The Biography* (London: Virgin, 2007), p.98.

round (sic) ball'.[29] There was no doubt that 'O'Neill had developed into a Gaelic football player of rare ability, but there was a problem; he had also signed to play association football for Irish League side Distillery'.[30]

The same dilemma was to confront Neil Lennon (b.1971) some years later. Having grown up in Lurgan, County Armagh, Lennon made 40 appearances for Northern Ireland. He writes, 'the people of Lurgan lived for their sport. Football, or rather soccer, was followed avidly in the town, but there was also a great deal of interest in horse racing and boxing, and in Nationalist areas of the town, Gaelic football was played with a passion'.[31] According to Lennon, 'there were quite a few of us who played both Gaelic football and soccer, though in some parts of Ireland that was very much frowned upon'.[32]

Indeed, when he first went to St Michael's school, 'it became clear that I faced something of a problem, one that almost got me expelled from the school and nearly ended my career in soccer almost before it started'.[33] He continues, 'tradition meant everything to Sister St Anne. As far as she was concerned, it was to be Gaelic football or no football at all'.[34] Lennon, 'on the other hand, just could not envisage life without soccer'[35] and 'despite my Gaelic football success, soccer was more and more the main focus of my life'.[36]

Only Tully and McParland grew up in the era when the Gaelic Athletic Association sought to exclude those found guilty of watching or playing 'foreign' games. Nevertheless, each of these former Northern Ireland soccer players had grown up with Gaelic games. The decision to pursue a career in soccer was taken for two main reasons – a preference for the sport and

29   Ibid., p.99. It should be noted that a round ball is used in both soccer and Gaelic foot-ball, although the author here seems to presume that the Gaelic ball is different.
30   Ibid., p.106.
31   N. Lennon, *Man and Bhoy* (London: HarperSport, 2006), p.32.
32   Ibid.
33   Ibid., p.40.
34   Ibid., p.41.
35   Ibid.
36   Ibid., p.45.

an acknowledgment that it offered greater opportunities. It was seldom an easy decision, not least because it involved loosening an attachment to a movement that was recognized in the players' respective communities as the main, legitimate vehicle for an embodied expression of Irishness. Compensation could always be found, however, in other physical and social expressions of Irish Catholic identity.

Catholic/Nationalist Relationships – Habitus Matters

Writing about English-born soccer players who have represented the Republic of Ireland, Holmes and Storey argue that there is 'a need to move beyond a conception of national identity that is intrinsically linked to Ireland as a bounded space' and 'to conceive of Irish identity in diasporic terms; an identity that is no longer place-bound or contained by the actual borders of Ireland'.[37] An important related point about Irish migrants in the United States is made by veteran Gaelic games commentator, Micheál Ó Muircheartaigh, who observes that 'most of them never saw home again, but it would be true to say that Ireland seldom left their minds'.[38] Indeed, he recalls a telephone conversation with one emigré of whom he had asked why he had never returned home in fifty years:

> His reply was most revealing: 'I have indeed. Every single night before going to bed I walk out the door at home – up Bóthar na Seán and into every single field before returning home and then in my mind going to bed in Dún Síon.'[39]

---

37   M. Holmes and D. Storey, 'Who are the Boys in Green? Irish Identity and Soccer in the Republic of Ireland', in A. Smith and D. Porter (eds), *Sport and National Identity in the Post-War World* (London: Routledge, 2004), pp.88–104, p.100.

38   M. Ó Muircheartaigh, *From Dún Síon to Croke Park: The Autobiography* (Dublin: Penguin Ireland, 2004), p.21.

39   Ibid.

Noting that all social relations are enshrined, not simply reflected, in space, Henri Lefebvre writes:

> [...] social relations, which are concrete abstractions, have no real existence save in and through space. *Their underpinning is spatial.* In each particular case the connection between this underpinning and the relations it supports calls for analysis.[40]

In relation to national habitus, the significant space is often that territory which is contained within national boundaries. For the diaspora, however, the national territory becomes boundless. Within that boundless space though, we must also take account of those domestic spaces such as cellars, drawers and wardrobes wherein are located material evocations of the national 'home' – photographs, items of clothing, souvenirs of first holy communions and confirmations, old hurley sticks and so on. It is in 'this material paradise'[41] that we acquire a heightened sense of self – in this case, national self. In such ways are memories of the 'old country' formed for, as de Certeau points out, 'like those birds that lay their eggs only in other species' nests, memory produces in a place that does not belong to it. It receives its form and its implantation from external circumstances, even if it furnishes the content (the missing detail)'.[42]

The footballers discussed in this chapter all left Ireland to pursue their professional careers. But each of them found ways by which to maintain a direct connection with Catholic Ireland. In the case of Tully, O'Neill and Lennon, there was the personal involvement with Celtic Football Club – 'The Good Ship Celtic', as Tully describes it[43] – which was founded by Irishmen and has been closely linked to Ireland and to the Irish diaspora ever since. Tully recalls, 'It took me, personally, three hours to decide on the Timaloys as opposed to the English glamour teams [including Liverpool, Manchester United and Arsenal]. It wasn't only the fact that I liked the

40 H. Lefebvre, *The Production of Space* (Oxford: Blackwell, 1991), p.404.
41 G. Bachelard, *The Poetics of Space* (Boston, MA: Beacon, 1994), p.7.
42 M. de Certeau, *The Practice of Everyday Life* (Berkeley, CA: University of California Press, 1988), p.86.
43 Tully, *Passed to You*, p.18.

terms, but that it had always been an ambition of mine to play for the great Scottish club'.[44] Others have had similar feelings. According to his biographer, 'the pleasure O'Neill took from his appointment as Celtic manager, walking in the footsteps of his heroes, could be described as wide-eyed'.[45] For Lennon, 'Pulling on the hoops for the first time was a magical feeling, and taking part in my first huddle [...] confirmed there was no going back. "This is it, you are here and it's not a dream" were my thoughts'.[46] Lennon has subsequently gone on to be appointed as Celtic manager.

Those players who had no association with Celtic in the course of their professional career sought other ways of maintaining an attachment to Ireland in a 'foreign' country. It is worth noting, for example, that it was the Irish connection that allowed McParland to settle in England after a period of homesickness. Recalling the significant role played by a compatriot, McParland writes, 'My early days at Villa Park were not altogether smooth ones. At first I had a little trouble over my "digs". I was lucky, however. That wonderful character Joseph Cornelius Martin – popularly known as "Con" – asked me to stay at his house, and it proved a big help to me in settling down in Birmingham'.[47] Similarly, Jennings refers to 'joining the "London Irish"' (at Arsenal).[48]

In addition to playing for Celtic, Tully also betrays his emotional ties with Catholic Ireland when identifying important people in his international career. He describes the Northern Ireland manager, Peter Doherty as 'the great gentleman'[49] and 'a pre-match genius'[50] with 'off-field magic'.[51] He adds tellingly, 'before every Irish game, Peter Doherty gives us the "It's all for the glory of Ireland" talk. It may sound silly to the staid Englishmen

44   Ibid., p.16.
45   Montgomery, *Martin O'Neill*, p.83.
46   Lennon, *Man and Bhoy*, p.191.
47   McParland, *Going for Goal*, p.19.
48   Jennings, *Pat Jennings*, p.67.
49   Tully, *Passed to You*, p.70.
50   Ibid., p.25.
51   Ibid., p.26.

– yet I'm sure it puts all the players in the right frame of mind'.[52] Another man he remembers with much affection is Gerry Morgan, one of the few Catholics to have been closely associated with Belfast's Linfield FC until the contemporary era and the Northern Ireland team's trainer. According to Tully, 'with his genial smile and unending flow of witticisms, Gerry did much to build up the tremendous team spirit which ran through the Irish team'.[53]

Playing International Football

Soccer is something of an exception in the world of Irish sport inasmuch as most so-called 'foreign' games are organized on an all-Ireland basis and 'national' teams represent the whole of Ireland. This explains why Ulster unionists finish up representing an entity (a thirty-two county Ireland) which they would not wish to see being given constitutional legitimacy. Previous research has examined the attitudes of rugby players from an Ulster unionist background who have represented Ireland at rugby union.[54] Their background and upbringing explain why this did not prove problematic for most of them and also why their unionism remained unaffected by their sporting allegiance, just as the latter was largely unaffected by their political views. If the only way to play international rugby or cricket is to play for an all-Ireland team, then so be it. Thus former Irish international rugby player, Willie John McBride, asserted:

52   Ibid., p.73.
53   Ibid., pp.24–5. For more on Morgan's perhaps unique contribution to football in Northern Ireland, see A. Bairner and G. Walker, 'Football and Society in Northern Ireland: Linfield Football Club and the case of Gerry Morgan', *Soccer and Society*, vol. 2, no. 1 (2001), pp.81–98.
54   See A. Bairner, 'Political Unionism and Sporting Nationalism'; also A. Bairner, 'Sport, Irishness and Ulster Unionism'.

> I stand for anyone's national anthem and when I pulled on the green shirt I was playing for Ireland. It was about the performance on the field. I want nothing to do with politics. I am not a flag waver and never will be.[55]

In this comment, there are clear traces of sporting pragmatism. Indeed in that respect there are even higher ambitions than merely playing for Ireland. As Nigel Carr commented, 'The greatest honour I had in the game was to play for the Lions because less people get picked for the Lions than for Ireland and similarly Ulster'.[56] Furthermore, sporting expediency need not be taken as evidence of political uncertainty. For example, Davy Tweed, the former Irish player, once a highly visible member of the Democratic Unionist Party (DUP), certainly did not become any less of a unionist as a result of his time with the Irish rugby squad:

> Well I think everyone wants to play as high a standard as they can. I always was an Ulsterman and got a huge sense of pride playing for Ulster. The pride I got playing in my Ulster jersey and I would have died in it. Not taking anything away from the Ireland jersey that meant a terrible lot, but to answer your question I would say that the Ulster jersey meant more to me.[57]

Perhaps Tweed's reservations take us closer to the mindset of those northern Catholic footballers who represent Northern Ireland in the knowledge that the team itself receives little support from the community in which they grew up.

It is worth noting that throughout the autobiographies almost all of the references are to Ireland and not Northern Ireland. During the era when Tully and McParland were playing this terminology was commonplace and used by unionists as much as by nationalists. This practice was part of the legacy of the IFA having been the pre-partition governing body for football throughout Ireland and the fact that until the 1950s, Northern Ireland teams still drew upon players from the whole island. One wonders, however, if this preference for 'Ireland' over 'Northern Ireland' reflects

---

55   Interviewed by Simon Mason, 6 February, 2000. Quoted in Bairner, 'Sport, Irishness and Ulster Unionism', p.169.
56   Ibid.
57   Ibid.

something more. Reading Martin O'Neill's biography that would seem unlikely. According to his biographer, '... O'Neill was never happier than when he was playing for his country'.[58] In the autobiographies, however, a rather different picture emerges.

Jennings recalls, 'I thought it was a dream come true when I made my international debut at Windsor Park, but I was appalled by some of the remarks shouted at me from behind the goal. "Go back where you belong" was the mildest form of abuse hurled in my direction'.[59] 'Being a Catholic', he adds, 'was no popularity boost'.[60] Even by those standards, however, Lennon's experience was unique. He writes, 'I was proud to play forty times for my country, but at the end it all turned very sour indeed and a lot of happy memories have been permanently blighted'.[61]

On 28 February 2001, shortly after Neil Lennon, a regular in the home side, had been transferred from Leicester City to Celtic, Northern Ireland played Norway at Windsor Park. Despite attempts by other fans to drown out the noise, a sizeable section of the Northern Ireland support shouted abuse at Lennon throughout the first half of the game. Referring to his team manager, Sammy McIlroy, Lennon comments, 'It was as though he did not understand what lay at the heart of the whole situation'.[62] By contrast, Lennon also makes reference to Martin O'Neill, his former club manager at Leicester and subsequently his Celtic manager. 'I know what Martin O'Neill would have done', he writes, '– he would have addressed that section of the crowd who were abusing me and told them to cease their activities forthwith'.[63]

A year and a half later, on 21 August 2002, Northern Ireland were due to play Cyprus, again at Windsor Park, and Lennon had been asked to captain the team. He realized that this would be seen as a controversial choice:

58   Montgomery, *Martin O'Neill*, p.127.
59   Jennings, *Pat Jennings*, p.185.
60   Ibid., p.186.
61   Lennon, *Man and Bhoy*, pp.273–4.
62   Ibid., p.7.
63   Ibid.

For better or worse, I had become a controversial figure, both in Scotland and in
Northern Ireland. I was a symbol for one side, the epitome of what was wanted in a
Celtic man dedicated to the club he loved, whereas for the other side I was something
to despise. I could see the two sides would never meet on common ground, and that
there would always be extremists who simply could not tolerate my presence in a
Northern Ireland jersey.[64]

He admits that he may have contributed to this situation:

Some pundits would later say that I had been ill-advised to call for the football teams
of Northern Ireland and the Republic to be united, but not for the first or last time,
they were misquoting or misunderstanding what I had said in an interview some
weeks before the match. I had said that a team drawn from all of Ireland's thirty-two
counties would do better than the two separate teams. In saying that I was only recognizing that in rugby union, all Ireland played as one and did so very successfully.
But at no point did I say the two countries should unite, in football or politically.
In fact, I was only stating the same position as the late George Best, the greatest of
all Northern Ireland players. But then he didn't play for Celtic.[65]

In the lead-up to the Cyprus game, a threat was made on Lennon's life and
he made the decision not only to withdraw from the squad, playing only
a couple of times thereafter, but subsequently to bring his international
football career to an end. The treatment of Lennon had more to do with
the fact that he had become a Celtic player than because he was a Catholic.
His unease with the idea of a Northern Ireland 'national' football team
was, of course, another contributory factor although, as he points out, he
is by no means the only former Northern Ireland player to have expressed
a desire for a united Ireland team.

Jennings argues the case as follows:

Ireland should field one soccer team in international football matches, including
players from all 32 counties. I know that statement will infuriate a lot of people, but
I make it without any political or religious bias. I am aware that a lot of administrative obstacles and a great deal of prejudice must be overcome before it is realized,
but it can't be impossible. There's just one Irish XV playing Rugby Union: if the

64   Ibid., p.15.
65   Ibid., p.21.

rugger types can make it work, surely the soccer authorities on both sides of the border can get together.[66]

He adds, 'All I know is that I'm sorry I've never had the opportunity to play for an all-Ireland team at international level'.[67] In fact, Jennings did play in the charity game against Brazil in 1973 in which a united Ireland team in the guise of Shamrock Rovers played the visitors but his dream of an official all-Ireland team seems as far away as ever. As a republican prisoner once suggested to the author, 'a united Ireland will be easier to achieve than a united Ireland football team'. With the consolidation of Northern Ireland's constitutional status as a consequence of the Good Friday Agreement, one might be tempted to add that the two are equally unattainable in the foreseeable future.

Conclusion

Events surrounding the end of Neil Lennon's international career are hugely influential in terms of Catholic attitudes towards the Northern Ireland team. It should be noted, however, that only towards the end of his career, and for very specific reasons, did Lennon sever his links with the Northern Ireland team. Like the others, he had previously performed conscientiously for the side. Both Jennings and he, however, explicitly favoured a united Ireland team. O'Neill's biographer hints at little controversy and, indeed, points to his subject's passion for the 'national' team. An O'Neill autobiography would almost certainly offer additional insights. The autobiographies of Tully and McParland are less controversial overall and especially with regard to international football than those of Jennings or Lennon. But they played their professional football in the pre-Troubles era. That said, it is apparent from all of the books examined here that each of the players had a particularly close affinity with their Catholic and nationalist roots.

66 Jennings, *Pat Jennings*, p.182.
67 Ibid.

In the early stages of their life stories, this is most clearly demonstrated in their negotiation of the rival attractions of Gaelic games and football. The point is further established by adult relationships which are recognized as important – relationships with individuals or, in several cases, with Celtic. These examples of the influence of a Catholic/nationalist habitus highlight the extent to which Northern Ireland has been and remains (as shown in the case of Lennon) a divided society (not least in relation to residence and education).[68]

These footballers' stories suggest that there is more evidence of division than of convergence – signs of a Northern Irish football consciousness, perhaps, but not of an emergent Northern Irish political consciousness, far less a 'national' identity. The Good Friday Agreement has done much to strengthen the constitutional status of Northern Ireland. Ironically, however, it has also simultaneously allowed for greater freedom and more opportunities than in the past to choose one's own national allegiance. Thus, in an era when the political leaders of Irish nationalism and republicanism are helping to govern Northern Ireland as a constituent part of the United Kingdom, young players such as Darren Gibson have chosen the Republic of Ireland over Northern Ireland for their own reasons.

The peace process has achieved a great deal not least in terms of the reduction of violence and human suffering. But to what extent do people now identify with Northern Ireland as a political and cultural entity? In relation to football, the next stage of the conflict transformation process will dictate whether a Northern Irish identity is sufficiently robust amongst a majority of the population of the six counties for a Northern Ireland team to attract support from both communities. Sport is often used in nation-building processes. In this case, however, it may be that the nation-building process must precede the football nation-building process. If the former fails, then we may not have heard the last of calls for an all-Ireland team and, in the short term at least, of more Catholic players expressing a desire to pursue an international career influenced more by an Irish national identity than by a Northern Irish consciousness.

68   See P. Shirlow and B. Murtagh, *Belfast: Segregation, Violence and the City* (London: Pluto, 2006).

Bibliography

Amossy, R. 'Autobiographies of Movie Stars: Presentation of Self and its Strategies', *Poetics Today*, vol. 7, no. 4 (1986), pp.673–703.

Bachelard, G. *The Poetics of Space* (Boston, MA: Beacon, 1994).

Bairner, A. 'Political Unionism and Sporting Nationalism: An Examination of the Relationship between Sport and National Identity within the Ulster Unionist Tradition', *Identities: Global Studies in Culture and Power*, vol. 10, no. 4 (2003), pp.517–35.

——. 'Sport, Nationality and Postcolonialism in Ireland', in J. Bale and M. Cronin (eds), *Sport and Postcolonialism* (Oxford: Berg, 2003), pp.159–74.

——. 'Sport, Irishness and Ulster Unionism', in A. Bairner (ed.), *Sport and the Irish: Histories, Identities, Issues* (Dublin: UCD Press, 2005), pp.157–71.

—— and G. Walker. 'Football and Society in Northern Ireland: Linfield Football Club and the Case of Gerry Morgan', *Soccer and Society*, vol. 2, no. 1 (2001), pp.81–98.

Brown, M. J. *Is Taiwan Chinese? The Impact of Culture, Power, and Migration on Changing Identities* (Berkeley, CA: University of California Press, 2004).

Ching, L. T. S. *Becoming 'Japanese': Colonial Taiwan and the Politics of Identity Formation* (Berkeley, CA: University of California Press, 2001).

Corcuff, S. (ed.) *Memories of the Future: National Identity Issues and the Search for a New Taiwan* (Armonk, NY: M. E. Sharpe, 2002).

Cosgrove, B. 'Not Cricket?', in E. Longley, E. Hughes and D. O'Rawe (eds), *Ireland (Ulster) Scotland: Concepts, Contexts, Comparisons*, Belfast Studies in Language, Culture and Politics, no. 7 (Belfast: Cló Ollscoil na Banríona, 2003), pp.61–4.

De Certeau, M. *The Practice of Everyday Life* (Berkeley, CA: University of California Press, 1988).

Fulton, G. 'Northern Catholic Fans of the Republic of Ireland Soccer Team', in A. Bairner (ed.), *Sport and the Irish: Histories, Identities, Issues* (Dublin: UCD Press, 2005), pp.140–56.

Goffman, E. *The Presentation of Self in Everyday Life* (New York: Harper, 1959).

Green and White Army, <http://www.ourweecountry.co.uk/greenwhitearmy.html> (accessed 1 June 2008).

Hassan, D. 'Sport, Identity and Irish Nationalism in Northern Ireland', in A. Bairner (ed.), *Sport and the Irish: Histories, Identities, Issues* (Dublin: UCD Press, 2005), pp.123–39.

Holmes, M. and D. Storey, 'Who are the Boys in Green? Irish Identity and Soccer in the Republic of Ireland', in A. Smith and D. Porter (eds), *Sport and National Identity in the Post-War World* (London: Routledge, 2004), pp.88–104.

Hornung, A. and E. Ruhe. *Postcolonialism and Autobiography* (Amsterdam: Rodopi, 1994).

Howe, S. *Ireland and Empire: Colonial Legacies in Irish History and Culture* (Oxford: Oxford University Press, 2000).

Jennings, P. *Pat Jennings: An Autobiography* (London: Panther, 1983).

Kiberd, D. 'Modern Ireland: Postcolonial or European?', in S. Murray (ed.), *Not on Any Map: Essays on Postcoloniality and Cultural Nationalism* (Exeter: University of Exeter Press, 1997), pp.81–100.

Lefebvre, H. *The Production of Space* (Oxford: Blackwell, 1991).

Lennon, N. *Man and Bhoy* (London: HarperSport, 2006).

Macintyre, A. *Good Friday: The Death of Irish Republicanism* (New York: Ausbo, 2008).

McParland, P. *Going for Goal* (London: The Soccer Book Club, 1960).

Montgomery, A. *Martin O'Neill: The Biography* (London: Virgin, 2007).

Ó Muircheartaigh, M. *From Dún Síon to Croke Park: The Autobiography* (Dublin: Penguin Ireland, 2004).

Shirlow, P. and B. Murtagh. *Belfast: Segregation, Violence and the City* (London: Pluto, 2006).

Sugden, J. and A. Bairner. *Sport, Sectarianism and Society in a Divided Ireland* (Leicester: Leicester University Press, 1993).

Todd, J., N. Rougier, T. O'Keefe and L. C. Bottos. 'Does Being Protestant matter? Protestants and the Re-making of Ethno-religious Identity after the Good Friday Agreement', *National Identities*, vol. 11, no. 1 (2009), pp.87–99.

Tully, C. *Passed to You* (London: The Soccer Book Club, 1958).

Weiner, G. 'Disrupting Autobiographical Narratives: Method, Interpretation, and the Role of Gender', <http://www.educ.umu.se/~gaby/autobiography.html> (accessed 12 May 2008).

GYOZO MOLNAR

Chapter 11
Rediscovering Hungarian-ness:
The Case of Elite Hungarian Footballers

Introduction

In this chapter, I will focus on the migratory experiences of Hungarian footballers and their particular way of coping with the challenges and anxieties
of living abroad. I will approach the analysis of these experiences by outlining and discussing a possible interplay between migration and national
identity. By considering aspects of migration and national identity, I will
outline the process of what I have termed 'rediscovering Hungarian-ness',
which was the mode of response to the challenges of migration and the
consequent experience of foreignness by the participants in this study. It is
important to highlight at this point that, like migration – 'a process which
affects every dimension of social existence, and which develops its own
dynamics'[1] – identity formation, equally, is a process. This perception moves
away from a more traditional approach, which views identity as a monolithic, established structure, to recognize, as Kosic describes, that 'identity
is not a stable set of characteristics attached to an individual but is hybrid,
multiple and shifting.'[2] Fortier further explains that 'identity is always

1   S. Castles and M. J. Miller, *The Age of Migration: International Population in the
     Modern World* (3rd edn; Basingstoke: Palgrave Macmillan, 2003), p.21.
2   A. Kosic, 'Migrant Identities' in A. Triandafyllidou (ed.), *Contemporary Polish
     Migration in Europe: Complex Patterns of Movement and Settlement* (Lampeter:
     Edwin Mellen, 2006), pp.245–66, p.246.

producing itself through the combined process of being and becoming'.[3] Hence, rediscovering one's identity, national identity in this case, is also a process that takes place and changes over time. In this particular instance, it is a form of self-defence mechanism that protects the integrity of the individual migrant's identity, thereby maintaining the security of his or her self, what Giddens calls 'ontological security'.[4]

It has been argued that we live in the era of migration, where the movement of people has reached unprecedented proportions and complexity.[5] The growing significance of migrations is often associated with globalization, modernity and technology. That is, migrations are connected to other social processes such as globalization and regionalization, which are currently taking place within the European Union (EU).[6] For instance, Appadurai clearly identifies ethnoscapes, the global movement of people, as one of the dimensions of globalization.[7] Consequently, if we indeed live in a global age,[8] and in the age of migration,[9] then we must understand how these social processes idiosyncratically affect people moving across borders and cultures.

Globalization and modernity, and the migratory flows and experiences triggered by them, create new challenges and anxieties. Giddens observes that: 'modernity radically alters the nature of day-to-day social life and affects the most personal aspects of our [social] experience'.[10] In other words, 'modernity [...] brings about major changes in the external

3   A.-M. Fortier, *Migrant Belongings: Memory, Space, Identity* (Oxford: Berg, 2000), p.2.
4   A. Giddens, *Modernity and Self-Identity: Self and Society in the Late Modern Age* (Cambridge: Polity, 1990), Ch. 2.
5   Castles and Miller, *The Age of Migration*.
6   See B. Edgar, J. Doherty and H. Meert, *Immigration and Homelessness in Europe* (Bristol: Polity, 2004).
7   A. Appadurai, 'Disjuncture and Difference in the Global Cultural Economy', *Theory, Culture and Society*, vol. 7, no. 2 (1990), pp.295–310, p.295.
8   M. Albrow, *The Global Age* (London: Polity, 1996), p.2.
9   Castles and Miller, *The Age of Migration*, p.5.
10   Giddens, *Modernity and Self-Identity*, p.1.

social environment of the individual['s self]'.[11] Migration, by definition, incorporates the transfer of one's self to a foreign environment and the encounter with different peoples, cultures and identities. When people migrate, they often undergo a close encounter with another culture, leading to a range of issues, including identity crises and the development of personal insecurities. Ahmed et al. observe that research suggests that 'migrancy destabilizes identities [...] as they detach identity from place',[12] thereby creating nomadic identities. This is a critique of what can be called the 'worn-out assumption' of migration, which presumes that the spatio-cultural transition of the self is 'a linear process of integration, acculturation and assimilation'.[13] This view presupposes docile identities accepting and embracing the features and practices of the host environment without much resistance. However, Fortier argues that, on the contrary, 'displaced people deploy strategies of "dwelling" in the new environment' while 'actively engaging in shaping and negotiating their immediate circumstances to fit their own needs'.[14] That is, migrants consciously interact with their host environment and create an active, ever-changing relationship, based on the socio-cultural interplay between themselves and the new surroundings. Consequently, when studying migration we must consider the spatial, cultural and emotional relocation and needs of the self, and the consequent changes within the self. Ahmed et al. observe that 'although migrants often move across vast geographic distances, the greatest movement often occurs within the self'.[15] In late modernity, this geographical relocation, leading to destabilized identities, happens to many divided and disoriented individuals who have had to contend with the changes and uncertainties of the modern social world.[16]

---

11   Ibid., p.12.
12   S. Ahmed, C. Castaneda, A.-M. Fortier and M. Sheller, *Uprootings/Regroundings: Questions of Home and Migration* (Oxford: Berg, 2003), p.2.
13   Fortier, *Migrant Belongings*, p.19.
14   Ibid.
15   Ahmed et al., *Uprootings/Regroundings*, p.5.
16   A. D. Smith, *National Identity* (London: Penguin, 1991), p.17.

Sport-related migrations and migrants are no exceptions. We know that the relevance and scale of sport-related migrations are growing and so is the academic literature on the subject.[17] However, when I began this project I realized that there was a gap concerning the migratory experiences of Central and Eastern European athletes.[18] Most of the research centres on Western European countries and their athletes or athletes working in Western European countries. Interestingly, this gap regarding the contemporary migratory experiences of Central and Eastern Europeans is not exclusive to the sport literature. In migration literature more generally, there is a lack of research into and discussion of the experiences of current migrants from Central and Eastern Europe. Such studies as do exist are mainly survey-type investigations, exploring migratory macro or meso-structures.[19] While it is important to explore patterns of migration, in general, and in Central Europe, in particular, a survey-type data collection approach does not provide sufficient depth or pay appropriate heed to the personal issues and anxieties migrants actually face while abroad. The existence of this lacuna regarding the individual experiences, epic journeys and personal struggles that migrant players often undergo triggered and underpin this project.

17   See J. Bale and J. Maguire (eds), *The Global Sport Arena: Athletic Talent Migration in an Independent World* (London: Frank Cass, 1994); J. Magee and J. Sugden, 'The World at Their Feet: Professional Football and Labour Migration', *Journal of Sport and Social Issues*, vol. 26, no. 4 (2002), pp.421–37, p.421; M. Taylor, 'Global Players? Football, Migration and Globalization, c.1930–2000', *Historical Social Research*, vol. 31, no. 1 (2006), pp.7–30, p.7.

18   G. Molnar and J. Maguire, 'Hungarian Footballers on the Move: Issues of and Observations on the First Migratory Phase', *Sport in Society*, vol. 11, no. 1 (2008), pp.74–89, p.74.

19   C. Wallace and D. Stola, 'Introduction: Patterns of Migration in Central Europe', in C. Wallace and D. Stola (eds), *Patterns of Migration in Central Europe* (Basingstoke: Palgrave, 2001), pp.3–44. However, for a comprehensive account of contemporary Polish migrants and their experiences, see A. Triandafyllidou (ed.), *Contemporary Polish Migration in Europe: Complex Patterns of Movement and Settlement* (Lampeter: Edwin Mellen, 2006).

As a result of the enlargement of the EU – a process of regionalization – the cross-country movement of people, including athletes and coaches, has been changing.[20] The free movement of labour within the EU has impacted on migration patterns and, consequently, identities. Although, in the case of the participants in this study, we cannot properly talk of emerging identities, but rather of a re-emerging identity which has been triggered by the regrounding experiences of migration.[21]

The Participants

There is no need for a lengthy methodological discussion, but to facilitate a better understanding of this case study, a brief outline of information about the participants and of the method employed follows.

Participants ($n = 14$) were contacted through their club officials, to whom I had sent letters describing the study and requesting agreement for interviews to be conducted with individual footballers. Interviews took place at three professional football clubs in Hungary, whose managers had granted permission for the study to be undertaken. All of the players were volunteers and consisted exclusively of white male Hungarian professional footballers with extensive migratory experience. All of the participants had spent at least one season in a foreign elite, first or second, division team, but most of them had played abroad for several years and in more than one foreign country.[22] In other words, all of the players belong in

---

20   J. Maguire and D. Stead, 'Border Crossings: Soccer Labour Force Migration and the European Union', *International Review for the Sociology of Sport*, vol. 33, no.1 (1998), pp.59–73, p.59.

21   See Ahmed et al., *Uprootings/Regroundings*, p.1.

22   For further information on the migration patterns of Hungarian players, see G. Molnar, 'Mapping Migrations: Hungary Related Migrations of Professional Footballers after the Collapse of Communism', *Soccer & Society*, vol. 7, no. 4 (December 2006), pp.463–85, p.463.

the category of migrant since they moved from one country to another with the intention of residing in the country of destination for a specific period of time.[23] In terms of marital status, all the participants, except two, were married or engaged prior to moving abroad, which resulted in direct family support for most players. All of the footballers began playing at an early age and considered it to be the most important part of their lives. The personal details and impressions gained from the interviews indicated that the interviewees were mature (average age = 30 years), formally educated and had sufficient knowledge and self-awareness to understand and make sense of their own migratory experiences.

Verbal Data: Semi-Structured Long Interviews

Data were gathered through semi-structured long interviews. The long interview is a type of semi-structured interview that possesses all the general features of a semi-structured design,[24] but it enables the researcher to gain a deeper insight into social phenomena without extensive and intimate involvement in the life of the community under investigation. McCracken defines the long interview as follows:

> The long interview departs from participant observation insofar as it is intended to accomplish certain ethnographic perspectives without committing the investigator to intimate, repeated, and prolonged involvement in the life and community of the respondent. It departs from [focus] group methods of qualitative research [...] insofar as it is conducted between the investigator and a single respondent. It departs from the 'depth' interview practised by the psychological inquirer insofar as it is concerned with cultural categories and shared meanings rather than individual affective states.[25]

---

23   D. Jary and J. Jary, *Collins Dictionary: Sociology* (Glasgow: Harper Collins, 2000), p.385.

24   See, for example, T. May, *Social Research: Issues, Methods and Process* (3rd edn; Buckingham: Open University Press, 2001); U. Flick, *An Introduction to Qualitative Research* (London: Sage, 2002).

25   G. McCracken, *The Long Interview* (London: Sage, 1988), p.7.

That is, the long interview allows the researcher to achieve the above through a multi-step method of inquiry by going through stages of familiarization and defamiliarization.[26] As a corollary, one can argue that interviewing is an (inter)active data collection technique that gathers in-depth information about social interactions through the dialogue between an interviewer and an interviewee.[27] Hence, the data are not collected, in the traditional sense, but co-authored, meaning that conducting semi-structured interviews is not a passive process, but an inter-subjective enterprise.[28]

The analysis consisted of the transcripts and field notes – these were taken without interrupting the flow of the interview – being repeatedly read to achieve further familiarization with the data in attempting an empathetic perspective. This perspective was enhanced by theoretical coding that consists both of personal knowledge (familiarity) and disciplinary knowledge (manufacturing distance).[29] At the end of this analysis, the developed patterns and themes became the foundation of the interpretation which will be evidenced below in a discussion of the personal struggles to preserve Hungarian-ness.

Understanding Migrants

As a result of the analysis of interview data, national identity and the struggle of the participants with their national identity appeared to be a recurring theme. This is an issue that had been indicated by previous research

26   Ibid., pp.33–4.
27   See also J. Butt and G. Molnar, 'Involuntary Career Termination in Sport: A Case Study of the Process of Structurally Induced Failure', *Sport in Society*, vol. 12, no. 2 (March 2009), pp.240–57, p.240.
28   S. Kvale, *Interviews: An Introduction to Qualitative Research* (London: Sage, 1996), p.183.
29   N. K. Denzin and Y. S. Lincoln, *Strategies of Qualitative Inquiry* (Thousand Oaks, CA: Sage, 1998).

which had observed migration's effect on identity.[30] In fact, the relation between identity and migration is multi-fold, leading to the laborious process of uprooting and regrounding.[31] Therefore, what was interesting was the way in which Hungarian footballers reacted to the anxieties and challenges of migration, reactions which I could readily relate to and was in a good position to reflect on analytically as a consequence of my own status, being myself a migrant.

I would not argue that a researcher must be a migrant to understand migration, other migrants and their life experiences, but I would suggest, rather, on the basis of the empirical phase of this research, that having a considerable degree of sensitivity to the issues and insight into them helps. Having or acquiring migrant status does not directly assist the gaining of access to migrants, but it may help in accessing their experiences, including particularly the sensitive information and sometimes painful memories that they have. When I began interviewing participants, I was not fully aware of my status – as a fellow migrant – and the advantage (cultural capital) it would provide. However, I noticed during the data collection phase of the research that participants opened up more easily and often went into great depth in sharing migration-related personal information. Moreover, they often alluded to the 'common ground' they identified between themselves and me, and made statements such as: 'But you know yourself how it is'; 'I am sure you have had the same issues living in England'; and 'I don't think I need to tell you if you have lived abroad for so long'. I came to recognize the advantage afforded by my migrant status during the course of conducting interviews, including the potential significance of connecting with migrant participants on the level of shared experience. This migration-based common denominator factor emerges even more clearly in Fortier's work on *Migrant Belongings* (2000).[32]

---

30   See, for example, D. Stead and J. Maguire, 'Rite de Passage or Passage to Riches? The Motivation and Objectives of Nordic/Scandinavian Players in English League Soccer', *Journal of Sport and Social Issues*, vol. 24, no. 1 (2000), pp.36–60, p.36; Fortier, *Migrant Belongings*.

31   See Ahmed et al., *Uprootings/Regroundings*, p.1.

32   Fortier, *Migrant Belongings*.

Fortier investigated an Italian community in London and was concerned about being able to gain access to and be accepted by migrant Italians. However, when she was in the field, after making initial contacts, she swiftly gained acceptance and access because of her status as another migrant in London. It is worth quoting her observation at length:

> As it turned out, being Italian did not really matter for my integration within London Italian associative life. Initially, it did come as a surprise to the people I came in contact with that I, a non-Italian French-Canadian from Québec, was [conducting...] research on Italians in London. But this was not the basis of exclusion [...]. My ethnic identity was part of negotiations between myself and the men and women I interacted with in order to 'locate' me in relation to them. The outcome was that we met on the terrain of our common status as foreigners in Britain [...]. I was included in the folds of this cultural minority. And it seemed to override Italianness.[33]

In a similar vein to Fortier, I would argue that observation of this nature has multiple methodological implications regarding migration and ethnic studies. Although Fortier acknowledges a range of potential implications, it is, indeed, the cultural capital accumulated through shared identities as and with migrants that was relevant to my research, without which I could not have achieved the desired richness of data, which affords insight into the personal feelings and struggles of migrant Hungarian footballers.[34] One of the key issues was related to preserving national identity, which is discussed below.

National Identity Rediscovered

Why is national identity such an important aspect of migrations? According to Smith, a sense of national identity is a powerful means of defining and locating individual selves in the world.[35] This shared and unique culture

33   Ibid, p.7.
34   Ibid.
35   Smith, *National Identity*, p.17.

enables us to know 'who we are' in the modern world. And, by rediscovering our culture, we 'rediscover' ourselves, the 'authentic self', which is often taken for granted. Hungarian players in this study unequivocally admitted that they rediscovered their own culture and national identity as they were facing a range of challenges whilst abroad.

All the participants indicated that the most demanding aspect of being a migrant was being away from home, with all its implications, such as missing friends, family, and Hungarian cuisine, and withstanding the lure of Hungary and of their town or city of origin. In addition to these issues, participants expressed their attitude to the host environment. One player explained:

> Austrians are nice, but cold. I could never get used to that. I would never be able to live in a country like Austria, although it is much more advanced. The standard of living is quite high and they are well off. But neither I nor my girlfriend could get used to that kind of coldness. I would not be able to live in Austria, or in any other country, for that matter, because I and my Hungarian mentality would not change enough to settle somewhere else.

He also specified that, although Austria represents more advanced social and perhaps footballing conditions, he never considered it as his 'home' and would not think of settling there. Stead and Maguire made similar observations regarding the theme of 'feeling at home' in the host environment when claiming that Scandinavian footballers 'retained a strong commitment to their [cultural] roots'.[36] In other words, home is not something we simply leave behind; rather, migration entails the (re-)creation and regrounding of home in the host environment.[37] Homing desires[38] are consequently achieved by 'physically or symbolically (re-)constituting spaces which provide some kind of ontological security in the con-

36   Stead and Maguire, 'Rite de Passage or Passage to Riches?', p.55.
37   Ahmed et al., *Uprootings/Regroundings*.
38   See A. Brah, *Cartographies of Diaspora: Contested Identities* (London: Routledge, 1996).

text of migration'.[39] Although the process of regrounding one's home may indeed lead to achieving a higher degree of ontological security, it does not necessarily mean that migrants themselves feel 'at home'.

Correspondingly, regardless of the host country and the quality of reception in it, all the interviewees pointed out that Hungary or a specific town or city in Hungary constituted *home* throughout their foreign careers. To one of the participants, home was 'Hungary, evidently. I felt I was a total stranger [abroad]'. In a similar vein, another footballer expressed that he never felt at home abroad: 'Nothing meant real home. The place [abroad] where I went home to, and, unfortunately stayed alone, meant a medium level of security'. Although he liked the host country and intended to spend some more time there, he would not consider settling there:

> Home is always Hungary. Despite the fact that I would love to go back to [abroad]... and stay there for a longer period, I could not leave Hungary forever because I am a Hungarian. I do not have any other reasons. I love Hungary.

Others too admitted that: 'I love [the foreign natives]... but, regardless, I love to be at home [in Hungary]'. Although, most of the players meant Hungary when they talked about 'home', some of the players were more particular about the location of home, which reflected a certain degree of *Heimat*.[40] As one of the participants expressed it: 'To me Szombathely [a city in the north-western part of Hungary] is always *home*'. Another demonstrated the same sense of *Heimat* when specifying the location of 'home': 'When I am done [with football] then it is Pécs [a city in the south-western part of Hungary]. I am from Pécs and I want to go back there. I try to direct my life to end up there'.

All of these quotations illustrate that Hungarian players, regardless of the experience they underwent in the host country and club, want to return

39   A.-M. Fortier, 'Making Home: Queer Migrations and Motions of Attachment', in S. Ahmed, C. Castaneda, A.-M. Fortier and M. Sheller, *Uprootings/Regroundings: Questions of Home and Migration* (Oxford: Berg, 2003), pp.115–35, p.115.

40   J. Maguire, 'Blade Runners: Canadian Migrants and Global Ice-Hockey Trials', *Journal of Sport and Social Issues*, vol. 20, no. 3 (1996), pp.335–60, p.335; J. Maguire, *Global Sport: Identities, Societies, Civilizations* (Cambridge: Polity, 1999).

and settle in Hungary. This was reinforced by the future plans of the participants, most of whom admitted that they would like to have a few more years of foreign football, but all of them wanted ultimately to return to and settle in Hungary. It was said that: 'I would like to spend next year abroad and come back [to Hungary] after that and do something football-related'. Another footballer mentioned that: 'I will return to Szombathely after my career ends abroad'. One of the interviewees also expressed his intention of remaining in Hungary and Hungarian football: 'I am thirty years old. I would like to stay here [the south-eastern part of Hungary]. I still have two and a half years on my contract and I want to spend that here'.

The common desire of Hungarian players to return and settle in Hungary can be linked to the manner in which they behaved and perceived themselves in the host environment. As has been observed, most of the footballers never truly felt at home in the host country and Hungary, or a particular city or town, constituted home even for those players who had positive experiences abroad, such as better pay and/or more advanced footballing circumstances.[41] The feeling of being both culturally and spatially displaced prompted Hungarian players to talk extensively about 'home' and their missing what used to constitute 'home'. The frequent reference to feeling 'homeless' whilst abroad suggests a degree of anxiety with which participants in this study had to cope. Boym explains this as follows:

> When we are home, we don't talk about it … To feel at home is to know that things are in their place and so are you; it is a state of mind that doesn't depend on an actual location. The object of longing, then, is not really a place called home but this sense of intimacy with the world.[42]

This sense of intimacy or, in fact, the lack of it is directly linked to the way Hungarian players depicted their private lives and sense of Hungarian-ness – their national identity – whilst abroad.[43] All of the participants noted that they remained Hungarians and that their sense of national identity

---

41   Cf. Stead and Maguire, 'Rite de Passage or Passage to Riches?'.
42   S. Boym, *The Future of Nostalgia* (New York: Basic, 2001), p.251.
43   See also Maguire, *Global Sport*.

never declined. In fact, most of the players pointed out that their degree of Hungarian-ness was heightened and they became hyper-sensitive and somewhat nostalgic about Hungary and related issues whilst abroad. A player reflected upon his attitude towards Hungary as follows:

> I am very proud to be a Hungarian and whenever I was asked I immediately said that I was a Hungarian. It happened that some people had negative opinions about Hungarian football and Hungary ... but I was like a defence lawyer and told them all about the circumstances.

Another illustrated the strengthening of his Hungarian-ness in this fashion:

> I became really patriotic. This really emerged in me. I was very sensitive when someone said something bad and was proud when there was something good about Hungary. Everything interested me about Hungary ... I was proud of everything good that happened in Hungary.

This strengthened national identity was present in all the footballers. They admitted that spending some time in a foreign country made them re-evaluate Hungarian culture: 'There [abroad] you can really learn to appreciate the value of Hungarian food. One night I just drove around [my home town] and I was thinking whether people liked and appreciated this city or just get up in the morning and go to work?' They clearly explained the way they came to re-evaluate Hungary and their Hungarian-ness:

> I would say that its [Hungary's] value has grown. When I get on a bus I feel differently because I see the things of the city. They are different. In the old days, when I went to school by bus and I got on that bus, I took it for granted. Now I see it a bit differently... now I am so far from it I am very happy if I can take a walk in that park and sit on that bench. Simply, its value has grown.

One player added that: 'We go to a Hungarian restaurant when my wife has a birthday or name-day. That is a very good feeling'. It was also specified that, although footballers had to accept and accommodate to the rules and customs of the host club, they tended to resist some part of the foreign culture and assumed an escapist attitude in their private lives through creating a small Hungarian cocoon or carapace in the host setting. Boym explains that 'ordinary exiles [and migrants] often become artists of their lives, remaking themselves and their second home with great integrity [...] this doesn't mean that there is no nostalgia for the homeland, only that this kind of nostalgia precludes restoration of the past'.[44] This restoration meant the regrounding of Hungarian culture and cultural practices. A participant expressed this as follows: 'I eat Hungarian food and live like a Hungarian man. Nothing has changed in this regard. So I am in a small cocoon abroad'. He also mentioned that: 'We eat Hungarian dishes at home'. Then another noted his intention of preserving his Hungarian-ness abroad: 'They [the football club] really try to force upon me this [foreign] stuff [food] but I cannot and do not want to switch. I would go bananas. My body would not know what's up!'

Based upon the evidence presented, it can be observed that migrant Hungarian footballers always considered Hungary as home, never intended to settle in foreign countries, developed an enhanced sense of Hungarian-ness abroad and (re-)created and perpetuated a little Hungary in the host environment.[45] These observed phenomena outline a process which migrant Hungarian footballers underwent whilst abroad. This process, illustrated by Diagram 11.1 and discussed below, can be termed rediscovering national identity – Hungarian-ness in this particular case.

According to Anthony Smith, 'a sense of national identity provides a powerful means of defining and locating individual selves in the world'.[46] This shared and unique culture enables us 'to know "who we are" in the contemporary world'.[47] Each nation is assumed to have a specific identity, which is a part of the culture and explains what it means to belong to that nation.[48] When people migrate, they often go through identity crises or

44   Boym, *The Future of Nostalgia*, p.252.
45   See the typology devised by Molnar and Maguire, 'Hungarian Footballers on the Move', p.86.
46   Smith, *National Identity*, p.17.
47   Ibid.
48   M. Pickering, *Stereotyping: The Politics of Representation* (New York: Palgrave, 2001).

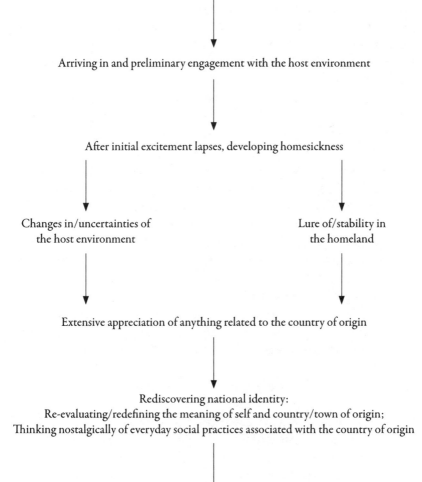

Diagram 11.1. The process of rediscovering national identity

develop personal insecurities in facing other cultures. A way of coping with cultural challenges is to 'rediscover ourselves' through our original culture. In other words, 'by rediscovering ... [our] culture, we "rediscover" ourselves, the "authentic self"... [as] it has happened to many divided and disoriented individuals who have had to contend with the vast changes and uncertainties of the modern world'.[49]

Migration led to a crisis in the identity of Hungarian footballers or, as Giddens calls it, in their ontological security.[50] Because of the anxieties of migration that had pierced the protective carapace of Hungarian football-ers in this study, they developed a self-defence mechanism to withstand the challenges of the foreign environment. Consequently, they reclaimed their home which was part of their regrounding themselves. This aspect of regrounding, Ahmed et al. call it 'homing', is a process of re-establishing the home while abroad.[51] They argue that home is not something that you leave behind; rather, it can be uprooted and, when required, regrounded, meaning that we can take our home with us. This symbolizes that a home is more than just material objects and through the process of homing we can reclaim and repossess habits, objects and histories which have been uprooted. By regrounding our home we create what Hoffman called 'soils of significance', which help us reduce the anxieties brought on by migra-tion and restore the protective cocoon which may have been damaged during migration.[52]

After presenting the Hungarian footballers' dispositions in the host countries, it can be argued that they underwent a process of rediscovering themselves and their national identities in order to cope with the challenges presented by the modern football world and foreign cultures. Diagram 11.1, based on interview-generated evidence, illustrates this process, through which they developed a sense of amplified national identity, which, in tandem with the regrounding of their home, assisted the preservation of their self-integrity and the restitution of their ontological security.

49   Smith, *National Identity*, p.17.
50   Giddens, *Modernity and Self-Identity*, Ch. 2.
51   Ahmed et al., *Uprootings/Regroundings*, p.9.
52   E. Hoffman, *Lost in Translation: Life in a New Language* (London: Minerva, 1989).

The process of rediscovering national identity begins with the actual migration of individuals who move away from their country and culture of origin and attempt to settle in a foreign host environment. In doing so, they engage with the host environment in many different ways and at varying levels. The type and degree of engagement is unique to the migrant and his or her migratory circumstances and can either facilitate or hinder the potential assimilation of the migrant into the host environment. In this study, as the footballers indicated, after the initial excitement, prompted by factors such as new accommodation, new culture and people, migrants tend to reflect on their position and develop severe homesickness. As Boym observes: 'when the initial hardships are over [...] the immigrant can afford the luxury of leisurely reflection.'[53] This reflection is induced by, on the one hand, challenges in and uncertainties about the host environment and, on the other, the lure of and stability in the original home land.[54] Footballers reacted to the blend of these impacts by developing an extensive admiration for anything related to their country of origin – food especially appeared to be a marker of national identity, through which they rediscovered their original national identity, and which had been taken for granted prior to migration.[55] In other words, instead of assimilating into the host culture, they held on to and revisited their original cultural values and practices.

In the case of footballers, rediscovering national identity meant re-evaluating and redefining, that is, regrounding themselves and their country of origin. This laborious process of regrounding homes and lives[56] was manifested in thinking nostalgically about everyday social practices in the home environment, such as travelling on the bus and sitting on a bench in Hungary, and appreciating national cuisine. The way for Hungarian footballers to cope with and survive the host culture – a type of self-defence mechanism – was to create a nationalistic, nostalgic cocoon in the host environment in which they could preserve their rhapsodic[57] national identity

---

53   Boym, *The Future of Nostalgia*, p.254.
54   Maguire, *Global Sport*.
55   See also Stead and Maguire, 'Rite de Passage or Passage to Riches?'
56   Ahmed et al., *Uprootings/Regroundings*.
57   The word 'rhapsodic' is used in the sense of expressing and experiencing powerful emotions. See R. Teleky, *Hungarian Rhapsodies: Essays on Ethnicity, Identity and Culture* (Seattle: University of Washington Press, 1997).

and escape from the realm of foreignness. Ahmed et al. observe that 'for those who have left their homes, a nostalgic relation to both the past and home might become part of the lived reality in the present.'[58] That is, participants in this study regrounded their home, which became their sanctuary, representing Hungary, and themselves, in the foreign terrain; a place to which they could retreat and find solace and security in familiar national elements such as language, food, photographs and customs. They (re)created their home, a 'private enclave where one can be free and in control of one's life',[59] in order to regain, at least partially, the intimacy of their original dwelling. However, after returning to their country of origin, this rhapsodic nationalistic sentiment began to decline and then, as anxieties triggered by foreignness were fading away, was reduced to the level participants had had prior to migrating.

A similar observation to the above with regard to Hungarian migrants creating a culturally protective cocoon can be found in a piece of exile literature, in a novel by John Marlyn.[60] *Putzi, I Love You, You Little Square* (1981) is set in Canada (Winnipeg specifically), within a Hungarian migrant community, and tells a story about a precocious talking foetus on the verge of being born. The work is ostensibly about the quest of the (male) foetus to find a proper father for himself, but behind this conceit there lies a meta-narrative. The foetus, Putzi, speaks only English, but perceives himself as Hungarian in the womb of his mother. It can be argued that Putzi represents the second generation of those Hungarian migrants who had been living in a hermetically and culturally sealed Hungarian community (an effective and affective womb). They themselves struggle with their own identity, as they still think of themselves as Hungarians, but simultaneously feel the allure of the dominant identity. To succumb to the latter would also be a way of escaping certain Hungary-related stereotypes. The tension lies in the process of 'giving birth', which is, in reality, a re-birth

---

58   Ahmed et al., *Uprootings/Regroundings*, p.9.
59   M. Csikszentmihalyi and E. Rochberg-Halton, *The Meaning of Things* (Cambridge: Cambridge University Press, 1981).
60   J. Marlyn, *Putzi, I Love You, You Little Square* (Toronto: Coach House, 1981).

(leaping out of their cultural cocoon) for that Hungarian community, through extensively embracing the dominant culture and reforming their identity. The anxiety derives from the first generation, which is afraid of leaving the (Hungarian) 'womb' (protective carapace) and integrating into dominant cultural practices.

Participants in this study displayed similar attitudes in terms of being reluctant fully to engage with the host culture. Therefore, despite the fact that the model represented by Diagram 11.1 has been developed on the basis of data collected from migrant Hungarian footballers, it may be argued that other Hungarian migrants have the tendency to exhibit similar dispositions to what is described by Marlyn. This observation would support the conclusions of other migration-related research, which has already claimed that, in relative terms, Hungarians are not significantly inclined to migrate, nor, for those who do migrate, to settle in the host country, in comparison with the populations of other Central European countries.[61] Other sport migration-related research, however, has detected comparable migratory behaviour patterns. For instance, Maguire and Stead came to the conclusion regarding cricket migrants that: 'Home for most of the players is still their native country'.[62] Furthermore, Stead and Maguire made the following observation regarding Scandinavian migrant footballers in England: 'The Nordic/Scandinavian players may have been crossing geographical boundaries, but culturally, they were not doing so'.[63] These examples indicate that other migrants also maintain strong ties with their culture of origin. This practice is not exclusive to athletes and athletic talent migration,[64] as Boym makes the following observation regarding migrants in general: 'Sometimes the immigrants themselves, particularly those who

---

61   See, for example, Wallace and Stola, 'Introduction: Patterns of Migration in Central Europe'.

62   J. Maguire and D. Stead, 'Far Pavilions? Cricket Migrants, Foreign Sojourns and Contested Identities', *International Review for the Sociology of Sport*, vol. 31, no. 1 (1996), pp.1–24, p.13.

63   Stead and Maguire, 'Rite de Passage or Passage to Riches?', p.55.

64   See E. Probyn, *Outside Belongings* (London: Routledge, 1996); Fortier, *Migrant Belongings*.

came to the developed countries not for political but for economic reasons
and were not subjects of persecution, reconstitute a mini nation-state on
foreign soil.'[65] Hungarian migrant footballers in this study followed the
pattern suggested by Boym and did not merely 'retain their original roots',
but developed an amplified sense of Hungarian-ness, built a mini nation-
state and lived in a culturally sealed cocoon or carapace, (re-)creating and
regrounding a strong sense of little Hungary.

Conclusion

Migration, by definition, incorporates the transfer of oneself (and one's
self) to a foreign environment and the encounter with different peoples,
identities and cultures. That is, migration studies often consider various
degrees of cultural encounters, the clash of various local, regional and global
identities and/or habituses.[66] In this chapter, I have discussed the way in
which Hungarian footballers commonly react to the host environment
in private life, which reflects the fact that they possess well-functioning
cultural self-defence mechanisms.

Interviewees indicated that their national identity, their 'Hungarian-
ness', was rediscovered abroad. This happens regularly with migrants who
learn to re-evaluate their self-identity in a foreign environment.[67] Nevertheless, this was not the only attitude observed in this case. Participants
also indicated that they tended to create a Hungarian cocoon in the host
environment which was an isolated setting, a refuge, where they could
eliminate the feeling of foreignness. That is, instead of embracing the host
environment, and going through a process of integration, acculturation and

---

65   Boym, *The Future of Nostalgia*, p.254.
66   See N. Elias, *The Germans* (New York: Columbia University Press, 1996), p.2; Castles
      and Miller, *The Age of Migration*.
67   See also Stead and Maguire, 'Rite de Passage or Passage to Riches?'

assimilation, Hungarian footballers guarded their rhapsodic Hungarian-ness and tried to eliminate the impact of foreign culture on their private life. This behaviour pattern is a way of coping with the anxieties brought on by modernity and migratory social situations, and may also be charac-terized by a historically rooted, amplified self-defence mechanism, which takes effect when Hungarian players are forced outside their comfort zone of Hungarian-ness. The social discomfort experienced by the participants launches the process of rediscovering national identity, which was char-acteristic of the Hungarian footballers interviewed. This disposition may have been triggered by 'residues of very vigorous defensive processes [...] which have become dissociated from their original situations [...] and have developed into permanent character traits',[68] character traits which Hungar-ian footballers tend to display while living and working abroad.

Since the data collected is limited to generalizing the observed behav-iour pattern to Hungarian male footballers, it would be an intriguing project to explore further the possible historical roots that may have triggered this self-defence mechanism and whether this can be observed with regard to other sports or, perhaps, to the entire Hungarian population. In this way, the findings of this research could be extended and particular aspects of Hungarian national identity, which have often been questioned and deemed questionable in recent times, could be further illuminated.[69]

Investigations of this kind might be able to establish that it is not only Hungarian footballers who rediscover and reinforce their original national identity and learn to view it nostalgically through the 'rose-tinted glasses' of geographical distance in order to cope with the challenges of the modern world and the host country. This would be of importance in the contemporary era of globalization, in which local and national identities are often seen to be subjugated by globally conveyed identities, with their

68 A. Freud, *The Ego and the Mechanism of Defence* (rev. edn; London: Hogarth, 1968), p.33.

69 See, for instance, G. Csepeli, *National Identity in Contemporary Hungary* (New York: Columbia University Press, 1997); G. Kosztolanyi, 'Hungarian Identity, Globalization and EU Accession', *Central Europe Review*, vol. 2, no. 6 (2000), <http://www.ce-review.org/00/6/essay6.html> (accessed 1 June 2009).

concomitant and locally experienced global uncertainties. That is, in the era of modernity, 'the question of "How shall we live?" has to be answered in day-to-day decisions about how to behave, what to wear and what to eat – and many other things',[70] driven by the individual's ever changing social circumstances.

Bibliography

Ahmed, S., C. Castaneda, A.-M. Fortier and M. Sheller (eds). *Uprootings/Regroundings: Questions of Home and Migration* (Oxford: Berg, 2003).

Albrow, M. *The Global Age* (London: Polity Press, 1996).

Appadurai, A. 'Disjuncture and Difference in the Global Cultural Economy', *Theory, Culture and Society*, vol. 7, no. 2 (1990), pp.295–310.

Bale, J. and J. Maguire (eds). *The Global Sport Arena: Athletic Talent Migration in an Independent World* (London: Frank Cass, 1994).

Boym, S. *The Future of Nostalgia* (New York: Basic, 2001).

Brah, A. *Cartographies of Diaspora: Contested Identities* (London: Routledge, 1996).

Butt, J. and G. Molnar. 'Involuntary Career Termination in Sport: A Case Study of the Process of Structurally Induced Failure', *Sport in Society*, vol. 12, no. 2 (March 2009), pp.240–57.

Castles, S. and M. J. Miller, *The Age of Migration: International Population in the Modern World* (3rd edn; Basingstoke: Palgrave Macmillan, 2003).

Csepeli, G. *National Identity in Contemporary Hungary* (New York: Columbia University Press, 1997).

Csikszentmihalyi, M. and E. Rochberg-Halton. *The Meaning of Things* (Cambridge: Cambridge University Press, 1981).

Denzin, N. K. and Y. S. Lincoln. *Strategies of Qualitative Inquiry* (Thousand Oaks, CA: Sage, 1998).

Edgar, B., J. Doherty and H. Meert. *Immigration and Homelessness in Europe* (Bristol: Polity, 2004).

Elias, N. *The Germans* (New York: Columbia University Press, 1996).

70   Giddens, *Modernity and Self-Identity*, p.14.

Flick, U. *An Introduction to Qualitative Research* (London: Sage, 2002).

Fortier, A.-M. *Migrant Belongings: Memory, Space, Identity* (Oxford: Berg, 2000).

——. 'Making Home: Queer Migrations and Motions of Attachment', in S. Ahmed, C. Castaneda, A.-M. Fortier and M. Sheller (eds), *Uprootings/Regroundings: Questions of Home and Migration* (Oxford: Berg, 2003), pp.115–35.

Freud, A. *The Ego and the Mechanism of Defence* (rev. ed.; London: Hogarth, 1968).

Giddens, A. *Modernity and Self-Identity: Self and Society in the Late Modern Age* (Cambridge: Polity, 1990).

Hoffman, E. *Lost in Translation: Life in a New Language* (London: Minerva, 1989).

Jary, D. and J. Jary. *Collins Dictionary: Sociology* (Glasgow: Harper Collins, 2000).

Kosic, A. 'Migrant Identities' in A. Triandafyllidou (ed.), *Contemporary Polish Migration in Europe: Complex Patterns of Movement and Settlement* (Lampeter: Edwin Mellen, 2006), pp.245–66.

Kosztolanyi, G. 'Hungarian Identity, Globalization and EU Accession', *Central Europe Review*, vol. 2, no. 6 (2000), <http://www.ce-review.org/00/6/essay6.html> (accessed 1 June 2009).

Kvale, S. *Interviews: An Introduction to Qualitative Research* (London: Sage, 1996).

Magee, J. and J. Sugden. 'The World at their Feet: Professional Football and Labour Migration', *Journal of Sport and Social Issues*, vol. 26, no. 4 (2002), pp.421–37.

Maguire, J. 'Blade Runners: Canadian Migrants and Global Ice-Hockey Trials', *Journal of Sport and Social Issues*, vol. 20, no. 3 (1996), pp.335–60.

——. *Global Sport: Identities, Societies, Civilizations* (Cambridge: Polity, 1999).

——and D. Stead. 'Far Pavilions? Cricket Migrants, Foreign Sojourns and Contested Identities', *International Review for the Sociology of Sport*, vol. 31, no. 1 (1996), pp.1–24.

——. 'Border Crossings: Soccer Labour Force Migration and the European Union', *International Review for the Sociology of Sport*, vol. 33, no. 1 (1998), pp.59–73.

Marlyn, J. *Putzi, I Love You, You Little Square* (Toronto: Coach House, 1981).

May, T. *Social Research: Issues, Methods and Process* (3rd edn; Buckingham: Open University Press, 2001).

McCracken, G. *The Long Interview* (London: Sage, 1988).

Molnar, G. 'Mapping Migrations: Hungary Related Migrations of Professional Footballers after the Collapse of Communism', *Soccer & Society*, vol. 7, no. 4 (December 2006), pp.463–85.

——and J. Maguire. 'Hungarian Footballers on the Move: Issues of and Observations on the First Migratory Phase', *Sport in Society*, vol. 11, no.1 (2008), pp.74–89.

Pickering, M. *Stereotyping: The Politics of Representation* (New York: Palgrave, 2001).

Probyn, E. *Outside Belongings* (London: Routledge, 1996).

Smith, A. D. *National Identity* (London: Penguin, 1991).

Stead, D. and J. Maguire. 'Rite de Passage or Passage to Riches? The Motivation and Objectives of Nordic/Scandinavian Players in English League Soccer', *Journal of Sport and Social Issues*, vol. 24, no. 1 (2000), pp.36–60.

Taylor, M. 'Global Players? Football, Migration and Globalization, c.1930–2000', *Historical Social Research*, vol. 31, no. 1 (2006), pp.7–30.

Teleky, R. *Hungarian Rhapsodies: Essays on Ethnicity, Identity and Culture* (Seattle: University of Washington Press, 1997).

Triandafyllidou, A. (ed.) *Contemporary Polish Migration in Europe: Complex Patterns of Movement and Settlement* (Lampeter: Edwin Mellen, 2006).

Wallace, C. and D. Stola. 'Introduction: Patterns of Migration in Central Europe', in C. Wallace and D. Stola (eds), *Patterns of Migration in Central Europe* (Basingstoke: Palgrave, 2001), pp.3–44.

DILWYN PORTER

Chapter 12
Cornwall and Rugby Union:
Sport and Identity in a Place Apart

Writing in 2000, a Cornish schoolgirl summed it up neatly. 'Cornwall', she explained, 'is a separate place, cut off from England by the [River] Tamar, the rest surrounded by sea. We have our own music, our own festivals and events, and our own culture'. The Cornish people also had their own language, rescued by a small but determined minority.[1] There were echoes here of the nineteenth-century schoolboy, asked to describe Cornwall's location, who answered: 'he's kidged to a furren country by the top hand'.[2] At the start of the twenty-first century Cornwall remains 'kidged' (stuck) to 'furren' (foreign) England, and through England to the rest of the United Kingdom, but its past has been characterized by the persistence of difference. This is rooted in 'the Cornish paradox' whereby Cornwall is both an English county and, for some, the territorial space inhabited by a Celtic nation.[3]

At various times rugby has allowed the Cornish to show that they are different from their English neighbours. In 1908, when Cornwall won the English county championship for the first time, there was an explosion of quasi-patriotic fervour, 'almost as if a land – or a very old nation – was

1   F. Coles, 'Why Cornwall Is Special to Me', in P. Payton (ed.), *Cornwall For Ever! Kernow Bys Vyken!* (Truro: Cornwall Heritage Trust, 2000), p.228.

2   Cited in P. Payton, *The Making of Modern Cornwall: Historical Experience and the Persistence of 'Difference'* (Redruth: Dyllansow Truran, 1992), p.93.

3   See B. Deacon, D. Cole and G. Tregidga, *Mebyon Kernow and Cornish Nationalism* (Cardiff: Welsh Academic Press, 2003) pp.1–13.

rediscovering itself'.[4] The crowds that followed the Cornish team in the late 1980s and 1990s, when it enjoyed success in the same competition, seemed to behave in much the same way as their Edwardian predecessors. They sang 'Trelawny', the Cornish anthem, and cheered when a giant pasty (Cornwall's contribution to English fast food) was tied to the crossbar. They also waved the black and white flag of St Piran, which had been adopted in the late twentieth century to signify Cornwall as a place apart.

Geography was an important influence. Cornwall's remote location has underpinned the persistence of difference, especially in the political sphere where centre-periphery relations are mainly determined. The county's status as a duchy under the English crown dates from an accommodation reached in the fourteenth century which allowed for a degree of autonomy, symbolized in Cornwall by the privileges granted to tin miners via Stannary law.[5] As the state grew more powerful, the erosion of peripheral autonomy generated resentment and resistance. 'If the national movement had not survived and grown', observed Gwynfor Evans in the context of Wales, 'the nation of Cymru could have been Britished out of existence'.[6] Though resistance in Cornwall has generally taken cultural rather than political forms, the existence of *Mebyon Kernow* (MK), founded in 1951, is an important indicator of difference bred, at least in part, by peripheralism. 'No other apparently English county', as MK's historians have observed, 'has been the setting for a permanent political party demanding territorial devolution and some form of autonomy'.[7]

One of the problems of communities on the peripheries of modern states is how to achieve visibility at the centre. Being out of sight has often meant being out of mind. The condescending entry in the 1884 edition of the *Encyclopaedia Britannica* – 'for Wales: see England' – was indicative

---

4   T. Salmon, *The First Hundred Years: The Story of Rugby Football in Cornwall* (Illogan: Cornish Rugby Football Union, 1983), p.7.

5   Deacon, *Cornwall*, pp.98–9; Payton, *Making of Modern Cornwall*, pp.50–2; Payton, *Cornwall*, pp.84–6.

6   G. Evans, *The Fight for Welsh Freedom* (Talybont: Y Lolfa, 2000), p.124.

7   Deacon, Cole and Tregidga, *Mebyon Kernow*, p.2.; on peripheralism, see Payton, *Making of Modern Cornwall*, pp.7–40.

of this kind of metropolitan thinking.[8] So too, a hundred years later, was the tendency, in regional planning and the provision of public services, to disregard Cornish claims for separate treatment based on cultural difference and territorial integrity. The so-called 'Devonwall' project of the 1990s, which sought to create a single regional entity from England's two most south-westerly counties, trampled on Cornish sensitivities. Statistical invisibility, arising from the habit of aggregating totals for Cornwall and Devon, also prompted resentment, not least because it prejudiced Cornwall's case for funding from the European Union.[9]

Rugby could not address these essentially political concerns but it helped to make Cornwall more visible 'upcountry' and especially in London. After the 1998 final, which Cornwall lost, a local newspaper reported that there was 'a sense of achievement, of having shown the Cornish flag to the English'.[10] Though it was an 'all-England' competition, the championship seems to have been especially important for counties remote from the metropolis.[11] As the most distant of all competing counties, the competition meant more to Cornwall than to any of its rivals, according to the Cornwall Rugby Football Union (CRFU).[12] A review of the evidence, not merely relating to matches that Cornwall played but to the exuberant exhibitions of Cornishness that accompanied them, suggests that this claim was justified. 'In Cornwall', as Andy Seward has argued, 'rugby football [...] has been imbued from the beginning with Cornish meaning'.[13]

8   K. O. Morgan, *Rebirth of a Nation: Wales 1880–1980* (Oxford: Oxford University Press, 1981), p.3.

9   See P. Payton, 'Territory and Identity', in P. Payton (ed.), *Cornwall since the War* (Redruth: Institute of Cornish Studies / Dyllansow Truran, 1993), pp.224–52; also Deacon, Cole and Tregidga, *Mebyon Kernow*, pp.85–7; Deacon, *Cornwall*, pp.224–7.

10 *Cornishman* (Penzance), 23 April 1998, p.8.

11 See C. B. Powell and E. W. Moses, *Durham County Rugby Union: Sixty Years Records of the County Fifteen* (Newcastle-upon-Tyne: Andrew Reid, 1936), p.200.

12 K. Pelmear, *Rugby in the Duchy: an Official History of the Game in Cornwall* (Falmouth: Cornwall Rugby Football Union, 1960), p.71.

13 See A. Seward, 'Cornish Rugby and Cultural Identity: a Socio-Historical Perspective', *Cornish Studies*, (2nd series), no. 5 (1997), pp.164–79; also in *The Sports Historian*, vol. 18, no. 2 (1998), pp.78–94.

1908 and All That

Football in a recognizably modern form arrived in Cornwall in the 1870s just as the county's industrial economy passed its peak. That rugby prevailed owes much to the influence of English public schools. The Redruth club was formed in 1875 by a local banker who had come down from Marlborough and a fellow enthusiast who had learned the game at Clifton, schools where the handling code prevailed. However, though the influence of public-school old boys was critical, there were not enough of them to keep the game to themselves. It was necessary, therefore, to undertake some missionary work by introducing rugby to miners, fishermen and other Cornish working men. A pre-existing tradition of folk football, known as 'hurling' in Cornwall, may have helped prepare the way.[14] The basis for rugby as a cross-class sporting activity was thus established in Cornwall at an early stage in the game's development. Cornish popular culture, shaped for working men by the physicality of hard labour, readily assimilated a tough physical-contact sport.

Cornwall fielded a representative fifteen for the first time in 1883, but did not make a significant mark for some time. Though the English county championship started in 1888, it was not until 1892 that Cornwall entered and a further eight years before a match was won.[15] Cornish interest in rugby before the championship season of 1907–1908 appears to have focused primarily on local rivalries. 'The principle of hating your next-door neighbour held good all over Cornwall', the Cornish-born historian A. L. Rowse later recalled. Penryn and Falmouth were 'at daggers drawn', and the mining centres of Redruth and Camborne nurtured 'the most notorious dislike of all'.[16] This ensured that matches between rival clubs were fiercely contested. The Falmouth-based *Cornish Echo*, after a match at Redruth, complained

14   Seward, 'Cornish Rugby', pp.166–8.
15   For Cornwall's playing record, see Salmon, *First Hundred Years*, pp.115–20. For a history of the competition, see O. L. Owen, *The History of the Rugby Football Union* (London: Rugby Football Union / Playfair, 1955), pp.322–30.
16   A. L. Rowse, *A Cornish Childhood: Autobiography of a Cornishman* (London: Grey Arrow, 1942; edn cited 1962), p.21.

'of the unfair treatment meted out to the Falmouth team by the Redruth players and a large section of their supporters'.[17] Rugby-related violence on the way to and from matches was not unknown. In 1908, two Newlyn fishermen were attacked on a train by seven men from St Ives shouting 'Let's kill 'em!'[18] In Cornwall, it seems, behaviour both on and off the field was similar to that found in other places where rugby was embedded in working-class culture and buttressed by intense local rivalries.[19]

That Cornwall had a robust rugby culture could not be denied. It was the county championship of 1908, however, that cemented the relationship between rugby and identity. By then the industrial society that had largely defined Cornishness in the mid-nineteenth century was in retreat. Copper mining had virtually disappeared; tin mining, declining from the 1870s, was in a precarious state. Meanwhile Cornwall's fishing industry fell away as the pilchard abandoned its coastal waters and competition for mackerel intensified.[20] New industries were developing, notably clay and shipbuilding, but only partially compensated for what had been lost. Tourism was also beginning to make an impact, encouraged by the Great Western Railway's (GWR) campaign to promote 'the Cornish Riviera' from 1904, though there were as yet only slim pickings for those fishermen who 'rowed the "foreigners" out of the harbour to catch mackerel they would otherwise be catching themselves'.[21]

The consequences of mass emigration, as people left home to seek work, were profound. Cornwall's population, 369,390 in 1861, had fallen to 318,591 forty years later.[22] Over the same period 44.8 per cent of Cornish males and 26.2 per cent of females between the ages of fifteen and twenty-

17   *Cornish Echo* (Falmouth), 24 January 1908, p.6.
18   *Cornubian* (Redruth), 16 January 1908, p.5.
19   T. Collins, *A Social History of English Rugby Union* (London: Routledge, 2009), p.91; G. Williams, *1905 and All That: Essays on Rugby Football, Sport and Welsh Society* (Llandysul: Gomer, 1991), pp.74–5.
20   Payton, *Cornwall*, pp.215–24; Deacon, *Cornwall*, pp.165–6.
21   J. Betjeman, 'Cornwall', in J. Guest (ed.), *The Best of Betjeman* (Harmondsworth: Penguin, 1978), pp.194–7, p.196.
22   Census statistics for Cornwall at <http://www.statistics.gov.uk?census2001/bicentenary/pdfs/cornwall/pdf>(accessed 5 September 2009).

four went overseas; large numbers also left for other parts of the UK.[23] It is important, however, not to overstate the rapidity of industrial decline and the extent to which it paralysed Cornish society. The downward trend in population was temporarily reversed in the first decade of the twentieth century as the local economy revived. The clay and shipbuilding industries were thriving and rising prices encouraged some tin mines to reopen. Few in the 1900s would have concurred with the idea that Cornwall's industries were dead and buried.[24] If Cornish rugby in its *annus mirabilis* was an expression of Cornish identity, it was because it sat comfortably alongside the mine, the chapel and other surviving features of nineteenth-century industrial society.

Philip Payton has argued that the idea of Cornish native genius – Trevithick's locomotives and Davy's safety lamp – was central to how the Cornish thought of themselves. 'At its most developed', he notes, 'the pride in Cornish achievement verged on arrogance or even chauvinism.'[25] Though this had been dented as staple industries declined, it was still very much in evidence in the 1900s. Local newspapers celebrated the thriving rugby scene alongside articles that reminded readers of Cornwall's contribution to the industrial revolution. 'The Early Life of Trevithick' and 'The Cornish Miner 40 Years Ago' were typical of this *genre*. They also reported the weekly round of chapel activities, pausing to reflect on the disproportionate number of Cornishmen entering the Methodist ministry.[26] '*Wha's like us?*', as the Scots would say, and success at rugby simply underlined the point. 'And who will dispute that we are a wonderful people', asked the *Cornishman*, 'after the great inter-county rugby football match on Saturday [...]?'[27]

---

23   Payton, *Cornwall*, p.224.
24   Deacon, *Cornwall*, pp.169–74; also M. Williams, 'Why is Cornwall Poor? Poverty and In-Migration since the 1960s', *Contemporary British History*, vol. 17, no. 3 (2003), pp.57–9.
25   See Payton, *Cornwall*, pp.194–6.
26   *Cornubian*, 16 January 1908, p.9; 23 January 1908, p.9; 2 April 1908, p.3.
27   *Cornishman*, 2 April 1908, p.4.

Even before Cornwall had secured its place in the final, there were indications that rugby was contributing to growing self-confidence and pride in Cornishness. 'Football Fancies', a column of rugby-related gossip in the *Cornubian*, reported that one local hero, now playing in faraway Leicester, had recently been to 'the little village of London'. This segued into a story about some 'Cornish lads' who had visited the capital and ventured on to the 'Tuppenny Tube':

> The lift did seem a long time coming up, and one lad anxiously inquired of the 'checker in' how long they had to wait for 'the skip'. Once in the lift and going down! down!! down!!! the Cornubians felt at home again and everything was 'all kiff' – until she pulled up with a bump and the gates rolled back. 'Hold on, partner', said the tall un, 'this is our level – and here comes "the tram"'.[28]

The story and the insider's language in which it was told are redolent of cultural self-sufficiency. Nothing London could offer – even its new-fangled underground railway – was likely to impress a Cornishman. Cornwall in 1908 could still look the capital in the face.

Beating Middlesex, the strongest of the metropolitan counties, in the semi-final in March 1908 was thus no more than Cornish lads would have expected, especially as the Cornwall fifteen combined so effectively. Middlesex were 'very fast, powerful and clever, as well as tricky, but they were not so much *together* as the Cornish side'. Maybe there was something after all in Cornwall's 'One and All' tradition?[29] Two weeks later, after Durham had been defeated in the final in front of 17,000 spectators at Redruth, the links between rugby and Cornishness were made more explicit. In Wales at this time there was a tendency to regard prowess at rugby as a distinctively Welsh characteristic and to attribute the famous nation-making victory over New Zealand in 1905 to indigenous Celticity.[30] Similar sentiments

28 *Cornubian*, 23 January 1908, p.3.
29 *Cornubian*, 19 March 1908, p.3, my emphasis. 'One and All' is a traditional rallying cry, signifying Cornish unity.
30 Williams, *1905 and All That*, p.72; D. L. Andrews, 'Welsh Indigenous! And British Imperial? – Welsh Rugby, Culture and Society, 1890–1914', *Journal of Sport History*, vol. 18, no. 1 (1991), pp.335–49, pp.338–44.

informed coverage of the 1908 county championship. Cornwall had won, according to the *Cornubian*, because '[its] players and officials displayed to a remarkable extent the grit and determination characteristic of the residents in the most western county in the country.'[31]

The *Cornishman* ('A Newspaper for One and All') was equally happy to celebrate Cornishness, but went further:

> [...] notable Cornish athletes have their place in the life of the nation. To be the best centre or back, wing or 'skipper' of the 'scrum' in all England is something to be proud of and something which cannot be attained without the possession and exercise of that virility and tenacity which has enabled the Anglo-Saxon and Celtic peoples to dominate the rest of the world.[32]

This reference raised important questions. Were the Cornish people English or were they Celts? And, if they were Celts, how did this impact on Cornwall's relationship with England, the UK and the British Empire beyond?

Cornwall's Celtic revivalists had answers to both these questions, though their influence at the time was limited. Romantic in outlook, they turned their backs on industrial Cornwall, seeking inspiration in pre-industrial Cornwall and its ancient language. If the Celtic-Cornish Association, founded in 1901, had a political aim it was simply to establish Cornwall's Celtic credentials to the satisfaction of the Pan-Celtic movement. They achieved some success in this respect, mainly through the efforts of Henry Jenner, whose *Handbook of the Cornish Language* was published in 1904. Yet the most important feature of the Cornish-Celtic movement at this time was its rejection of political nationalism. There was, as Jenner explained later, 'no wish on anyone's part to translate the Irish political expression *Sinn Féin* into Cornish, to agitate for Home Rule for Cornwall [...] [or to] foment disloyalty to England's King or to the British Empire.'[33] This stance precluded the development of a Cornish equivalent of the home rule movements in Scotland and Wales.

31   *Cornubian*, 2 April 1908, p.3.
32   *Cornishman*, 2 April 1908, p.4.
33   Cited in Deacon, Cole and Tregidga, *Mebyon Kernow*, p.16. *Sinn Féin* translates as 'Ourselves Alone'.

From time to time revivalists sought to engage with a wider Cornish public through the local press. That it was necessary to explain in 1908 that *Curnow* (sic) translated as 'Cornwall' suggests that they faced an uphill task in their efforts to Celticize Cornish culture.[34] More important, perhaps, was their failure to develop a political space where concerns regarding Cornwall's relationship with England could be raised. To some extent rugby union, a topic with which Cornishmen of all classes were familiar after 1908, helped to fill this gap. Celtic revivalists and Cornish politicians might have little to say on centre-periphery relations, but Cornwall's status as rugby's champion county raised the issue in a new form. The CRFU now complained that its players were routinely overlooked when the Rugby Football Union (RFU) selected England teams. Former president Dr Hichens 'could not but help thinking that the Cornishmen had been slighted by the authorities above'. It was, he observed at the post-match banquet, 'a mystery [...] that they had not one representative in the English team'. These views were echoed a few days later, ironically at an event to honour a Redruth player who *had* been selected to tour with England. Cornwall, one speaker claimed, was still under-represented:

> He would like to have seen Cornwall play an English team on their ground, and then they would have shown the committee what capabilities the men of Cornwall possessed – (applause). Some people said Cornwall was out of England – (applause) and this appeared to be the prevailing opinion amongst the authorities above – (renewed laughter).[35]

Clearly, the idea of squaring-up to England on equal terms was appealing, while the reference to Cornwall being 'out of England' indicated a view of centre-periphery relations characterized by metropolitan disdain and Cornish resentment.

34 *Cornubian*, 23 January 1908, p.9.
35 *Cornubian*, 2 April 1908, p.3; see also Salmon, *First Hundred Years*, p.9; *Cornubian*, 9 April 1908, p.7; speech attributed to S. Howard Lanyon.

'Do They Always Carry On Like This?'

These complaints may have had some effect, for the RFU turned to Cornwall later in 1908 when it was obliged to find a team at short notice to
represent the UK at the London Olympics. The tournament, reduced to a
single match against Australia, proved an unhappy experience for Cornwall
in every respect.[36] This setback notwithstanding, it was clear after 1908 that
rugby provided a space where Cornish people could make a public display
of their distinctive cultural identity. At a basic level this required no more
than wearing the Cornish black and gold when watching a county match
and joining in when 'Trelawny' was sung. Remembering '1908' – or at least
being aware of its significance – was also important. Bert Solomon, whose
fleet-footed brilliance helped secure the famous victory, became 'as firmly
fixed in the Cornish consciousness as are Richard Trevithick and Humphry
Davy'.[37] As 1908 receded into the historical distance, anyone who could
say 'I was there' connected Cornwall's present with its past. One Redruth
man, up for the 1958 final, wore the same rosette that he had sported fifty
years earlier. Another, aged 103, who attended the 1991 final, was celebrated
in the Cornish press as the only person living to have seen the county win
the championship twice.[38]

Not that it was necessary to have 'been there' to 'remember'. Match-
day behaviour, passed down from one generation to another, helped to
sustain a link with the past. After the 1908 final, Durham's mascot, a toy
monkey, having accompanied the team for many seasons without mishap,
had been torn apart by a Cornish spectator.[39] A minor incident, perhaps,
but visiting teams learned that crowds west of the Tamar were passion-

36   See I. Buchanan, 'Rugby Football at the Olympic Games', *Journal of Olympic History*,
     vol. 5, no. 1 (1997), pp.12–14, pp.12–13; also *The Fourth Olympiad: Being the Official
     Report of the Olympic Games of 1908* (London: British Olympic Association, 1909),
     pp.179–80.
37   A. Buckley, *Bert Solomon: a Rugby Phenomenon* (Truro: Truran, 2007), p.42.
38   *Coventry Evening Telegraph*, 8 March 1958, p.16; *Western Morning News* (Plymouth),
     20 April 1991, p.34; *Cornishman*, 25 April 1991, p.1.
39   *Cornishman*, 2 April 1908, p.4.

ate in demonstrating their support for the black and gold. Spectators at Redruth, especially those who gathered at 'Hellfire Corner', were said to give Cornwall a distinct edge when playing at home. 'An atmosphere of impending doom to all challengers has existed for so long', observed London's *Daily Telegraph* in 1969, 'that one might be inclined to scoff at the idea of any visiting county side winning in Cornwall'.[40] Two years earlier the excesses of some Cornish supporters had attracted criticism. Previewing the 1967 semi-final at Redruth, the *Telegraph* noted that Surrey would have to contend with 'the fervour of 13,000 [Cornish] partisans'. 'One admires them for it', the correspondent added, 'but hopes that the unsporting barracking when the opposition were taking place kicks in the quarter-final will not be repeated'.[41]

The implication was clear enough: crowds in Cornwall were both less polite and more committed than those that followed rugby union in most other parts of England. It was a difference that persisted and was especially noticeable when local differences were set aside in support of the county team. As an expression of identity that was specifically Cornish, it was not transferable. After 1924, the CRFU was no longer awarded matches against Australia, New Zealand and South Africa. Instead, a joint Devon and Cornwall team took on the tourists, an unhappy compromise as far as Cornwall was concerned, especially as most of the matches were staged in Devon. Spectators, accustomed to cheering for Cornwall, could not identify with a hybrid fifteen in the same way. 'Few of us knew what to shout', explained the journalist J. C. Trewin, reflecting on a match against South Africa in 1931:

> We began promisingly. We shouted for 'The Counties!' But, as the game proceeded, our good intentions vanished, and whilst some shouted for 'The Whites!' others cried 'Devon!' or 'Cornwall!', according to the counties of their choice, and glanced uncomfortably at their neighbours the while.[42]

40 *Daily Telegraph*, 11 January 1969, p.9.
41 *Daily Telegraph*, 4 February 1967, p.7.
42 University of Reading Special Collections, J. C. Trewin MS, 4739/271, 'The Critic in the Grandstand', undated cutting from the *Western Independent* [22 November 1931].

Trewin, Cornish by upbringing, had worked for the Plymouth-based *Western Independent* since 1925. He had seen enough county rugby to recognize its special importance for Cornwall.

Applying 'Devonwall' principles precluded unambiguous expressions of Cornish identity. Cornish crowds at inter-county games were not subject to such constraints and were passionate in support of their team. They also owned a stock of invented tradition on which they drew for cultural sustenance. Trewin later recalled the match-day atmosphere when Cornwall played away from home between the wars:

> [...] opponents would be alarmed by the arrival of a small regiment of Cornishmen in their rosettes of black and gold: it was their habit to chant 'Trelawny' before the game, and to cheer frantically to the end. Few things could have heartened a side more than that massed Cornish roar.[43]

One match, a semi-final against Middlesex in 1928, played at Richmond, in deepest London suburbia, left an indelible mark. It seems to have been the Cornish equivalent of 'the Celtic invasion of London', when an army of Welsh supporters had descended on Twickenham for an England-Wales match a year earlier.[44]

It was not what happened on the field that caused Trewin to remember this particular encounter; it was the behaviour of the crowd, especially 'the wild Cornish roar when Cornwall beat Middlesex by five points to three'.[45] The main body of the Cornish contingent comprised 1200 who had travelled up from the south-west by special train; a further 800 were London-based exiles. Trewin's report described a sustained demonstration of Cornishness before, during and after the match. At the final whistle, 'all the visitors' assembled in front of the pavilion to sing 'Trelawny'. When they eventually dispersed, some 'roamed the streets of Richmond singing the

---

43   J. C. Trewin, *Up from the Lizard* (London: Carroll and Nicholson, 1948), p.197.

44   H. Richards, *The Red and the White: The Story of England v Wales Rugby* (London: Aurum, 2009), pp.84–5.

45   J. C. Trewin and H. J. Willmott, *London-Bodmin: an Exchange of Letters between J. C. Trewin and H. J. Willmott* (London: Westaway, 1950), p.86.

County anthem and shouting "war cries".[46] Inter-county rugby reminded the Cornish of 1908 and of their own cultural identity. Given the generally disappointing performances of the Cornish team in the inter-war period, a match in the London area was a rare opportunity to remind the capital that Cornwall existed. Significantly, the thick description of Trewin's match report was not matched by *The Times*, which simply noted that Cornwall had been 'urged on by their supporters'.[47] With the metropolitan gaze averted, the Cornish periphery remained largely invisible from the centre, even when it manifested itself at the end of the District Line.

'Do they always carry on like this?', a perplexed Londoner had asked. 'No one troubled to reply to him', Trewin recalled, 'but the answer was simple. They do.'[48] It was easier, however, to make an impression on a provincial city than on the capital. A few weeks later, Cornwall's first appearance in a final for twenty years saw another 'small regiment' travel to Yorkshire. Despite a round-trip of over 700 miles, the Cornish supporters never really left home. Having been conveyed to Bradford by a GWR 'special', they wandered the streets together. For those who were weary, Camborne's Methodist superintendent had made arrangements for the Men's Institute to provide a place of rest, and the local Cornish Association was a reassuring presence throughout. 'Cornish excursionists to Bradford next Saturday need not be lonely', the *Cornish Post* observed rather unnecessarily.[49] Bradford's *Telegraph and Argus* clearly found the visitors exotic, reporting on their loud progress around the city centre under the headline 'TRELAWNEY (sic) COMES TO BRADFORD AND SINGS THAT HE SHALL NOT DIE'. A party from Camborne was said to have lamented a lack of pasties in the city's shops, though their bulging pockets suggested that they had come prepared. The pasty, Yorkshire readers were informed, 'is as popular

46 *Western Independent* (Plymouth), 5 February 1928, p.19; see also *West Briton* (Truro), 9 February 1928, p.3.

47 *The Times*, 6 February 1928, p.6.

48 Trewin MS, 4739/268, 'County Pride of the Cornish', undated cutting from the *Western Independent* [1928].

49 *Cornish Post* (Redruth), 3 March 1928, p.8; *West Briton*, 8 March 1928, pp.3, 7; *Yorkshire Post*, 10 March 1928, p.23.

in Cornwall as Yorkshire pudding is in the county of the broad acres'.[50] Traditionally consumed by tin miners at work, it was a convenient way of carrying Cornish identity 'upcountry'. In the event, Yorkshire earned a narrow victory in a match played in a snowstorm. The consolation, for those who had travelled, was that they could now make their own contribution to Cornish rugby's oral tradition. 'Little sleep did we have', one recalled years later, '– not that we expected it for our excitement was tremendous'.[51]

Thirty years were to pass before Cornwall next reached the final. In the intervening years, much of what was left of the county's nineteenth-century industrial economy disappeared in the economic blizzard of the 1930s. All its industrial staples suffered; mining and fishing more than most. Output of clay halved in the three years after 1929 as demand from overseas collapsed. Though the tourist industry expanded it did not grow quickly enough to compensate for the loss of employment elsewhere. Unemployment rates remained higher than the UK average, and this encouraged a new exodus, more often now to more prosperous parts of England than abroad. Whereas the decline of Cornwall's population had been arrested between 1901 and 1911, it now resumed, reaching its twentieth-century low point at 317,968 in 1931. Bernard Deacon has argued that the evidence for economic and socio-cultural paralysis in the inter-war years is 'overwhelming'.[52] The best that could be hoped for was to 'make do' or 'get by'.

There are strong indications that the cultural base to which Cornish identity was linked remained largely unchanged. Parliamentary elections in which Liberals, rather than Labour, still confronted Conservatives suggested a fossilized political culture where the chapel remained an important influence. That the Cornish were in some important ways different from their English neighbours was not in doubt. Celtic revivalists continued to remind them of their non-English past via the Federation of Old Cornish Societies, founded in 1925, and a more impatient strain was evident in the political agenda sketched out by *Tyr ha Havas* (Land and Language) after

---

50   *Bradford Telegraph and Argus*, 10 March 1928, p.7.
51   See Salmon, *First Hundred Years*, p.107; Pelmear, *Rugby in the Duchy*, p.82.
52   Deacon, *Cornwall*, pp.195–99; see also Payton, *Cornwall*, pp.237–41.

1932.[53] Yet despite or perhaps because of the extreme hardship to which the county was exposed, it was the culture of industrial Cornwall that predominated, even if it was now defined by the decommissioned trawler, the shut pithead and the dole queue.

By 1958, when 5,000 Cornish supporters made their way to Coventry to support their team against Warwickshire in the county championship final, these conditions no longer applied, not least because the county was benefiting from the full employment of the post-war period and relative affluence. Yet, as Ronald Perry has argued, it 'was still – historically, culturally, politically and economically – something of a tight little island, a land apart'.[54] As the midland city prepared for what was inevitably described as an 'invasion', its local newspaper took the precaution of employing a 'Cornish correspondent'. He was able to confirm that it would be 'the first time that some of the younger men have ever crossed the border into England'. Indeed, by 1958, more people from the Midlands were likely to have crossed the border into Cornwall. 'Since the demise of tin mining and the decline of fishing', he explained, 'Cornwall has become predominantly a tourist county'.[55] Certainly, it no longer had an industrial economy on the nineteenth-century model; the largest employer was now the service sector, with 15 per cent of jobs linked to tourism.[56]

Despite these changes a kind of cultural inertia prevailed. Cornishness manifested itself in the same ways that had been seen at Richmond and Bradford thirty years earlier. Before the match, black and gold bedecked supporters congregated in the city centre 'shouting and singing their war song'. At the stadium, a party of Cornishmen 'paraded round the pitch holding their pasty aloft'. Later, in the city's pubs, the Cornish drowned

53   See G. Tregidga, 'The Politics of the Celto-Cornish Revival, 1886–1939', *Cornish Studies* (2nd series), no. 5 (1997), pp.142–6; Deacon, Cole and Tregidga, *Mebyon Kernow*, pp.22–4.

54   R. Perry, 'Cornwall Circa 1950', in Payton, *Cornwall since the War*, pp.22–46, p.44.

55   *Coventry Evening Telegraph*, 6 March 1958, p.15.

56   Perry, 'Cornwall Circa 1950', p.30; see also A. Williams and G. Shaw, 'The Age of Mass Tourism', in Payton, *Cornwall since the War*, pp.84–97.

their sorrows – they had lost again – and regaled locals with 'Trelawny', along with 'well-known hymns'.[57] The influence of the Methodist chapel, an integral component of Cornwall's old industrial society, may yet have survived in vestigial form. The Cornish, according to one account, 'took possession of the city'.[58] It was an impressive display and a clear indication that difference persisted. Yet, even within the narrow context of English rugby, it remained difficult for peripheral Cornwall to make its mark at the centre. E. W. Swanton, *Daily Telegraph* writer and self-appointed high priest of England's middle-class sports establishment, was especially dismissive. The presence of 'thousands of bedecked patriots' had ensured that the match was fiercely contested, but it had also encouraged 'instances of Cornish over-exuberance among the forwards [which] had tended to dilute neutral sympathies'.[59]

The Last Hurrah? Rugby and Cornish Identity at the End of the Century

Cornish Methodism was an almost spent force as the county's supporters prepared to travel 'upcountry' for the county championship final at Twickenham in 1989. The Porthleven circuit was about to close nine of its thirteen chapels.[60] South Crofty, Cornwall's one remaining tin mine, was still being worked, but production was heavily subsidized. When support was withdrawn in 1997, it closed.[61] By then Cornwall's old industrial economy, along with its Methodist congregations, had all but disappeared. So, too, had many of the branch factories established by national companies

57   *Coventry Evening Telegraph*, 8 March 1958, p.16; 10 March 1958, p.6.
58   Pelmear, *Rugby in the Duchy*, p.92; see also Salmon, *First Hundred Years*, pp.27–9.
59   *Daily Telegraph*, 10 March 1958, p.5.
60   *Western Morning News*, 31 March 1989, p.7.
61   Payton, *Cornwall*, pp.295–6.

from the 1950s onwards.[62] By the 1980s, the illusion of Cornwall's 'second industrial revolution' was manifest, leaving the county's economy more dependent than ever on tourism, where employment was largely seasonal and low-paid. However, whereas industrial decline had previously been accompanied by falling population, the late twentieth-century experience was different. Cornwall's population rose from 342,301 in 1961 to 468,631 in 1991 as in-migrants, often retired people who had first visited as tourists, cashed in on higher property values elsewhere and set up home in the south-west. In-migration brought some economic benefits, but these were outweighed by unemployment, low wages and a higher rate of business failure than anywhere else in the UK.[63]

The unholy alliance of population growth and economic decline fostered a siege mentality among those who regarded themselves as native Cornish. 'If the English influx continues at the present rate', MK's *Cornish Nation* warned in 1973, 'the very existence of *Kernow*, the Cornish homeland, is under threat as a cultural, national entity'.[64] As the economic downturn of the early 1980s began to bite, the resulting pressures on the housing and labour markets reinforced these anxieties. In these conditions, MK, reluctantly at first, transformed itself from a pressure group into a political party. Though its electoral impact was modest, its emergence as a political force helped to shape a pro-Cornish, anti-metropolitan agenda that the major parties ignored at their peril. Liberal and Liberal Democrat candidates, for example, campaigned with some success under the banner of 'A Fair Deal for Cornwall'. Though most electors remained impervious to the politics of separatism, MK was able to secure 50,000 signatures in favour of a devolved Cornish assembly in 2000–1. Dean Shipton, who had captained Cornwall's fifteen to a county championship victory in 1999, was a much-publicized signatory.[65]

---

62 Deacon, *Cornwall*, pp.209–10; Payton, *Cornwall*, pp.274–5.
63 Williams, 'Why is Cornwall Poor?', p.56.
64 Cited in Deacon, Cole and Tregidga, *Mebyon Kernow*, p.61.
65 Deacon, Cole and Tregidga, *Mebyon Kernow*, p.107; see also Deacon, *Cornwall*, p.229, Payton, *Cornwall*, p.297.

Such high-profile support was important in view of the part played by rugby in the broad-based Cornish cultural renaissance of the late 1980s and 1990s. The crisis of identity that had propelled MK into political activism manifested itself in a number of ways. Local dialect, for example, was deemed to be under threat, diluted by incomers and the influence of the mass media.[66] Those who sought to preserve it were no doubt heartened by the success of the Celtic revivalists in promoting the use of the Cornish language from the late 1960s. There were around 500 speakers of varying proficiency by 1980 and, though this was a modest total, it has to be set against the claim that 'the Cornish language is perhaps the only example in linguistic history of a wholly defunct vernacular being successfully resuscitated'.[67] Though progress faltered after 1987 as the language movement fragmented, the revivalists of the late twentieth century made a bigger impact than their predecessors in creating a wider awareness of the specifically Celtic, non-English elements of Cornish culture. Perhaps this was most clearly demonstrated by the widespread adoption of St Piran's flag, once regarded as 'MK's flag', but increasingly used to assert Cornish identity in contexts ranging from the formal to the banal. It flew over County Hall alongside the standards of the UK and the EU; it appeared in advertisements and business logos, and on car stickers.

It was much in evidence as supporters made their way to Twickenham for the county finals in 1989, 1992 and 1998, when Cornwall lost, and 1991 and 1999, when they won. The revival of Cornish rugby at this time owed something to contingency. Once leading English clubs had begun to compete for league titles after 1987, county rugby was increasingly regarded as an anachronistic distraction. Professionalization, when it arrived in 1995, simply reinforced this effect, as clubs were reluctant to release their players. Metropolitan critics were quick to point out that the tournament was now

66   A. Sharp, 'The Institute of Cornish Studies Survey of Cornish Dialect: A Progress Report', *Journal of the Institute of Cornish Studies*, no. 6 (1978), pp.9–16, pp.12–13.
67   M. Combellack, 'Twelve Years Progress in Unified Cornish, 1967–79', *Journal of the Institute of Cornish Studies*, no. 6 (1978), pp.45–51, p.45. See also P. Payton and B. Deacon, 'The Ideology of Language Revival', in Payton, *Cornwall since the War*, pp.271–90.

second-rate. John Reason, reporting the 1989 final for the *Sunday Telegraph* was unimpressed by what he had seen: 'Up and unders only went up. Miss moves missed everything. So did common or garden passes', he recorded. 'The standard of play was awful', was his withering assessment of the 1992 match.[68] For the *Daily Telegraph's* correspondent in 1991, when Cornwall won the championship for the first time since 1908, it was a huge mystery. 'What is the attraction of county rugby, an increasingly isolated section of the game which has been successively devalued by leagues and the unloved divisional competition?'[69] The more important question, however, as even sympathetic observers recognized, was why it should mean so much to Cornwall when it attracted so little attention elsewhere?

Close observers of the Cornish scene were in no doubt as to the significance of these events. Having signed off his *Making of Modern Cornwall* on St Piran's Day (5 March) 1992, Philip Payton, Director of the Institute of Cornish Studies, was so struck by what happened at Twickenham a few weeks later that he was moved to add a postscript. Cornwall had failed to achieve 'back-to-back' championship victories, but the outcome of the match was almost incidental. The county's 'small regiment' of travelling supporters, encouraged by reaching the final in 1989 and then actually winning it in 1991, had morphed into the self-styled – and 40,000 strong – 'Trelawny's Army'. Time-honoured match-day rituals were duly performed, black and gold was worn, 'Trelawny' was sung and pasties were consumed, not simply to ward off hunger but as a signifier of Cornish identity. 'That's not a Cornish pasty', exclaimed one foot-soldier as he rejected the pale imitation he had been offered on his way to the 1991 final. 'It's got carrot in it'.[70] Tradition, however, was reinforced by some new influences, most evident, perhaps, in the adoption of the ubiquitous 'Mexican wave', with which crowds at sporting events in the late twentieth century learned to celebrate themselves. Women were present in larger numbers than before, and the Falmouth Marine Band added a smidgen of post-modern irony. What

68 *Sunday Telegraph*, 2 April 1989, p.47; 19 April 1992, p.26.
69 *Daily Telegraph*, 20 April 1991, p.29.
70 *Western Morning News*, 22 April 1991, p.1.

Payton saw in all this was 'an unnerving demonstration of "Cornishness" by some ten per cent of the Duchy's population [...] [which] served to impress not only the rugby fraternity but also a far wider world'.[71]

Trelawny's Army was a powerful restatement of Cornish cultural identity. The fact that so many people would travel long distances to cheer on their team in a competition of little interest to anyone else was itself an indication that they were different. That the opposition was provided by counties that were uncompromisingly English simply accentuated a Cornish sense of otherness for which rugby had become a vehicle. By the late twentieth century, the game's central place in the popular culture of modern Cornwall was underpinned by its relationship with each of the components of modern Cornish identity. A sentimental link with industrial Cornwall remained in place. There were no miners in the fifteen that started the 1991 final; most of the players worked in the service sector, and there was room on the substitutes' bench for an art student. Yet the *Western Morning News*, in a leading article, felt obliged to single out Brian Andrew, now a pub manager but the only player who could claim a connection 'with the almost abandoned tradition of tin-mining, in which he once worked'.[72] The relationship between Celticity and Cornish rugby had been sealed a year earlier when the Cornish *Gorsedd* decided to present a special trophy to the CRFU, signifying bardic approval for the county's sporting achievement.[73] There were even indications that recent incomers might find a place alongside the Cornish-born in Trelawny's Army, a development that paralleled MK's movement towards a more inclusive civic nationalism.[74]

It was also important to raise awareness, not least because Cornwall had become by the 1990s one of the poorest regions in both the UK and the EU. One exile, writing home before the 1998 final, hoped that Trel-

---

71   Payton, *Making of Modern Cornwall*, p.244; see also Deacon, *Cornwall*, pp.219–20.

72   *Western Morning News*, 18 April 1992, p.4.

73   *Cornishman*, 2 May 1991, p.14.

74   *Western Morning News*, 22 April 1991, p.14; Deacon, Cole and Tregidga, *Mebyon Kernow*, p.116.

awny's Army would use the occasion 'to demonstrate our difference, and celebrate our history, language and culture'. He concluded:

> We are a 'little land', as A. L. Rowse put it, and have often been ignored or poorly treated, a process that still continues, but Twickenham will give us an opportunity to remind 'upcountry' that we are here, different and resilient. We should take that opportunity.[75]

If it was now more difficult for the metropolitan centre to discount the Cornish periphery, Trelawny's Army was partly responsible.[76] Having witnessed the carnival of Cornish popular culture at English rugby union's 'HQ' in 1989, at least some London-based opinion formers now recognized a political dimension. *The Guardian* detected a 'lusty spirit of national independence' that was 'alive and flourishing in the undeclared republic of Cornwall'.[77]

Conclusion

Community identities are rooted in living cultures, shaped by common experience and subject to change over time. As industrial Cornwall, moulded by mining and Methodism, faded away, the tourist industry and the settlement of incomers from 'foreign' England helped to modify what it meant to be Cornish. Celtic revivalism – its advocates seeking a place for *Kernow* in the Celtic family of nations – was also important in that it legitimized an alternative version of cultural identity that owed nothing to Cornwall's relationship with England. There is clearly some mileage in the argument that rugby was periodically deployed to facilitate the collective

75 *Cornishman*, 16 April 1998, p.26, letter from M. J. Daniels.
76 *Western Morning News*, 19 April 1991, p.1.
77 *The Guardian*, 2 April 1989, cited in Payton, *Cornwall*, p.271.

expression of 'enduring Cornishness in an otherwise changing world'.[78] It is important, however, to recognize that Cornish identity is in itself a rather complex phenomenon. Though the proportion of the county's residents self-identifying as 'Cornish' rather than 'English' or 'British' (44 per cent in 2004) is a strong indication that difference persists, this does not readily translate into electoral support for MK, which remains a minority party. 'The Cornish', as Bernard Deacon has argued, 'can be intensely "Cornish" but also unthinkingly "English"'.[79]

The rugby union county championship provided opportunities for the Cornish to express their distinctive identity within the context of an 'all-England' competition. It allowed Cornish people to be both 'of England' and 'not of England' at the same time, while intermittently making peripheral Cornwall more visible at the centre. Thus rugby could function as an expression of Cornish identity and as a perfect encapsulation of the Cornish paradox in which it was rooted. A downgraded competition, however, was no longer fit for this purpose. By the end of the 1990s this was becoming apparent, even to Trelawny's army. Whereas it had comprised most of the 56,000 crowd at Twickenham in 1991, only 22,000 attended the 1999 final.[80] Whatever magic the county championship had ever possessed was wearing very thin and within a few years it had almost disappeared. 'The successes of Cornwall's team in their black and gold have always been an important part of Cornwall's national identity', observed MK's *Cornish Nation* in 2008, 'but sadly the opportunities for representative rugby in Cornwall are now very limited'.[81] Whether a Cornish club side – the Cornish Pirates currently compete in the second tier of the English professional game – could focus popular support in the same way as the county fifteen remains an open question.

---

78   Seward, 'Cornish Rugby', p.174.
79   Deacon, *Cornwall*, pp.220–1. MK polled 7 per cent of the votes in Cornwall at the elections for the European parliament in 2009; <http://www.mebyonkernow. org/?=news/207> (accessed 5 September 2009).
80   *Sunday Telegraph*, 23 May 1999, p.12 (Sport).
81   *Cornish Nation*, no. 47, April 2008, p.10.

Bibliography

Andrews, D. L. 'Welsh Indigenous! And British Imperial? – Welsh Rugby, Culture and Society, 1890–1914', *Journal of Sport History*, vol. 18, no. 1 (1991), pp.335–49.

Betjeman, J. 'Cornwall', in J. Guest (ed.), *The Best of Betjeman* (Harmondsworth: Penguin, 1978), pp.194–7.

British Olympic Association. *The Fourth Olympiad: Being the Official Report of the Olympic Games of 1908* (London: British Olympic Association, 1909).

Buchanan, I. 'Rugby Football at the Olympic Games', *Journal of Olympic History*, vol. 5, no. 1 (1997), pp.12–14.

Buckley, A. *Bert Solomon: A Rugby Phenomenon* (Truro: Truran, 2007).

Coles, F. 'Why Cornwall Is Special to Me', in P. Payton (ed.), *Cornwall For Ever! Kernow Bys Vyken!* (Truro: Cornwall Heritage Trust, 2000), p.228.

Collins, T. *A Social History of English Rugby Union* (London: Routledge, 2009).

Combellack, M. 'Twelve Years Progress in Unified Cornish, 1967–79', *Journal of the Institute of Cornish Studies*, no. 6 (1978), pp.45–51.

Deacon, B. *Cornwall: A Concise History* (Cardiff: University of Wales Press, 2007).

——, D. Cole and G. Tregidga. *Mebyon Kernow and Cornish Nationalism* (Cardiff: Welsh Academic Press, 2003).

Evans, G. *The Fight for Welsh Freedom* (Talybont: Y Lolfa, 2000).

Morgan, K. O. *Rebirth of a Nation: Wales 1880–1980* (Oxford: Oxford University Press, 1981).

Owen, O. L. *The History of the Rugby Football Union* (London: Rugby Football Union / Playfair, 1955).

Payton, P. (ed.) *Cornwall since the War* (Redruth: Institute of Cornish Studies / Dyllansow Truran, 1993).

——. *The Making of Modern Cornwall: Historical Experience and the Persistence of 'Difference'* (Redruth: Dyllansow Truran, 1993).

——. *Cornwall: A History* (Fowey: Cornwall Editions, 2004).

—— and B. Deacon. 'The Ideology of Language Revival', in Payton, *Cornwall since the War*, pp.271–90.

Pelmear, K. *Rugby in the Duchy: an Official History of the Game in Cornwall* (Falmouth: Cornwall Rugby Football Union, 1960).

Perry, R. 'Cornwall Circa 1950', in Payton, *Cornwall since the War*, pp.22–46.

Powell, C. B. and E. W. Moses. *Durham County Rugby Union: Sixty Years Records of the County Fifteen* (Newcastle-upon-Tyne: Andrew Reid, 1936).

Richards, H. *The Red and the White: The Story of England v Wales Rugby* (London: Aurum, 2009).

Rowse, A. L. *A Cornish Childhood: Autobiography of a Cornishman* (London: Grey Arrow, 1942; edn cited 1962).

Salmon, T. *The First Hundred Years: The Story of Rugby Football in Cornwall* (Illogan: Cornwall Rugby Football Union, 1983).

Seward, A. 'Cornish Rugby and Cultural Identity: A Socio-Historical Perspective', *Cornish Studies* (2nd series), vol. 5 (1997), pp.164–79; repr. in *The Sports Historian*, vol. 18, no. 2 (1998), pp.78–94.

Sharp, A. 'The Institute of Cornish Studies Survey of Cornish Dialect: A Progress Report', *Journal of the Institute of Cornish Studies*, no. 6 (1978), pp.9–16.

Tregidga, G. 'The Politics of the Celto-Cornish Revival, 1886–1939', *Cornish Studies* (2nd series), vol. 5 (1997), pp.125–50.

Trewin, J. C. *Up from the Lizard* (London: Carroll & Nicholson, 1948).

——and H. J. Willmott. *London-Bodmin: an Exchange of Letters between J. C. Trewin and H. J. Willmott* (London: Westaway, 1950).

Williams, A. 'Why is Cornwall Poor? Poverty and In-Migration since the 1960s', *Contemporary British History*, vol. 17, no. 3 (2003), pp.55–70.

——and G. Shaw. 'The Age of Mass Tourism', in Payton, *Cornwall since the War*, pp.84–97.

Williams, G. *1905 and All That: Essays on Rugby Football, Sport and Welsh Society* (Llandysul: Gomer, 1991).

PART 5

The New Sporting Europe

ARND KRÜGER

Chapter 13
Sport and Identity in Germany since Reunification

It is not customary to put sport into the context of national identity in a country that considers itself a land of poets and thinkers (*Dichter und Denker*). It was probably done for the first time on the occasion of the 1936 (Berlin) Olympics, when Germans acted in a way they liked to see themselves, open to the world, friendly, enthusiastic – albeit within the Nazi state.[1] The Games were considered the emotional highlight of the Nazi period, so much so that many (particularly after the war) saw them as a well-orchestrated show to hoodwink world public opinion about the reality of Nazism.[2] The Games of 1936 also show that such an event has many different meanings for different people, but they certainly constitute realms of memory (*lieux de mémoire*)[3] for the German people.[4]

National identity is a concept difficult to grasp in any country, but in post-war Germany it is particularly complicated. Hollywood movies reminded Germans constantly that they were a nation of perverts, so that

1   A. Krüger, *Die Olympischen Spiele 1936 und die Weltmeinung: Ihre aussenpolitische Bedeutung unter besonderer Berücksichtigung der USA* (Berlin: Bartels and Wernitz, 1972); for a general account, see J. MacClancy (ed.), *Sport, Identity and Ethnicity* (Oxford: Berg, 1996).
2   A. Krüger and W. Murray (eds), *The Nazi Olympics: Sport, Politics and Appeasement in the 1930s* (Champaign, IL: University of Illinois Press, 2003).
3   P. Nora (ed.), *Les lieux de mémoire* (3 vols; Paris: Gallimard, 1984; 1986; 1992).
4   A. Krüger, "'What's the Difference between Propaganda for Tourism and for a Political Regime?' Was the 1936 Olympics the First Postmodern Spectacle?', in J. Bale and M. Krogh Christensen (eds), *Post-Olympism? Questioning Sport in the Twenty-First Century* (Oxford: Berg, 2004), pp.33–50; see A. Smith and D. Porter (eds), *Sport and National Identity in the Post-War World* (London: Routledge, 2004).

a sense of the historical continuity of the nation was difficult to achieve. East Germans learned to identify with those Germans who had been persecuted for political reasons during the Nazi period and individuals could thus avoid being perceived as a Nazi or the child of one – but as many disassociated themselves from the leading doctrine, they developed an even more peculiar relationship with the past. While the 8th of May soon came to be celebrated in the German Democratic Republic (GDR) as the Day of Liberation from Hitlerian Fascism, in the West it was the day of Germany's surrender. While the East celebrated the victory of the Red Army, the West learned about the victorious Americans (and to a lesser extent the British and even less so the French).[5] It has been assumed that the creation of the *Deutschmark* in 1949 and winning the Football World Cup in 1954 (*Das Wunder von Bern* – The Miracle of Bern) did more for the national identity of the young Federal Republic than the German constitution (*Grundgesetz*), the flag or the national anthem.[6]

In this chapter, I will look particularly at the FIFA World Cup 2006 in Germany, as here can be found – for the first time as a mass movement – a new flag-waving German patriotism.[7] This can be interpreted as a sign of a different form of national identity – and it certainly helped to impress external observers and seems to have had a longer-lasting effect on the foreign press than any planned political activity.[8] In what follows, I will

5   P. Hurrelbrink, 'Befreiung als Prozess: Die kollektiv-offizielle Erinnerung an den 8. Mai 1945 in der Bundesrepublik, der DDR und im vereinigten Deutschland', in G. Schwan, J. Holzer et al. (eds), *Demokratische Identität: Deutschland, Frankreich, Polen im Vergleich* (Wiesbaden: Verlag für Sozialwissenschaften, 2006), pp.71–120.

6   W. Pyta, 'Der Beitrag des Fussballsports zur kulturellen Identitätsstiftung in Deutschland', in W. Pyta (ed.), *Der Lange Weg zur Bundesliga* (Münster: LIT, 2004), pp.1–30; A. Tomlinson and C. Young (eds), *German Football: History, Culture, Society* (London: Routledge, 2006); for the general problem of sport in divided societies, see J. Sudgen and A. Bairner (eds), *Sport in Divided Societies* (Aachen: Meyer and Meyer, 1999).

7   D. H. Jütting (ed.), *Die Welt ist heimgekehrt: Studien zur Evaluation der FIFA-WM 2006* (Münster: Waxmann, 2007).

8   S. Laetsch, *Sind wir Deutschland?* (Hamburg: Diplomica, 2008); for Great Britain, see K. Och, *Hat die Fussball-WM 2006 den Stahlhelm verbannt? Das Deutschlandbild in der Sportberichterstattung britischer Tageszeitungen* (Marburg: Tectum, 2008).

try to put German identity since unification into the context of 'banal nationalism' in order to understand why a sporting event can have such a result.[9] This will also lead us to the questions of agency and control with regard to national identity.

Historical Problems of Identity

Germany is a fluid concept. The year 2009 was celebrated as the *Varus Year*, as 2,000 years ago Arminius, a Cheruscian prince, brought together numerous northern Germanic tribes to defeat the Roman troops under the leadership of Quinctilius Varus, thus ensuring that the Rhine remained the Germanic border in the North-West and a common Germanic identity began to emerge.[10] But if one considers German national identity over the course of the last 140 years, that is to say since German unification within the Prussian-dominated Empire, one may well conclude that for most of the period any sense of national identity in Germany remained underdeveloped. There were certainly times when there was a high degree of aggressive nationalism, but for the most part one can more easily identify a local or regional identity and only after that a national identity and to some extent a sense of a European and a world identity.[11] As a result of the war of 1870–1 against France, the German Empire was constructed under Prussian domination, yet still with a degree of sovereignty granted to the twenty-five separate German states.[12] It was not at the time an obvious choice to create what was then known as the *lesser* German state (Klein-

9   M. Billig, *Banal Nationalism* (2nd edn; London: Sage, 1997).

10 M. Gödecke and K. Schafmeister, 'Die lippischen Beiträge zum Varusjahr 2009', *Lippische Mitteilungen aus Geschichte und Landeskunde*, vol. 77 (2008), pp.201–5.

11 M. Featherstone, 'Global and Local Cultures', in J. Bird, B. Curtis et al. (eds), *Mapping the Future: Local Cultures, Global Change* (London: Routledge, 1993), pp.169–87.

12 H.-U. Wehler, *Das Deutsche Kaiserreich: 1871–1918* (Göttingen: Vandenhoeck and Ruprecht, 1988).

deutschland), as the German-speaking Austrian territories, whose representatives had been very influential in the German Parliament of 1848, were not included.[13]

Despite the fact that within the smaller Germany, many separate identities remained strong, there is a general consensus that German nationalism became sufficiently militant to play a major role in starting the First World War in 1914.[14] As this nationalist sentiment was also very visible in the field of physical exercise,[15] it can be safely assumed that its development during those first forty-two years helped to maintain – if not strengthen – German nationalism and a sense of national identity as regards the new German Empire. Until the turn of the twentieth century, there were German championships in Vienna and Austrian-based federations such as the *Deutscher Turnerbund* (German Association of Gymnasts) had regional sections in Germany. But did the old identities not disappear?[16] If you asked a person from Eichsfeld, the then border area of Prussia and Thuringia – today of Lower Saxony and Thuringia – he would declare his personal identification with the Catholic enclave of Eichsfeld, surrounded by Protestants, and with its historical struggle against Prussia, the Nazis and the German Democratic Republic.[17] What makes a nation a community? As Balibar observes, 'Every social community reproduced (solely) by the functioning of its institutions is imaginary'.[18] For a collective national identity one needs at least:

13   H. Schulze, *Der Weg zum Nationalstaat: Die Deutsche Nationalbewegung vom 18. Jahrhundert bis zur Reichsgründung* (Munich: DTV, 1992).

14   H. Herzfeld, *Der 1. Weltkrieg* (Munich: DTV, 1968); G. Mai, *Das Ende des Kaiserreichs: Politik und Kriegsführung im Ersten Weltkrieg* (Munich: DTV, 1993).

15   A. Krüger, '"Der olympische Gedanke in der modernen Welt hat uns zu einem Symbol des Weltkrieges verholfen": Die internationale Pressekampagne zur Vorbereitung auf die Olympischen Spiele 1916', in N. Gissel (ed.), *Öffentlicher Sport: Die Darstellung des Sports in Kunst, Medien und Literatur* (Hamburg: Czwalina, 1999), pp.55–67.

16   For the different forms of nationalism, see B. Giesen (ed.), *Nationale und kulturelle Identität* (Frankfurt: Suhrkamp, 1991).

17   P. Aufgebauer, E. Denecke et al., *Das Eichsfeld: Ein Deutscher Grenzraum* (Duderstadt: Mecke, 2002).

18   See E. Balibar, 'The Nation Form: History and Ideology', in P. Essed and D. T. Goldberg (eds), *Race Critical Theories* (London: Blackwell, 2001), pp.220–30.

- A definite territory, helping to define the borders of the community;
- A common language;
- A common past, which has created a sufficiently large collective memory, that is, common realms of memory.[19]

The boundaries of the territory of Germany have been continually subject to change over time. To call the unification of the GDR with the Federal Republic 'reunification' is to employ one of those Gramscian words used to create or maintain a myth.[20] Only between 1945 and 1949 were the then borders, determined by the victors, the same as the current borders. The first verse of the German national anthem still alludes to a Germany that would include much of Poland, the Russian enclave of Kaliningrad, half of Denmark, parts of the Netherlands, parts of Austria and the Alto Adige region of Italy. But, at all times, most of Germany's borders (except for the North Sea and the Baltic) have been artificial.

Although the varieties of the German language used in the two post-war German states began to diverge, they were still mutually comprehensible. It was still the language into which Luther (living in what later became East Germany) translated the Bible. GDR German diverged less from Luther's German (albeit adding many acronyms for GDR organizations), while the West German language was flooded with Anglicisms. But today, there is a common territory and a common language. The question that remains is the matter of a common past, a common interpretation of the past, collective memory and a common realm of memory.

This dimension of identity does not develop overnight. Hobsbawm and Ranger argue that the invention of traditions can be a significant factor in assisting the development of such an identity.[21] But the earlier identities

19　For the problems of collective memory in a German context, see A. Krüger, 'Sieben Arten in Vergessenheit zu geraten', in A. Krüger and B. Wedemeyer-Kolwe (eds), *Vergessen Verdrängt Abgelehnt: Zur Geschichte der Ausgrenzung im Sport* (Münster: LIT, 2009), pp.4–16.
20　M. Michael, *Constructing Identities* (London: Sage, 1996).
21　E. J. Hobsbawm and T. Ranger (eds), *The Invention of Tradition* (Cambridge: Cambridge University Press, 1984).

do not disappear overnight either. Indeed, many would argue that even today they have not yet gone away. The 'Wall' that still exists in the heads of many, between an East German identity and a West German identity, has its origin in strong German regionalism, which has been reinforced by the political and cultural rift of the Cold War period. Berlin was never able to achieve such a central position as Paris had for France. Not even the major Prussian cities accepted the dominance of the capital,[22] and many forms of local,[23] regional and national notions of *Patrie* have long existed side by side in Germany.[24] The establishment of the former GDR saw the creation of a strong additional identity. The cleavages that exist between East and West are particularly marked, as they are based on traditional regional identities, which have been strengthened due to cultural, political and economic differences.[25]

After World War II, the eleven western states of the Federal Republic of Germany found themselves in the comfortable position of being integrated into the broader West. This helped to pave the way for access to the international sports world, while the GDR had to wait for more than twenty years before being admitted with a separate team, with its own colours, hymn and flag. In the Olympic field, it was not until 1972 that the GDR had its own team. German unity existed for a long time in language, culture, religion – and even to some extent in sports. Western television programmes were available in most of the East, but due to separation by

22   H. Beckstein, *Städtische Interessenpolitik: Organisation und Politik der Städtetage in Bayern, Preussen und im Deutschen Reich, 1896–1923* (Düsseldorf: Droste, 1991).

23   I do not want to go into the proposition here that historical knowledge can always be considered *local*, as only in this sense does it have a living meaning, see A. Biersack, 'Local Knowledge, Local History: Geertz and Beyond', in L. Hunt (ed.), *The New Cultural History* (Berkeley, CA: University of California Press, 1989), pp.72–96.

24   To some extent the alternatives have become visible in the German Federation, see H. Seiler, 'Der Deutsche Bund als Forschungsproblem, 1815–1960', in *Wiener Beiträge Geschiche zur der Neuzeit*, vol. 16, no. 7 (1990), pp.31–58.

25   The notion of cleavages has been introduced into the discussion by Stein Rokkan, see P. Flora and E. Fix (eds), *Stein Rokkan: Staat, Nation und Demokratie in Europa – Die Theorie Stein Rokkans aus seinen gesammelten Werken* (Frankfurt: Suhrkamp, 2000); S. Rokkan, *Vergleichende Sozialwissenschaft: Die Entwicklung der inter-kulturellen, inter-gesellschaftlichen und inter-nationalen Forschung* (Frankfurt: Ullstein, 1972).

the Wall, the idea of unity faded in the hearts and minds of the younger generation. National unity was celebrated in 1989–90 with flag-waving, but the unification party was soon over and was followed by daily differences and disillusionment.[26]

The German constitution assumes 'equal living conditions' in all of Germany, the 'Blühende Landschaften' (prospering landscapes) promised at the time of unification did not materialize as fast as people expected. The cleavages between East and West, *Ossis* and *Wessis*, became obvious in many areas of social, cultural and economic life. Nobody knows how long the 'wall in the head' will last in the form of separate German identities in the former West and East. Alesina and Fuchs-Schündeln (2007) have sought to demonstrate in a comprehensive study that in the absence of decisive developments speeding up unity it will take another twenty to forty years before a joint identity will be reached in the field of expectations and basic social assumptions.[27] Süssmuth, Heyne and Maennig (2009) have shown that an event like the FIFA World Cup 2006, which helped to create a common identity for a month, may accelerate the process. But the authors wrote their paper before the current economic crisis, so that its effects are not included, and it remains a matter for speculation whether the national measures to overcome the crisis constitute a factor which will promote or undermine unity.[28]

According to Schmidt and Blank (2003), Germans are patriotic and nationalistic, but 'a substantial proportion of Germans feel no pride in being German.'[29] In an international comparison of national pride, Smith and Kim (2006) ranked East Germany last of 22 nations and West Germany

---

26 For the scepticism of the older generation, see P. Glotz, 'Die Identität des grösseren Deutschlands', in P. Glotz, *Der Irrweg des Nationalstaates: Europäische Reden an ein deutsches Publikum* (Stuttgart: DVA, 1990), pp.127–60.

27 A. Alesina and N. Fuchs-Schündeln, 'Good-Bye Lenin (or Not?): The Effect of Communism on People's Preferences', *American Economic Review*, vol. 97, no. 4 (2007): pp.1507–28.

28 B. Süssmuth, M. Heyne and W. Maennig, *Induced Civic Pride and Integration* (CESIFO Working Paper, no. 2582; Munich: IFO, 2009).

29 P. Schmidt, T. Blank et al. (eds), 'National Identity in Europe', *Political Psychology*, vol. 24, no. 2 (2003), pp.233–401, p.298.

only nineteenth.[30] This was already noted in international comparisons by Noelle-Neumann and Köcher (1987)[31] and Smith and Jarkko (1998).[32] Moreover, the mean scores for pride in 'German history' are the lowest of all countries polled in a representative sample. In Germany, success in sport is a stronger motive for showing pride than Germany holding a leading role in Europe. Most notably, there was a significant decrease in national pride between 1995 and 2004, according to the data of Smith and Kim (2006), which includes sport.[33] Sport can be seen as a contested field, in that Evans and Kelley (2002) found little pride in West German sporting success, although a little more in East Germany, yet still far below, for example, the United States or Ireland.[34]

Among East Germans, the positive evaluation of success in sport is significantly higher than among West Germans. This can be explained by the fact that competitive sports were a crucial element of the GDR's national self-image. Although most respondents agree that Germany has a strengthened role in international decision-making due to its economic superiority, there is a comparatively strong tendency to object to the statement that German morale could be a role model for other nations. More West Germans than East Germans consider their country, however, to be the best in the world.

30   T. W. Smith and S. Kim, 'National Pride in Comparative Perspective: 1995/96 and 2003/04', *International Journal of Public Opinion Research*, vol. 18, no. 1 (2006), pp.127–36.

31   E. Noelle-Neumann and R. Köcher, *Die verletzte Nation* (Stuttgart: DVA, 1987).

32   T. W. Smith and L. Jarkko, *National Pride: A Cross-national Analysis* (GSS Crossnational Report no. 19; Chicago: NORC, 1998).

33   Smith and Kim, 'National Pride in Comparative Perspective'.

34   M. D. R. Evans and J. Kelley, 'National Pride in the Developed World: Survey Data from 24 Nations', *International Journal of Public Opinion Research*, vol. 14, no. 3 (2002), pp.303–38; p.319.

Sport and National Identity

Substantial amounts of post-unification government money have been invested in research into East German sport. It has been well documented that success in sport in the GDR was often achieved by illegitimate means, such as doping, including the doping of children and young people, which by most standards is immoral if not criminal. Even today, coaches from the former East Germany are discriminated against if they have been involved in doping practices, while no effort has been made to expose their West German counterparts, who similarly benefited from pharmacological manipulation.[35]

Success in the Olympic Games was therefore regarded with some scepticism, as it was largely based on athletes from the former GDR, whose doping past was regarded critically. Although there was considerable pride in the success of local heroes, national success did not bring about any major shift in this scepticism. The GDR system of doping was organized by the government, and it did not include any serious attempt to inform the athletes of the health risks involved. Performance-enhancing drugs were given to children and young athletes without the consent of their parents or guardians, and doping was so well documented on a GDR level that many of the people involved were subsequently exposed. But even before the revelation of unethical practices among the GDR sporting elite, spectators in East Germany had lost interest in the highly privileged elite sport system. Directly after the opening of the border, spectators shied away from international sporting events in the former GDR. Nonetheless, in a wave of 'ostalgia' (nostalgia for the things of the East), former stars of the early pre-state-doping GDR like the cyclist Täve Schur maintained their hero status.

To ensure 'equal living conditions', out-of-competition doping checks were introduced in Germany (together with Norway) in 1990, the earliest

35 G. Spitzer, *Doping in der DDR: ein historischer Überblick zu einer konspirativen Praxis; Genese – Verantwortung – Gefahren* (3rd edn; Cologne: Sport und Buch Strauss, 2004).

in the world. It was assumed that by this means the approach to doping in the East and the West – which had not been symmetrical – would merge into a common German system. In a transitional period of three years, two complete sets of nationally subsidized athletes and coaches were financially supported with the help of taxpayers' money, totalling approximately 7,000 (the pre-unification total for the two countries) instead of 3,500 athletes.[36] Ireland introduced out-of-competition doping checks only in 2000; in many American sports they have not yet been introduced, as most American athletes compete most of the year for their school or university, to which World Anti-Doping Agency (WADA) rules seldom apply. By systematic dope-testing, doping practices have been curtailed across Germany, but the German international success rate is declining. However, sporting success based on cheating is clearly problematic as a basis for the formation of national identity.

Identification typically happens with sports stars or with teams. Identification with individual sports stars from the former GDR in the new united Germany has been made very difficult because of the previous doping practices. The GDR's top sprinter, Katrin Krabbe, would have had star potential, but was convicted of doping. The success of Nils Schumann at the Olympic Games was not followed up by consistent achievement. Jan Ullrich, an East German who reached stardom in the international cycling world, has been discredited due to his involvement in doping affairs. Only swimming medallist Franziska van Almsick, too young to be identified with the GDR doping system, was able to achieve star status.[37]

Football was different.[38] The *Bundesliga* (Federal League) celebrated local identities and national cleavages. It epitomized the 'time of the tribe',[39]

36   A. Krüger, 'Grundlagen der Doping-Prophylaxe', in R. Kauerhof, S. Nagel and M. Zebisch (eds), *Doping und Gewaltprävention* (Leipzig: Leipziger Universitätsverlag, 2008), pp.143–66.

37   J. Mährlein, *Der Sportler als Marke: Entwicklung, Vorteile, Erfolgsfaktoren* (Düsseldorf: VDM Müller, 2004); J. Mährlein, *Der Sportstar in Deutschland: die Entwicklung des Spitzensportlers vom Helden zur Marke* (Göttingen: Sieke, 2009).

38   R. Giulianotti, *Football: A Sociology of the Global Game* (Cambridge: Polity, 1999).

39   M. Maffesoli, *The Time of the Tribe: The Decline of Individualism in Mass Society* (London: Sage 1996); A. King, *The European Ritual: Football in the New Europe* (Aldershot: Ashgate, 2003), pp.191–222 ('Localism').

and with it the readily changing sense of identity in Germany. Very few of the GDR clubs were able to maintain a first-division presence in the new Germany, but top players such as Thon, Sammer, Ballack, Schneider and Doll were able to make their mark in the *Bundesliga* and in the national team.

Football-related integration functioned in the same way as the integration of East Germans into West Germany had functioned in the years between 1945 and 1961, before the Berlin Wall was built. Individuals who dared to leave almost everything behind but their knowledge and skills migrated individually from East to West and then integrated individually, leaving their East German identity mostly behind. The collective integration of East German soccer into the western-dominated Football Federation took place relatively easily in lower level football, but in professional football East Germany had no role to play.

Towards the end of the war, or soon after it, about 12 million Germans from those parts of Germany that are now in Poland or further east had to move westward. About 8 million went to West Germany, about 4 million to East Germany. In 1947, the then Soviet Occupied Zone had 19.1 million inhabitants. Of these, about 3 million migrated to the West up to 1961, when the Wall was built and emigration was made very difficult. Yet, despite the difficulties, another 600,000 emigrated up to 1988, making a total 3.6 million East Germans living in the West. In the last twenty years, more westward migration has taken place, so that today 7 per cent of the West German population originally came from the East. Only 0.7 per cent of the population in the current East came from the West. In addition, there are about 500,000 intra-German commuters, 400,000 from East to West and 100,000 in the opposite direction. These data do not include movements within Berlin, nor emigration to foreign countries.[40] With so little internal exchange of population within Germany, it has been very difficult to develop a joint German identity.[41]

40   R. Geissler, 'Struktur und Entwicklung der Bevölkerung', in *Informationen zur politischen Bildung*, no. 269 (2nd edn; Bonn: Bundeszentrale für politische Bildung, 2004), pp.1–3.
41   For the problems of identity of those who migrated and the over four million late arrivals from Russia, see P. Gilroy, 'Diaspora and the detours of identity', in K. Woodward (ed.), *Identity and Difference* (London: Sage 1997), pp.301–46.

When German unification was discussed within the sport system in 1990, it was the West German (DSB) and the East German (DTSB) federations that negotiated what they could learn from each other – until it became clear how German unification would take place: the territory of the GDR would dissolve itself into the original five Länder (states) and all would then be absorbed as new states in the German Federal Republic. For the DSB, this meant that it stopped negotiating with the (unpopular) DTSB and waited for the five new regional eastern state federations to apply for membership. Knowledge and skills from the East German sport system were thus not used at first, but individuals could bring their skill to the West and many other countries. It is an open question whether a different form of integration, for example at the level of the two existing national bodies, would have made a difference in terms of a new and somewhat different national identity. In all probability afterwards neither the East nor the West would have felt comfortable within the new entity. If national integration had taken place in a different way, perhaps with a new joint constitution rather than integration by copying the West, a very different Germany might have developed.[42] Sport just followed suit. Even if GDR sport lost its mouthpiece in 1990, the unification process did not suppress the pride in East Germany about its former athletic successes, above and beyond doping. Klaus Huhn's series of *Beiträge zur Sportgeschichte* (Articles on the History of Sport; 1995–present) shows that this is still alive in the older generation.[43]

The special importance of football in the process of national identity construction has already been noted. The enthusiastic patriotism of the German fans at the FIFA World Cup in Germany in 2006 raises questions as to why it did not emerge earlier and why the process took place at all. When Denmark became European Football Champions in 1992, the same kind of happy non-aggressive patriotism had been visible. This showed

42   J. Braun and M. Barsuhn, 'Schussfahrt in die Einheit', *Horch und Guck*, vol. 14, no. 51 (2005), pp.33–9.
43   K. Huhn, *Beiträge zur Sportgeschichte* (Berlin: Spotless, 1995–present).

how enthusiasm could be transferred from a team to the fans. What the Danes called their 'rooligans', like the Dutch 'Oranji' and Scottish 'Tartan Army', were not dissimilar to the German fans of 2006: creative, happy, colourful, sociable, gregarious and boisterous, but non-violent.[44] Was it that the event took place in Germany, was it the style of the team, was it the perfect weather, or was Germany, all of Germany, just ready to behave normally and enjoy football like a big party?

The FIFA World Cup in Germany (2006)

The enthusiastic German patriotism on the occasion of the FIFA World Cup has been placed in the context of the German past beyond the sports world. In 2006, German flags sold out, probably for the first time since 1933. Flag producers were taken by surprise, as Germans, in contrast to Americans, do not have flags displayed so extensively. Germans have so many problems with their country's past that the Former President of the Federal Republic, Gustav Heinemann, when asked whether he loved Germany, answered: 'No, I love my wife.'[45] If you had asked most German fans in 2006, they would probably have answered differently. The flag-waving, anthem-singing fans obviously loved Germany. But this was no longer a unified block of marching fans; it was a German national celebratory party, a 'love parade' of football, a football-carnival across the whole of Germany.

44 H. Heinonen, 'Finnish Soccer Supporters Away from Home: A Case Study of Finnish National Team Fans at a World Cup Qualifying Match in Liverpool, England', *Soccer & Society*, vol. 3, no. 3 (2002), pp.26–50.

45 N. Strohbach, '"Is this love?" Liebe und Ähnliches in der (griechischen) Antike' in Y. Niekrenz and D. Villanyi (eds), *Liebeserklärungen: Intimbeziehungen aus soziologischer Perspektive* (Wiesbaden: Verlag für Sozialwissenschaften, 2008), pp.23–39, p.28.

Nobody knows why football created the 'Sommermärchen' (summer fairy tale) of 2006. In 2004, Sönke Wortmann's movie *Das Wunder von Bern* was a national success, linking football and the myth of German national identity. It celebrated the victory of the German football team in 1954, intertwining it with a family history. The father of the family, who had recently returned a broken man after ten years as a Soviet POW, finds his strength and courage (and the respect of his son and family) when he takes his son to watch Germany win the World Cup in Berne.[46] This is a classic case of the invention of a tradition as proposed by Hobsbawm and Ranger – and it certainly paved the way for the 2006 World Cup. To what extent did the two million foreign spectators who came to Germany for a big party evoke a reaction among German fans? Was it the fact that a new generation was going to see football with a different attitude towards the German past and flag than the previous two generations? The fans in the stadium were on average thirty-four years old, those attending big-screen viewings thirty-one. The spectators were relatively well educated, and very few of them seemed disposed to violence.

An analysis of the fans on the occasion of the FIFA World Cup in Korea and Japan in 2002 is instructive. Manzenreiter pointed out the difference as regards the first international championships in those two countries (in both cases the Olympic Games). The first such Games had been serious, professional, with relatively little outward display of enthusiasm. There were very few signs of overt nationalism. It had been a demonstration of control by the government and of well-behaved spectators. The year 2002 was different. Big-screen public viewings had become very important, as far more people wanted to be part of the show than there were places for in the stadium. One could argue about the extent to which these viewings were genuinely 'public', as often an admission fee was charged and spectators had to pass through a security check.[47]

---

46   F. Breitmeier, 'Ein Wunder, wie es im Drehbuch steht: Die WM 1954 – ein deutscher Erinnerungsfilm' in W. Pyta (ed.), *Der lange Weg* (Münster: LIT, 2004), pp.127–50.

47   W. Manzenreiter, 'Sport Spectacles, Uniformities and the Search for Identity in Late Modern Japan', *Sociological Review*, vol. 54, no. S2 (2006), pp.144–59.

In our context one can see, however, that there had been a flood of national symbols, such as had hitherto been used sparingly. Now these symbols were used openly, but in a non-threatening manner. The Japanese flag (*Hinomaru*) is considered a controversial symbol as it also stands for the country's militaristic past. After World War II, flying the *Hinomaru*-flag was at first severely restricted by the American occupation forces and contested by many as it stood for right-wing imperialism; it was only reintroduced officially by an act of the Japanese parliament in 1999.[48] In 2002, it was present everywhere. While the organizers stressed the friendly character of the World Cup and its international flavour, the fans were dressed like the fans of a football club (or an American university team) in one colour, in one seating-block, and gave a splendid show of their nationalism. However, if you looked at that block more closely, you could discern a wide variety of individual shirts. All were red in Japan or blue in Korea, but some had official team vests, some older team vests, some just T-shirts in the appropriate colour.

The first big international post-war sporting events in Germany were as official and 'serious' as in most other countries. But the 2006 World Cup in Germany was even more colourful than in the Far East: the German flag is the Black-Red-Gold tricolour of the 1848 Revolution, but the colours of the football federation are the Black-White-Red of the German Empire (and thus the colours of the Swastika). The foreign fans wore their colours, but many Germans wore the green team jersey of German away games (the home-game jersey often having sold out), or just the jersey of the football club they supported throughout the year. This created a very colourful prospect. While the French still shout their 'Allez les Bleus', thus foregrounding a national colour, there were no unitary colours in this sea of Black-Red-Gold flags. Just as at a big party, everybody dressed up individually; there was more face-painting than ever before – imitating the foreign fans. While the organizers in Japan and Korea and also in Germany had planned to create a demonstration of the power of the state, the fans created

48   R. Goodman and K. Refsing (eds), *Ideology and Practice in Modern Japan* (London: Routledge, 2002), p.32.

big parties. In Germany, there had been endless discussions about preventive security measures, suspending the Schengen Treaty to assure thorough border checks for known hooligans, and, in response to fears that as many as 50,000 East European prostitutes would flood the country, providing 'Verrichtungsboxen' [custom-built sex cabins large enough to accommodate cars] for them and their male customers. In the end, the government, just like the media, were overwhelmed by the enormous turnout of friendly, happy fans and their show of patriotism.[49]

Some basic facts may illuminate what made this new realm of memory so important. The eighteenth World Cup took place from 9 June to 9 July 2006 in Germany. No less than 198 national teams attempted to qualify for the final in Germany. The thirty-two qualifying teams each stayed in a different German town, thus spreading more football enthusiasm and an international flavour all over the country. The 3.36 million spectators watched in the twelve different stadiums, themselves nicely distributed across Germany, with a complete sell-out in almost all matches. About 14,000 journalists reported on the World Cup. At times, as many as 16.9 million spectators were watching the televised matches outside the home, mainly out on the streets at big-screen events, but also at neighbourhood or garden parties, making this the biggest party in Germany. Among all Germans, 99 per cent thought that Germany was a good host; 93 per cent enjoyed the foreign fans. There were no differences between young and old, East and West. Some forty-eight of the sixty-four football matches were shown on German public television, while 83 per cent of all Germans watched at least one match. A total of 21 million Germans watched ten or

49   Bundesregierung (ed.), *Fussball-WM 2006: Abschlussbericht der Bundesregierung* (Berlin: Presse und Informationsamt der Bundesregierung, 2006); for the mass media and their role in exploiting nationalism and national peculiarities, see A. Daalmann, *Fussball und Nationalismus: Erscheinungsformen in Presse- und Fernsehberichten in der Bundesrepublik Deutschland und den Vereinigten Staaten von Amerika am Beispiel der Fussball-Weltmeisterschaft 1994* (Berlin: Tischler, 1999); S. Inthorn, 'A Game of Nations? Football and National Identities', in A. Tomlinson and C. Young (eds), *German Football: History, Culture, Society* (Oxford: Taylor and Francis, 2007), pp.155–267.

more Games, with 8.8 million watching twenty-one or more. Most impressively, 30 million Germans watched the semi-final between Germany and Italy, giving it a market share of 84.1 per cent, the highest percentage of any television audience since the introduction of audience participation surveys in 1975. Even matches with no German participation were watched on average by 10 million people.[50]

Internationally, the FIFA World Cup presented a mixed picture. The matches were shown on 376 television stations, more than any previous World Cup. There were 43,600 broadcasts totalling 73,000 hours aired in 214 countries, which if shown on a single station would be the equivalent of eight years of continuous telecast. There were 26.29 billion in-home and 2.1 billion out-of-home viewers, the same numbers as four years previously in Japan and Korea. The cumulative European audience in 2006 was 5.33 billion (up 29.6 per cent over 2002), with Germany and Italy contributing 31.5 per cent of the total.[51] German newspapers informed the fans about public reaction abroad, thus creating a feedback system, as Germans celebrated themselves and saw that their show of national identity was widely appreciated.[52]

50 S. Geese, C. Zeughardt and H. Gerhardt, 'Die Fussballweltmeisterschaft 2006 im Fernsehen', *Media Perspektiven*, vol. 24, no. 6 (2006), pp.454–64.
51 Fédération Internationale de Football Association, 'No. 1 Sports Event', FIFA InfoPlus, <http://www.fifa.com/mm/document/fifafacts/ffprojects/ip-401_06e_tv_2658.pdf> (accessed 8 July 2009).
52 M. Voeth, I. Tobies and C. Niederauer, *Fussball-Weltmeisterschaft 2006 – Was die Deutschen denken und dachten* (Stuttgart: Förderverein für Marketing, 2006); for a general view on audiences, see N. Abercrombie and B. Longhurst, *Audiences* (London: Sage, 1998).

Identity between Agency and Control

Peter Lösche (2002) has shown that football is not the cause of social change, but rather that it is an expression of public change taking place.[53] Previous interpretations have led us to believe that football changed the course of history, while in reality it is a sphere in which a general mood has the chance to express itself more freely than in many others areas of public life. No other area has such opportunity to create identity, in spite of all of the cleavages, as football. It is appreciated across all social, political and regional specificities. It helps to create identity as the individual becomes part of that imagined community of Germans or of the fans of a particular club. In football, allegiance is relatively stable, but it can shift from the smaller to the bigger entity rapidly.[54] If Schalke plays, one is a Schalke fan, but if Germany plays, a German fan. The stadium is one of the last places in which Germans of all classes can meet, although VIP lounges are making such meetings more and more difficult.

The *Wunder von Bern* is more present in the mind of the younger generation (up to age 24) than the Holocaust.[55] As Rahn notes, 'Politics is more interesting to people who are committed to some kinds of collective identities, e.g., partisan or national identities, because the self is more emotionally invested in objects that have a public or political nature.'[56] The

53 P. Lösche, 'Sport und Politik(Wissenschaft): Das dreidimensionale Verhältnis von Sport und politischem System der Bundesrepublik Deutschland', *Jahrbuch für Europa- und Nordamerikastudien*, no. 5 (2002), pp.45–63.

54 V. Scheuble and M. Wehner, 'Fussball und nationale Identität', *Der Bürger im Staat*, vol. 56, no. 1 (2006), pp.26–31.

55 Forschungsgruppe Wahlen e.V. (ed.), *Deutschen Geschichte – Ergebnisse einer repräsentativen Bevölkerungsumfrage* (Mannheim: Forschungsgruppe Wahlen, 2005), p.15ff. Sönke Wortmann's film on the 1954 World Cup broke box office records in Germany on its release in 2003. Wortmann also directed a film on the 2006 World Cup, *Deutschland: Ein Sommermärchen* (Germany, 2006).

56 W. M. Rahn, 'Feeling, Thinking, Being, Doing: Public Mood, American National Identity and Civic Participation', paper prepared for presentation at the Annual Meeting of the Midwest Political Science Association, Chicago, IL, 17 April 2004,

conversion of the football stadiums to all-seater arenas, and the fact that two-thirds of all tickets were given to sponsors and football federations, tremendously increased the role of public viewing at 'Fan-Fest' events. With all sorts of security measures, the stadiums as well as the Fan-Fests were planned to be a demonstration of the omnipresent state. Nothing seemed to be left to chance.[57] The disaster of the 1972 Munich Olympics (yet another sports-related realm of memory) is still in the minds of many of those responsible for public safety. Nobody expected such a turnout of supporters, with the fans taking over the streets.

The role of industry has not been studied yet. Although the exclusive rights of the sponsors have been discussed, merchandizing has had an influence in establishing an image of identity.[58] While England played under the Union Jack at early football world cups, the team now plays under the St George's Cross to differentiate itself and its supporters from the Scottish fans with their St Andrew's Cross,[59] as, in that particular context, all that is required is a flag and an anthem. This process of selection as applied to national symbols mirrors that of the traditional Japanese flag, which was similarly first used in the world of sport. However, the extent to which such collective symbols are taken up by the individual must, inevitably, remain unclear. How does an individual feel when he or she buys the jersey of a national team or of one of the players of that team? What does one feel as a German if the *Bildzeitung* (a German daily with a circulation of about 4 million and a readership of about 10 million) announces in a banner

<http://www.allacademic.com//meta/p_mla_apa_research_citation/0/8/2/3/4/pages82345/p82345-1.php> (accessed 8 July 2009), p.22; see also F. Manning, *The Celebration of Society: Perspectives on Contemporary Cultural Performance* (Bowling Green, KY: Bowling Green University Press, 1983).

57 B. Ufer, 'Emotionen und Erlebnisse beim Public Viewing: Explorative interdisziplinäre Analyse eines gesellschaftlichen Phänomens' (unpublished PhD thesis, University of Göttingen, 2009).

58 D. Hesmondhalgh, *Cultural Industries* (London: Sage 2002); P. du Gay and M. Pryke (eds), *Cultural Economy* (London: Sage, 2002).

59 S. Reichl, 'Flying the Flag: The Intricate Semiotics of National Identity', *European Journal of English Studies*, vol. 8, no. 2 (2004), pp.205–17.

headline on its front page *'Wir sind Papst'*? (We Are the Pope) – or in 2006 *'Schwarz-Rot-Geil'* (Black-Red-Cool)?[60]

As in many fields involving the clash of private and public matters, football is at the crossroads of agency and control. Germany has a long tradition of a predominance of control. Fans enjoy the odd mixture, as they watch something that is controlled by the referee, and by the coaches, yet where players deliver brilliant individual performances within the rules of the game and a controlled team strategy. In the end, it is the result that counts, that is it is the agency of the players that matters. The fans have been relatively lightly controlled for some time now, but the club, the police and private security providers try to prevent excesses of agency. If a stadium is all-seater, there is less agency than on the terraces. In 'Fan-Fests' the control is significantly lighter. Of course, great care was taken with the preparations for the big party. There was not just an official national anthem, but also an unofficial song that was specially produced for the World Cup;[61] the mascot, however, played only a minor role.

Two years later at the European Football Championship, German enthusiasm seemed to be less expressive. The German team itself played less enthusiastically, and in a more controlled way. So the question arises as to whether the enthusiasm of 2006 was also (partly) due to the charismatic team manager Jürgen Klinsmann, and the attacking and committed style of football he drew from his team. Or was it the general social climate that influenced the context of the World Cup? Was the enthusiasm less pronounced in 2008 as the Championships did not take place in Germany, which thus lacked the presence of thirty-one other national teams and their fans? After all, these foreign fans may have stimulated the reaction of the German fans, just as the fans of rival football clubs stimulate each other. At the Olympic Games or other international championships, the foreign athletes tend to live in an Olympic village, in a single location, thus the enthusiasm of the fans is concentrated on that spot, to the exclusion of the rest of the country.

60   Using 'geil' instead of 'gold' (both starting with a 'g') is a clever semantic trick: 'geil' is part of the youth language, signifying 'cool', 'horny', 'lustful', and thus also 'happy'.

61   The song *'54, '74, '90, 2006*, by the Sportfreunde Stiller, made it to number one in the German single charts for two weeks.

It is difficult to determine the reasons for the enthusiasm on the part of the 2006 fans. Whatever its source, it certainly helped to increase a sense of national identity beyond the East-West divisions.[62] The fans were also individuals, so it is difficult to come to any generalized conclusions. The constant commentary on and descriptions of fans in the mass media have made them into symbols of an imagined community. Such 'imagined communities' are part of national identity. One can therefore safely assume that the FIFA World Cup in 2006 will stay in the collective memory of Germans as one of the realms of memory to which Nora refers.[63] Media events such as the FIFA World Cup are a part of both individual and mass communication. The communication in 2006 was not only verbal, but also symbolic, as there were more cars and bicycles showing German flags (about 24 × 54 cm, on a small plastic shaft, 'Made in China') and more people wearing national shirts than ever before.

Conclusion

This discussion has been a social constructionist attempt to analyse German identity. Was the reception really identical in the East and the West? Did the East German fans feel differently about the team captain Michael Ballack and the sterling player Bernd Schneider, as these two players were products of the GDR's talent selection system? We have not analysed the language of the fans' chants or the television commentaries to show how an imagined community is reinforced. Or was this just a feedback system,

---

62   GDR football supporters have often been fans of the West German team. GDR football hooligans demonstrated to the average citizen the limits of the GDR police force, see J. Braun and U. Hagemann (eds), *Deutschland einig Fussballland? Deutsche Geschichte nach 1949 im Zeichen des Fussballs* (Hohengehren: Schneider, 2008); M. Dennis, 'Soccer Hooliganism in the German Democratic Republic', in Tomlinson and Young, *German Football*, pp.52–71.

63   B. Anderson, *Imagined Communities: Reflections on the Origin and Spread of Nationalism* (London: Verso, 1983); P. Nora, *Les Lieux de mémoire*.

that strengthened an existing identity, or did it actually create that identity in the first place? The emotional communication potential of the individual matches has not been analysed either. The number of TV spectators viewing out-of-home varied between 10 and almost 17 million. Television is capable of massaging the masses,[64] and this increases the awareness of the imagined community. We do not know to what extent the postmodern patchwork-identity has an influence on national identity.

Which of these activities can legitimately be considered a part of agency, and what was manipulated or forced upon the spectators by group or mass behaviour? FIFA negotiated with the German government and the German football federation and its organizing committee under the chairmanship of football idol Franz Beckenbauer. The German government and FIFA stand for absolute control, in which only the sponsors are permitted to interfere.[65] The German authorities were preoccupied by a potential hooligan threat, and thus not alive to the carnivalesque potential of the event.[66] They did not anticipate the fans taking over, converting what the officials had presumed to be a 'serious' national event into a gigantic carnival. This shift of control from government and federations, the official Germany, to the fans showed that the young generation of Germans has a very different attitude towards the 'nation' from the older generation, now preferring government by the governed. The German fans were far more colourful than any previous World Cup football fans; does this also symbolize the fact that the new German identity is colourful and resents the previous uniformity? When the late Peter Glotz demanded that post-unification Germany should become more like the Netherlands, more liberal, easier on the 'aesthetics of the state', with much less emotional rhetoric, less declamatory nationalism, he was not thinking about football fans.[67] What has been

64   F. Rötzer, 'Mediale Massage', *Telepolis: Magazin der Netzkultur*, vol. 11, no. 6 (2006), <http://www.heise.de/tp/r4/artikel/22/22842/1.html> (accessed 8 July 2009).

65   J. Sugden and A. Tomlinson, *Who Rules the Peoples' Game? FIFA and the Contest for World Football* (Cambridge: Polity, 1998); Maurice Roche, *Mega-Events and Modernity: Olympics and Expos in the Growth of Global Culture* (London: Routledge, 2000).

66   R. Giulianotti, 'Football and the Politics of Carnival: An Ethnographic Study of Scottish Fans in Sweden', *International Review for the Sociology of Sport*, vol. 30, no. 2 (1995), pp.191–220.

67   Glotz, *Die Identität des grösseren Deutschlands*, p.152.

described as the *campanilismo* of Italian football, happy national unity on the basis of very strong local patriotism, is also present in Germany.[68] Italian unity came at a similar time to Germany's in the nineteenth century, and so the historical basis of the social and political fabric has been similar.[69] But this postmodern German identity which incorporates the many cleavages characterized by being individual and multi-faceted is sceptical about heavy-handed government and simply enjoys a big party when there is one. There have been a large number of official 'image campaigns' aimed at maximizing the positive legacy of the FIFA World Cup in Germany. Although these should be seen as the background to the fans' behaviour, none of them really made the kind of impact the fans made themselves.[70] In this respect, the FIFA World Cup 2006 was certainly influential in shaping postmodern German identity, but this national identity turned out to be significantly different from the previous perceptions and assumptions of the German (and other) authorities and the media.

Bibliography

Abercrombie, N. and B. Longhurst. *Audiences* (London: Sage, 1998).

Alesina, A. and N. Fuchs-Schündeln. 'Good-Bye Lenin (or Not?): The Effect of Communism on People's Preferences', *American Economic Review*, vol. 97, no. 4 (2007), pp.1507–28.

Anderson, B. *Imagined Communities: Reflections on the Origin and Spread of Nationalism* (London: Verso, 1983).

---

68 R. de Biasi and P. Lanfranchi, 'The Importance of Difference: Football Identities in Italy', in G. Armstrong and G. Giulianotti (eds), *Entering the Field: New Perspectives on World Football* (Oxford: Berg, 1997), pp.87–104.

69 A. Krüger, 'The Influence of the State Sport of Fascist Italy on Nazi Germany, 1928–1936', in J. A. Mangan and R. Small (eds), *Sport, Culture, Society* (London: Spon, 1986), pp.145–65.

70 K. Kamps and J.-U. Nieland, 'Weltschaufenster Fussball: Kampagnen aus Anlass der WM 2006', in J. Mittag and J.-U. Nieland (eds), *Das Spiel mit dem Fussball: Interessen, Projektionen und Vereinnahmungen* (Essen: Klartext, 2007), pp.579–86.

Aufgebauer, P., D. Denecke et al. *Das Eichsfeld: Ein Deutscher Grenzraum* (Duderstadt: Mecke, 2002).

Balibar, E. 'The Nation Form: History and Ideology', in P. Essed and D. T. Goldberg
(eds), *Race Critical Theories* (London: Blackwell, 2002), pp.220–30.

Beckstein, H. *Städtische Interessenpolitik: Organisation und Politik der Städtetage
in Bayern, Preussen und im Deutschen Reich, 1896–1923* (Düsseldorf: Droste,
1991).

Biersack, A. 'Local Knowledge, Local History: Geertz and Beyond', in L. Hunt (ed.),
The New Cultural History (Berkeley, CA: University of California Press, 1989),
pp.72–96.

Billig, M. *Banal Nationalism* (2nd edn; London: Sage, 1997).

Braun, J. and M. Barsuhn. 'Schussfahrt in die Einheit', *Horch und Guck*, vol. 14, no.
51 (2005), pp 33–9.

Braun, J. and U. Hagemann (eds). *Deutschland einig Fussballland? Deutsche Geschichte
nach 1949 im Zeichen des Fussballs* (Hohengehren: Schneider, 2008).

Breitmeier, F. 'Ein Wunder, wie es im Drehbuch steht: Die WM 1954 – ein deutscher
Erinnerungsfilm', in W. Pyta (ed.) *Der Lange Weg zur Bundesliga* (Münster: LIT,
2004), pp.127–50.

Daalmann, A. *Fussball und Nationalismus: Erscheinungsformen in Presse- und Fernsehberichten in der Bundesrepubik Deutschland und den Vereinigten Staaten
von Amerika am Beispiel der Fussball-Weltmeisterschaft 1994* (Berlin: Tischler,
1999).

De Biasi, R. and P. Lanfranchi. 'The Importance of Difference: Football Identities in
Italy', in G. Armstrong and R. Giulianotti (eds), *Entering the Field: New Perspectives on World Football* (Oxford: Berg, 1997), pp.87–104.

Dennis, M. 'Soccer Hooliganism in the German Democratic Republic', in A. Tomlinson and C. Young (eds), *German Football: History, Culture, Society* (London:
Routledge, 2006), pp.52–71.

Deutsche Bundesregierung (ed.) *Fussball-WM 2006: Abschlussbericht der Bundesregierung* (Berlin: Presse und Informationsamt der Bundesregierung, 2006).

Du Gay, P. and M. Pryke (eds). *Cultural Economy* (London: Sage, 2002).

Evans, M. D. R. and J. Kelley. 'National Pride in the Developed World: Survey Data
from 24 Nations', *International Journal of Public Opinion Research*, vol. 14, no.
3 (2002), pp.303–38.

Featherstone, M. 'Global and Local Cultures', in J. Bird, B. Curtis et al. (eds), *Mapping the Future: Local Cultures, Global Change* (London: Routledge, 1993),
pp.169–87.

Fédération Internationale de Football Association, 'No. 1 Sports Event', FIFA Info-
Plus, <http://www.fifa.com/mm/document/fifafacts/ffprojects/ip-401_06e_
tv_2658.pdf> (accessed 8 July 2009).

Flora, P. and E. Fix (eds). *Stein Rokkan: Staat, Nation und Demokratie in Europa – Die Theorie Stein Rokkans aus seinen gesammelten Werken* (Frankfurt: Suhrkamp, 2000).

Forschungsgruppe Wahlen e.V. (ed.) *Deutschen Geschichte – Ergebnisse einer repräsentativen Bevölkerungsumfrage* (Mannheim: Forschungsgruppe Wahlen, 2005).

Geese, S., C. Zeughardt and H. Gerhardt. 'Die Fussballweltmeisterschaft 2006 im Fernsehen', *Media Perspektiven*, vol. 24, no. 6 (2006), pp.454–64.

Geissler, R. 'Struktur und Entwicklung der Bevölkerung', *Informationen zur politischen Bildung*, no. 269 (2nd edn; Bonn: Bundeszentrale für politische Bildung, 2004), pp.1–3.

Giesen, B. (ed.) *Nationale und kulturelle Identität* (Frankfurt: Suhrkamp, 1991).

Gilroy, P. 'Diaspora and the Detours of Identity', in K. Woodward (ed.), *Identity and Difference* (London: Sage, 1997), pp.301–46.

Giulianotti, R. 'Football and the Politics of Carnival: An Ethnographic Study of Scottish Fans in Sweden', *International Review for the Sociology of Sport*, vol. 30, no. 2 (1995), pp.191–220.

——. *Football: A Sociology of the Global Game* (Cambridge: Polity, 1999).

Glotz, P. 'Die Identität des grösseren Deutschlands', in P. Glotz (ed.), *Der Irrweg des Nationalstaates: Europäische Reden an ein deutsches Publikum* (Stuttgart: DVA, 1990), pp.127–60.

Gödecke, M. and K. Schafmeister. 'Die lippischen Beiträge zum Varusjahr 2009', *Lippische Mitteilungen aus Geschichte und Landeskunde*, vol. 77 (2008), pp.201–5.

Goodman, R. and K. Refsing (eds), *Ideology and Practice in Modern Japan* (London: Routledge, 2002).

Heinonen, H. 'Finnish Soccer Supporters Away from Home: A Case Study of Finnish National Team Fans at a World Cup Qualifying Match in Liverpool, England', *Soccer & Society*, vol. 3, no. 3 (2002), pp.26–50.

Herzfeld, H. *Der 1. Weltkrieg* (Munich: DTV, 1968).

Hesmondhalgh, D. *Cultural Industries* (London: Sage, 2002).

Hobsbawm, E. J. and T. Ranger (eds). *The Invention of Tradition* (Cambridge: Cambridge University Press, 1984).

Huhn, K. *Beiträge zur Sportgeschichte* (Berlin: Spotless, 1995–present).

Hurrelbrink, P. 'Befreiung als Prozess: Die kollektiv-offizielle Erinnerung an den 8. Mai 1945 in der Bundesrepublik, der DDR und im vereinigten Deutschland', in G. Schwan, J. Holzer et al. (eds), *Demokratische Identität: Deutschland, Frankreich, Polen im Vergleich* (Wiesbaden: Verlag für Sozialwissenschaften, 2006), pp.71–120.

Inthorn, S. 'A Game of Nations? Football and National Identities', in A. Tomlinson and C. Young (eds), *German Football: History, Culture, Society* (London: Routledge, 2006), pp.155–67.

Jütting, D. H. (ed.) *Die Welt ist heimgekehrt: Studien zur Evaluation der FIFA-WM 2006* (Münster: Waxmann, 2007).

Kamps, K. and J.-U. Nieland. 'Weltschaufenster Fussball: Kampagnen aus Anlass der WM 2006', in J. Mittag and J.-U. Nieland (eds), *Das Spiel mit dem Fussball: Interessen, Projektionen und Vereinnahmungen* (Essen: Klartext, 2007), pp.579–86.

King, A. *The European Ritual: Football in the New Europe* (Aldershot: Ashgate, 2003), pp.191–222.

Krüger, A. *Die Olympischen Spiele 1936 und die Weltmeinung: Ihre aussenpolitische Bedeutung unter besonderer Berücksichtigung der USA* (Berlin: Bartels and Wernitz, 1972).

——. 'The Influence of the State Sport of Fascist Italy on Nazi Germany, 1928–1936', in J. A. Mangan and R. Small (eds), *Sport, Culture, Society* (London: Spon, 1986) pp.145–65.

——. '"Der olympische Gedanke in der modernen Welt hat uns zu einem Symbol des Weltkrieges verholfen": Die internationale Pressekampagne zur Vorbereitung auf die Olympischen Spiele 1916', in N. Gissel (ed.), *Öffentlicher Sport: Die Darstellung des Sports in Kunst, Medien und Literatur* (Hamburg: Czwalina, 1999), pp.55–67.

——. '"What's the Difference between Propaganda for Tourism and for a Political Regime?" Was the 1936 Olympics the First Postmodern Spectacle?', in J. Bale and M. K. Christensen (eds), *Post-Olympism? Questioning Sport in the Twenty-First Century* (Oxford: Berg, 2004), pp.33–50.

——. 'Grundlagen der Doping-Prophylaxe', in R. Kauerhof, S. Nagel and M. Zebisch (eds), *Doping und Gewaltprävention* (Leipzig: Leipziger Universitätsverlag, 2008), pp.143–66.

——. 'Sieben Arten in Vergessenheit zu geraten', in A. Krüger and B. Wedemeyer-Kolwe (eds), *Vergessen Verdrängt Abgelehnt: Zur Geschichte der Ausgrenzung im Sport* (Münster: LIT, 2009), pp.4–16.

——and W. Murray (eds). *The Nazi Olympics: Sport, Politics and Appeasement in the 1930s* (Champaign, IL: University of Illinois Press, 2003).

Laetsch, S. *Sind wir Deutschland?* (Hamburg: Diplomica, 2008).

Lösche, P. 'Sport und Politik(Wissenschaft): Das dreidimensionale Verhältnis von Sport und politischem System der Bundesrepublik Deutschland', *Jahrbuch für Europa- und Nordamerikastudien*, no. 5 (2002), pp.45–63.

MacClancy, J. (ed.) *Sport, Identity and Ethnicity* (Oxford: Berg, 1996).

Mährlein, J. *Der Sportler als Marke: Entwicklung, Vorteile, Erfolgsfaktoren* (Düsseldorf: VDM Müller, 2004).

——. *Der Sportstar in Deutschland: die Entwicklung des Spitzensportlers vom Helden zur Marke* (Göttingen: Sieke, 2009).

Maffesoli, M. *The Time of the Tribe: The Decline of Individualism in Mass Society* (London: Sage, 1996).

Mai, G. *Das Ende des Kaiserreichs: Politik und Kriegsführung im Ersten Weltkrieg* (Munich: DTV, 1993).

Manning, F. *The Celebration of Society: Perspectives on Contemporary Cultural Performance* (Bowling Green, KY: Bowling Green University Press, 1983).

Manzenreiter, W. 'Sport Spectacles, Uniformities and the Search for Identity in Late Modern Japan', *Sociological Review*, vol. 54, no. S2 (2006), pp.144–59.

Michael, M. *Constructing Identities* (London: Sage, 1996).

Noelle-Neumann, E. and R. Köcher. *Die verletzte Nation* (Stuttgart: DVA, 1987).

Nora, P. (ed.) *Les Lieux de mémoire* (3 vols; Paris: Gallimard, 1984; 1986; 1992).

Och, K. *Hat die Fussball-WM 2006 den Stahlhelm verbannt? Das Deutschlandbild in der Sportberichterstattung britischer Tageszeitungen* (Marburg: Tectum, 2008).

Pyta, W. 'Der Beitrag des Fussballsports zur kulturellen Identitätsstiftung in Deutschland', in W. Pyta (ed.), *Der Lange Weg zur Bundesliga* (Münster: LIT, 2004), pp.1–30.

Rahn, W. M. 'Feeling, Thinking, Being, Doing: Public Mood, American National Identity, and Civic Participation', paper prepared for presentation at the Annual Meeting of the Midwest Political Science Association, Chicago, IL, 17 April 2004, <http://www.allacademic.com//meta/p_mla_apa_research_citation/0/8/2/3/4/pages82345/p82345-1.php> (accessed 8 July 2009).

Reichl, S. 'Flying the Flag: The Intricate Semiotics of National Identity', *European Journal of English Studies*, vol. 8, no. 2 (2004), pp.205–17.

Roche, M. *Mega-Events and Modernity: Olympics and Expos in the Growth of Global Culture* (London: Routledge, 2000).

Rötzer, F., 'Mediale Massage', *Telepolis: Magazin der Netzkultur*, vol. 11, no. 6 (2006), <http://www.heise.de/tp/r4/artikel/22/22842/1.html> (accessed 8 July 2009).

Rokkan, S. *Vergleichende Sozialwissenschaft: Die Entwicklung der inter-kulturellen, inter-gesellschaftlichen und inter-nationalen Forschung* (Frankfurt: Ullstein, 1972).

Scheuble, V. and M. Wehner. 'Fussball und nationale Identität', *Der Bürger im Staat*, vol. 56, no. 1 (2006), pp.26–31.

Schmidt, P. and T. Blank (eds). 'National Identity in Europe', *Political Psychology*, special issue, vol. 24, no. 2 (2003), pp.233–401.

Schulze, H. *Der Weg zum Nationalstaat: Die Deutsche Nationalbewegung vom 18. Jahrhundert bis zur Reichsgründung* (Munich: DTV, 1992).

Seier, H. 'Der Deutsche Bund als Forschungsproblem, 1815–1960', *Wiener Beiträge Geschiche der Neuzeit*, vol. 16, no. 7 (1990), pp.31–58.

Smith, A. and D. Porter (eds). *Sport and National Identity in the Post-War World* (London: Routledge, 2004).

Smith, T. W. and L. Jarkko. *National Pride: A Cross-national Analysis* (GSS Cross-national Report no. 19; Chicago: NORC, 1998).

Smith, T. W. and S. Kim. 'National Pride in Comparative Perspective: 1995/96 and 2003/04', *International Journal of Public Opinion Research*, vol. 18, no. 1 (2006), pp.127–36.

Spitzer, G. *Doping in der DDR: ein historischer Überblick zu einer konspirativen Praxis; Genese – Verantwortung – Gefahren* (3rd edn; Cologne: Sport und Buch Strauss, 2004).

Strohbach, N. '"Is this love?" Liebe und Ähnliches in der (griechischen) Antike', in Y. Niekrenz and D. Villanyi (eds). *Liebeserklärungen: Intimbeziehungen aus soziologischer Perspektive* (Wiesbaden: Verlag für Sozialwissenschaften, 2008), pp.23–39.

Sugden, J. and A. Tomlinson. *Who Rules the Peoples' Game? FIFA and the Contest for World Football* (Cambridge: Polity, 1998).

Sugden, J. and A. Bairner (eds). *Sport in Divided Societies* (Aachen: Meyer and Meyer, 1999).

Süssmuth, B., M. Heyne and W. Maennig. *Induced Civic Pride and Integration* (CESIFO Working Paper, no. 2582; Munich: Ifo, 2009).

Tomlinson, A. and C. Young (eds). *German Football: History, Culture, Society* (London: Routledge, 2006).

Ufer, B. 'Emotionen und Erlebnisse beim Public Viewing: Explorative interdisziplinäre Analyse eines gesellschaftlichen Phänomens' (unpublished PhD thesis, University of Göttingen, 2009).

Voeth, M., Tobies, I. and C. Niederauer. *Fussball-Weltmeisterschaft 2006 – Was die Deutschen denken und dachten* (Stuttgart: Förderverein für Marketing, 2006).

Wehler, H.-U. *Das Deutsche Kaiserreich, 1871–1918* (Göttingen: V and R, 1988).

JAMES RIORDAN

Chapter 14
Sport and Politics in Russia and the Former Soviet Union

The Role of Sport in a Totalitarian State

In a society of cataclysmic transformation and authoritarian dictatorship – which Russia has been for over a hundred years – sport has acquired a unique meaning for ordinary people in terms of identity and Platonic 'empathy and catharsis'. Nikolai Starostin, one-time Soviet football captain and Gulag victim came close to explaining this role when he talked of Soviet football in the 1920s and 1930s:

> I think that the pre-war social role and significance of football grew out of the special relationship the public had with it. People seemed to separate it from all that was going on around them. It was like the utterly unreasoned worship by sinners desperate to seek oblivion in their blind appeal to divinity. For most people football was the only, and sometimes the very last, chance and hope of retaining in their souls a tiny island of sincere feelings and human relations.[1]

This is a perceptive comment on the role of sport under a totalitarian regime, and it applies to sportsmen and women, as well as fans, in all such countries, whether Nazi Germany, Fascist Italy, Falangist Spain or any of the one-time or current communist states.[2]

---

1   N. Starostin, *Futbol skvoz gody* [Football Down the Years] (Moscow: Sovetskaya Rossiya, 1989), p.83.
2   See P. Arnaud and J. Riordan (eds), *Sport and International Politics: The Impact of Fascism and Communism on Sport* (London: Spon, 1998).

Further, the relationship between sport and the public has special significance for Russians, who, in the last twenty years, have moved from being Soviet citizens in a multi-ethnic state to Russian citizens in 'Mother Rus'. This is not a reversion to the pre-1917 situation because under the tsars Russia was an inland empire that embraced over a hundred different nationalities. Now, for the first time, Russians have a country (more or less) to themselves, stretching half way round the world to the Sea of Japan in the east, the Arctic Ocean in the north and the mountains in the south that separate the country from China and Mongolia. In such a vast land, Russians today make up some 80 per cent of the population (in the USSR they comprised nearly 49 per cent).

The Early Days of Organized Sport in Russia

Russian sport has its roots deep in Russian history, in the people's traditions, the climate, fears about internal and external foes (in a land which borders on a dozen foreign states), in the organized sports pioneered mainly by Britain, the gymnastics schools of Germany (Jahn), Scandinavia (Ling and Nachtegal) and the Czech lands (Tyrs), as well as in Prussian military training. In 1917, when the Bolsheviks came to power, the new leadership inherited from tsarist Russia an incipient sports movement that differed in a number of ways from that which had developed in the West. In Britain particularly, individual enthusiasts from among the leisured class had pioneered the development of certain organized sports, given them their rules and conventions and often made them exclusive to their social, racial and gender group. There were thus established single-sport clubs (for tennis, golf, football, etc.) and governing bodies for individual sports separate from one another and from government, based for purposes of control and, to a large extent, of finance on their members.[3]

---

3   See J. Riordan, 'Amateurism, Sport and the Left: Amateurism for All Versus Amateur Elitism,' in T. Collins and D. Porter (eds), *Sport in History*, special issue, 'Amateurism in Britain: For the Love of the Game?' (London: Routledge, 2006), pp.468–84.

In Russia, on the other hand, as in the economy, the tsarist state had to some extent discouraged individual enterprise; it had created some control over the organization of sport – in schools, the armed forces, the national federations and the Olympic Committee (Russia being a founder member of the International Olympic Committee). It had set up the Office of the Chief Supervisor of Sport headed by an army officer, General Voyeikov, to coordinate the sports movement. Moreover, most Russian clubs became multi-sport centres, in so far as the organization of Russian sport developed in close association with the Olympic model; and these sports complexes were linked to local and central government. This enabled the regime to maintain close supervision over the development of organized sport and to prevent it being used for anti-monarchist, liberal or revolutionary purposes (as the Turner movement in Germany and the Sokol movement in the Czech lands had been). In Russia, some rebel groups formed illegal *dikie* – 'outlaw' – clubs which practised shooting and unarmed combat on remote fields.

Revolutionary Sport

The new Soviet government in 1917 was therefore able to take over a ready-made state organization of sport without having to dismantle a wide-ranging structure of autonomous sports clubs and federations, or to counter any firmly rooted amateur values. What is more, with the sweeping away of a leisured class, there were no members of the upper or middle classes left in Russian society to develop sport for their own disport, as they had in, say, Britain.

The functions of sport were seen as raising physical and social health standards, socializing people into the new system of values, encouraging a population in rapid transition from country to town to identify themselves with wider communities (including the 'Soviet nation') and, after World War II, facilitating international recognition and prestige. This was a pattern of sports development common to many other modernizing societies during the twentieth century, especially in Africa, Asia and Latin America.

Essentially, however, sport during the first few years came to be geared to the needs of the war effort. All the old clubs and their equipment were commandeered for the Universal Military Training Board (*Vsevobuch*) whose main aim was to supply the Red Army with contingents of trained conscripts as quickly as possible.

A second major consideration was health. Regular participation in physical exercise was to be a means of improving health standards swiftly and of educating people in hygiene, nutrition and exercise. This could only succeed, in the opinion of Nikolai Podvoisky, head of *Vsevobuch*, if the emotional attractions of competitive sport were fully exploited – this at a time when influential groups were agitating against competition and record-breaking. For example, the 'Hygienists' were totally against competitive sport and the playing of any sport that was harmful (mentally and physically) to the human organism (such as boxing, weightlifting or rugby). The 'Proletkult' (Proletarian Culture group) believed that a completely new sports superstructure should develop upon society's socialist base. The advocates of both movements in the 1920s became 'left-deviationist' victims of the purges in the late 1930s.[4]

A third function of sport was integration of the many nationalities into a single socialist federation. The significance, therefore, of the First Central Asian Olympics, held in Tashkent over ten days in early October 1920, may be judged from the fact that this was the first time that Uzbeks, Kirgiz, Kazakhs and other Turkic peoples, as well as Russians and other Europeans, had competed in any sporting event together.[5]

4   See Z. Starovoitova, *Istoriya fizicheskoi kultury* [History of Physical Culture] (Moscow: Partizdat, 1969), pp.139–40; A. V. Lunacharsky, *Mysli o sporte* [Thoughts on Sport] (Moscow: Partizdat, 1930), p.72.

5   D. Yeshchin and A. Pustovalov, *Natsionalny vopros v fizkulturnom dvizhenii* [The National Issue in the Physical Culture Movement] (Moscow-Leningrad: Izdatelstvo, 1938), p.12.

Impact on Sport of Industrialization, Collectivization and Political Dictatorship

The implications for the sports movement of the economic and political processes (rapid industrialization, collectivization of agriculture and political dictatorship) of the late 1920s and early 1930s were extremely important, for it was then that the organized pattern of Soviet sport was formed – with the nationwide sports societies, sports schools, national fitness programme and the uniform rankings system for individual sports. The new society saw the flourishing of all manner of competitive sports with spectator appeal, of leagues, cups, championships, popularity polls and cults of sporting heroes. All were designed to provide recreation and diversion for the fast-growing urban populace. The big city and security forces (*Dinamo*) teams, with their substantial resources, dominated competition in all sports. Thus, the premier league of 1938 included nine Moscow and six *Dinamo* teams from the cities of Moscow, Leningrad, Kiev, Tbilisi, Odessa and Rostov out of its twenty-six clubs.[6]

A relatively close tie was re-established in the 1930s between sport and the military, stemming from the conviction that a state surrounded by unfriendly powers (especially with the rise of Fascism in Italy and Germany) must be militarily strong. Sport openly became a means of providing pre-military training and achieving a relatively high standard of national fitness and defence. The two largest and most successful sports clubs were those run by the armed forces and the security forces: the Central House of the Red Army (later to become the Central Sports Club of the Army, *TsSKA*) and *Dinamo*, respectively. After 1931, moreover, the national fitness programme, the *GTO*, was expressly intended to train people, through sport, for military preparedness and work – the Russian abbreviation *GTO* – *Gotov k trudu i oborone* – standing for 'Prepared for Labour and Defence'.

---

6   See N. A. Kiselyov (ed.), *70 futbolnykh let* [70 Football Years] (Leningrad: Lenizdat, 1970); also J. Riordan, *Sport in Soviet Society* (Cambridge: Cambridge University Press, 1977), pp.124–8.

The junior fitness programme was called 'Be Prepared for Labour and Defence', giving a clue to its origin. The initial fitness targets were based on Baden-Powell's Boy Scout badges for 'Athlete' and 'Marksman', taken from his book *Scouting for Boys* (1909) – though this was never attributed to him in Soviet times.[7]

Post-War Sports Competition with the West

With the conclusion of the war and the setting of a new national target – to catch up with and overtake the most advanced industrial powers in sport as in all else – the Soviet leaders felt it possible to demonstrate the pre-eminence of sport in Soviet socialist society. Given the limited opportunities elsewhere, sport seemed to offer a suitable medium for pursuing this goal as an area in which the USSR did not have to take second place to capitalist states. This aim presupposed a level of skill in a wide range of sports superior to that existing in the leading Western states.

This trend towards proficiency was reinforced after the war by mobilization of the total, if limited, resources of the entire sports system, by creating full-time, well-remunerated athletes and teams, and by giving them considerable backing (including, after 1960, some forty sports boarding schools). Soviet leaders saw sport as 'one of the best and most comprehensible means of explaining to people all over the world the advantages of the socialist system over capitalism'.[8]

7   The Young Pioneers took over from the Scouts their motto 'Be Prepared', their salute and their emblem – the *fleur de lys* – which later evolved into three flames. It was said that the motto came not from Baden Powell, but from Lenin who had once said that 'Workers Must Always Be Prepared for Action'. See *Pedagogicheskaya entsiklopediya* [Pedagogical Encyclopaedia] (vol. III; Moscow, 1968), p.853.
8   See N. Romanov, *Trudnye dorogi k Olimpu* [Difficult Roads to Olympus] (Moscow: Fizkultura i sport, 1987), p.57.

By the Second World War, Soviet sport was approaching international standards in a few sports. In football it had evidently reached it, as demonstrated by the four-match unbeaten tour of Britain by the Moscow *Dinamo* team in the autumn of 1945. It was not long, however, before the Soviet Union was to become the most successful and versatile nation in the history of sport, particularly in amateur sports at the Olympic Games. The USSR dominated the summer and winter Olympics, from its Helsinki debut in 1952, as well as some non-Olympic sports, like chess (chess and draughts were defined as 'sports' in the Soviet Union and included in the Uniform Rankings as well as, in the case of chess, in sports boarding schools). On the other hand, the Soviet Union never seriously challenged the world's leading football teams (after 1945). Soviet football failed to gain a place among the world's leading nations or clubs. The same might be said of professional basketball, tennis and cycling, though not ice hockey, where the Soviet national team took on and beat the leading National Hockey League clubs in the first hockey 'summit' of 1972 and went on to do well in the rest of the 1970s and 1980s.

And yet, at the very moment of reaching the pinnacle of sporting glory, the Soviet Union precipitously (and, to most people, unexpectedly) started to fall apart. Two years after the Moscow-hosted Olympic Games, the Soviet President, Leonid Brezhnev, died; three years and two more presidents later, Mikhail Gorbachev came to power with the radically new policies of 'perestroika' (rebuilding the economy) and 'glasnost' (political openness). It was too little, too late. Four years after that, the communist edifice crumbled throughout the eight nations of Eastern and Central Europe. The Soviet Union followed suit and ceased to exist as a unitary state in late 1991. It would be a mite extravagant to blame the Moscow Olympics for the demise of communism. Yet for many citizens of communist states, the 1980 Olympics brought tensions to a head, especially as the public was able to see those tensions in its own backyard. It is noteworthy that when the revolutions swept across Eastern Europe in late 1989, there was an intense debate about sport. Far from being at the periphery of politics, sport was right at the core.

The rapidity of post-totalitarian change in all areas, sports included, in Eastern and Central Europe and the one-time Soviet Union would seem to indicate that the elite sports system and its attainments, far from inspiring national pride and patriotism, tended to provoke resentment among many people. This appeared to be more evident in those countries – Hungary, Poland, Romania, Bulgaria and the GDR – which had 'revolution' and an alien sports system and values thrust upon them that were contrary to their indigenous traditions. A similar mood has been apparent, too, in Islamic (Uzbekistan, Kazakhstan, Turkmenistan, Tadzhikistan and Kirghizia) and Baltic (Lithuania, Latvia and Estonia) areas of the old USSR.

Sports stars were seen as belonging to a private, elite fiefdom within the overall domain; they were not part of a shared national achievement, let alone heritage. That is not to say that, in societies of hardship and totalitarian constraint, and in the face of Western arrogance and attitudes that were sometimes tantamount to racial prejudice, the ordinary citizen obtained no vicarious pleasure in her/his champion's or team's performance. But, overall, the dominant attitude was one not entirely different from British class attitudes to sports and heroes which are not 'ours'.

On the other hand, in countries like the now defunct Yugoslavia and Czechoslovakia, as well as the Slav regions of the old Soviet Union (Ukraine, Belarus and Russia), the patriotic pride in sporting success and heroes would appear to have been genuine. One reason for this may be that the socialist revolution of 1917 in the old Russian empire, and of 1946 and 1948 in the cases of Yugoslavia and Czechoslovakia, came out of their own experience and had some popular support. The same might be said of China and Cuba.

Sport in Contemporary Russia

During the 1980s, radical changes had begun to appear in Soviet sport, breaking the mould of its functionalized and bureaucratic (plan-fulfilment) structure. Until then, not only had the state-controlled, utilitarian system hampered a true appraisal of realities that lay beneath the 'universal' statistics and 'idealized' veneer, it had prevented concessions to particular groups in the population – the 'we know what's best for you' syndrome whereby the fit tell the disabled that sport is not for them; men tell women what sports they should play; the old tell the young they can play only on their (old) terms, in their clubs, using their facilities; the leaders, mindful of international prestige, decide that competitive Olympic sports are the only civilized form of culture. It also entailed Moscow (via the Warsaw Pact military alliance) telling other European communist countries that they were to boycott the Los Angeles Olympics of 1984 (though Yugoslavia and Romania demurred) as a quid pro quo for the US attempted boycott of the Moscow Games in 1980.

Once people saw journalists writing about the past and exposing the realities of elite sport, they started to question the very morality of sport, the price that society should pay for talent. Many expressed their distaste at what they felt was a race for false glory, the cultivation of irrational loyalties, the unreasonable prominence given to the winning of victories, the setting of records and the collecting of trophies – an obsessive fetishism of sport. This was the very criticism made of 'sport' by opposition groups back in the 1920s, such as the 'Hygienists' and the Proletarian Culture advocates.

This is, of course, an issue not unknown in other societies, especially those of scarcity. But for a population that had been waiting years for decent housing, phones and cars, that saw the Russian economy collapsing, and that felt that sporting victories were being attained for political values they did not share – that is, that sports 'heroes' were not *theirs* and that they were somehow accomplices in gilding the lily of the Communist Party – the vast sums being lavished on ensuring a Grand Olympic Show represented the straw that broke the camel's back.

Having allowed the nation to bare its soul, the leaders in the post-communist, post-Gorbachev era radically changed their scale of priorities. They no longer saw the need to demonstrate the advantages of socialism since they were trying to distance themselves from the command economy that had failed so badly and from the totalitarian political system that had accompanied the imposition of communism from above. Once the curtain came down on communism, the international challenge was diluted through lack of state support; the free trade union sports societies, as well as the ubiquitous *Dinamo* and armed forces clubs, mostly gave way to private sports and recreation clubs; women's wrestling and boxing extracted more profit than women's chess and volleyball; the various nationalities preferred their own independent teams to combined effort and success. So *Dinamo* Kiev opted to compete in a Ukrainian league (with similar competition to that in the Scottish premier league where Celtic and Glasgow Rangers annually vie for top spot), Tbilisi *Dinamo* in a Georgian league (ditto), and Russian clubs in the Russian Football League set up in 1991.

Putin and Sport

When he took over the presidency of Russia in 2000, Vladimir Putin seized on sport as a means to restore Russia's pride, power and dignity after the international humiliation it had received in the Gorbachev and Yeltsin eras. The erstwhile president (a top-class athlete himself: holder of a black belt in judo, as befits a former top agent in the security forces!) was mindful of the prestige that had accrued to the USSR through its sporting success at the Olympic Games. Putin's aim has been more ambitious, encompassing the world's top professional sports as well as the old amateur Olympic events. He set about clawing back the nation's assets from the oligarchs and forcing them to invest their vast fortunes at home, especially in Russian sport.

Soon after the Russian oligarch Roman Abramovich took control of the London football club Chelsea, he and other Russian businessmen were criticized by the then President of the Russian Football Association, Vyacheslav Koloskov who said that he 'would have preferred Abramovich and his business colleagues to invest their money in Russian football in so far as they had made their fortune by extracting and selling the country's natural resources [...] I hope that the oligarchs will help Russian clubs to right their financial situation which at the moment leaves much to be desired'.[9] It is not clear whether the warning came from on high or from the Russian Football Association, but shortly after the announcement, several oligarchs signed agreements to invest in the leading Russian football teams and the development of grass-roots football.

To give but one example. Roman Abramovich, owner of Chelsea FC, is obliged to invest substantial funds in Russian domestic football. Besides paying most of the $1.3 million annual salary of the former Russian team manager, Guus Hiddink, he has covered the construction costs ($30 million) of a new national stadium and contributed the lion's share to the building of ten new world-class stadiums (each costing some $170 million). He is also the chief investor in 'Operation Excellence', a scheme involving the creation of 75 artificial grass pitches and 9000 football youth academies.

The results have been impressive:

- In the last few years, Moscow's TsSKA (2005) and Zenit St Petersburg (2008) have won the UEFA Cup and the Super Cup. The Russian national team has risen from fifteenth to third/fourth (with Germany) in UEFA league rankings. In the 2008–9 season, the Russian Premier League moved up three places in UEFA rankings, to sixth among European leagues (behind England, Spain, Italy, France and Germany). Whereas only recently some top Russian teams fielded 11 foreigners, now all teams by law field mainly Russians. Russia is likely to rival England in bidding to stage the 2018 World Cup.
- In 2008, TsSKA won the European club basketball title.
- The Russian ice hockey team has celebrated victory in the hockey world championships, beating Canada (in Canada) in the 2008 final for the first time in 18 years.
- At the Beijing Olympics, Russia came third behind China and the USA, and fourth in the Paralympic medal table.
- Russian tennis players provide more men and women in the ranking tables than any other nation.

9   V. Koloskov, 'Oligarchs in Russian Football', quoted in *Sport-Express*, 9 September 2008.

Such developments undoubtedly leave Russians with mixed emotions. To some, participation in the global market for sports kudos and talent is seen as part of living in a 'normal' and 'civilized' world. Yet the process of sports globalization, with its concomitant 'boom and slump' (which the now disfavoured Karl Marx so accurately forecast), only goes to confirm Russia's subordinate status in the world. This is deeply resented by some people. Post-communist television has fostered the same kind of globalization and homogenization ('dumbing-down') in all forms of popular culture. Russian nationalism is wounded by the international sports and pop culture that accompanies the country's decline as a world power.

No wonder that some of the older generation hark back to the 'good old days' of Soviet 'high culture' and relative security. There were no 'hit' killings, no drain of talent abroad, no take-overs by oligarchs, no American-style culture. The great bulk of Russians believe the oligarchs stole the people's assets (oil, metals, gas) and left the Russian population worse off today than they were during the last thirty years of communism.

The sporting diaspora of Russian athletes and the nefarious activities of the oligarchs who own sports clubs have caused the same kind of nationalistic ire against multinational juggernauts and billionaire owners as they have caused elsewhere in the world. It has also had the effect of forcing fans to turn away from sport altogether. Football is one example. It has long been the most popular spectator sport during Russia's summer months (ice hockey and, increasingly, five-a-side indoor football take over in winter). In Soviet times, during the 1970s and 1980s, the major stadiums were packed to capacity, with an average of 35,000 fans at premiership matches. Today, the six major Moscow teams average just over 7000 spectators a game– a pitiful figure by any European standards.

The problem today is made more complex because athletes are part of an international monoculture of wealthy and privileged elite performers, many of whom have no patriotic loyalty to their country of birth and refuse to play for Russia (as in cycling, boxing and weightlifting) or change nationality when the money is right (as in athletics and swimming). In Soviet times, there was undeniably a different attitude in sportsmen and women, who, in any case, were banned from playing for non-Soviet teams or, as in tennis, had to hand over most of their fees to the sports ministry. Today, the astonishing rise of Russian tennis stars has much to do with the new image of women (and, to some extent, men), with its link to glamour and show business. Unlike in Soviet times, promising young tennis players can travel the world to train and compete in the best conditions (like to California, where Maria Sharapova lived from a young age) and earn fortunes by endorsing products and exploiting their allure and sex appeal.

Many Russians of the older generation find this hard to accept. Vladimir Rodionov, General Secretary of the Russian Football Federation, looks nostalgically back to the time when '[w]e were proud, we were patriotic, we played for love of our sport and our country. Now it's all about money. It affects everything'.[10] The American Robert Edelman makes a similar point in regard to sports consumers: 'Soviet citizens created an arena of popular culture that was human and genuine, spontaneous and playful. In the vortex of globalized sport, that difference has been lost'.[11]

In football, while some fans might look to the national team as representing a new Russian nationhood with which they might identify, the players often regard themselves, as Russia's one-time captain, Alexei Smertin, recently told me, as 'gypsies who roam the world looking for a hook on which to hang their kit: one year Bordeaux, the next Chelsea, then Portsmouth, back to Chelsea, then Charlton, Fulham. God knows where I'll be next year.' In fact, today, in his mid-thirties, he is plying his trade in Washington.

Looking Back and Looking Forward

The radical shift in sports policy generally has obscured many of the positive features of communist sport. The old system was broadly open to the talents in most sports, probably more so than in the West. It provided

---

10   G. Marcotti, 'Russia's flawed foreign policy', *The Times*, 15 November 2004, p.23.
11   R. Edelman, 'There Are No Rules on Planet Russia: Post-Soviet Spectator Sport', in A. Barker (ed.), *Consuming Russia: Popular Culture, Sex and Society since Gorbachev* (Durham, NC: Duke University Press, 1999), p.238.

opportunities for women to play and succeed, if not on equal terms with men, at least on a higher plane than Western women. It gave an opportunity to the many ethnic minorities and relatively small states within the USSR to do well internationally and help promote that pride and dignity that sports success in the glare of world publicity can bring. Nowhere in the world was there, since the early 1950s, such reverence for the Olympic movement, for Olympic ritual and decorum. One practical embodiment of that was the contribution to Olympic solidarity with modernizing nations: the training of Third World athletes, coaches, sports officials, medical officers and scholars at colleges and training camps. Much of this aid was free. None of it was disinterested; but it also went to those who were clearly exploited, with the collusion of the West, as was the case with the Soviet-led campaign against apartheid in sport.

Russia today is a society in transition, including in sport. Fixing the economy, cleaning up corruption, stopping the outflow of Russia's wealth, restoring a sense of pride and community, even introducing a modicum of democracy, would certainly contribute to a healthier society and sports system. It would also help Russians develop a sense of identity with something they could feel really was 'theirs' and not an appendage of a corrupt political system.

What an examination of Russian sport also reveals is the way the state can use sport to pursue socio-political ends. In the Soviet years (1917–91), sport was an agent of social change in the process of nation-building, with the state as pilot. In the post-Soviet and the Putin era, the ends have been mainly to try to restore Russian pride and power after the humiliation of the break-up of the USSR and the loss of control over near neighbours in Central and Eastern Europe. The leaders are able to use sport in this way because of Russia's conversion from state socialism to state capitalism, including the state direction of sport.

Bibliography

Arnaud, P. and J. Riordan (eds). *Sport and International Politics: The Impact of Fascism and Communism on Sport* (London: Spon, 1998).

Edelman, R. 'There Are No Rules on Planet Russia: Post-Soviet Spectator Sport,' in A. Barker (ed.), *Consuming Russia: Popular Culture, Sex and Society since Gorbachev* (Durham, NC: Duke University Press, 1999).

Kiselyov, N. A. (ed.) *70 futbolnykh let* [70 Football Years] (Leningrad: Lenizdat, 1970).

Koloskov, V. 'Oligarchs in Russian Football,' quoted in *Sport-Express*, 9 September 2008.

Lunacharsky, A. V. *Mysli o sporte* [Thoughts on Sport] (Moscow: Partizdat, 1930).

Marcotti, G. 'Russia's flawed foreign policy,' *The Times*, 15 November 2004, p.23.

Pedagogicheskaya entsiklopediya [Pedagogical Encyclopaedia] (vol. III; Moscow, 1968).

Riordan, J. *Sport in Soviet Society* (Cambridge: Cambridge University Press, 1977).

——.'Amateurism, Sport and the Left: Amateurism for All Versus Amateur Elitism,' in T. Collins and D. Porter (eds), *Sport in History*, special issue, 'Amateurism in Britain: For the Love of the Game?' (London: Routledge, 2006), pp.468–84.

Romanov, N. *Trudnye dorogi k Olimpu* [Difficult Roads to Olympus] (Moscow: Fizkultura i sport, 1987).

Starostin, N. *Futbol skvoz gody* [Football Down the Years] (Moscow: Sovetskaya Rossiya, 1989).

Starovoitova, Z. *Istoriya fizicheskoi kultury* [History of Physical Culture] (Moscow: Partizdat, 1969), pp.139–40.

Yeshchin, D. and A. Pustovalov. *Natsionalny vopros v fizkulturnom dvizhenii* [The National Issue in the Physical Culture Movement] (Moscow-Leningrad: Izdatelstvo, 1938).

JOHN BALE

Chapter 15
Europeans Writing the African 'Olympian'

This chapter explores colonial attitudes to an indigenous African body culture. Central to such a project is the European *representation* of the native by means of the colonialists' written words, rumours, painting, sketching, photography and filming. I adopt a postcolonial approach in the sense that that my analysis (a) provides an alternative reading of conventional colonial wisdoms and dominant meanings; (b) shows a concern with the re-writing of colonial texts; (c) explores aspects of colonial relations between the colonizer and the colonized; and (d) shows a willingness to seek out the 'density, contradiction and ambiguity of colonial discourse'.[1] This categorization is suggestive of *how* postcolonial studies of 'sport' might proceed, but how might postcolonial sports be defined?[2] There is, I suggest, a spectrum between what may be termed 'hybrid sportoids', in which two body-cultures become mixed when indigenous people meld a sport into their own games (such as Trobriand cricket),[3] and, at the other end of the scale, sports that are imposed and adopted by the colonized without any basic changes to the colonialists' sporting practices (such as British cricket and football). What follows explores a third scenario, where pre-colonial body-cultures survived colonialism (at least during part of the colonial period) and were never colonized and 'sportized'.

---

1   S. Ryan, *The Cartographic Eye* (Cambridge: Cambridge University Press, 1966), p.15.
2   See J. Bale and M. Cronin (eds), *Sport and Postcolonialism* (Oxford: Berg, 2003), pp.4–7.
3   On Trobriand cricket, see B. Malonowski, *Coral Gardens and Their Magic* (vol. 1; London: Allen and Unwin, 1935), p.211; H. A. Powell, 'Cricket in Kiriwina', *The Listener*, 4 September 1952, pp.384–5.

Rwanda and Its 'Spring Artists'

At the beginning of the twentieth century there were at least four configurations of vertical jumping worldwide. These included the British and North
American model of serious, competitive, achievement sport, including
the high jump. The second form of jumping was the 'gymnastic' model,
familiar in Germany and the Nordic nations, in which posture was more
important than performance. Thirdly, throughout many parts of Europe,
there were acts involving jumping in music halls and circuses where laughter and burlesque were popular characteristics. And fourthly, there were a
number of African and Asian configurations of vertical jumping that were,
at the time, being chronicled in Europe for the first time. It is this fourth
form of jumping that, between 1907 and the late 1950s, was recorded by a
large number of colonial writers, who, from the small nation of Rwanda,
brought back to Europe astonishing records of a form of 'high jumping'
called (by the native people) *gusimbuka-urukiramende*. The accounts of
this Rwandan jumping appeared in a variety of texts including travellers'
tales, anthropological research, missionary reports, and track and field
manuals.

Native Rwandan jumping differed in several ways from the 'Western'
and other models. First, athletes performed on unprepared sites, making
their jump from a raised mound, log or stone. They jumped feet first and
landed on the same kind of surface as that from which they took off. Secondly the jumpers, who often ran together in a line, jumped, one after
another, over a carefully placed reed which rested on two upright reeds
that sloped away from the on-coming jumper (see Figure 15.1). Thirdly, it
was not necessarily competitive, lacking in measured records, with only
Europeans retaining measurements of performances during the colonial
period. Standardized equipment was not used and 'results', therefore, lacked
comparability. It was not a modern sport, but it was easily constructed as
one – as an 'imaginative sport' (*pace* Said), that is, one represented in those
writings about parts of the world that reflected a European imagination.[4]

---

4   E. Said, *Orientalism* (London: Penguin, 1995).

But European writing of this African athleticism was far from monolithic and consisted of a variety of discursive practices that were often ambivalent. It is the variety of rhetorical modes used to describe *gusimbuka* that forms the focus of this chapter.

The first Europeans to witness and record this Rwandan form of athleticism are thought to have been members of the Duke of Mecklenburg's expedition to central and east Africa.[5] The Mecklenburg party also claimed to be the first expedition to photograph this form of an African corporeality. Indeed, there is a strong suggestion that members of the Mecklenburg expedition arranged this photographic event themselves. The weighted rope, identical to German gymnastic jumping, is not shown in any other photographs that I have seen (Figure 15.2).[6] Subsequent travellers, scientists and tourists who recorded the Rwandan high jumpers in various media, invariably named the young men who performed *gusimbuka* 'a Tutsi', rather than Hutu or Twa (the two other groups of people making up the *Banyarwanda*) and continued to do so for a half century or more. Fifty years after the Mecklenburg photograph was taken the basic form of *gusimbuka* had barely changed (Figure 15.3).

Gusimbuka seems to have been practised in three contexts. The first was as a part of manly training (by groups of selected youths or *intore*) at the 'court' of the 'king' (*mwami*) or of chiefs. The *intore* were disbanded by the Belgian colonial administration in 1922 as the result of their growing indiscipline and thereafter *gusimbuka* was most widely performed in a second context, namely at celebratory gatherings such as royal festivals and weddings. A third, less well-documented, context is thought to have been as a local form of popular recreation.[7] The *mwami* and the major chiefs of Rwanda were invariably members of the Tutsi elite, and during the colonial period Tutsi represented about twelve per cent of the Rwandan population (*Banyarwanda*) though there were considerable regional variations in the

5   A. Mecklenburg, *In the Heart of Africa* (London: Cassell, 1910); J. Czekanowski, *Forschungen im Nil-Congo-Zwischengebiet* (vol. 3; Leipzig: Kinkhardt and Biermann, 1911).
6   J. Bale, *Imagined Olympians* (Minneapolis: University of Minnesota Press, 2002).
7   J. Maquet, *The Premise of Inequality in Rwanda* (London: Oxford University Press, 1961), p.21.

balance of population. The Hutu majority were also recruited as *intore* but were rarely associated with *gusimbuka* by European writers. In this sense, references to *gusimbukaka* as a Tutsi body-culture served to assist the stereotyping of Tutsi as super athletes and Hutu, through omission, as ordinary by comparison. It could be read as contributing to an ideology that instilled among the *Banyarwanda* a 'premise of inequality'.[8] The traditions of a half-century of Tutsi rule, under German, and then Belgian patronage, were collapsing as Hutu assumed power in the 1940s and 1950s. *Gusimbuka*, represented as a Tutsi icon, had disappeared by the mid-1960s.

Traditional ways of representing Africa and 'the African' were as 'other', as 'natural' and 'living in the past', but there was no single colonial gaze over the Rwandan corporeal landscape. David Spurr has suggested that twelve rhetorical modes – 'basic tropes' or 'a kind of repertoire for colonial discourse' – may be used in colonial textual discourse to describe non-Western people.[9] I employ four of Spurr's modes: *surveillance, appropriation, idealization* and *negation*. Each of these is applied to the representation of the athleticism of Rwandan men. The strength of Spurr's approach is its ability to show the process of essentialization as much more than pejorative stereotyping. Instead, different rhetorics are juxtaposed. The following analysis will illustrate how a Rwandan corporeality was constructed for, and communicated to, the European world. In addition, and specifically, it will show how a Rwandan corporeal practice was transformed by a Western imagination into a familiar and reductive cultural form – 'the Tutsi high jump'. Spurr's basic question is one that asks how Western writers construct representations of the strange and (to the writer) often incomprehensible realities confronted in the non-Western world. What are the cultural, ideological or literary presuppositions upon which such constructs are based?[10]

8   Ibid.
9   D. Spurr, *The Rhetoric of Empire* (Durham, NC: Duke University Press, 1993). Spurr's twelve rhetorical modes are: surveillance, appropriation, aestheticization, classification, debasement, negation, affirmation, idealization, insubstantialization, naturalization, eroticization, and resistance.
10   Ibid.

This discussion will be presented in four sections, each focusing on one of Spurr's rhetorical modes, though these should not be interpreted as mutually exclusive. Of the four categories selected, surveillance also merges with classification, and idealization merges with three other categories – aestheticization, naturalization and eroticism, while negation merges with debasement.

Rhetoric of the Record

Visual observation is widely regarded as the essential starting-point of the Western record of 'the African'. The commanding view of the colonizer provides the source of both information (and with it, authority) and aesthetic pleasure. The written and quantified records of the African body were essential parts of the modernist project of bringing order to Africa. The quantified record *of gusimbuka-urukiramende* was a form of surveillance and through the use of accurate quantification and measurement the European could codify differences in customs that would be represented as fixed and normalized.

Imperialism involved the quantitative measurement of the imperial realm – a means of recording that frequently collided with idealized or naturalized modes. The measuring of various parts of the African's body was widespread and led to the growth of the sub-discipline of anthropometry. The Rwandan 'high jump' performances were measured via a similar ideological lens. Providing that the height of the mound or stone forming the take-off point could be deducted, measurement of the 'net height' jumped could be readily made. Mecklenburg recorded, allegedly with 'exact evidence', a Tutsi athlete who jumped 2.50 metres with 'young boys' clearing 1.50 to 1.60 metres.[11] In the decades between 1910 and 1950 other

---

11   A. Ndjuru, *Studien zur Rolle der Leibesübungen in der traditionellen Gesellschaft* (Cologne: University of Cologne, 1983), p.128. See also Mecklenburg, *In the Heart of Africa*.

visitors recorded a wide variety of measurements. At an event witnessed by
William Roome, six athletes were said to have beaten the 'world's record'
of 6 feet 7 inches. Two of them 'must have cleared a height of eight feet', a
measurement which Roome was 'careful to take clear above the stone from
which they jumped'.[12] Atilio Gatti claimed that he recorded one performance with particular accuracy, measuring the height *exactly* at 8 feet 1⅛
inches from the ground'.[13] These performances were aided by a run-up to
the point of take-off that also encouraged measurement. Its length was
variously recorded at about 10 yards, 13 yards, 15 yards and 20 paces.[14]

The height of the mound or stone from which the athletes jumped was
likewise measured. Various heights were recorded, ranging from two and a
half inches to over three feet.[15] It was consistently reported that the jumpers could only achieve such heights with the help of the take-off mound,
which suggests a lurking sense of negation and a refusal unequivocally to
acknowledge Tutsi athleticism. When Ernst Jokl, an esteemed sports sci-
entist, compared the African leap to the European jump, he estimated that
the elevated take-off points gave the Tutsi jumpers an advantage of about
6 inches.[16] However, by taking a 'small anthill into account' a clearance of
7 feet 10 inches was reduced to one of 6 feet 4 inches.[17] The concern that
everything should be accurately measured reflected the European obsession for detail. Measurement was central to the European description of
the non-European world. It reflected a European 'way of seeing' – authori-
tative, powerful and appropriative despite – or, perhaps, because of – its

12   W. Roome, *Tramping through Africa* (London: Black, 1930), p.103.
13   A. Gatti, *South of the Sahara* (London: Hodder and Stoughton, 1946), p.171.
14   L. Catlow, *In Search of the Primitive* (New York: Little Brown, 1966), p.21; M.
      Birnbaum, 'Reception in Ruanda', *Natural History*, vol. 44, no. 5 (1939), pp.298–
      307, see p.307 for the length specified; P. Balfour, *Lords of the Equator* (London:
      Hutchinson, 1937), p.242; Roome, *Tramping through Africa*, p.103.
15   Bale, *Imagined Olympians*, p.72.
16   E. Jokl, 'High Jump Technique of the Central African Watussis', *Journal of Physical
      Education and School Hygiene*, no. 33 (1941), pp.145–9. On Jokl, see J. Bale, 'The
      mysterious Professor Jokl', in J. Bale, M. Christensen and G. Pfister (eds), *Writing
      Lives in Sport* (Aarhus: Aarhus University Press, 2004), pp.25–39.
17   P. Smith, 'Aspects de l'esthétique au Ruanda', *L'Homme*, no. 25 (1927), p.11.

mathematical or quantitative representation in apparently neutral and value-free terms. Quantification and the record were part of the language of achievement sport that was imposed on the pre-sportified oral world of Rwanda via the lens of the achievement orientation of the Western sports enthusiast. Generalizations and 'models' would additionally help to minimize imprecision. Diagrammatic representations (Figure 15.4) scientifically replaced the sentiment of the written word. The diagrams can be read as spatial analysis, collapsing the human athlete into a set of depersonalized lines and trajectories. The diagrams serve to generalize Tutsi and the awkward presence of any extraneous Europeans is erased.

Even if those who took measurements were not sports fans, the urge to measure and record was undeniable. The athletics statistics of the European were, like the map, an imperial technology of ordering which allowed a form of homogeneous recording to appropriate the African for the European realm. The Rwandan body was valued for ethnological and scientific advances; it was also valued for its athleticism and its potential Olympism. Its value was best estimated by measuring it (that is, its output) in terms of quantified records and in this way it could be located within the expanding empire of international achievement sport.

Claiming by Naming

Colonial discourse implicitly claims the place surveyed for the colonizer. A basic feature of colonialist discourse was the '*transferability* of empire's organizing metaphors'.[18] Like colonial landscapes, the African body was 'brought within the horizon of European intelligibility through the multiple practices of naming'.[19] The application of European terms to African

---

18   E. Boehmer, *Colonial and Postcolonial Literature* (Oxford: Oxford University Press, 1995), p.52.

19   D. Gregory, *Geographical Imaginations* (Cambridge: Blackwell, 1994), p.171.

body-culture revealed the problem of translating something from one culture to another. Rwanda was dispossessed of its indigenous corporeal culture, the possibility of an indigenous athleticism was effaced by the widespread application of terms like 'high jump', *hoogspringen*, *Hochsprung*, and *saut en hauteur*. The term 'high jump' connoted competitive, modern sport. The French term makes 'height' as well as 'jump' explicit. Here were familiar words or terms of reference from sources of the colonial gaze and it is possible to view the Europeans in Rwanda as being confronted with nothing so much as an image of themselves. Naming had acted as norming.[20] Exactly the same conclusions, of course, could be applied to the widespread use of the term 'sport' to *gusimbuka*. 'Sport' could bring 'the African' and 'the European' together. The athletic prowess of the 'muscular Christian' Captain Geoffrey Holmes (a British Military Cross recipient, member of the British Olympic team, captain of the army ice hockey team and later an ordained priest) was thought to constitute *a common bond* that in some way united the two worlds of British and Rwandan body-culture. Somehow this bond 'enabled him, in such a large measure, to win the friendship of the *sport loving* Batusi'.[21] 'Sport' in the 1920s was a slippery term, continuing to carry some of its nineteenth-century connotations and being applied to many disparate activities, ranging from elephant-shooting to cricket and from pig-sticking to high jumping.

For most European observers, the Rwandan version of high jumping *was* unquestionably a 'sport' and one in the achievement-oriented, Olympian mould. An introductory textbook from the mid-1920s generalized Tutsi as practising sports such as archery, javelin and discus throwing and high jumping 2.20 metres without a 'springboard'.[22] It was confidently

20   L. Berg and R. Kearns, 'Naming as Norming: Race, Gender and Identity Politics of Naming Places in Aotearoa/New Zealand', *Society and Space*, vol. 14, no. 1 (1996), pp.99–122.

21   J. Roome, *Through the Lands of Nyanza* (London: Marshall, Morgan and Scott, 1931), p.134 (my emphasis, J. B.).

22   A. Michiels and N. Laude, *Notre Colonie: Géographie et Notice Historique* (Brussels: A. Dewit, 1924), p.6.

described as the 'favourite sport' in Rwanda.[23] If it was a sport it would also need to have its 'champions', a title that was applied to Kanyamuhunga – 'the champion jumper of Ruanda'[24] and 'possibly the world'.[25] European representations of the indigene resulted in a reductive construction of colonial subjectivity – a 'type' such as 'native', Tutsi or 'savage' and the use of the man's name accepted 'the necessary cultural and personal individuation that selfhood generally presumes'.[26] With 'sport' also came the 'record'. Mecklenburg found it necessary to add a footnote comparing the Tutsi performance of 2.50 metres with the existing 'American world record' of 1.94 metres.[27] Rwandan performances only meant anything when compared with the records of the West, a comparison that was itself an appropriation.[28] Europeans saw the natural (including human) resources of colonized lands as rightfully belonging to 'civilization' and 'mankind' rather than to the indigenous peoples. The notion of Africa as the colonizer's inheritance is reflected in the way in which African culture was recorded and perceived. The European view looked forward in time as well as out in space and European texts projected and transformed the African landscape into a familiar cultural terrain. Hence, whereas Henry Morton Stanley's gaze had constructed the English country village out of the East African landscape,[29] those who viewed *gusimbuka* had constructed an imaginative sports landscape made up of the Olympic Games, champions and world records.

23   Roome, *Through the Lands of Nyanza*, p.134.

24   Roome, *Tramping through Africa*, p.102.

25   S. Smith, 'A Journey into Belgian Ruanda', *Ruanda Notes*, no. 21 (1927), pp.9–13, p.11.

26   H. Gilbert and J. Tompkins, *Post-Colonial Drama: Theory, Practice and Politics* (London: Routledge, 1996), p.165.

27   Mecklenburg, *In the Heart of Africa*, p.59.

28   The people of Rwanda did not read *gusimbuka* as a Western sport – how could they? It contained none of the characteristics of Western sports: record-seeking standardization, bureaucratization, equality of opportunity and quantification. See A. Guttmann, *From Ritual to Record* (New York: Columbia University Press, 1978).

29   M. Pratt, *Imperial Eyes* (London: Routledge, 1992), p.208.

Frequent allusions were made to the Olympics. Patrick Balfour reck-
oned that 'they could walk off with the high jump contests at the Olympic
Games',[30] while Ellen Gatti hoped that 'some enterprising entrepreneur
will bring a bunch of these lads' to the same Games.[31] The possibility of
witnessing Tutsi athletes competing against the 1948 Olympic 100 metres
champion from the United States, the sprint-hurdler Harrison Dillard, was
also welcomed.[32] Ernst Jokl thought that although Rwandan women did
not take part in the jumping, they possessed even greater Olympic potential than the men. He was a consistent supporter of the sportification *of
gusimbuka*[33] and in 1950 suggested to Dr Ralph Bunche, then in charge
of the UN Trusteeship Council in New York, that 'a modern system of
Physical Education and coaching be introduced to Rwanda and that an
effort he made to enter a Watusi team' (not, notice again, a team from
Rwanda) in the Olympic Games.[34] Likewise, in 1954 the performance of
the Rwandan 'high jumpers' attracted missionaries and athletic coaches
from the USA, hoping that they could recruit native boys to their athletic
squads, 'hire a great jumper' and 'persuade him to agree' to compete in the
1956 Melbourne Olympics.[35]

Representing *gusimbuka* as a version of something that was already
known would be seen by Edward Said as a way of controlling the threat
that it represented,[36] in this case a threat of the established view of the
world sporting order. But with the Rwandan high jumpers the threat was
seemingly impossible to avoid. It was the misperceived congruence of
gusimbuka with the sportized high jump that led a prominent German

---

30   Balfour, *Lords of the Equator*, p.241.
31   E. Gatti, *Exploring we would go* (London: Robert Hale, 1950), p.79.
32   M. Akeley, *Congo Eden* (London: Gollancz, 1951), p.59.
33   E. Jokl, *Medical Sociology and Cultural Anthropology of Sport and Physical Education*
     (Springfield, IL: Thomas, 1964), p.26.
34   Ibid., pp.126–7.
35   B. Dozier, 'Tribesman Jumped 7' 6"', *Track and Field News*, vol. 7, no. 11 (1954),
     p.4.
36   Said, *Orientalism*, p.59.

physician to ask: 'What, then, will be left of our world records?'[37] The 'high jumpers' of Rwanda were seen as ideal bodies awaiting the body manage-ment of Western sport and, given their perceived skills at high jumping, it was automatically assumed that European sports – and by implication, the universal space of Olympism – could be easily introduced into the region. Olympism would lead to refined performance. Hence, despite the fact that the Europeans saw the Tutsi as superior high jumpers, it is implied that they could be further improved within the global sports system. Roome noted that if they were trained in the European manner they would 'jump equally well' without the aid of the raised take-off, a case of the seamless conversion of indigene to athlete.[38]

Like African 'art', *gusimbuka* reflected simply a 'stage' in the 'devel-opment' towards a 'civilized' body-culture.[39] The way in which it was read also presumed the continuing vitality of Tutsi society and its corporeality. Drawing on observations on African art, such writing *rewards Africa* for conforming to a European image of athletics, for acting as a mirror in which the European can contemplate a European idea of sport.[40] The European witnesses of the 'Tutsi high jump' found in the Africans' corporeality the possibility of bridging the gap between the African past and the global present. While in many situations the differences between the African and the Occidental were vast, European observers viewed *gusimbuka* as a kind of 'meeting-ground'. The statistics were the sporting equivalent of a universal currency. The male European gaze had prepared the bodies of Rwandans (written as 'the Tutsi') for entry into the spaces of Western sport. Such a world could be read as 'liminal' in character – 'a topsy-turvy reflection of home, in which constructions of home and away are temporarily disrupted

37   Quoted in J. Hoberman, *Darwin's Athletes* (Boston, MA: Houghton Mifflin, 1997), p.46.
38   Roome, *Tramping through Africa*, p.103.
39   B. Ashcroft, G. Griffiths and H. Tiffin, *The Empire Writes Back* (London: Routledge, 1989), p.158.
40   C. Miller, 'Theories of African', in H. Gates (ed.), *'Race', Writing and Difference* (Chicago: University of Chicago Press, 1985), p.290.

before being reinscribed or reordered, in either case reconstituted'.[41] The
fantasies that projected the Tutsi on to the global sports stage suggest how
occidental writing tried to minimize cultural differences through the unifying power of Western cultural institutions such as the Olympic Games and
the sports record. The narrowness of vision of the Europeans' conceptual
framework was exposed in their misconceptions, and in the poverty of
their vocabulary and imagery which led them to see 'Tutsi high jumpers'
as potential world record breakers or Olympic athletes.

It is important to stress that the attitudes and perceptions noted above
were not entirely uncontested. Some European explorers seemed to be less
uncertain (or less rash) about the semantic ordering or location of *gusimbuka* and alternative signifiers were, on occasion, used in its representation.
For example, it was described as a 'traditional Watusi *art*'[42] but much more
interesting, I think, is the use of the word 'Springkünstler' (jumping artist
or artiste) in the title of a paper on Tutsi athleticism published in 1929.[43]
Whereas the term 'high jump' blurred the distinction between 'home' and
'away', representations of 'non-sportified' body-culture signified something
quite different. The jumper as artist/artiste rather than as athlete immediately connotes a performance rather than a result, a participant rather than
a winner, an entertainer rather than an athlete, sensuousness rather than
seriousness. 'Springkünstler' explicitly acknowledges artistry rather than
sport and athleticism. It fits much better into the world of entertainment
and display that seems to have formed the context in which *gusimbuka*
was most often represented; that is, in its festive rather than its military
form. But the application of the term 'jumping-artistry' was never widely
adopted, despite the fact that it was arguably much more suitable.

But it was the term 'high jump' that (while correctly describing what
was happening) appropriated *gusimbuka* through its Olympian connotations. In other words (literally), by looking to the world of sport for

41   R. Phillips, *Mapping Men and Empire* (London: Routledge, 1997), p.13.

42   O. Meeker, *Report on Africa* (London: Chatto and Windus, 1955), p.151 (original
     emphasis).

43   H. Kna, 'Die Watussi als Springkünstler', *Erdball*, no. 12 (1929), pp.459–62.

language to describe what was being observed, there is the danger of falling into a trap of simple appearances. *Gusimbuka* became 'high jumping' – a body-culture *for* Europe. The application of the designation 'high jump' brought Tutsi closer to European. At the same time, the Western view exemplified a paradox of colonial discourse with appropriation lying alongside other traditional tropes – the debasement and negation of the African – as part of the desire to stress racial difference.

Noble Athletes

A common tendency among nineteenth-century and early twentieth-century Euro-Americans was to deny African body-culture and to see 'the African' as nothing more than a savage. J. A. Mangan observed that the 'overestimation of Western tradition resulted in underestimation of indigenous customs'.[44] But I think Mangan overestimates the extent of the Western devaluation of the African and one only needs to read the extravagant language used to describe the grace of Tutsi high jumpers to see that the African was esteemed. To be sure, it was possible to negate Tutsi athletic performances, as we will see, but it seems that the ambivalence of colonial discourse is reflected in a frequent willingness to describe the physicality of the African in highly idealized terms. After all, the high jump performance witnessed by Mecklenburg was something that the Occident had yet to achieve. So while cultural difference could be claimed for the 'Tutsi high jumper', cultural retardation and physical inferiority were less easily adduced and the 'natural' categories of 'Europe' and 'Africa' became blurred. Here the African performed better than the European at something the Europeans perceived as theirs. Tutsi were also seen as having crossed an unmarked boundary, transgressing the 'sport-space' of the white American and European.

44   J. A. Mangan, *The Games Ethic and Imperialism* (London: Viking, 1986), p.1.

Mecklenburg described the jumping as 'noteworthy', 'remarkable' and 'wonderful'. The athletes had 'slender', 'splendid figures'; the jump of 2.50 metres was 'incredible'.[45] Gatti noted that 'we saw *slim* figures take a few *easy* steps, *effortlessly* abandon the ground and [...] *soar* high over a thin reed, descending in *graceful* curves, landing *lightly, composedly*'.[46] These effortless jumps were seen to have been made by natural athletes; 'the Tutsi' were a 'race of natural athletes', which meant that without training they could clear their own heights.[47] This was not the lazy, disadvantaged native of the environmental determinist's Africa. Far from it: presented here are images of the naturalized and idealized African – physically perfect, naturally gifted, graceful and able to outperform the best the Occident could offer. Yet the philosophy that explained the slothfulness of the native African – that of environmental determinism – was also used, in large part, to explain how nature had endowed 'the Tutsi' (but seemingly not 'the Hutu') with natural athletic prowess. Kna noted that young cattle herders learned early in life to quickly, and *effortlessly*, climb steep slopes. It was the nature of the terrain and topography which was the principal factor contributing to their musculature and their resulting high jumping abilities. Mecklenburg made similar observations, stating that the leg muscles and sinews of the mountain dwellers were far better developed than those of the people of the plains.[48]

45   Mecklenburg, *In the Heart of Africa*, pp.59–60. The 'record' of 2.50 metres became the definitive height, mainly as a result of Mecklenburg's written and visual 'evidence' of a Tutsi high jumper who was shown jumping over the heads of Mecklenburg and his adjutant and subsequently published in a variety of sources. However, other writers contest the view that the athlete jumped 2.50 metres, for example Jan Czekanowski (who gives a height of 2.35m) and the German sports historian Carl Diem (who claims '2.53m', a probable misprinting of 2.35m); see Bale, *Imagined Olympians*, p.71. For an analysis of 'the Mecklenburg photograph', see J. Bale, 'Partial Knowledge: Photographic Mystifications and Constructions of "the African Athlete"', in M. Phillips (ed.), *Deconstructing Sport History* (Albany, NY: State University of New York, 2006), pp.95–126.

46   Gatti, *South of the Sahara*, p.170 (my emphasis, J. B.).

47   H. Bernatzik, *Afrika: Handbuch der Angewandten Völkerkunde* (Innsbruck: Schüsselverlag, 1947), p.896.

48   Quoted in Kna, 'Die Watussi als Springkünstler', p.460.

The Tutsi could jump 2.50 metres at a time when the European view of the 'world record' was only 1.97 metres. Jokl observed that:

> [...] these primitive people carry out a technically complicated athletic movement which modern athletes can only learn to perform gradually during a prolonged and scientifically supervised period of training. The Watussis, on the other hand seem to conceive the control of the movement patterns underlying advanced high jumping rather complexly. They apparently have found an autodidactic short cut which enables them to acquire mastery of the jumping technique without taking recourse to the analytical process of learning which we have to go through in our athletic training.[49]

Tutsi athletes were also seen as being what Western athletes could have been, had they not fallen into an implied state of physical degeneracy. They were not only different from the Western athletes but, having failed to be overtaken by the machine age, they were also better athletes. This could be seen as an example of 'healthy primitivism in the application of what was deemed to be a simple pastoral culture ... [and] the natural masculine outdoor life of sport'.[50] In Rwanda the healthy primitivism of the Tutsi could be viewed as embodying imperial dreams, perhaps even impulses for Western regeneration.[51] The British track and field coach, F. A. M. Webster reflected such atavistic tendencies, referring to 'a tribe in the far interior who had been said to be capable of clearing over 7 ft', adding that the 'efficiency of these native high jumpers probably owes much to the fact that nature and natural environment, without the cramping and distorting engines of civilization in the shape of ill-made and badly fitting footwear, have allowed the feet full play for development and growth, so that flexibility and spring have been retained unimpaired'.[52] It was more than simply sympathy for black African culture when he added that 'what black men are doing today I suppose our own white ancestors were able to achieve

49   Jokl, 'High Jump Technique of the Central African Watussis', p.146.
50   G. Low, *White Skins, Black Masks: French and British Orientalism* (London: Routledge, 1996), p.30.
51   Boehmer, *Colonial and Postcolonial Literature*, p.127.
52   F. A. M. Webster, *Athletes of Today* (London: Warne, 1929), p.184.

when they too enjoyed the freedom of savagery'.[53] Like other bourgeois males who travelled to Africa, Webster seems to have been disenchanted with a rational social order and the urban and overdeveloped culture of the machine. His final words appear to be seeking a re-making of the 'natural body', innocent and pre-modern, following its cultural depletion. For some, the apparent subordination of the competitive spirit that was observed in *gusimbuka* provided a hint of a kind of primitive communism. For example, in the case of Rwandan jumping 'rivalry has its well-defined limits' and jumping stopped when the athletes felt tired, 'leaving the field with their arms around each others necks'.[54]

Champions Denied

The fourth rhetorical mode, that of negation, might be regarded as the most common form of representing Africa and 'the African' from the eighteenth century onward. Africa was seen, for example, as an empty space waiting to be appropriated and then filled or 'developed'. Negation is often allied to the rhetorical mode of debasement (and denial). It is possible to negate African corporeality by defining it out of existence or re-writing history. Negation is the negative stereotype and the polar opposite of the positive that is found (though with equivocation) in rhetorical modes such as idealization and naturalization. 'African' corporeality, like other aspects of their non-Western otherness, were paradoxically negated and 'ridiculed for their attempt to imitate the forms of the West'.[55] But modes of negation were often more difficult (though far from impossible) to apply to *gusimbuka*, with representational problems resulting when Europeans encountered 'native' body-cultures that appeared to be similar to those

53   Ibid.
54   M. Severn, *Congo Pilgrim* (London: Travel Book Club, 1952), pp.195–6.
55   Spurr, *The Rhetoric of Empire*, p.84.

of Europe, exacerbated if such body-cultures could, apparently, produce superior performances to those of the European, belying European expectations of racial superiority.

The most negative form of recording *gusimbuka* is to deny it. That there was no sport at all in pre-colonial Africa often ran parallel to the view, noted earlier, that 'the African' was a *natural* sportsman. This contradiction can be explained by Spurr's observations that 'the concept of *nature* must be available as a term that shifts in meaning, for example, by idealizing or degrading the savage, according [*sic*] as the need arises at different moments in the colonial situation'.[56] The contradiction also arose because the fluidity of the word 'sport' encouraged both alterity and mimesis. On the one hand it could be applied to events of the modern global sports system which, when seemingly absent from the African context (via the rhetorical mode of negation), could be used to maximize the cultural distance between the African and the European. On the other hand, when physical form was divorced from social function, the visible similarities of indigenous body-cultural practices with those of Europe could be used to exemplify the Rousseauvian view of the 'noble savage' and the appropriation of the 'natural athlete' for the sportized European realm. Yet the 'natural' could also be read negatively. Combined with the imagery of the 'giant' – the title of one of Gatti's papers was 'The Jumping Giants of Rwanda' – a freakish quality could be attributed to Tutsi.[57] Such freakishness moderated the idealized view that was also painted of them and rendered their apparently outstanding athletic performances less significant. Their supposed natural ability could also be read as giving them an unfair advantage over the European.

Negation is illustrated in the writing of Karl Reutler who, in 1940, claimed that the Duke of Mecklenburg himself denied that *gusimbuka* was an indigenous body-culture. Reutler claimed that in an interview:

56   Ibid., p.168.
57   A. Gatti, 'The Jumping Giants of Rwanda', *The Negro Digest*, December 1945, pp.25–7.

The Duke clearly stated that the Tutsi have only done this high jumping once — to be precise, on the day of the Duke's visit — and as a result of his proposal. The Duke emphasized that the Tutsi had never before, and probably never since, done the high jump [*Die Watussi haben niemals vorher und wohl auch niemals mehr später den Hochsprung gemacht*]. [...] In summary, the Tutsi high jump was a unique European experiment [*ein einmaliger Versuch von Europäern*]. The assertion of Professor Weule, that the high jump is the main sport of the Tutsi, is a mistake and basically false. The high jump had nothing to do with their economic and racial characteristics, it has not developed, it did not remain with them, nor has it been adapted to their way of life nor been adopted.[58]

Mecklenburg had claimed *gusimbuka* as a Tutsi (yet again, I stress, not as a Rwandan) tradition in 1928, but its negation by Reutler would be fully consistent with the prevailing Nazi body-cultural ideology. The academic conventions of a racist state in which the selection of scholars had become Aryanized (Jews being ineligible for university posts from 1933) seriously influenced aspects of representation. In situations where it was undeniable that Africans could defeat 'Aryans', they were simply read as being nearer to animals than to athletes. This was part of a 'total' theory within which a wide range of attributes formed the basis for the categorization of people in macro-groups, for example, 'Negroes'.[59]

The juxtaposing of the modes of negation and appropriation is exemplified in a much later example of the denigration of Rwandan jumping achievements. Rummelt obtained 'scientific evidence' which, he claimed, showed that if factors such as the uneven surface of the ground and the take-off mound were taken into account the laws of mathematics and physics would predict that Rwandan performance would have been modest by Western standards. By employing scientific advice and simple mathematical calculations, he was able to conclude that the jump of 2.50 metres claimed by Mecklenburg could be converted from one culture to another and become equivalent to a modern high jump performance of between 1.87 and 1.89 metres. My interest here is not the accuracy of his claims but in the fact

58   K. Reutler, *Über die Leibesübungen der Primitiven* (Rostock: Carl Hinstorff, 1940), pp.51–2.

59   J. Hoberman, *Sport and Political Ideology* (London: Heinemann, 1984), pp.164–5.

that he had first to appropriate *gusimbuka* in order to compare it with the Western model, before being able to negate it as a *Hochsprunglegende* (high-jump legend).[60]

Absence, denial and legends: this rhetoric exemplifies the mode of negation that privileged European athletic prowess over that of 'the African'. The Rwandan high jumpers were projected as fantastical, freakish or, having been scrutinized by Western objectivity, simply not as good as first impressions may have suggested. Negation and naturalization combined to prepare the way for the excesses of the European sports model. On the one hand, 'sport' did not exist and an empty Africa awaited colonization by Western athleticism; but on the other, the 'natural athletes' were available to be processed for the anticipated world of achievement sports.

Conclusion

This chapter has considered the various modes of colonial rhetoric that were applied to an African body-culture and communicated to a European public by a variety of media. Such 'imagined sports', like Said's 'imaginative geographies of Empire', were 'verbal acts'.[61] The rhetorical modes selected to structure this chapter show that the European projection of an African corporeality in the early twentieth century was far from one of negation, a mode that is frequently associated with much colonial writing. The continent was not always represented as 'empty' or as 'nothingness'. In it were found natural athletes and super-humans whose physicality exposed the white man as feeble by comparison. However, colonial discourses conflicted with one another. The juxtaposition of the quantified record of *gusimbuka* with the idealized naturalization of Tutsi 'athletes' demonstrated vividly

---

60   P. Rummelt, *Sport im Kolonialismus – Kolonialismus im Sport* (Cologne: Pahl-Rugenstein, 1986), p.91.
61   G. Olsson, *Birds in Egg/Eggs in Bird* (London: Pion, 1980), p.12.

that in travel writing 'science and sentiment code(d) the imperial frontier in the two externally clashing and complementary languages of bourgeois subjectivity'.[62] This chapter also shows how colonial discourse about Africa was not only a 'European discourse about non-European worlds' but also a sportized discourse about non-sportized worlds.[63] Those who read Tutsi as future Olympians failed to see the significance of almost everything except sports. Such a view ignored history, anthropology, linguistics and politics, and, I should stress, it was almost always Tutsi who were rhetorically privileged as athletes. How could the writers of the aforementioned texts have been so sure that there were no Hutu among them?

The main aim of this analysis has been to explore the messy discourse of an African athleticism. But if politics underlie the textual images of *gusimbuka-urukiramende*, it is possible to privilege the mode of idealization, for it can surely be conceived as part (albeit a small part) of a European complicity in the construction of 'Tutsi-ness', something that has been seen as being far from unrelated to the Tutsi genocide. Some observers aver that 'racist prejudice was a structural feature of Rwandan society'[64] claiming that 'Rwanda is unique in the sheer abundance of traditions purporting to show the superiority of the Tutsi over the other castes [sic]'.[65] Hutu, while numerically outnumbering Tutsi and Twa, were negated in Tutsi and European representations and, especially during the period of Belgian colonization, were crudely described in numerous writings as 'races'.[66] I suggest that the positive stereotyping of Tutsi, through their apparent athletic prowess, can clearly be seen as a display of 'racial' superiority. Devoid of any military overtones and replacing power with grace, what better symbol of 'racial' authority could there be than that of 'the Tutsi high jumper'?

From the perspective of modern sports, the imaginary Olympians of Rwanda never corresponded to the pictures that the Europeans had painted of them. Jokl's certainty that 'the Tutsi' were 'bound to play an increasingly important role in the Olympic Games in the future' was never reflected in

---

62   Pratt, *Imperial Eyes*, p.39.
63   Ibid, pp.34–5.
64   P. Uvin, 'Prejudice, Crisis and Genocide in Rwanda', *African Studies Review*, vol. 40, no. 2 (1997), pp.91–115, p.91.
65   R. Lemarchand, *Rwanda and Burundi* (London: Pall Mall, 1970), p.34.
66   See, for example, Gatti, 'The Jumping Giants of Rwanda', p.164.

actuality.[67] The 'high jumpers' of Rwanda never competed in the Olympic Games, and when, in the 1950s, pressure was put on Rwandan people to adopt Western body-cultures, *gusimbuka* prevailed over the 'modern' high jump that was bureaucratized by the International Amateur Athletics Federation (IAAF). The 'official' Rwandan high jump record today stands at 1.90 metres. Tutsi did not break the official world record of the Western sports system and instead their records remain as inscriptions in colonialist writing and photography – testaments to a European culture which was able to acculturate Tutsi only as a way of seeing.

Bibliography

Akeley, M. *Congo Eden* (London: Gollancz, 1951).

Ashcroft, B., G. Griffiths and H. Tiffin. *The Empire Writes Back* (London: Routledge, 1989).

Bale, J. *Imagined Olympians* (Minneapolis: University of Minnesota Press, 2002).

——. 'The mysterious Professor Jokl', in J. Bale, M. Christensen and G. Pfister (eds), *Writing Lives in Sport* (Aarhus: Aarhus University Press, 2004), pp.25–39.

——. 'Partial Knowledge: Photographic Mystifications and Constructions of "the African Athlete"' in M. Phillips (ed.), *Deconstructing Sport History* (Albany, NY: State University of New York, 2006), pp.95–126.

—— and M. Cronin (eds). *Sport and Postcolonialism* (Oxford: Berg, 2003).

Balfour, P. *Lords of the Equator* (London: Hutchinson, 1937).

Bernatzik, H. *Afrika: Handbuch der Angewandten Völkerkunde* (Innsbruck: Schüsselverlag, 1947).

Berg, L. and R. Kearns, 'Naming as Norming: Race, Gender and Identity Politics of Naming Places in Aotearoa/New Zealand', *Society and Space*, vol. 14, no. 1 (1996), pp.99–122.

Birnbaum, M. 'Reception in Ruanda', *Natural History*, vol. 44, no. 5 (1939), pp.298–307.

Boehmer, E. *Colonial and Postcolonial Literature* (Oxford: Oxford University Press, 1995).

Catlow, L. *In Search of the Primitive* (New York: Little Brown, 1966).

67 E. Jokl, *Medical Sociology*, p.70.

Czekanowski, J. *Forschungen im Nil-Congo-Zwischengebiet* (vol. 3; Leipzig: Kinkhardt and Biermann, 1911).

Dozier, B. 'Tribesman Jumped 7' 6''', *Track and Field News*, vol. 7, no. 11 (1954), p.4.

Gatti, A. 'The Jumping Giants of Rwanda', *The Negro Digest*, December 1945, pp.25–7.

——. *South of the Sahara* (London: Hodder and Stoughton, 1946).

Gatti, E. *Exploring We Would Go* (London: Robert Hale, 1950).

Gilbert, H. and J. Tompkins. *Post-Colonial Drama: Theory, Practice and Politics* (London: Routledge, 1996).

Gregory, D. *Geographical Imaginations* (Cambridge: Blackwell, 1994).

Guttmann, A. *From Ritual to Record* (New York: Columbia University Press, 1978).

Hoberman, J. *Sport and Political Ideology* (London: Heinemann, 1984).

——. *Darwin's Athletes* (Boston, MA: Houghton Mifflin, 1997).

Jokl, E. 'High Jump Technique of the Central African Watussis', *Journal of Physical Education and School Hygiene*, no. 33 (1941), pp.145–9.

——. *Medical Sociology and Cultural Anthropology of Sport and Physical Education* (Springfield, IL: Thomas, 1964).

Kna, H. 'Die Watussi als Springkünstler', *Erdball*, no.12 (1929), pp.459–62.

Lemarchand, R. *Rwanda and Burundi* (London: Pall Mall, 1970).

Low, L. *White Skins, Black Masks: French and British Orientalism* (London: Routledge, 1996).

Malonowski, B. *Coral Gardens and Their Magic* (vol. 1; London: Allen and Unwin, 1935).

Mangan, J. A. *The Games Ethic and Imperialism* (London: Viking, 1986).

Maquet, J. *The Premise of Inequality in Rwanda* (London: Oxford University Press, 1961).

Mecklenburg, A. *In the Heart of Africa* (London: Cassell, 1910).

Meeker, O. *Report on Africa* (London: Chatto and Windus, 1955).

Michiels, A. and N. Laude. *Notre Colonie: Géographie et Notice Historique* (Brussels: A. Dewit, 1924).

Miller, C. 'Theories of African', in H. Gates (ed.), *'Race', Writing and Difference* (Chicago: University of Chicago Press, 1985).

Ndjuru, A. *Studien zur Rolle der Leibesübungen in der traditionellen Gesellschaft* (Cologne: University of Cologne, 1983).

Olsson, G. *Birds in Egg/Eggs in Bird* (London: Pion, 1980).

Phillips, R. *Mapping Men and Empire* (London: Routledge, 1997).

Powell, H. A. 'Cricket in Kiriwina', *The Listener*, 4 September 1952, pp.384–5.

Pratt, M. *Imperial Eyes* (London: Routledge, 1992).

Reutler, K. *Über die Leibesübungen der Primitiven* (Rostock: Carl Hinstorff, 1940).

Roome, J. *Through the Lands of Nyanza* (London: Marshall, Morgan and Scott, 1931).

Roome, W. *Tramping through Africa* (London: Black, 1930).

Rummelt, P. *Sport im Kolonialismus – Kolonialismus im Sport* (Cologne: Pahl-Rugenstein, 1986).

Ryan, S. *The Cartographic Eye* (Cambridge: Cambridge University Press, 1966).

Said, E. *Orientalism* (Penguin: London, 1995).

Severn, M. *Congo Pilgrim* (London: Travel Book Club, 1952).

Smith, P. 'Aspects de l'esthétique au Ruanda', *L'Homme*, no. 25 (1927), p.11.

Smith, S. 'A Journey into Belgian Ruanda', *Ruanda Notes*, no. 21 (1927), pp.9–13.

Spurr, D. *The Rhetoric of Empire* (Durham, NC: Duke University Press, 1993).

Uvin, P. 'Prejudice, Crisis and Genocide in Rwanda', *African Studies Review*, vol. 40, no. 2 (1997), pp.91–115.

Webster, F. A. M. *Athletes of Today* (London: Warne, 1929).

Notes on Contributors

PADDY AGNEW has lived and worked as a professional journalist in Rome since 1986, covering a wide canvas that stretches from football to the Vatican, taking in Italian politics and the Mafia along the way. Since 1992, he has been Rome correspondent for the *Irish Times*, whilst for 15 years he worked as a TV football commentator for the Italian state broadcaster, RAI. On football, he is a regular contributor to the BBC, RTÉ, TalkSport and many other radio stations, whilst he is the Italian correspondent for the monthly magazine, *World Soccer*. Agnew is also the author of the acclaimed work, *Forza Italia: A Journey in Search of Italy and its Football* (London: Ebury Press, 2006).

ALAN BAIRNER is Professor of Sport and Social Theory at Loughborough University. He is co-author of *Sport, Sectarianism and Society in a Divided Ireland* (Leicester: Leicester University Press, 1993) and author of *Sport, Nationalism and Globalization: European and North American Perspectives* (Albany, NY: State University of New York Press, 2001). He edited *Sport and the Irish: Histories, Identities, Issues* (Dublin: University College Dublin Press, 2005), and is joint editor (with John Sugden) of *Sport in Divided Societies* (Aachen: Meyer and Meyer, 1999), (with Jonathan Magee and Alan Tomlinson) of *The Bountiful Game? Football Identities and Finances* (Aachen: Meyer and Meyer, 2005) and (with Gyozo Molnar) of *The Politics of the Olympics: A Survey* (London: Routledge, 2010). He serves on the editorial boards of the *International Review for the Sociology of Sport* and the *International Journal of Sport Policy*.

JOHN BALE is Emeritus Professor of Sports Studies at Keele University and an honorary professor at Queensland University, Australia. He has authored many books and articles on various aspects of sports, including *Imagined Olympians* (Minneapolis: University of Minnesota Press, 2002) and *Anti-Sport Sentiments in Literature* (London: Routledge, 2007), and co-edited, with Tony Bateman, *Sporting Sounds* (London: Routledge, 2008). He is currently writing a book on Lewis Carroll's engagement with sports.

SEÁN CROSSON is Programme Director of the MA in Film Studies in the Huston School of Film & Digital Media at the National University of Ireland, Galway. He has published widely on various aspects of Irish studies, from film to literature, and his current research interest concerns the representation of sport in film, the subject of several recent and forthcoming publications, including the book *Sport and Film* (London: Routledge, 2011). He is also guest co-editor with Philip Dine of a forthcoming special issue of the journal *Media History* on 'Sport and the Media in Ireland'.

SÉBASTIEN DARBON is a researcher at the French National Centre for Scientific Research (CNRS) and works at the Institut d'Études Méditerranéennes, Européennes et Comparatives (IDEMEC) in Aix-en-Provence. He is a specialist in sports anthropology and has published many articles and several books, especially on rugby, cricket and baseball. His most recent book is *Diffusion des sports et impérialisme anglo-saxon: De l'histoire événementielle à l'anthropologie* (Paris: Maison des Sciences de l'Homme, 2008).

PAUL DIETSCHY is Senior Lecturer in Sports Studies at the Université de Franche-Comté (Besançon) and a researcher at the Centre d'Histoire de Sciences Po, Paris, where he coordinates (with Patrick Clastres) a research group on sport, cultures and societies in Europe in the twentieth century. His publications include the following recent books: (with Yvan Gastaut and Stéphane Mourlane) *Histoire politique des Coupes du monde de football* (Paris: Vuibert, 2006); (with Patrick Clastres) *Sport, société et culture en France du XIXe siècle à nos jours* (Paris: Hachette, 2006); (with David-Claude Kémo-Keïmbou) *Le Football et l'Afrique* (Paris: EPA/FIFA, 2008); also published in English as *Football and Africa* (Paris: EPA/FIFA, 2008); and *Histoire du football* (Paris: Perrin, 2010).

PHILIP DINE is Senior Lecturer in French at the National University of Ireland, Galway. He has published widely on representations of the French colonial empire, including particularly decolonization, in fields ranging from children's literature to professional sport. Other published research includes a history of *French Rugby Football* (Oxford: Berg, 2001), as part of a broader reflection on leisure and popular culture in that country. The present volume is one of the outcomes of a thematic project on sport and identity in France and Europe for which he acted as co-ordinator and which was funded by the Irish Research Council for the Humanities and Social Sciences (2006–2009).

MARCUS FREE is Lecturer in Media and Communication Studies at Mary Immaculate College, University of Limerick. He has published widely on constructions of gender and national identity in sport, sport media and fandom, and in television drama and film. He is co-author (with John Hughson and David Inglis) of *The Uses of Sport: A Critical Study* (London: Routledge, 2005).

BORJA GARCÍA is Lecturer in Sport Policy and Management at Loughborough University's School of Sport, Health and Exercise Sciences. His research interests include the European Union's sports policy and the transformation of European sport's governance structures. He has published articles in journals such as the *International Journal of Sport Policy* and the *Journal of Contemporary European Research*. He has recently published an edited book titled *The Transformation of Football: A Case of Europeanization?* (Manchester: Manchester University Press, 2010). He is a founding member of the Association for the Study of Sport and the European Union and a member of the editorial board of the *Sport & EU Review*.

JEFFREY HILL is Emeritus Professor of Historical and Cultural Studies at De Montfort University, Leicester, where, until 2007, he was Director of the International Centre for Sport, History and Culture. His research interests include the cultural history of sport and leisure, and popular politics in Britain. Among recent publications are *Sport, Leisure and Culture in Twentieth-Century Britain* (London: Palgrave Macmillan, 2002) and *Sport and the Literary Imagination: Essays in History, Literature, and Sport* (Oxford: Peter Lang, 2006). *Sport: A Historical Introduction* is due from Palgrave Macmillan in 2010. He is also working, with Anthony Bateman, on the *Cambridge Companion to Cricket* for Cambridge University Press.

CATHAL KILCLINE completed his doctorate in French Studies at the National University of Ireland, Galway, in 2009. A Government of Ireland (IRCHSS) scholar (2007–2009), his research concentrates primarily on the representation of migrant and post-colonial identities. He has published a number of articles on sport and popular culture in France and received the Junior Scholar Award from the European Committee for Sports History (CESH) in 2007.

ARND KRÜGER is Professor of Sports Studies at the Georg-August-Universität, Göttingen. His research interests include twentieth-century sport in all its facets. He has co-edited (with William Murray) *The Nazi Olympics: Sport, Politics, and Appeasement in the 1930s* (Champaign, IL: University of Illinois Press, 2003) and (with Axel Dreyer) *Sportmanagement: Eine themenbezogene Einführung* (Munich: Oldenbourg, 2004). He is an International Fellow of the American Academy of Kinesiology and Physical Education and Editor-in-Chief of the journal *European Studies in Sports History*.

GYOZO MOLNAR is Senior Lecturer in Sports Studies in the Institute of Sport and Exercise Science at the University of Worcester. He completed his doctorate in the Sociology of Sport at Loughborough University and his research interests revolve around migration, globalization and national identity. His current publications include articles such as 'Mapping Migrations: Hungary Related Migrations of Professional Footballers after the Collapse of Communism', 'Involuntary Career Termination in Sport: A Case Study of the Process of Structurally Induced Failure' (with Joanne Butt) and a forthcoming book (edited with Alan Bairner) on *The Politics of the Olympics*.

DILWYN PORTER is Senior Research Fellow at the International Centre for Sports History and Culture at De Montfort University, Leicester, and was until recently co-editor of the journal *Sport in History*. He has published extensively on issues relating to sport, especially football, and English identity in the post-1945 period. In addition, he retains an interest in business history and has contributed a chapter on the transformation of British sport since 1960 to *Business in Britain in the Twentieth Century* (Oxford: Oxford University Press, 2009).

JAMES RIORDAN is Visiting Professor of Sports Studies at the University of Worcester and President of the College of Fellows of the European Sports History Association. His research interests include Russian and Soviet sport, and sport in communist societies. He has published widely on these subjects: his publications include *Sport in Soviet Society* (Cambridge: Cambridge University Press, 1977), *Sport, Politics and Communism* (Manchester: Manchester University Press, 1991), and *European Cultures in Sport* (edited with Arnd Krüger) (Bristol: Intellect, 2003).

ÁLVARO RODRÍGUEZ DÍAZ is Professor of Sociology at the University of Seville and the co-ordinator of the Committee on the Sociology of Sport of the Spanish Federation of Sociology. His research interests include Sports Spaces and the Sociology of Leisure. His publications include *El Deporte en la Construcción del Espacio Social* [Sport in the Construction of Social Space] (Madrid: Centro de Investigaciones Sociológicas, 2008) and numerous articles such as 'Football Fan Groups in Andalusia', in *Football Fans Around the World* (London: Routledge, 2007). He is also an editor of *Anduli*, a review of Social Sciences.

DAVID SCOTT holds a personal chair in French (Textual and Visual Studies) at Trinity College Dublin. He has written widely on literature, painting and semiotics, and has organized international exhibitions on art and design. His books include *Pictorialist Poetics* (Cambridge: Cambridge University Press, 1988 and 2009), *Paul Delvaux* (London: Reaktion, 1992), *European Stamp Design: A Semiotic Approach* (Chichester: Academy, 1995), *Semiologies of Travel* (Cambridge: Cambridge University Press, 2004) and *The Art and Aesthetics of Boxing* (Lincoln, NE: University of Nebraska Press, 2009). His translation of Mallarmé's sonnets appeared in 2008. He is currently completing a book entitled *Poetics of the Poster*. A former associate editor of *Word & Image*, he was president of IAWIS/AIERTI, 1999–2002.

ELENI THEODORAKI is Reader at Edinburgh Napier Business School and Director of the Edinburgh Institute for Festival and Event Management. She researches in the area of organizational analysis, governance and mega-events and is author of *Olympic Event Organization* (Amsterdam: Elsevier, 2007). She has worked for Olympic Games bid and organizing committees, and has undertaken commissioned/funded work for the International Olympic Committee on the role of women in management, the British Academy on sport development overseas, and East Potential on the impacts of the London 2012 Olympic Games preparations on social housing. In Spring 2010, the London Mayor appointed her Core Commissioner for a Sustainable London 2012.

Index

Cultural Identity Studies

Edited by
Helen Chambers

This series aims to publish new research (monographs and essays) into relationships and interactions between culture and identity. The notions of both culture and identity are broadly conceived; interdisciplinary and theoretically diverse approaches are encouraged in a series designed to promote a better understanding of the processes of identity formation, both individual and collective. It will embrace research into the roles of linguistic, social, political, psychological, and religious factors, taking account of historical context. Work on the theorizing of cultural aspects of identity formation, together with case studies of individual writers, thinkers or cultural products will be included. It focuses primarily on cultures linked to European languages, but welcomes transcultural links and comparisons. It is published in association with the Institute of European Cultural Identity Studies of the University of St Andrews.